IN THE COURT
OF PUBLIC OPINION

ALGER HISS

IN THE COURT OF PUBLIC OPINION

HARPER COLOPHON BOOKS
Harper & Row, Publishers
New York, Evanston, San Francisco, London

This book was originally published in a hardcover edition by Alfred A. Knopf in 1957.

First HARPER COLOPHON edition published 1972.

STANDARD BOOK NUMBER: 06-090293-0

TO P.H.

CONTENTS

ILLUSTRATIONS

Reproductions of material offered as evidence on the motion for a new trial will be found following page 374.

PREFACE TO THE COLOPHON EDITION

This reprint of my analysis of the facts and circumstances of my case is being issued without change.

In the Court of Public Opinion is part of my effort for the full vindication I have at all times anticipated. In the fifteen years since the book first appeared, my lawyers and I have continued to seek further evidence and to reexamine aspects of the case we had tended to neglect or take for granted. A number of independent investigators have also added their efforts, resulting in more than a score of books and magazine articles. At the moment, three new and quite divergent studies are in preparation; they will, I believe, add significant clarification.

The congressional hearings and the trials in my case took place at a time of public hysteria which served to usher in the McCarthy era. As the result of changes in American political attitudes since the trials and since the initial publication of this book, it may now receive a wider and more relaxed consideration than was possible in 1957. I am gratified that my own account of my case is again in the court of public opinion.

ALGER HISS
February 12, 1972

HEARINGS AND RELATED EVENTS IN 1948

August 3, HEARING: Whittaker Chambers's first appearance before Committee on Un-American Activities (PUBLIC SESSION).

August 5, HEARING: My first appearance (PUBLIC SESSION).

August 7, HEARING: Chambers's second appearance (EXECUTIVE SESSION).

August 16, HEARING: My second appearance (EXECUTIVE SESSION).

August 17, HEARING: Confrontation at Commodore Hotel, New York (EXECUTIVE SESSION).

August 18, HEARING: My wife's only appearance (EXECUTIVE SESSION at Commodore Hotel, New York).

       HEARING: Isaac Don Levine's first appearance (EXECUTIVE SESSION).

August 24, HEARING: Martha Pope's appearance (EXECUTIVE SESSION).

August 25, HEARING: My last appearance—public confrontation.

August 26, HEARING: William Rosen's appearance.

August 27:   Chambers's appearance on *Meet the Press* broadcast.

August 30, HEARING: Adolf A. Berle's appearance (EXECUTIVE SESSION).

September 27:   Filing of my libel suit in Baltimore against Chambers.

October 14 *and* 15:   Chambers denies knowledge of espionage before New York Grand Jury.

November 4:   First testimony by Chambers in Baltimore libel-suit proceedings.

November 17:   Chambers produces typed papers and my handwritten notes in Baltimore proceedings.

November 19:   Papers produced by Chambers turned over to the Department of Justice at my direction.

December 2:   Chambers at his farm turns over microfilm to representatives of Committee.

December 3:   New York Grand Jury reconvenes.

December 15:   Indictment.

IN THE COURT
OF PUBLIC OPINION

CHAPTER ONE

FIRST APPEARANCE
BEFORE THE COMMITTEE,
AUGUST 5, 1948

IN AUGUST 1948 I was living in New York City. For the preceding year and a half I had been president of the Carnegie Endowment for International Peace. To accept that position I had resigned from the State Department, where I was director of the office responsible for proposing and carrying out our policies in the United Nations.

My new work was closely related to what I had been doing in Washington, for the Endowment had decided to concentrate its activities on support of the United Nations as the appropriate means of furthering Andrew Carnegie's aim, stated in 1910, "to hasten the abolition of international war, the foulest blot upon our civilization." The Endowment was conducting research and publishing analyses of the proceedings of the United Nations. In addition we were preparing a series of technical studies to assist the newly created United Nations with its own organizational problems and with the questions coming before it and its affiliated agencies.

On Monday, August 2, 1948, I returned to work at the
Endowment's office in New York after a month's vacation
with my family in a small Vermont village where we had
spent our summers for many years. I had come down on the
train alone, as my wife and son were staying in Vermont for
a few more weeks. That evening a reporter reached me by
telephone at my apartment. He told me that, according to information coming from the Committee on Un-American Activities of the House of Representatives, a man named Chambers was going to appear before the Committee the next
morning and would call me a Communist. The reporter asked
whether I had any comment.

I did not. The untruthful charge of Communism had been
the lot of many who had been New Deal officials in the Washington of the 1930's and the early 1940's. I had not taken such
charges seriously when made against others and I saw no reason why I or anyone else should pay much attention to a
similar fanciful charge that might now be made against me.

The next morning, Tuesday, August 3, 1948, a witness
named Whittaker Chambers appeared before the Committee
and said that he was a senior editor of *Time* magazine but
that years before he had been "attached" to "an underground
organization of the United States Communist Party" in
Washington. He said that I had been a member of that group.
I received this information about Chambers's testimony, while
I was at work in my office, from numerous telephone calls
from reporters for the press services and for individual papers.
The volume of inquiry by the press was a surprise to me, but
I was still inclined to treat the charges as more of a nuisance
than anything else.

As I knew no one named Whittaker Chambers (I had
heard the man's full name only once before, about a year
earlier) and as I had belonged to no organization of the Communist Party, I told the newspapermen that what he said
about my association with him was completely untrue, and
that so far as I knew I had never even seen him.

At lunch I was advised by friends to ignore the Committee as a body whose activities were discounted by all sensible people. Nevertheless, I chose to make my denials not only to the newspapers but in the same setting where the charges had been made. Therefore, I sent a telegram to the Committee that same afternoon saying that I wanted to appear to deny Chambers's charges under oath. As I expected to be in Washington on Endowment business two days later, I suggested that I appear on that day, Thursday.

The interest of the press and my decision to appear before the Committee were matters that affected the Carnegie Endowment because of my position with it. I therefore called the Chairman of the Endowment's board of trustees, Mr. John Foster Dulles, and told him of what I had learned from the press and of my telegram to the Committee. I then tried to go on with my regular work in spite of the distraction of Chambers's strange story and the welcomed interruptions of friends who expressed their indignation and offered their support.

Chambers's testimony was given just three months before the 1948 Presidential and Congressional elections. A few days prior to Chambers's public debut Miss Elizabeth Bentley had told the Committee her tale of Communist conspirators in government. For some months before the taking of any testimony, the more sensational newspapers had carried reports of promised disclosures by the Committee. In March the Committee had received from Congress (the first Republican Congress since 1932) the largest appropriation ($200,000) it had ever received in its ten years of existence. The election year 1948 had been chosen as a period of increased activity for the Committee; and the selected theme of that activity was Communist espionage. The Chairman of the Committee, Mr. J. Parnell Thomas, Republican, of New Jersey, said later that the Republican National Committee Chairman "was urging me in the Dewey campaign [Governor Dewey's 1948 Presidential effort] to set up the spy hearings. At that time he was urging me to stay in Washington in order to put the heat on Harry Truman." [1]

In addition to the Chairman, the Committee had four other Republican members: Karl E. Mundt of South Dakota, John McDowell of Pennsylvania, Richard M. Nixon of California, and Richard B. Vail of Illinois. The Democrats were John S. Wood of Georgia, John E. Rankin of Mississippi, H. Hardin Peterson of Florida, and F. Edward Hébert of Louisiana. William S. White of *The New York Times* commented on August 15, 1948: "Likely as not, troubles for the Truman Administration will begin simultaneously with any hearing. The President has no really strong political supporter or close friend on the committee's Democratic panel of four, and in that same panel he has certainly one of his most violent detractors, Representative John E. Rankin of Mississippi."

Only Mr. Hébert is still in the House of Representatives. Mr. Mundt and Mr. Nixon later became Senators, Mr. Nixon still later being elected Vice President. Mr. Wood, nominated by President Eisenhower, became a member of the Subversive Activities Control Board in 1955.

The chief officer of the Committee's staff was Robert E. Stripling, whose association with the Committee dated back to his service as clerk to Representative Martin Dies, the first Chairman of the Committee. The *New York Times* analysis of August 15 described Stripling as "a powerful figure" in the Committee's proceedings who kept "always alert for the striking or sensational" in his choice of subjects for hearings. The director of research, Benjamin Mandel, was later named by Chambers as the man who had issued to him his Communist Party card. Upon Chambers's appearance before the Committee, the two, Chambers writes, were to "resume [a] close acquaintance." [2]

The Committee accepted the day I had suggested, Thursday, and I went on to Washington the evening before. On

[1] *The New York Times*, February 8, 1954.
[2] *Witness* (Random House, 1952).

arriving I obtained a transcript of Chambers's testimony. This gave me no more information as to what he was talking about than had the press accounts. He said nothing of the actual circumstances under which I had in fact met and known him by a different name, so that I still had no key to his identity, despite a slight sense of familiarity about some of his press photographs. An unknown man, with unknown motives, had chosen to call me a Communist. More specifically, he had asserted that I had been a Communist in the mid-1930's.

Although I found no clues to Chambers's identity or to his motivation in his testimony, I found in reading the transcript indications of the Committee's attitude. Mundt, presiding in Thomas's absence, had, I noticed, asked Stripling whether he knew "the reason why" I was "removed from the State Department." Though Stripling had made the correction that he had no record that I had been removed, Mundt later in the hearing had volunteered, without correction, another prejudicial statement about me:

There is reason to believe that he organized within that Department one of the Communist cells which endeavored to influence our Chinese policy and bring about the condemnation of Chiang Kai-shek, which put Marzani in an important position there. . . .

I had never known any Marzani. Not only had I never organized "cells" within the State Department, I had no connection with our China policy after 1944, a time when Chiang's pre-eminence was undisputed. My only functions before that time relating to China had been assisting in removing discriminatory aspects of our immigration policy, in negotiating a treaty of friendship with China, and in expediting lend-lease aid to China.

Upon bringing out my position with the Carnegie Endowment, Mundt had in addition contributed for the record the statement:

. . . Certainly there is no hope for world peace under the leadership of men like Alger Hiss.

Rankin, of the Democratic wing of the Committee, had remarked:

Under the New York FEPC [Fair Employment Practices Committee] law, you can't ask this man whether he is a Communist or not, or where he came from, or what his name was before it was changed. You can't even ask for his photograph. Of course, he can get into an institution of that kind in New York, but he couldn't do it in Mississippi.

Later he had asserted in question form:

. . . don't you think Mr. Carnegie, the rich Scotchman that developed this foundation, would turn over in his grave if he knew that kind of people were running the foundation?

It seemed to me plain enough that some members of the Committee were launched on a hunt for political sensations and that their attitude toward anyone charged with Communism would not be objective. I was annoyed at their biased comments about me, but I felt convinced that in spite of their attitude I would be able to show them promptly that they had been misled into hasty and unfair remarks. I had nothing to hide and, I thought, nothing to fear. A simple statement of facts would surely clear up the whole business.

On Thursday morning I appeared at the Committee's hearing room, the large caucus room in the Old House Office Building, and waited until I was called. During fifteen years of government service, and in my quasi-public work since then, I had attended many hearings of Congressional committees. I had acted as a drafting assistant, as a representative of government agencies, as an observer, as counsel—in a number of different capacities. But the atmosphere of this Committee was a new experience for me. The press coverage was greater than of any hearing I had attended before. Stripling has estimated that the hearing "drew perhaps the biggest turnout of reporters and spectators in the history of our inquiries."

At the beginning of my testimony, I said that I had never been a member of the Communist Party or of any of its front organizations nor had I followed its line. I said also that, so far as I knew, none of my friends was a Communist and went on to add:

> To the best of my knowledge, I never heard of Whittaker Chambers until in 1947, when two representatives of the Federal Bureau of Investigation asked me if I knew him and various other people, some of whom I knew and some of whom I did not know. I said I did not know Chambers. So far as I know, I have never laid eyes on him, and I should like to have the opportunity to do so.

The name had remained in my memory from that occasion a year earlier because I had been asked, first, if I knew anyone named Chambers and I had replied that one of my boyhood friends was named Chambers. I had then been asked if I knew Whittaker Chambers, who was not further identified. I told them I did not. As a law-school classmate and friend is named Whittaker, the combination of the last names of two friends stuck in my memory.

I had seen in the accounts of Chambers's testimony of August 3 several press photographs of him. There seemed to be a degree of familiarity about some of these. Perhaps I had met him at some large gathering and failed to catch, or now failed to recall, his name. Or perhaps he resembled someone I actually did know. At the time I had no further clues and I was curious to have a good look at him. I assumed that the Committee, having had for two days my request to testify, would have made arrangements for him to be present. My telegram had expressly stated: "I do not know Mr. Chambers. . . ." Had the procedure of confrontation been followed promptly to clear up the question of identity, I would in any colloquy that morning with Chambers unquestionably have been able, as I was two weeks later when I did see him, to recognize him as the free-lance writer George Crosley whom I had met fourteen years before, in the early days of the New Deal.

Chambers's identity preoccupied me. I could not be sure, without seeing him, whether I had ever met him. After my

initial statement and after I had answered routine questions as
to my education and employment, McDowell said that he had
"forgotten entirely what charge was made by Mr. Chambers."
Mundt, undertaking to summarize Chambers's testimony of
two days before and my denials, included the remark that I
had said I had never seen Chambers. I interrupted to correct
him, saying:

As far as I know, I have never seen him.

When Mundt's summary was over, I returned to the issue
of identity. Angered that the Committee had allowed this unknown man to attack me publicly before giving me an opportunity to challenge him, I said that I wished I could have
seen Chambers before he testified. Stripling, after asking when
I first heard of Chambers's allegations, inquired:

You say you have never seen Mr. Chambers?

I replied:

The name means absolutely nothing to me, Mr. Stripling.

Stripling then showed me a single close-up snapshot taken
by an Associated Press photographer during Chambers's testimony. This was a foreshortened picture that had been taken
at an angle, from below Chambers's chin. Stripling said that
Chambers had become much heavier than he had been in
1934 and 1935. I replied that I would rather see the man
than his picture and that I would not want to testify that I
had never seen him. I said I would like to see him, after
which I would be better able to tell whether I had ever seen
him before. I then asked the direct question: "Is he here today?"
When the Acting Chairman, Mundt, replied that he was not, I
remarked that I had hoped he would be.

The Committee went no further with the subject of
Chambers's identity. Following a brief series of questions about
Chambers's charges, Nixon expressed for the Committee the
need for a prompt confrontation. He said that when arrangements were made for Chambers's appearance, "the witnesses

[should] be allowed to confront each other so that any possibility of a mistake in identity may be cleared up." This was the obvious next step under the circumstances, as the Committee had failed to insure identification before permitting Chambers to testify publicly and had also failed to produce him at this hearing.

In fact, however, the obvious practical step of letting me see Chambers was not taken for some time. Instead the Committee proceeded two days later to interrogate Chambers in secret about his claims of familiarity with my personal habits and then, again in secret, to go over the same topics with me on August 16. This procedure obscured what had actually happened, that I had indeed met Chambers fourteen years before but under a different name and in entirely different circumstances from those he asserted. Worse, the Committee's course built up over a two-week period the false impression that I had denied ever knowing Chambers under any name and in any circumstances. Though they did not then make it public, the Committee knew two days after my testimony that I had never known Chambers by his own name. He admitted this at a secret session held on August 7, but I did not learn of this until nine days later. The entire procedure followed by the Committee was ill-suited to an objective inquiry into the basic and preliminary question of whether I had ever known the man at all.

The procedure that was adopted not only misled the public but also prevented me from promptly realizing that Chambers was Crosley. My memory depends a good deal on names to place people. I remember the names of acquaintances of other years whom I would not be able to recognize if I were to meet them face to face. I can see someone with a familiar face and be unable to place him until something suggests his name. And attributing the wrong name to such a face will block my recollection completely. It was twelve years since I had seen Crosley, and his face was no longer a familiar one. Nevertheless, had Chambers testified as Crosley, or had he said that during his acquaintance with me he had used that

name, I could have soon placed him even without seeing him.
I believe that I would have recalled him had he identified
himself merely by describing the circumstances under which
I had known him. Instead, to the displacement of name, that
important tag for recognition and for searching the files of
memory, was added the elimination of all the details of my
acquaintance with him. After twelve years the half-forgotten
face of George Crosley, whose name, even, had long ceased to
be in my active memory, was not called back by any mnemonic
signal.

Eleven days after my testimony I saw in a press item that
Chambers in his secret testimony of August 7 had said that
he had stayed in my house and had driven my car. This did
recall Crosley—for the first time. I had sublet my apartment
to Crosley and had also given him my old Ford roadster when
I bought a Plymouth sedan in 1935. I recognized then the
possibility that he might have some connection with the mystery of the unknown Chambers.

But I couldn't even then bring myself to believe that Crosley would have made up these charges against me. I had
treated him well. He had no reason to bear a grudge against
me. Chambers on August 3 hadn't said that he had been a
free-lance writer, as Crosley had been when I knew him. He
hadn't said he had subleased my apartment or that I had
given him my 1929 roadster. Surely if he were Crosley he
would have mentioned some of these facts at his first appearance.

The photographs I had seen of Chambers didn't remind
me of Crosley. Although Stripling had said that since the
1930's Chambers had gained thirty to forty pounds, the particular photographs I saw didn't look simply like an overweight
George Crosley. Crosley had had very bad teeth. None of the
photographs of Chambers that I saw showed poor teeth and
no reference had been made to Chambers's having had bad
teeth in the 1930's. Crosley's teeth were decayed and one of
them was split, the forward half having come away, leaving
the gleaming steel of a pivot against the darkened rear of the

broken tooth. The resulting disfigurement was the most striking aspect of Crosley's appearance; it deflected attention from
his other features, making them less apparent in observation,
less distinct in memory. (In fact, this most arresting feature
of his appearance when I knew him had in the intervening
twelve years been obliterated by new false teeth.) When on
August 16 I recalled Crosley, it did occur to me that perhaps
Chambers had known Crosley, another writer, and that in the
course of conversation Chambers had picked up some facts
about me. Perhaps this information had been supplemented
by others who knew me. I had noticed that Chambers in his
initial testimony was familiar with my recent positions and
duties in the State Department and with the nature of my
current activities in private life, though he did not claim to
have known me after 1937.

But on August 5, as Crosley had not yet been recalled to
my mind, these speculations had not yet occurred to me. I
knew merely that a stranger had unaccountably said that I had
been a member with him of a secret Communist group, that
he had eventually come to my house to ask me to break with
the Communist Party, that *I* had cried at separating from him,
that *he* was very fond of me. The situation seemed to me to
be in the realm of fantasy and for that very reason, I could
not but feel, would be dispelled by a simple assertion of
reality.

And so, indeed, the hearing seemed to go. My testimony,
which I have already summarized, was brief. The Acting Chairman, Mundt, expressed "the appreciation of the committee
for [my] very cooperative attitude, for [my] forthright statements, and for the fact that [I was] first among those whose
names were mentioned by various witnesses to communicate
with us asking for an opportunity to deny the charges." Even
Rankin said he wanted "to congratulate the witness that he
didn'tt [*sic*] refuse to answer the questions on the ground that
it might incriminate him, and he didn't bring a lawyer here to
tell him what to say." The practical step of letting me have
a prompt look at Chambers had been arranged, or so I thought.

It seems clear that some members of the Committee, however, had a political stake in seeing to it that this fantasy should not be dispelled. No meeting with Chambers was arranged. Their attitude was revealed in a series of articles by Stripling that appeared in the Hearst press some months later (January 30 through February 26, 1949) and in the fall of 1949 in book form as *The Red Plot Against America*, edited by Bob Considine of International News Service (Hearst). Stripling reports that in an executive session (Congressional terminology for a closed meeting of the Committee) that followed my testimony, "the members looked at one another for a time, and you could have cut the gloom with a knife. 'We're ruined!' one declared. . . . our espionage [3] inquiry plainly was tottering. President Truman took the occasion to call the hearing a 'red herring.'. . ."

Chambers, though not officially connected with the Committee, is also able to record this incident, adding the comment: "It was an election year, and the seat of every member of the Committee was at stake." Chambers further records that Nixon was "the man of decision who . . . made the Hiss Case possible" by insisting on additional hearings. Without apparent ironical intent, Chambers observes that the Committee "never faltered again." [4]

---

[3] Though Chambers had expressly stated in his August 3 testimony that those he named "were specifically not wanted to act as sources of information," Stripling here reveals that the Committee had predetermined that its inquiry was to be a hunt for spies. Thomas, too, spoke of setting up "the spy hearings" (see pp. 5–6).

[4] Both Stripling and Chambers have, however, disclosed an additional occasion on which the Committee "faltered," and which revealed again the heavy investment the Committee had made in presenting a prejudged case as opposed to following an objective quest for facts. See pp. 171–3.

CHAPTER TWO

SECOND APPEARANCE,
AUGUST 16

ONE week and a day after my appearance I heard from the
Committee again. Returning to my apartment on Friday evening, August 13, to pick up a few things before taking the train
to rejoin my family in Vermont, I found a telegram asking
me to meet the Committee in Washington on Monday. This
I took to be notice that the opportunity to see Chambers had
been arranged.

During the week as I awaited the Committee's next step,
I had been baffled by what to do next. I continued to believe
that the whole business was some kind of fantasy. But I wanted
to take steps to clear it up. I had consulted a number of friends
while I tried to keep the regular work of my office going at
the same time. I asked a family friend of many years' standing,
who was also a member of the firm with which I had been
associated when I practiced law in New York, about having
Chambers's history, record, and associations investigated by a
professional investigator. And I took up with him and with
other friends the status of lie-detector tests, following calls

from the press after the Committee had let it be known that
it might employ such tests. I also explored the possibility of
suing Chambers for libel or slander.

The results of my inquiries were that I received the informal opinion that Chambers's statements about me before
the Committee or to government agencies were privileged
against suit, that I was warned against lie detectors as unre-
liable booby traps, and that I was advised against a private investigation of Chambers as unsuitable at that time.

I also asked other friends whether I could not simply walk
in on Chambers at his *Time* office to satisfy my curiosity as
to who this assailant was. Closer inspection should clear up
the mystery as to whether I had ever met him. But here, too,
the advice was negative. Because it seemed evident that the
Committee would arrange for a prompt confrontation, I was
told that my curiosity about Chambers should wait.

From Vermont I called the family friend with whom I
had talked about investigating Chambers and told him of the
Committee's new initiative. Monday morning he boarded my
train in New York and continued on to Washington with me.
He brought along an associate who was technically familiar
with lie detectors and with private investigations. They had
with them copies of newspapers which had appeared over the
week end and which recounted some of the "secret" testimony
Chambers had given after my appearance of August 5. It was
in one of those papers that I saw then the item stating that
Chambers claimed to have stayed in my house and to have
driven my car. This was the item that brought George Crosley
back to mind.

Crosley was one of the large number of people I had met
while I was serving as counsel in 1934 and 1935 to the Senate
Committee Investigating the Munitions Industry, generally
known as the Munitions Committee or the Nye Committee.
That Committee, headed by Senator Gerald Nye of North
Dakota, had been established in 1934 as a result of public interest in widely reported activities of munitions manufacturers,
foreign and domestic, and their agents.

Hearings of the kind conducted by the Nye Committee occur but rarely and attract wide attention. Our hearings were regularly attended by a sizable press corps, including many representatives of foreign papers and news agencies. We of the staff gave much time to answering their questions; the Nye Committee, like other such bodies before and since, valued good press relations. It was my first assignment in public relations and I took pride in enlisting public support for the Committee's efforts.

Books and magazine articles were written on the subject of the Committee's inquiries. Their authors, too, came to the Committee staff for information. Students at work on theses, free-lance writers, editors of the publications of peace organizations, popular lecturers, and curious individuals without affiliation were attracted to the hearings and remained to ask questions, to examine the transcript of the hearings and the documents gathered as exhibits by the Committee. Staff members responded with missionary zeal to inquiries—and they were many—from all quarters. In addition we accepted invitations to speak to interested groups in and about Washington.

The Committee included in its membership Senator Arthur H. Vandenberg, who took an effective and vigorous part. Two other members, Homer T. Bone (now a Circuit Judge) and James P. Pope, later of the TVA, were also members of the Senate Committee on Agriculture. As a lawyer with the Department of Agriculture, I had frequently met with their Committee and had thus come to know them.

The Munitions Committee, despite the public interest in its field of investigation and the distinction of its membership, never received large appropriations. Its methods of operation reflected this combination of prestige and penury. Office rental was minimized by using the members' own offices for various Committee functions and by the temporary utilization of empty hearing rooms and of other temporarily vacant space in the Senate Office Building. The Secretary of the Committee, Mr. Stephen Raushenbush, and his receptionist-stenographer, Miss Elsie Gullender, had more or less permanent quarters.

The rest of the staff, often out of the city for interviews and for examination of records, made do when in Washington with what temporarily available rooms the members of the Committee could locate for us.

The Committee's payroll was also modest. All salaries were low, but the chief saving in this budget area was accomplished by borrowing personnel from the Executive Departments. The chief officials of the Executive Departments, as a favor to important Senators, detailed to the Committee members of their own staffs whose services were requested. Accountants, lawyers, stenographers, economists, army and navy officers were among those thus borrowed for varying periods. I was in this manner lent by the Department of Agriculture toward the end of July of 1934 to serve as counsel. By December I was engaged in presenting in public hearings before the Committee material on overseas sales activities of some of our large aircraft manufacturers. It was my duty to assemble documentary evidence bearing upon these activities and to examine witnesses who were familiar with the subjects under inquiry.

At that particular time, therefore, I was approached for information by a larger number of inquirers than usual. As the cases of other members of the staff were presented to the Committee, their public-relations functions increased in the same way. Crosley said he was a free-lance writer living in New York who planned to do a series of articles on the munitions investigation. He hoped to sell these to the *American Magazine.* I associate his initial inquiries with the aircraft hearings. From this I date my acquaintance with him as beginning toward the end of December 1934 or early in 1935. I saw him two or three times at the Senate Office Building, once or twice letting him go over the stenographic transcript and the exhibits we had so far introduced into the record. Printing of the hearings was protracted. It involved thorough editorial and proofreading work and it had no particular priority with the Government Printing Office. Pending delayed publication of the hearings, press representatives and others interested in our record had, therefore, frequent recourse to our proof sheets of the stenographic transcript and to our working file copies of the exhibits.

Members of the staff frequently lunched near by at a modest eating place, the States Restaurant. To minimize interruptions to my work at the office, I made luncheon appointments there with some of those who called to discuss the Committee's work. I had a couple of luncheons of this sort with Crosley. As it was my practice while a government official not to accept meals or gifts from members of the public with whom I had official dealings, I naturally made a point of paying my own check at these lunches. I remember Crosley as one of those with whom I had official contacts who waited for me to pay his check also.

After Crosley had turned up at the office a few times over a period of some weeks, he mentioned that he wanted to bring his family to Washington for several months so that he could write with less interruption. Except for the accidental fact that at just that time I had overlapping leases on a house and on an apartment, I should probably never have had more than an office and occasional business-lunch relationship with Crosley. My wife and I had rented a house on P Street in Georgetown to which we were moving in mid-April, but we still had a lease until July 1 on our small apartment in the Wardman Park region. During the Depression spring of 1935 the prospects were slight for renting the apartment for a period of less than three months of the beginning of a Washington summer. The chance of doing just this, and thereby saving the rent, came when I found that Crosley was eager to rent. It was an attractive financial proposition to me. Having accepted as unavoidable the duplication of rent, I had nothing to lose even if he might prove to be a poor risk. Consequently, I was glad to sublease the apartment to him for the same rent I paid ($60 a month) with no extra charge for the slight cost of the utilities. As the new house was partly furnished, we were able to let him use some of our furniture. I had, I thought, both recouped my rent and assisted one of the writers covering our hearings to find quarters.

When the Crosleys arrived to take over the apartment, Crosley told me that their things had not come from New York. We had not been able to leave chinaware, silver, kitchenware, or linen. Without such articles and without a crib and other necessaries for their infant, then about eighteen months old, they would not have been very comfortable, but he made no mention of going to a hotel. In the circumstances of his evident lack of funds, there was an implied request for help. There were two extra rooms on the top floor in the P Street house, and I chose not to rebuff the implied appeal; we put them up against the expected arrival next day of their belongings. In fact the delivery van didn't arrive the next day either, so that they spent two nights with us.

At this time we were the owners of a 1929 Ford roadster which we were then contemplating trading in for a new car. On one occasion that winter, before Crosley had subleased the apartment, I had mentioned to him that I was going to drive to New York. He asked for a ride, which I gave him. As my tenant he borrowed the old roadster once or twice that spring and also asked where he could rent a car. Having been told that the Ford, which was still sturdy if lacking in the comfort of a new car, had only $25 value, as scrap, for trade-in purposes, I preferred to let the old car continue to be put to use. Consequently, I told him he could have it as soon as we got our new car. I felt pleased that the old car would be used after we had finished with it.

This was the George Crosley I recalled as I went to Washington on Monday, August 16, 1948. Press photographs of Chambers that I had seen did not seem at all like the Crosley I recalled, a free-lance of the Depression. He had been an unkempt figure of the Jack London, Jim Tully stereotype, not a *Time* type. I kept returning to the possibility that Chambers, evidently also a writer, could have known Crosley and from him have learned something about me.

When I appeared at the specified room in the House Office Building, four members of the Committee and six staff members were assembled. As at the first hearing, I saw no occasion for having counsel with me. The members present were the Chairman, J. Parnell Thomas, and McDowell, Nixon, and Hébert. The session was executive—that is, closed to press and public. At the outset Thomas emphasized the secrecy of the proceedings as a reason why I could not be assured of a copy of the record, which I requested. He said that "everything is supposed to be right within these four walls." Stripling, Chief Investigator, identified each person to demonstrate that "Everybody here is either a member of the committee or attached to the staff. . . ." Three and a half hours later Thomas concluded the session by assuring me that every one of them had "stood up and raised his right hand and taken an oath that he will not divulge one single word of testimony given here this afternoon." Hébert added that the stenographic reporter had been instructed to transcribe the testimony personally and to allow no one in his office to see it.

Nixon did most of the questioning. He informed me for the first time that Chambers had told the Committee that during the period in question he was not known by his own name. The possible link to Crosley in my mind was, however, immediately snuffed out by Nixon's adding: "He has testified that he was known by the name of Carl. Do you recall having known an individual between the years 1934 and 1937 whose name was Carl?"

I replied that I knew two or three "Carls," but none of them "could remotely be connected with the kind of testimony Mr. Chambers has given." It then developed that Chambers had said he was known to me only as "Carl," with no last name whatsoever. I testified that I had never known anyone merely by the name of Carl.

After several questions as to whether I had seen six or seven named persons at the apartment of one of them, Nixon showed me two recent pictures of Chambers and asked if I remembered "that person." I reminded him that at the public hearing I had said that I couldn't swear that I had never seen him. I added: "Actually the face has a certain familiarity." I said again that "I would like very much to see the individual

face to face. I had hoped that would happen before. I still hope
it will happen today. . . . I certainly wouldn't want to testify
without seeing the man, hearing him talk, getting some much
more tangible basis for judging the person and the personality."

Nixon then asked if my answer would be different if the
individual had stayed overnight in my house on several occasions. Crosley had not been overnight in my house on several
occasions. The question seemed to preclude him. I replied:
". . . I would find it very difficult to believe that that individual
could have stayed in my house when I was there on several
occasions overnight and his face not be more familiar than it
is." I again repeated my hope that I would be given the opportunity to see Chambers, to which Nixon observed that *before*
arranging that, the Committee wanted "to be certain that
there is no question of mistaken identity," the very issue that
a confrontation would have effectively settled. A few moments
later he added the further reason that an open session would
involve "considerable" publicity "and we were thinking that
if that could be avoided, that it should be avoided." I had not
observed that any investigating committee—much less this
one—shunned publicity.

The reasons given for the procedure of separate secret
sessions did not seem persuasive, nor did they increase my
confidence in the Committee's objectivity. Nixon went on to
ask a series of detailed questions relating to my wife and my
children, which I answered as a matter of course. However,
when he asked the names of our servants from 1934 to 1937,
I observed that my testimony on such topics might reach
Chambers and enable him to fortify his apparent pose as
someone who knew me well. (Chambers did in fact subsequently interview our former maids. See pages 227–30, 338.
I repeated this objection several times in the ensuing colloquy.

So long as I could not satisfy myself that I had ever met
Chambers, I could only assume that he might be lying about
having known me, as he was lying about the Communist activities he ascribed to me. On the bare issue of establishing

personal acquaintance, familiarity on his part with my personal life was likely to seem persuasive, especially in the absence of cross-examination. I didn't wish to supply this adventurer, obviously bent on harming me, with any information that might assist him to do so. The preliminary, and in itself color-less, issue of acquaintance could, I knew, most promptly be settled by my having a chance to see him face to face. I knew also that, perversely, the Committee's procedure, ostensibly de-signed to resolve this very question, not only magnified its apparent importance by delaying its resolution, but confused it with the real and important issue of the truth or falsity of Chambers's accusation of Communist activities.

The question of whether I had known this man with the vaguely familiar face was being built up, I sensed, to carry the implication that if I had known him, I had been a fellow Communist with him.

In addition, I sensed a proprietary attitude toward Cham-bers, as though he were the Committee's witness and I an outsider. I raised the topic frankly: "I have seen newspaper accounts, Mr. Nixon, that you spent the week end—whether correct or not, I do not know—at Mr. Chambers' farm in New Jersey." Nixon replied: "That is quite incorrect." (In fact, the late Bert Andrews of the New York *Herald Tribune*, in a series of articles that appeared some years afterward, re-ported that Nixon had the day before, Sunday, August 15, driven to Chambers's farm in Maryland and had spent several hours conversing with Chambers in Andrews's presence.)

Nixon took affront at my concern over the Committee's attitude and at my concern over being asked to supply details —such as the names of servants—that could prove helpful to Chambers, should they come to his ears. He said that I was implying "that the committee's purpose in questioning you today is to get information with which we can coach Mr. Chambers so that he can more or less build a web around you." My thought had, of course, not gone so far, and I as-sured him that I had meant no such implication. His counter assurance that my testimony would be kept secret was, however, weakened by his ignoring the various newspaper accounts that had already appeared of Chambers's secret testimony of August 7: "The same assurance was given to Mr. Chambers," he added quite seriously.

When Stripling showed me still another recent photograph of Chambers, I protested:

. . . The face is definitely not an unfamiliar face. Whether I am imagining it, whether it is because he looks like a lot of other people, I don't know, but I have never known anyone who had the relationship with me that this man has testified to and that, I think, is the important thing here, gentlemen. This man may have known me, he may have been in my house. I have had literally hundreds of people in my house in the course of the time I lived in Washington.

The issue is not whether this man knew me and I don't remember him. The issue is whether he had a particular conversation [1] that he has said he had with me and which I have denied and whether I am a member of the Communist Party or ever was, which he has said and which I have denied.

If I could see the man face to face, I would perhaps have some inkling as to whether he ever had known me personally.

I have met within the past week a man who said he worked on the same staff in a confidential relationship at San Francisco that I did who definitely knew me, and I have no recollection of ever having seen that man.

To the Chairman's question as to whether I would recall someone who had been a week at a time at my house, I said that I would, but insisted:

. . . I am not prepared to testify on the basis of a photograph.

At this point Nixon stated that Chambers had told the Committee that he had spent a week in my house. The vague image of Crosley and his broken tooth returned. He must have some connection with the story Chambers was telling. But I

---

[1] At this time Chambers's testimony of August 3 was the only testimony of his that was available to me. As pointed out in Chapter I, he had asserted in that testimony (1) that I was a Communist in the mid-1930's and (2) that in 1937 he had had a conversation with me in which he had urged me to break with the Communist Party, which, he said, I had refused to do.

could not be sure what that connection was and I was therefore reluctant to cause Crosley the embarrassment that might come from mentioning his name. I replied:

I have written a name on this pad in front of me of a person whom I knew in 1933 and 1934 [Here, as on other occasions, I was inaccurate in my use of dates without prior reference to fixed events like my association with the Nye Committee, leases, contracts, and other matters of record. I didn't meet Crosley until late 1934 or early 1935.] who not only spent some time in my house but sublet my apartment. That man certainly spent more than a week, not while I was in the same apartment. I do not recognize the photographs as possibly being this man. If I hadn't seen the morning papers with an account of statements that he knew the inside of my house, I don't think I would even have thought of this name. I want to see Chambers face to face and see if he can be this individual. I do not want and I don't think I ought to be asked to testify now that man's name and everything I can remember about him. . . .

Nixon then asked where I was living in 1933 and 1934. I explained that I had not examined my old leases and had simply jotted down from recollection, while on the train that morning, a list of the places where I had lived during a ten-year period beginning in 1933. I restated my position that under the circumstances I didn't think I should be asked questions of this kind, but that if Nixon insisted, after knowing my objections, I would answer. He replied: ". . . I must insist."

Hébert at this point, in the course of a long statement, expressed agreement with a major part of my position: "I am not pressing you to identify a picture when you should be faced with the man. That is your right." He went on to support my other point: "For the record, the issue is whether Chambers did have the conversation with you. . . ." But formal admission of the validity of my contentions did not sway the Committee from its determined procedure of continuing the *ex parte* examination without confrontation. I felt it my duty to accede under protest:

. . . I can only repeat if this committee asks me to go on with this specific line of inquiry, I will certainly do it. I do not feel comfortable about being in a position to protect my own reputation because I don't think knowledge of any individual is the issue here.

As I had just told the Committee, their own public comments were increasing the confusion that necessarily resulted from the procedure upon which they insisted. I had put it as follows:

MR. HISS: . . . Today as I came down on the train I read a statement—I think it was in the New York News—that a member of this committee . . . had told the press man who wrote the article that this committee believed or had reason to believe from talking to Chambers that Chambers had personally known Hiss, not that Chambers had had the conversation which is the issue here, that Chambers had been in Hiss' house. That is not the issue before this committee. . . . I am not prepared to say on the basis of the photograph——

MR. HÉBERT: We understand.

MR. HISS:—That the man, that he is not the man whose name I have written down here. Were I to testify to that, what assurance have I that some member of this committee wouldn't say to the press that Hiss confessed [2] knowing Chambers?

My question was answered in just the way I anticipated within two weeks by the Interim Report of August 28, issued with the Committee's unanimous approval. By that time I had on August 17 been permitted to see and question Chambers and had therefore been able to identify him as Crosley. The report was misleading and inaccurate:

. . . In fact, it was not until our public hearings had proceeded for some time that it was definitely established that Alger Hiss and Whittaker Chambers knew each other personally and rather intimately during the precise period of time that Whittaker Chambers testified that their associations took place. . . .

---

[2] The printed record cannot disclose irony. I was, of course, stating the characterization which I feared the Committee would give any such testimony by me.

It should also be noted that the stark fact that Alger Hiss and Whittaker Chambers, a self-confessed paid Communist functionary and espionage agent,[3] were acquainted with each other and did have numerous transactions and associations together, is of far greater significance under the circumstances than whether Chambers was known to Hiss by the name of "Carl" or of "George Crosley." This fact has been established without challenge for the record by the public hearings of this committee, although through the years it had been established by no other investigation.

. . . .

One of the most difficult problems which has faced the committee has been that of resolving the conflict between the testimony submitted by Whittaker Chambers and Alger Hiss. Chambers testified on August 3 that Hiss was a member of a Communist underground group of Government workers during the period 1934–37 when Chambers was serving as a Communist Party functionary in Washington. On August 5 Hiss categorically denied the charges of Chambers that he was or ever had been a member of the Communist Party, and furthermore denied ever having known Chambers or "having laid eyes upon him." As a result of exhaustive investigation by the committee's staff and of hours of executive session testimony from Hiss, Chambers, and all others who had information concerning the conflicting stories, Hiss finally admitted on August 17 for the first time that he actually had known Chambers as George Crosley, during the period in question.

The full title of this prejudiced report was: "Interim Report on Hearings Regarding Communist Espionage in the United States Government." Under a subheading, "Identification of the Espionage Groups," there was a further listing: "Ware-Abt-Witt Group" with my brother Donald's name and my name printed in a column of nine names introduced by the phrase: "The members of this group, according to Mr. Chambers, and their governmental employment during the period concerned in the testimony, are as follows."

[3] This is another example of the Committee's predetermination to inject espionage into its proceedings. Chambers in his testimony up to the date of this report, and for two and a half months thereafter, expressly disclaimed the role of espionage agent.

This report and frequent less formal communications to the press by Committee members and the staff gave the public, necessarily unfamiliar with the unpublished testimony which the Committee purported to summarize, an increasingly erroneous impression of the actual facts and a bias with which to view future developments in the case.

After my protest, the questioning resumed with Nixon's asking again for the names of our servants during the period 1934 to 1937. I gave him the name of the only maid we had employed regularly in those years who, according to our information, was still alive. (Later we learned that her successor, who had stayed with us until ill-health had forced her to stop working, had not died during the war years, as we had wrongly understood her youngest son to say.) He then passed on to the houses in which we had lived. He had just asked for the number of rooms in the first house when the Committee called a brief adjournment and I was asked to withdraw.

When I returned, I realized that I had left at my place the pad on which I had written Crosley's name. I assumed that one of the Committee's staff might quite likely have noticed the name. Under those circumstances I thought I should complete what I had already said about Crosley by prompt mention of his name. I did so as soon as the session was reconvened, in the following brief statement:

The name of the man I brought in—and he may have no relation to this whole nightmare—is a man named George Crosley. I met him when I was working for the Nye committee. He was a writer. He hoped to sell articles to magazines about the munitions industry.

I saw him, as I say [misprint for "saw"], in my office over in the Senate Office Building, dozens of representatives of the press, students, people writing books, research people. It was our job to give them appropriate information out of the record, show them what had been put in the record. This fellow was writing a series of articles, according to my best recollection, free lancing, which he hoped to sell to one of the magazines.

There then followed a series of questions and answers in which I stated the circumstances of my coming to know Crosley in the winter of 1934–5:

MR. STRIPLING: What color was his hair?

MR. HISS: Rather blondish, blonder than any of us here.

MR. STRIPLING: Was he married?

MR. HISS: Yes, sir.

MR. STRIPLING: Any children?

MR. HISS: One little baby, as I remember it, and the way I know that was the subleasing point. After we had taken the house on P Street and had the apartment on our hands, he one day in the course of casual conversation said he was going to specialize all summer in getting his articles done here in Washington, didn't know what he was going to do, and was thinking of bringing his family.

I said, "You can have my apartment. It is not terribly cool, but it is up in the air near the Wardman Park." He said he had a wife and little baby. The apartment wasn't very expensive, and I think I let him have it at exact cost. My recollection is that he spent several nights in my house because his furniture van was delayed. We left several pieces of furniture behind.

The P Street house belonged to a naval officer overseas and was partly furnished, so we didn't need all our furniture, particularly during the summer months, and my recollection is that definitely, as one does with a tenant trying to make him agreeable and comfortable, we left several pieces of furniture behind until the fall, his van was delayed, wasn't going to bring all the furniture because he was going to be there just during the summer, and we put them up 2 or 3 nights in a row, his wife and little baby.

Nixon then took up the questioning and asked if I could describe Mrs. Crosley. I replied that she was strikingly dark, but that I didn't know whether I would recognize her again because I didn't see very much of her. The questions continued:

MR. NIXON: How tall was this man, approximately?

MR. HISS: Shortish.

MR. NIXON: Heavy?

MR. HISS: Not noticeably. That is why I don't believe it has any direct, but it could have an indirect, bearing.

MR. NIXON: How about his teeth? [4]

MR. HISS: Very bad teeth. That is one of the things I particularly want to see Chambers about. This man had very bad teeth, did not take care of his teeth.

MR. STRIPLING: Did he have most of his teeth or just weren't well cared for?

MR. HISS: I don't think he had gapped teeth, but they were badly taken care of. They were stained and I would say obviously not attended to.

MR. NIXON: Can you state again just when he first rented the apartment?

MR. HISS: I think it was about June of 1935. My recollection is— and again I have not checked the records—that is, I went with the Nye munitions committee in the early winter of 1934. I don't even remember now when the resolution was passed. In any event, I am confident I was living on Twenty-ninth [sic] Street from December 1934 to June 1935 and that coincided with my service with the Nye committee. . . .

Throughout this testimony I assumed that my lease on the 28th Street apartment was from September to September (the usual New York term) and that the few months in which that lease overlapped the P Street lease were, therefore, the summer months. (I failed after the lapse of fourteen years to recall even the address correctly. The apartment was on 28th Street, not 29th Street as I said.) My memory also misplaced by a similar period of months the time when we had bought a new car.

Mr. Stripling asked what kind of automobile Crosley had. I replied:

MR. HISS: No kind of automobile. I sold him an automobile. I had an old Ford that I threw in with the apartment and had been trying to trade it in and get rid of it. I had an old,

---

[4] It is evident from his question that Nixon had already established that in the 1930's Chambers's poor teeth were a major identification mark.

old Ford we had kept for sentimental reasons. We got it just
before we were married in 1929.

MR. STRIPLING: Was it a model A or model T?

MR. HISS: Early A model with a trunk on the back, a slightly
collegiate model.

MR. STRIPLING: What color?

MR. HISS: Dark blue. It wasn't very fancy but it had a sassy
little trunk on the back.

MR. NIXON: You sold that car?

MR. HISS: I threw it in. He wanted a way to get around and I
said, "Fine, I want to get rid of it. I have another car, and
we kept it for sentimental reasons, not worth a damn." I let
him have it along with the rent.

I also told the Committee: "I can't remember when it
was I finally decided it wasn't any use expecting to collect from
him, that I had been a sucker and he was a sort of deadbeat;
not a bad character, but I think he just was using me for a
soft touch."

When Nixon asked if I could recall any subjects of conversation with Crosley, I answered:

We talked backwards and forwards about the Munitions Committee work. He told various stories that I recall of his escapades.
He purported to be a cross between Jim Tully, the author, and
Jack London. He had been everywhere. I remember he told me he
had personally participated in laying down the tracks of the street
cars in Washington, D.C. He had done that for local color, or
something. He had worked right with the road gang laying tracks
in Washington, D.C.

At this point Stripling asked if Crosley's middle initial
was "L," a remark that suggests knowledge on his part that
Chambers had used the name George L. Crosley. My reply
was that I didn't know, and that there must be some record
of my subtenant's name with the real-estate people. (In fact
the agents for the apartment had destroyed even their old
leases, so no records that would contain information about
subtenants had survived.)

A little later I was asked what kind of bill of sale I had given Crosley for the Ford and replied:

I think I just turned over—in the District you get a certificate of title, I think it is. I think I just simply turned it over to him.

Still later I was asked if I had ever ridden in the Ford with Crosley and said that I thought I had driven him to the apartment, and I mentioned the time I had driven to New York and had given him a lift. I said I thought the apartment lease had expired in September and that I had seen him several times after that.

Nixon interjected: "Even though he didn't pay his rent you saw him several times?"

I answered: "He was about to pay it and was going to sell his articles. He gave me a payment on account once. He brought a rug over which he said some wealthy patron gave him. I have still got the damned thing." Later I added that my recollection was he had also paid perhaps $15 or $20.

Nixon asked if I had given Crosley anything, and I mentioned "a couple of loans" and added that I had never been repaid.

I told the Committee that I found it difficult to believe that Crosley was Chambers: "I can't identify him from the pictures and can't see any motive." A few moments later I repeated my doubt on this latter score: "I can't imagine a normal man holding a grudge because somebody had stopped being a sucker."

The remainder of the session was taken up by questions about my wife, my children, my mother, my brothers and sisters, the houses in which I had lived, my stepson's schools, my boyhood activities of selling spring water and squabs to neighbors, my amateur interest in ornithology.

One other topic was raised which I regarded as highly prejudicial because of the impression its casual mention by the Committee might make on a technically uninformed public. Nixon asked if I would be willing to take a lie-detector test. He added that Chambers had said he would. My answer was:

Mr. Nixon, several days after I testified two members of the press told me that there had been a report that the committee was considering asking various witnesses if they would take a lie detector test. When I was asked if I had any comment to make on that, I said I didn't think it was appropriate at the time to make any comment.

Since then I have talked about that to several friends who I think are knowledgeable. When I was practicing law actively, quite frankly we had very little confidence in the so-called lie detector tests. I would say that I would rather have you ask me formally if you think lie detector tests are valuable in terms of who would administer it, what expert it is, what type of test, because the people I have consulted—and I think I have consulted knowledgeable people—say there is no such thing; that it is an emotion recording test; that it is not scientific, and that nobody scientifically competent, including the [Federal] Bureau [of Investigation], regards it as a scientific test.

He replied that "the committee has contacted Mr. Leonardo Keeler." It was Keeler's polygraph machine I had had in mind. I commented as follows:

Would it seem to you inappropriate for me to say that I would rather have a chance for further consultation before I gave you the answer? Actually, the people I have conferred with so far say that it all depends on who reads, that it shows emotion, not truth, and I am perfectly willing and prepared to say that I am not lacking in emotion about this business.

I have talked to people who have seen, I think, Dr. Keeler's own test and that the importance of a question registers more emotion than anything else. I certainly don't want to duck anything that has scientific or sound basis. I would like to consult further.

I would like to find out a little more about Dr. Keeler. As I told you, the people I have consulted said flatly there is no such thing, that it is not scientifically established.

It was arranged that I would send my answer by letter to the Committee within two days. My reply [5] referred to the fact that no Federal court accepted any machine as capable

[5] See Appendix A.

of ascertaining truth, and left the subject open for further consideration. The Committee never again mentioned the subject to me, but the mere interjection of the subject undoubtedly had prejudicial effects with those who were unaware of the lack of scientific validity of such tests. (The prosecutor in the second of my subsequent trials deliberately emphasized the Committee's suggested use of a lie detector in the hope that the jury would draw a conclusion prejudicial to me on the essential issue of veracity. See page 332.

Just before the session ended, the Committee held a private executive session during which I was asked to withdraw. Upon my return the Chairman announced that the Committee had unanimously decided on a public hearing for Wednesday, August 25, in the large caucus room, where Chambers and I would "have an opportunity to confront one another."

I replied: "I will be very glad of the chance to confront Mr. Chambers."

Nixon then interjected a variant suggestion, and the following colloquy took place:

MR. NIXON: Would you prefer to have it done informally?

MR. HISS: My desire is to see the man face to face.

MR. STRIPLING: Executive or open?

MR. HISS: It doesn't matter.

MR. NIXON: Where does it serve your best purpose? You just want to see the guy?

MR. HISS: It seems to me appropriate that it be done under committee auspices under the circumstances.

MR. NIXON: We are honestly trying to get the right way. If you have a public session, it is a show. Say it will be a meeting on the 25th in this room.

MR. HISS: You want me here in this room at 10:30 a.m.?

THE CHAIRMAN: Yes.

MR. HÉBERT: I am sympathetic to your feelings about not wanting a big show, but the other witnesses wanted to confront accusers in public.

MR. HISS: I had not expressed a preference.

MR. HÉBERT: I wanted to clear that up. Unless you express a

preference I want it public. Is a public meeting all right with you?

MR. HISS: Yes.

The Chairman then directed me to be present "at 10:15 on that day," saying the Committee would then decide "whether or not we will go into a public hearing." Stripling said that "this is a kind of unprecedented proposition, and if you say it is going to be a public session, you know it will be ballyhooed into a circus." He went on to express a preference for an executive session.

I commented:

MR. HISS: I want to be clear that I am not asking for an executive session as opposed to public. As far as consideration to me after what has been done to my feelings and my reputation, I think it would be like sinking the Swiss Navy. No public show could embarrass me now. I am asking to see this man.

MR. STRIPLING: Do you have a preference?

MR. HISS: I think it is for the committee to decide.

MR. NIXON: Do you care?

MR. HISS: I think I prefer a public session.

MR. HÉBERT: That is the reverse.

MR. HISS: I don't think I said that.

THE CHAIRMAN: Which do you want?

MR. NIXON: Let him think it over.

MR. HISS: May I try to give it—

MR. NIXON: We will also give Mr. Chambers an opportunity.

MR. HISS: Further consideration?

THE CHAIRMAN: Yes.

MR. NIXON: Just say that it will be arranged at that time, that no decision has been made as to the type of hearing.

MR. HISS: In any event, you want me here at 10:15 a.m. in this room.

The last words of the transcript of this session were those of the Chairman: ". . . we will see you August 25."

At this session of August 16, 1948, my second appearance before the Committee, on the occasion of the first mention of my relations with Crosley I had withheld nothing about those relations. I have subsequently testified to the same events many times. There has been no reason to add or subtract incidents. Because based on fact, the account has been consistently the same, corrected only as to dates which I had then had no opportunity to verify.

CHAPTER THREE

———

ORIGIN OF THE
"GUILT BY CLOSE ASSOCIATION"
THEORY

AS THE August 16 session had ended with a clear commitment in time and place for me to see Chambers face to face, I again had a sense of having accomplished something. But no sense of satisfaction was warranted. The Committee's delay in bringing Chambers and me together and their substituted procedure of separate secret hearings proved far more damaging to me than I then realized.

I had been concerned because the impression was being created that I had categorically denied ever having met the man Chambers by any name or under any circumstances. With the loose practice of charging guilt by association then all too prevalent, I feared that if the familiarity of Chambers's press photographs proved to stem from my having at some time actually met him, the further impression would be created that I must also have been his fellow Communist. This concern I now know to have been misplaced, for most people,

after reflection, soon conclude that mere *acquaintance* sup-
plies no basis for imputing any such thing.

The damage to me from the delayed meeting and the
secret hearings was, however, most serious for other reasons.
By taking Chambers's testimony of August 7 in secret, where
it could not be promptly corrected by me, and by characterizing all of this testimony as accurate, the Committee created
an impression that Chambers and I had had a close association,
and that what one supposedly intimate friend did the other
might be expected to do also. This might be called a theory of
"guilt by *close* association." This theory of guilt by close association encouraged even sophisticated minds to accept inferences from circumstantial evidence which they would not
have drawn in calmer times. At the time I overlooked the
growth of this theory in my case because, knowing its major
premise to be untrue, I could not imagine acceptance of that
premise by others.

The questions of a personal nature that I was asked on
August 16 which related to the various members of my family
and to my own interests and hobbies were, from this point of
view, far more significant than I then guessed. They were not
asked, as I had assumed they were, merely to give the Committee a general picture of my background and personality.
They were topics that Chambers himself had touched upon
in his August 7 session with the Committee (and apparently
also in the conversation, described by Bert Andrews, that he
and Nixon had at Chambers's farm on the 15th). The Committee promptly used Chambers's statements of August 7
about my personal life, whether accurate (as some, gained from
our actual acquaintance, certainly were) or inaccurate (as
were those that might indicate more than mere acquaintance),
to promote the myth of a close relationship.

As I look back over the record of my testimony of the
16th, I can see now that the "close association" theory had
already come into being and was being deliberately promoted
by the Committee's tactics. Thus, Stripling told me that day,
speaking of Chambers's August 7 appearance: "He sat there

and testified for hours. [The record shows that the session lasted for 2 hours and 40 minutes. A variety of topics unrelated to my personal life took up nearly one third of the hearing, and the members' questions to Chambers took up about half of the remaining time.] He said he spent a week in your house and he just rattled off details like that. He has either made a study of your life in great detail or he knows you, one or the other, *or he is incorrect.*" [1] Stripling made no response to my inquiry: "Could I ask you to ask him some questions?" Later that same day he indicated a less open mind as to the possibility that Chambers was incorrect in some of the details he had rattled off:

> I am trying to determine why a man would come in before a committee of Congress under the penalties of perjury and just out of the blue make up a story and then have that story check almost in every minute detail, according to check. . . .

Hébert did not go quite that far on the 16th in certifying to the correctness of Chambers's account of my personal affairs. Still, he did say: ". . . we probed him, as Mr. Stripling says, for hours. . . . There wasn't a thing that came to our minds that we didn't ask him about, these little details, to probe his own testimony or rather to test his own credibility."

Chambers had indeed become the Committee's witness and was increasingly to be treated as such. In Stripling's account of the Committee's activities in his newspaper articles and in his book, he said that there was little optimism in the subcommittee that prepared to hear Chambers's testimony of August 7. It is with relation to this precise period that he recorded, as quoted earlier, that "our espionage inquiry plainly was tottering." At this point the tone changes; the Committee makes a fresh start in pursuit of its original objective. He writes of "the man's incredibly detailed account" and says that the subcommittee was "dazzled by detail." More, he writes that he assigned "a quiet, middle-aged woman on our research staff to check on each item. . . . Everything jibed except in

[1] Italics added.

minute instances." This expands his remark of August 16 that Chambers's story checked "almost in every minute detail." The supposed checking had thus been done in advance of my testimony of the 16th, which was evidently desired for some other purpose—namely, to attempt to extract from me some appearances of support for the Committee's new start.

The Committee's characterization of this early secret testimony by Chambers as demonstrating a close association was emphasized at the public hearing of August 25 (see Chapter V) and is quite explicit in the Interim Report of August 28 [2] (". . . it was definitely established that Alger Hiss and Whittaker Chambers knew each other personally and rather intimately . . ."; "It is also clear that Hiss knew Chambers very well . . ."). Stripling's later account is that Chambers's August 7 testimony contained "facts which only an extremely intimate friend of Hiss . . . could have provided." (The indicated omission is of an ironical parenthetical clause: "or one who had hired dozens of private detectives to compile a report on Hiss.")

The close-association thesis became a platform from which Chambers could launch a succession of expanding charges. It seemed to me that as we disposed of one set of assertions by careful investigation, Chambers would produce another new story that wiped out the effect of the demolishing of the first one. And, always, the close-association theory gave color to his new assertion. Already it was serving to buttress his assertion that I was a member with him of an underground Washington group, the alleged leader and founder of which was dead and hence unavailable to confirm or refute Chambers. It was to become a chief basis of the case presented to the two successive juries in the trials that grew out of still newer charges that Chambers first launched in mid-November 1948—charges that have been made by no other witness. In his final argument to the second jury, the jury that voted for conviction, the prosecuting attorney said:

[2] See pp. 26–7.

. . . I think you will agree that if there was a close association certain things probably followed. . . .

. . . It meant not only that they were friends but that they were in agreement on their basic philosophy, and if they were in agreement on their basic philosophy they were all Communists. . . . Now if there was a close association and if they were in agreement on their philosophy then it is probable that each Communist helped the other.

And how did Mr. Hiss help? He gave the documents.

The vote of the second jury indicated that some of the jurors may have accepted the characterization of a close association which was so plainly, continually, and forcefully asserted by Committee members from August 1948 through the succeeding months, in hearings, reports, articles, speeches, and remarks to the press.

What were "these little details," these details that "dazzled" the Committee, this "incredibly detailed account" that the Committee asserted were confirmed by the independent inquiry of an unnamed "quiet, middle-aged woman" on its research staff?

How many of the details that are substantially accurate simply demonstrate a recollection stemming from actual acquaintance and from a closeness of observation developed by habits of parasitism? Was this recollection perhaps recently refurbished in anticipation of this very recital? Was it added to by stories picked up here and there? (Chambers has testified that he no longer remembers what he has experienced himself and what has been told him by others.[3]) In the circumstances of our acquaintance Chambers had had opportunity to observe or to learn from me some true items. We had met and talked about a dozen times; in particular, he had been in my P Street

[3] His precise testimony, given in 1951, was: "I find it impossible, with the play of so many influences on my mind, because people are always asking me questions, bringing me information, and there are actually areas of my experience where I can no longer distinguish between what I once knew and what I have heard and learned in the course of testifying. . . ."

house for two nights, we had lunched together a couple of times, we had driven from Washington to New York, passing through my home town of Baltimore on the way.

It is now established that when Chambers sought me out at the Nye Committee, he was engaged in illegal activities. With this in mind it is not illogical to assume that he had an ulterior motive in making my acquaintance. Was this part of an attempt to make connections with those who could be used as scapegoats or as covers for his actual accomplices? (Certainly after his admission of espionage and perjury, his charges against me served these very purposes.) His sublease was a nucleus on which he could build a dossier of items about me.

No less important, how many of the details of August 7 are demonstrable embroideries on fact, or surmises from known or supposed fact, or bald inventions, demonstrating not a close relationship but a ready disregard of the truth?

1.   Chambers correctly stated that my stepson was a member of the household and gave his name and approximate age. (Chambers said he was "about 10 years old." Timothy was born in September 1926 and so was eight when I first knew Chambers and nearly ten when I terminated our acquaintance.) He also gave Timothy's father's name and occupation, but then invented a nonexistent relationship to Thornton Wilder.

He did not know the name of any school Timothy had attended. This lack he filled by the invention that in 1936 I had moved my stepson (whose school expenses he correctly stated were at that time being paid by Timothy's father) from one school to another with lower tuition, turning over the difference to the Communist Party. This fabrication was capable of immediate independent exposure by any objective investigation through Timothy's father, who had paid the school bills directly or on receipts I forwarded to him. Moreover, the actual progression of schools was to more expensive ones, the cost of which I in time shared, another easily ascertainable fact. Quite unaware of Chambers's fabrication, I gave the Committee on the 16th all the necessary factual leads to follow:

MR. NIXON: What schools do you recall your son attended in 1934 to 1937?

MR. HISS: Tim was in the Friends School briefly here.

MR. NIXON: Where did he go before that?

MR. HISS: It is going to be hard to be sure. He went to a small school called the Cobb School, I think, in Chevy Chase.

MR. NIXON: Is that called the Chevy Chase School also?

MR. HISS: I don't think so. I think it was just called the Cobb School, Mr. Cobb ran it. After Friends School he went to boarding school to George School in Pennsylvania near Doylestown, right near Newtown, Pa.

MR. NIXON: Is the Friends School a rather expensive school, would you say, or moderate-priced school?

MR. HISS: I would say moderate.

MR. NIXON: And Cobb's School the same?

MR. HISS: Yes. I might say Timmy's educational expenses were paid by his own father as part of the arrangement.

MR. NIXON: Was the Cobb School, do you recall, more expensive than the Friends School?

MR. HISS: I would guess that it was probably less because it didn't carry through the grades thoroughly. It was a preschool and early primary grades.

MR. NIXON: And you can't recall that there was a school in between that and Friends School?

MR. HISS: I don't recall it, Mr. Nixon. He went to the Landon School here for a while.

MR. NIXON: That is after Friends School?

MR. HISS: That is after he had been at Friends and before he went to George School but not between Cobb and Friends. He went to Landon School, which is off Connecticut Avenue out when you get to Bradley Lane. [Timothy entered Landon in September 1936 after one year at Friends. He was at Friends when I still knew Chambers.]

MR. NIXON: Is that more expensive than the other?

MR. HISS: That was a rather expensive school.

MR. NIXON: More so than Friends School?

MR. HISS: I think so.

MR. NIXON: You don't recall the school he went to immediately before Friends?

MR. HISS: No; I don't. [There was none, other than Cobb's.]

MR. NIXON: But you would say the Friends School was a moderate priced school?

MR. HISS: Yes.

MR. HÉBERT: Then you put him in a more expensive school?

MR. HISS: Landon was more expensive than Friends. He hadn't been getting along very well at Friends and we consulted friends and thought that Landon was better.

MR. HÉBERT: You put him in a more expensive school?

MR. HISS: That is correct.

Nonetheless, months after it must have been evident to him that this was a lie, Stripling repeated this tale of Chambers's about my son's educational expenses in his articles and book as if it were fact, one of the "facts which only an extremely intimate friend of Hiss . . . could have provided."

Ex parte recitals without indication of their falsity can, of course, seem persuasive of intimacy. So difficult is it to catch up with a lie once launched that I have never seen this lie of Chambers's adverted to and repudiated.

Chambers's claim at this time was that he had known us through 1937. (Later this was expanded by him to April 1938.) When pressed for my son's physical characteristics, his only reply, quite incorrect, was that "Timmie was a puny little boy, also rather nervous." Had he known us at all in 1937, he would certainly have known that in February Timothy was nearly killed by an automobile while riding his bicycle. For weeks he was bedridden and then cast-bound for months in the small house to which we had moved in July 1936. Chambers's glib assumption of the role of family friend familiar with my son's schooling is contradicted (as are the dates he set for the period he knew me) by the facts. Chambers testified that the new school "was somewhere in Georgetown. He [Timothy] came back and forth every day." The new school, Landon School, which Timothy entered in the fall of 1936—after I had ceased to know Chambers—was some miles out in the country, west of Bethesda, Maryland. The school that *is* practically in Georgetown is Friends School, where Timothy went in 1935 when Chambers still knew me.

2. My wife at times addresses me as "Hill," though more often she calls me simply by my given name. Rarely she adds a "y" to the occasional "Hill." Chambers testified at the secret hearing of August 7:

MR. NIXON: What name did Mrs. Hiss use in addressing Mr. Hiss?
MR. CHAMBERS: Usually "Hilly."
MR. NIXON: "Hilly"?
MR. CHAMBERS: Yes.
MR. NIXON: Quite often?
MR. CHAMBERS: Yes.
MR. NIXON: In your presence?
MR. CHAMBERS: Yes.
MR. NIXON: Not "Alger"?
MR. CHAMBERS: Not "Alger."
MR. NIXON: What nickname, if any, did Mr. Hiss use in addressing his wife?
MR. CHAMBERS: More often "Dilly" and sometimes "Pross." Her name was Priscilla. They were commonly referred to as "Hilly" and "Dilly."
MR. NIXON: They were commonly referred to as "Hilly" and "Dilly"?
MR. CHAMBERS: By other members of the group.
MR. NIXON: You don't mean to indicate that was simply the nicknames used by the Communist group?
MR. CHAMBERS: This was a family matter.
MR. NIXON: In other words, other friends and acquaintances of theirs would possibly have used these names?

I have never called my wife "Dilly" or anything remotely like it. We have never been known by anyone, whatever his politics, as Hilly and Dilly. No friend has ever used Hill or Hilly in addressing me. The quiet, middle-aged woman in her check on this item did not approach me or any member of my family, or, so far as I have heard, any friend of ours. Yet, on the 16th, Nixon introduced the subject of nicknames with special emphasis.

MR. NIXON: There are matters which I wish to go into now to which Mr. Chambers has given categorical answers. . . . It will be very helpful as the two records look together to see how accurate he is in this case.

I want to say first of all, so that it won't come up, that I realize that the matters which are covered are matters which third parties could corroborate. . . .

What were the nicknames you and your wife had?

MR. HISS: My wife, I have always called her "Prossy."

MR. NIXON: What does she call you?

MR. HISS: Well, at one time she called me quite frequently "Hill," H-i-l-l.

MR. NIXON: What other name?

MR. HISS: "Hilly," with a "y."

MR. NIXON: What other name did you call her?

MR. STRIPLING: What did you say?

MR. HISS: She called me "Hill" or "Hilly." I called her "Pross" or "Prossy" almost exclusively. I don't think any other nickname.

MR. NIXON: Did you ever call her "Dilly"?

MR. HISS: No; never.

MR. NIXON: Never to your knowledge in fun or otherwise?

MR. HISS: Never.

Stripling's chronicle of Committee activities nevertheless incorrectly lists as "facts" which could be known only by "an extremely intimate friend" that "Mrs. Hiss called her husband 'Hilly.' He called her 'Dilly' or 'Pross.' Members of the Communist group called them 'Hilly and Dilly' when they spoke of them."

Chambers correctly gave my wife's first and maiden names, but not her middle name. He said maliciously, and disclosing by his invention his own values, that my wife spoke of her first husband "almost with hatred," and, though he could not recall the color of her eyes, he described her as "a short, highly nervous, little woman" who blushes "fiery red" when "excited or angry." I have never heard of any attempt by the Committee to verify from friends or acquaintances any of these "dazzling" details, each of which is utterly out of character. My wife is, in fact, neither little nor nervous, but is, on the contrary, of medium height and composed in manner. She is invariably charitable and affirmative in her opinions of others and not given to hatred, excitement, or anger.

Chambers mistakenly asserted that my wife came from a Quaker family. My wife has for years taken an interest in the activities of the Society of Friends, but her father and mother were lifelong and active Presbyterians. Chambers also said that my wife "came from the Great Valley, near Paoli, Pa." She was born in Evanston, Illinois. In her childhood her family moved to St. David's and some ten years later to Frazer, Pennsylvania. St. David's, Paoli, and Frazer are all within close commuting range of Philadelphia, on the main line of the Pennsylvania Railroad. St. David's is between Wayne and Bryn Mawr, Frazer between Paoli and Downingtown. Chambers asserted that while "driving" she had shown him the road "down which their farm lay" (there was no such drive; he was not asked and did not volunteer the circumstances which would have led to his taking a drive west of Philadelphia on which my wife would be one of the passengers while she was a resident of Washington). My wife's father was in the life-insurance business with offices in Philadelphia and had residences first at St. David's and later at Frazer from which he commuted daily to Philadelphia. The house at Frazer was directly on the Lincoln Highway, not "down" any road.

Nixon, of course with Chambers's statements in mind, asked me on August 16 if my wife had lived in Paoli. When I said the place was Frazer, he asked if it were near Paoli. He then asked:

Did she live on a farm?

Unaware of what lay behind the question, I replied:

Her father was in the insurance business, and he acquired a small place—I suppose it could be called a farm—from which he commuted to his insurance business.

No doubt this was taken as verification of Chambers's embroidery upon his knowledge that my wife had lived on the Main Line.

3. Chambers described me as "about 5 feet 8 or 9, slender," with "blue or gray" eyes. Upon being pressed, he replied: "I think they change," then accepted Nixon's suggested "sort of a blue-gray" by concluding: "Blueish gray, you could say." He added that I walk with a slight mince "if you watch him from behind." [4] When Stripling unaccountably asked if Chambers remembered anything about my hands, the reply was: "He had rather long delicate fingers. I don't remember anything special."

I am in fact six feet in height and have always been slender. My eyes are blue. I have a thin man's thin fingers. I have no mince from before or behind, yet Stripling lists this, too.

Chambers's former Communist associate Mandel interjected at about this point in Chambers's testimony that a photograph of me, presumably a press photograph taken during the August 5 hearings, showed one hand cupped to an ear. Chambers promptly, but incorrectly, jumped to the conclusion that my hearing is defective (the fact is that occasionally it was necessary to exclude temporary distracting noises of scraping chairs and persons entering or leaving the hearing room to catch clearly what was being said to me):

MR. CHAMBERS: He is deaf in one ear.
MR. NIXON: Mr. Hiss is deaf in one ear?
MR. HÉBERT: Which ear?
MR. CHAMBERS: I don't know. . . .

To demonstrate conclusively the falseness of this item, after this testimony of Chambers's was made available on August 25, I had a specialist at the Columbia Medical Center examine my hearing. He certified that my hearing in both ears is normal. On the 16th I was asked:

MR. STRIPLING: Are you hard of hearing in your left ear?
MR. HISS: Not to my knowledge.
MR. STRIPLING: I noticed you had your hand up to your ear.
MR. HISS: If I have done that, it is only when I wanted to be sure I was hearing.

[4] See pp. 318–20.

MR. STRIPLING: You did that before the committee in open session and did then. If you are having difficulty, we can all move this way.

MR. HISS: I am not aware of it and never heard any doctor say so.

No other checking with me was ever done by the Committee or its staff on this "categorical answer" of Chambers's. Yet Stripling lists my being "slightly deaf in one ear" as part of Chambers's "incredibly detailed account."

When asked if I wore glasses, Chambers correctly recalled that I use glasses only for reading, with his recollection perhaps aided by the current photographs taken in and out of hearing rooms.

He remembered my having told him that as a boy I had collected spring water in Druid Hill Park, Baltimore, and distributed it to neighbors. I, for my part, recalled his having told me that he worked in the gang that laid the street railways in Washington.[5]

Upon being asked if I had any hobbies, Chambers replied that both my wife and I were "amateur ornithologists." We do, indeed, go in for bird watching and did at the time I knew Chambers. He had gone on to add:

MR. CHAMBERS: They used to get up early in the morning and go to Glen Echo, out the canal, to observe birds.

I recall once they saw, to their great excitement, a prothonotary warbler.

MR. MC DOWELL: A very rare specimen?

MR. CHAMBERS: I never saw one. I am also fond of birds.

On the 16th, I was in turn asked about my hobbies and replied:

MR. HISS: Tennis and amateur ornithology.

MR. NIXON: Is your wife interested in ornithology?

MR. HISS: I also like to swim and also like to sail. My wife is interested in ornithology, as I am, through my interest. Maybe I am using too big a word to say an ornithologist because I am pretty amateur, but I have been interested in it since I

[5] See pp. 31, 95.

was in Boston. I think anybody who knows me would know
that.

MR. MC DOWELL: Did you ever see a prothonotary warbler?

MR. HISS: I have right here on the Potomac. Do you know that
place?

THE CHAIRMAN: What is that?

MR. NIXON: Have you ever seen one?

MR. HISS: Did you see it in the same place?

MR. MC DOWELL: I saw one in Arlington.

MR. HISS: They come back and nest in those swamps. Beautiful
yellow head, a gorgeous bird.

McDowell was a better ornithologist than Chambers. Arlington is in Virginia across from Washington, and the prothonotary nests in swamps along the Potomac River as far
south of Arlington as Glen Echo is *north* of Washington. The
prothonotary was to become, in magazine articles and in statements emanating from the Committee and its staff, the prime
alleged proof of a close relationship between Chambers and me
—as if an enthusiast boasts of his finds only to intimate friends.

4. Chambers, assuming that my mother was living at home
in Baltimore when he knew me, correctly located her house
(my birthplace) as being "on or near Linden Street." The
house is at 1427 Linden Avenue. Chambers lived for some
months in 1935 and 1936 on Eutaw Place, which is one block
west of Linden Avenue, perhaps the reason "Linden" remained
in his memory. My mother was not living at home from the
fall of 1934 until the fall of 1937, but her name and address
appeared in the Baltimore telephone directory each year.

Chambers correctly stated that I had a sister. He added,
incorrectly, that when he knew me she lived with my mother
in Baltimore. In fact my sister had by 1934 been living in
Texas for a number of years as a member of the staff of the
University of Texas. By that time, indeed, she had become
head of the department of physical education, a position she
still holds. Hébert, a Louisianan, was perhaps aware of my sister's career. It was he who on August 7 had, in one of his in-

frequent questions, asked Chambers whether I had brothers or sisters in addition to the brother whose name had already been mentioned. He had persisted:

MR. HÉBERT: What did the sister do?

MR. CHAMBERS: I don't think she did anything besides live with her mother. Whether he had any more than that I don't know. [An older brother and another sister had died in 1926 and 1928, respectively.]

MR. HÉBERT: You know he referred to. at least one sister?

MR. CHAMBERS: He did.

MR. HÉBERT: Do you recall her name?

MR. CHAMBERS: No.

MR. HÉBERT: And you don't recall what the sister did?

MR. CHAMBERS: No; I don't think she did anything.

MR. HÉBERT: Did it ever come up in conversation that the sister was interested in athletics?

MR. CHAMBERS: No.

MR. HÉBERT: Was he interested in athletics?

MR. CHAMBERS: I think he played tennis, but I am not certain.

MR. HÉBERT: With the sister now—it is very important—you don't recall the sister?

MR. CHAMBERS: We merely brushed that subject.

MR. NIXON: You never met the sister?

MR. CHAMBERS: No; nor never met the mother. My impression was his relations with his mother were affectionate but not too happy. She was, perhaps, domineering. I simply pulled this out of the air in the conversation.

On the 16th, Hébert asked me about my sister in the following passage:

MR. HÉBERT: Where does your sister live?

MR. HISS: She lives in Austin, Tex., department of physical education at the university.

MR. HÉBERT: University of Texas?

MR. HISS: Yes.

MR. HÉBERT: Where did she live before she went to the University of Texas?

MR. HISS: In Baltimore.

MR. HÉBERT: With whom?

MR. HISS: With my mother.

MR. HÉBERT: Just your mother and sister?

MR. HISS: Yes. She went straight to Texas, I think, on graduation from physical training school, may have had one intermediate position.

MR. HÉBERT: What year?

MR. HISS: She is a good deal older than I am. I think she has been in Texas about 20 years.

MR. HÉBERT: She has been in Texas about 20 years?

MR. HISS: Yes.

MR. HÉBERT: Would she have been living in Baltimore in the years in question with your mother?

MR. HISS: No, definitely no. She was in Texas at that time.

Chambers volunteered a statement about my sister-in-law's father which, if accurate, might have indicated more than casual knowledge of my family affairs: "Donald Hiss was married, I think, to a daughter of Mr. Cotton, who is in the State Department." My sister-in-law's maiden name was Jones; her father died when she was an infant. Yet the index to the Committee's Hearings, despite the asserted checking on Chambers's statements, reads: "Hiss, Mrs. Donald (nee Cotton)."

Stripling asked at one point if I went to church:

MR. STRIPLING: Did he go to church?

MR. CHAMBERS: He was forbidden to go to church.

MR. STRIPLING: Do you know whether he was a member of a church?

MR. CHAMBERS: I don't know.

In fact when we moved to P Street we attended near-by Christ Church, an Episcopal church whose rector was a college mate of mine. Timothy was a choirboy there at the time of his accident in 1937. I have been a lifelong member of the Episcopal Church.

5. Chambers was asked to describe the houses in which I had lived during the time that he claimed to know me, and to de-

scribe my furniture and furnishings. He recalled that when he first knew me I was living in the 28th Street apartment and correctly recalled the apartment house and that the apartment was on the top floor, though he did not point out that he had leased the apartment from me for several months in the spring of 1935. His description of its location was perhaps meant to sound more like that of a frequent visitor than that of a one-time occupant:

MR. CHAMBERS: . . . It seems to me when I first knew him he was living on 28th Street in an apartment house. There were two almost identical apartment houses. It seems to me that is a dead-end street and this was right at the dead end and certainly it is on the right-hand side as you go up.

It also seems to me that apartment was on the top floor. Now, what was it like inside, the furniture? I can't remember.

MR. MANDEL: What was Mr. Hiss' library devoted to?

MR. CHAMBERS: Very nondescript, as I recall.

Had Chambers been correct in his assertion that he knew me well, and as late as 1937, wouldn't he (as did my actual friends) have known at least of a prized volume which came to me at the end of June 1936? This is a facsimile of Justice Oliver Wendell Holmes's notebook which lists all the books the Justice (whom I had served as secretary) had read in his lifetime. Wouldn't a bookish fellow, a writer, remember some book in a "close friend's" house if indeed he had, as Chambers had said earlier, made that house "a kind of informal headquarters" where he had "stayed overnight for a number of days . . . from time to time," even having "stayed there as long as a week"?

The thinness of Chambers's pretense is emphasized by the answer he gave in an attempt to brazen out his statement that he had stayed in my house a number of days together from time to time, "as long as a week" at a time:

MR. NIXON: A week one time. What would you be doing during that time?

MR. CHAMBERS: Most of the time reading.

The inquiry concerning my books was but one of a series of routine questions about our tastes in food, articles of our furniture, and the like. Questions of this kind are standard procedure for prompting a real memory. Chambers demonstrated a lack of any real memory by answers that were as uninformative and question-begging as had been his statement that my books were "very nondescript." Occasionally he apparently sought to compensate for his unenlightening replies by irrelevant digressions:

MR. NIXON: Was there any special dish they served?

MR. CHAMBERS: No. I think you get here into something else. Hiss is a man of great simplicity and a great gentleness and sweetness of character, and they lived with extreme simplicity. I had the impression that the furniture in that house was kind of pulled together from here or there, maybe got it from their mother or something like that, nothing lavish about it whatsoever, quite simple. [Had he known us as well as he pretended, he might have recalled that not long after his two days' stay at P Street I received from the estate of Justice Holmes a large and handsome Queen Anne mirror which thereafter hung in the P Street hallway. It has since been rather noticeable wherever we have lived and was a subject of interest to our friends when we received it.]

Their food was in the same pattern and they cared nothing about food. It was not a primary interest in their lives.

Doesn't everyone have some favorite food? Even if it is as lackluster as my liking for all rice dishes?

Following the passage about my interest in ornithology and another about the cars I had had (a subject dealt with later in this chapter), Nixon continued:

MR. NIXON: Did they have a piano?

MR. CHAMBERS: I don't believe so. I am reasonably sure they did not.

When Chambers first knew us we had an old upright, which we gave away when we moved to P Street. At 30th Street when we no longer knew Chambers, but where he claimed to have been a constant visitor, we acquired a new piano which, though of spinet size, was a bulky object in the small living room.

MR. NIXON: Do you recall any particular pieces of furniture that they had?

MR. CHAMBERS: The only thing I recall was a small leather cigarette box, leather-covered cigarette box, with gold tooling on it. It seems to me that box was red leather.

MR. NIXON: Red leather cigarette box with gold tooling?

MR. CHAMBERS: That is right.

MR. NIXON: Do you recall any particular piece of bedroom furniture they had?

MR. CHAMBERS: No.

MR. NIXON: Do you recall possibly what the silver pattern was, if any? Was it sterling?

MR. CHAMBERS: I don't recall.

MR. NIXON: Do you recall what kind of chinaware they used?

MR. CHAMBERS: No. I have been thinking over these things and none of that stands out.

MR. NIXON: What kind of cocktail glasses did they have?

MR. CHAMBERS: We never drank cocktails.

MR. NIXON: Did they drink?

MR. CHAMBERS: They did not drink. They didn't drink with me. For one thing, I was strictly forbidden by the Communist Party to taste liquor at any time.

MR. NIXON: And you didn't drink?

MR. CHAMBERS: I never drank.

Again Chambers was incorrect as to our habits. As any friend would know, we are neither heavy drinkers nor are we abstemious. This testimony of his is itself an indication that his stay in my house was not that of an ordinary house guest, who would certainly have been offered a drink. I think it is indeed likely that there happened to be no occasion for me to have a drink with him in or out of my house. Chambers's colorful embellishment of this fact served the purpose of interrupting the rather monotonously unproductive questioning as to the houses in which I had lived. Several pages of testimony later on Nixon returned to that theme:

MR. NIXON: Getting back to Alger Hiss for the moment, do you recall any pictures on the wall that they might have owned at the time?

MR. CHAMBERS: No; I'm afraid I don't.

On August 16, I was not asked about any striking or unusual pieces of furniture, books, or other possessions—not even whether I owned a red leather cigarette box (like many other households, ours has often harbored leather cigarette boxes, but I recall no red one). The only questions of this kind related to stuffed birds and pictures of birds:

MR. STRIPLING: Do you have a collection of stuffed birds or anything?

MR. HISS: No.

MR. STRIPLING: Pictures of them?

MR. HISS: I have bird books with pictures; photographs that I had taken; no.

MR. STRIPLING: Just pictures of different birds not in books?

MR. HISS: I have several Audubon prints hanging in my house, of birds.

On August 7, Mr. Hébert at the end of the session had returned once more to the theme of the houses in which I had lived:

MR. HÉBERT: I am interested in the houses he lived in. You said several houses. How many houses? Start from the beginning.

MR. CHAMBERS: As well as I can remember, when I first knew him he was living on Twenty-eighth Street. . . . From there I am not absolutely certain the order of the houses, but it seems to me he moved to a house in Georgetown—that I know; he moved to a house in Georgetown—but it seems it was on the corner of P Street, but again I can't be absolutely certain of the streets.

MR. HÉBERT: It was on a corner?

MR. CHAMBERS: Yes; and as I recall, you had to go up steps to get to it. [The P Street house, where Chambers stayed two nights while waiting for his household effects and where he came to see me more than once thereafter, is not, as a matter of fact, a corner house. It does have a flight of steps up to the front door.]

MR. MANDEL: How many rooms were there in that house?

MR. CHAMBERS: I don't know offhand, but I have the impression it was a three-story house. I also think it had a kind of a porch in back where people sat. [It had three stories plus a basement dining room and kitchen; and it had a rear terrace and garden.]

Then if I have got the order of the houses right, he moved to a house on an up-and-down street, a street that would cross the lettered streets, probably just around the corner from the other house and very near to his brother Donald.

MR. HÉBERT: Still in Georgetown?

MR. CHAMBERS: Still in Georgetown. I have forgotten the reason for his moving. That was a smaller house and, as I recall, the dining room was below the level of the ground, one of those basement dining rooms; that it had a small yard in back.

I think he was there when I broke with the Communist Party.

In the spring of 1936 we found another house. The reason, striking enough to our intimates, was the collapse of the entire heating system at P Street during a winter cold spell while I was recovering from pneumonia. The new house *was* smaller and *was* on a north-and-south street, a numbered street, though Chambers failed to mention that obvious identification. Like the P Street house, it, too, had the familiar Georgetown basement kitchen and dining room, the kitchen in front and visible from the sidewalk. It was a bit over three blocks from the P Street house, not just around the corner from it. Like the neighboring duplicate house (whose yard was visible from the sidewalk), it had a small back yard, as Chambers said. The renovations to this house, 1245 30th Street, were finished later than originally scheduled. Consequently, that spring—instead of overlapping leases, as a year earlier—we had a hiatus in leases and spent the last two weeks of June at the Hotel Martinique on 16th Street, a fact of which Chambers, unlike our close friends, at no time seems to have been aware. As the spring of 1936 was the time when I terminated my ac-

quaintance with him, he very likely did know of our plans to
move to a near-by house that was then being renovated, and
may have passed it in coming to see me at P Street, though I
am quite sure that he never called on me at the new house. I
should add that it was very near my brother's house. He was the
only other Hiss with a residential address in the Washington
telephone book; Chambers may have noticed there what near
neighbors we were, or I earlier may have mentioned my brother's address to him in conversation. In any event, Chambers
has never claimed to have been in my brother's house. However obtained, his knowledge of its location doesn't come
from having *frequented* it, and the same is true of his knowledge of my 30th Street house.

Chambers's secret testimony of August 7 on houses continued for a little more:

MR. HÉBERT: Three houses? [Chambers had mentioned the apartment and only two houses up to this time.]

MR. CHAMBERS: But I went to see him in the house he later
moved to, which was on the other side of Wisconsin Avenue.
[At the end of 1937 we moved to 3415 Volta Place, which
is west of Wisconsin Avenue whereas the P Street and 30th
Street houses are east of it. I do not know how or why
Chambers learned that I moved, after I ceased to know him,
to a place he was able only thus vaguely to locate. Perhaps
he had ascertained that by 1938 I no longer lived on 30th
Street. This would have been an elementary precaution in
order not to make an obvious blunder in connection with his
testimony that he had come to see me after a long separation
to ask me to break with Communism. I know only that he
never came there while I was there.]

MR. HÉBERT: Three houses in Georgetown?

MR. CHAMBERS: One [the apartment] on Twenty-eighth Street.

MR. HÉBERT: The last time you saw him when you attempted to
persuade him to break away from the party——

MR. CHAMBERS: That was beyond Wisconsin Avenue.

MR. HÉBERT: Did you ever see their bedroom; the furniture?

MR. CHAMBERS: Yes; but I don't remember the furniture.

MR. HÉBERT: Did they have twin beds or single beds?

MR. CHAMBERS: I am almost certain they did not have twin beds.
MR. HÉBERT: In any of the four houses?
MR. CHAMBERS: I can't be sure about the last one, but I am reasonably sure they did not have twin beds before that.

Chambers lived at the apartment and stayed two nights at P Street. His recollection from that vantage point that we did not have twin beds is correct.

6. Chambers was also asked about our maids and whether we had pets:

MR. NIXON: Did the Hisses have a cook? Do you recall a maid?
MR. CHAMBERS: As nearly as I can remember, they had a maid who came in to clean, and a cook who came in to cook. I can't remember they had a maid there all the time or not. It seems to me in one or two of the houses they did.
    In one of the houses they had a rather elderly Negro maid whom Mr. Hiss used to drive home in the evening.
MR. NIXON: You don't recall the names of the maids?
MR. CHAMBERS: No; I don't.
MR. NIXON: Did the Hisses have any pets?
MR. CHAMBERS: They had, I believe, a cocker spaniel. I have a bad memory for dogs, but as nearly as I can remember it was a cocker spaniel.
MR. NIXON: Do you remember the dog's name?
MR. CHAMBERS: No. I remember they used to take it up to some kennel. I think out Wisconsin Avenue.
MR. NIXON: They took it to board it there?
MR. CHAMBERS: Yes. They made one or two vacation trips to the Eastern Shore of Maryland.
MR. NIXON: They made some vacation trips to the Eastern Shore of Maryland?
MR. CHAMBERS: Yes, and at those times the dog was kept at the kennel.

On the 16th, I was asked, as I have already pointed out, about our maids from 1934 to 1937. I replied:

I am not sure how helpful I can be. The first maid we had when we were in Washington as far back as 1929, I think, was with us for a while when we returned in 1933. She was a Negro maid. Her name was Martha Pope.

We never had more than one maid at a time. We never had an elderly maid until wartime, years after the period at issue. There had been no occasion to take any of the maids home after work as a regular pattern. Martha lived too far for that; her successor too near to need it.

I wasn't able at the moment to be sure how long Martha had stayed on our return to Washington. Her health began to fail and she had to stop work. I now know that she had remained with us well into 1935 while we were living on P Street. The maid who replaced Martha came to us when we were living on P Street and remained with us through the moves to 30th Street and to Volta Place. Her name was Claudia, or "Cleide," Catlett, a woman in her mid-thirties when she first came to us. She, too, was forced to stop work through ill-health, and during the war we understood that she had died some years after she had left us. (I, therefore, did not mention her in my testimony on the 16th.) We were mistaken; together with Martha Pope she testified for the defense in both trials.

Nixon inquired further:

MR. NIXON: If you had taken one of these servants home, would you be able to tell us where she lived, for example, from time to time?

MR. HISS: Yes. You mean if I had driven a servant to where she lived?

MR. NIXON: Yes; that is common practice. I do it, for example, with the woman who works for us.

MR. HISS: I have done that.

MR. NIXON: Does that refresh your memory?

MR. HISS: I remember the area where Martha Pope lived. She lived over near Howard University. I have been over there to ask if she were available, if she were sick. I may have even taken her home. I don't remember.

Later Nixon returned to the subject:

MR. NIXON: You testified you took your servants home?

MR. HISS: I have on occasions.

MR. NIXON: Do you recall the age of this particular woman, Mrs. Pope, by any chance?

MR. HISS: Martha, I would say she was probably in her 40's and very plump, very, very, plump, large cheerful plump woman.

MR. NIXON: Was she a cook or housekeeper?

MR. HISS: Cook and waitress. We never had more than one maid at a time.

The Committee was able to locate Martha on the basis of the information I gave, and took her testimony eight days later, August 24, in an executive session:

MR. NIXON: . . . Do you recall where the Hisses were living when you last worked for them?

MRS. POPE: On P Street.

. . . .

MR. NIXON: Where had she [Mrs. Hiss] lived before they moved to P Street?

MRS. POPE: Before they lived on O Street, and then they moved from O Street to Twenty-eighth Street.

MR. NIXON: Did you work for them when they lived on Twenty-eighth Street?

MRS. POPE: I did.

MR. NIXON: That was an apartment, was it not?

MRS. POPE: Yes.

MR. NIXON: And after they left Twenty-eighth Street, do you recall when they moved from there?

MRS. POPE: They moved from Twenty-eighth Street to P Street.

MR. NIXON: To P Street?

MRS. POPE: Yes.

MR. NIXON: And how long did you work for them while they lived on P Street. That is, how long do you recall working in the P Street house?

MRS. POPE: I just do not remember.

MR. NIXON: Just to the best of your recollection, if you can recall, was it a year or was it a month or something?

MRS. POPE: It was longer than a month.

MR. NIXON: Longer than a month.

MRS. POPE: I just do not remember how long it was.

MR. NIXON: Do you remember when they moved from that apartment on Twenty-eighth Street to P Street. Did you help them to move?

MRS. POPE: I was working with them; yes.

MR. NIXON: I see. Did you help them pack their dishes and things when they were moving at that time?

MRS. POPE: They left the apartment furnished; they moved to that P Street house, it was furnished.

· · · ·

MR. STRIPLING: Do you remember the time of year that was when they moved from the apartment on Twenty-eighth Street to the house on P Street?

MRS. POPE: I don't know whether it was spring or fall; I don't remember that.

· · · ·

MR. NIXON: Do you remember whether it was the spring or the winter?

MRS. POPE: It was not the winter, it was either the spring or the fall. I just do not remember now.

MR. NIXON: I see.

MR. STRIPLING: Mrs. Pope, when did you first go to work for the Hisses?

MRS. POPE: Soon after they were married.

MR. STRIPLING: Well, about what year was that?

MRS. POPE: That I cannot tell you. I don't remember.

· · · ·

. . . I had been working for them off and on nearly 5 years.

· · · ·

MR. STRIPLING: When you worked for them, what were your duties? Did you cook?

MRS. POPE: I did general house work.

MR. STRIPLING: General house work. Did you also cook?

MRS. POPE: Yes, sir.

MR. STRIPLING: What time did you get there in the morning?

MRS. POPE: 7:30.

MR. STRIPLING: 7:30 in the morning. What time did you leave in the afternoon?

MRS. POPE: 7:30 or 8 o'clock.
MR. STRIPLING: You were there all day?
MRS. POPE: Yes.

. . . .

MR. STRIPLING: Who moved into the apartment?
MRS. POPE: I don't know.
MR. STRIPLING: Did you ever hear them discuss that?
MRS. POPE: No; I never heard them discuss that.

. . . .

MR. NIXON: Did you work every day or did you have a certain number of days off?
MRS. POPE: I worked every day except Thursday.
MR. NIXON: Thursday was your day off?
MRS. POPE: Yes.
MR. NIXON: Did you work Saturday?
MRS. POPE: Yes.
MR. NIXON: Do you recall during that period just before you left, the year before you left the Hisses, that you were out because of illness or anything of that sort?
MRS. POPE: Yes.
MR. NIXON: When was that? Were you out for a long time?
MRS. POPE: I was out for, it might be, 2 or 3 weeks, I think, something like that. It was a good time that I was out.
MR. NIXON: Do you remember the time that was? Where were they living during that period?
MRS. POPE: Twenty-eighth Street.
MR. NIXON: At the apartment; I see. But you do not recall any time when you were out after they moved over to P Street?
MRS. POPE: I do not remember.

Stripling then showed Martha two photographs of Chambers "holding a baby" and a large photograph of Chambers, presumably a current press photo, which he said "was taken 12 years later, taken 14 years later" than the others.

MR. STRIPLING: . . . Now, did you ever at either the apartment on Twenty-eighth Street or at the home on P Street, did you ever see that person or that baby?
MRS. POPE: I do not remember.
MR. STRIPLING: You do not remember ever seeing it?

MRS. POPE: No; I do not.

MR. STRIPLING: Now, the baby's mother is a very dark woman, and they visited in the home of Mr. and Mrs. Hiss on P Street. They were there for several days.

MR. NIXON: They stayed overnight. Do you recall seeing them?

MRS. POPE: No; nobody stayed overnight, as I remember.

. . .

MR. STRIPLING: Do you remember the man?

MRS. POPE: No; I do not.

MR. STRIPLING: Never saw him?

MRS. POPE: I only saw it in the picture recently in the paper.

MR. STRIPLING: Who was the picture you saw in the paper?

MRS. POPE: I mean, here recently.

MR. STRIPLING: Who was the person that you saw?

MRS. POPE: Chambers; is it not?

MR. STRIPLING: The picture you are referring to is Whittaker Chambers.

MRS. POPE: That is the reason I say I saw his picture in the paper recently.

MR. STRIPLING: Does this look anything like the person you saw in the paper? . . . is that the person you saw in the paper?

MRS. POPE: It might be; I don't know.

MR. STRIPLING: Does it look like him?

MRS. POPE: It looks like—something like.

MR. STRIPLING: Does this person look like the one you saw in the paper?

MRS. POPE: It does not.

MR. STRIPLING: It does not look like the one you saw in the paper?

MRS. POPE: No; just this looks something like him, that is all.

MR. STRIPLING: This one [presumably the current photograph] looks something like him [i.e., was recognizable as the man whose photographs had appeared in the newspapers], but these [apparently the snapshots taken in 1934] do not look anything like him.

. . .

MR. STRIPLING: When did you last see Mr. Hiss?

MRS. POPE: When I last seen Mr. Hiss he lived at the Thirtieth Street house.

MR. STRIPLING: No; but when did you last see him? When was the last time that you saw Mr. Hiss?

MRS. POPE: When they lived at Thirtieth Street.

MR. STRIPLING: No; when was the last time you saw Mr. Hiss, Mr. Alger Hiss?

MR. NIXON: Not where was the last time you worked for him.

MRS. POPE: No; I am not saying—I never worked at the Thirtieth Street house.

MR. STRIPLING: When was the last time you saw him?

MRS. POPE: I am telling you now that was the last time, because I went there when the little boy got hurt, and I went to the house and saw the boy and I saw him then, and I have not seen him since.

MR. STRIPLING: When was the last time you talked to him?

MRS. POPE: Then.

MR. STRIPLING: At that time, you have not talked to him on the telephone?

MRS. POPE: No; I have not.

. . . .

MR. STRIPLING: When was the last time you saw Mrs. Alger Hiss?

MRS. POPE: When I went back to see the boy when he got hurt.

MR. STRIPLING: On Thirtieth Street?

MRS. POPE: Yes.

MR. STRIPLING: When was the last time you saw him? Do you think that was the last time?

MRS. POPE: When I went back.

MR. NIXON: Mrs. Pope, have you discussed this matter of your testimony here this morning with your employer, your present employer?

MRS. POPE: I just told him this morning that I remembered that I—I remembered the P Street house.

MR. NIXON: You discussed it with Mrs. Howard [of the Committee's staff], too, did you not?

MRS. POPE: I discussed it with her coming down.

MR. NIXON: She asked you some questions. Who else have you discussed this with?

MRS. POPE: No one else.

MR. NIXON: You are sure of that?

MRS. POPE: I am sure of that.

MR. NIXON: The first time you have discussed it was with Mrs. Howard and your present employer?

MRS. POPE: Yes, sir.

MR. NIXON: You have never talked on the telephone with Mr. Hiss?

MRS. POPE: No.

MR. NIXON: Or last year?

MRS. POPE: No; I have not seen Mr. Hiss or talked to him—wait a minute. I talked to Mrs. Hiss about several years ago. She wanted me to come back to work for her. But that was all in the case. That is all. She just wanted me to come back, and did not say anything else.

MR. NIXON: Did you talk to a friend of Mr. Hiss' lately?

MRS. POPE: No.

MR. NIXON: You have not?

MRS. POPE: I have not.

MR. NIXON: You are sure of that?

MRS. POPE: I am sure of that.

MR. NIXON: Did you talk to an attorney for Mr. Hiss?

MRS. POPE: I have not. I don't know his attorney.

MR. NIXON: They have not come to see you?

MRS. POPE: No; nobody has come to see me.

Perhaps Nixon had lost interest by this time in checking Chambers's reference to "a rather elderly Negro maid whom Mr. Hiss used to drive home in the evening." At all events, he did not question her on that, as one would have expected in view of his prior interest in that topic.

Nixon did continue, however, to try to establish the date Martha stopped working for us:

MR. NIXON: . . . you left the Hisses probably at the end of 1935, is that correct, in about December 1935; does that sound about right to you?

MRS. POPE: I do not know. It could have been. . . . It is so long that I could not remember that, just what time I left them.

MR. NIXON: But you did not take a vacation between the time you left the Hisses and went to work for these other people?

MRS. POPE: Yes; I was idle for a while.

MR. NIXON: About how long were you idle? That is the point.

MRS. POPE: About a couple of months or something like that.

MR. NIXON: About a couple of months of idleness. . . . So, you could have left them in October, and you do not recall when you worked at P Street, whether it was summer or winter or fall? . . . Do you remember whether you had to put up the shutters for the wintertime, or whether there was snow which was tramped in?

MRS. POPE: There was not any snow.

MR. NIXON: No snow.

Did the Hisses ever have any guests who stayed overnight at the P Street house?

MRS. POPE: Not as I know of.

This is one independent check of Chambers's dazzling details of which there is a public record. Yet I have never seen a Committee statement that Martha failed to bear out Chambers's most concrete assertion of a close friendship—namely, his saying that he had made my house an informal headquarters, had stayed overnight as long as a week at a time and while there had devoted his time mainly to reading. (Cleide Catlett, Martha's successor, was with us until some years after the period Chambers claimed to have known me. When she turned up, Cleide also made it clear that Chambers had had no such entree to my house.)

On the 16th, I was asked not only about our maids, but also about vacations and pets:

MR. NIXON: Where did you spend your vacations during that period?

MR. HISS: . . . My son went to a camp over on the Eastern Shore of Maryland. I am partly an Eastern Shore man myself. Part of my family came from there. When he was at camp we spent two summers, I think, during this period in Chestertown, Md.

MR. NIXON: On the Eastern Shore?

MR. HISS: On the Eastern Shore of Maryland. He went to a camp of friends of ours who lived just outside of Chestertown. For two summers we took a small apartment.

MR. NIXON: Did you have pets?

MR. HISS: We had a brown cocker spaniel we had before we came to Washington, was with us all during that period, and lived to be so old she died of old age.

MR. NIXON: What did you do with the dog when you went on your vacations; do you recall?

MR. HISS: I think we took Jenny over on the Eastern Shore . . .
when we went there. She did spend some time in the kennels
when we were away.
MR. NIXON: You can't recall for sure?
MR. HISS: We had a very good vet out near Rock Creek Park.

I made trips to the Eastern Shore, winter or summer,
whenever I could get away long enough to warrant the two-
hour car trip each way. Rock Creek Park is not "out Wisconsin
Avenue." In fact the cocker spent the summers with Timothy
at camp, and when we moved to 30th Street we acquired for
the winter a second and very lively cocker. Had Chambers ever
visited that tiny house, he would not have limited his recollection of our pets to the dog he saw at P Street.

These, then, are the "facts which only an extremely intimate friend" of mine could have provided. Had I had the
chance for a prompt identification of Chambers, and had his
testimony of August 7 been given in my presence and in public, where my corrections would have received equal attention,
the myth of close association would never have started.

To summarize briefly: Chambers on August 7 knew a
number of facts about me and the members of my household,
including the locations of some of our residences. These facts
were invariably of a kind that he could easily have learned either from his acquaintance with me in 1935 and the first half
of 1936 or from standard reference books.[6] But he was consistently ignorant of or entirely inaccurate about precisely those
items that a close association would have disclosed. In addition, he was ignorant of all events that occurred after the first
half of 1936 (with the single exception that he knew the general location of the house I moved to at the end of 1937). Yet
his contention was that he had known me throughout 1937.

[6] The then current *Who's Who in America* gave Baltimore as my birthplace, my wife's first and maiden names, her former married name, and the
name of my stepson. It also had a listing for my wife's former husband and
gave his occupation. *Current Biography* in 1947 added that I was an amateur
ornithologist and liked to play tennis.

Toward the close of the session Nixon suggested the use of a lie-detector test for the testimony Chambers had just given, and Chambers said he would, "if necessary," take such a test, for he was "telling the truth." Chambers's reply suggests that this early he felt assured of the Committee's protection and was confident that no proposal by the Committee would be permitted to result in injury to him. In the light of the Committee's subsequent failure to make any objective independent check of Chambers's statements at that hearing, such confidence on his part would not seem to have been misplaced. The lie-detector incident, coupled with the Committee's unwarranted assertions that it had independently verified Chambers's stories in detail, illustrates the arbitrary relation between the world of fact and the public impression created by the Committee—an impression based on undue emphasis upon items selected out of context, bolstering of inventions by flat assertions of verification, and even a proposal to rely on gadgets instead of standard procedures to create an aura of credibility for Chambers.

On August 7, Chambers mentioned three other topics related to me. Only one of them added to the claim of close relations. He began his testimony that day by admitting that I had not known him by the name of Whittaker Chambers and asserting that I had known him only by the pseudonym or "party name" of "Carl." The Committee's checking of Chambers's stories did include telephoning to the resident manager of the 28th Street apartment, Mrs. Jeffries, whose name appears in the hearings record as Mrs. W. M. Jeffers. When I later talked to her, I found that the Committee's representative had apparently been quite satisfied with her initial response that she had no recollection of me or of my subtenant after I had left, and had not asked her whether she recalled any subtenant in her entire residence at the 28th Street building whose name was not known to her or to the other tenants.

Chambers's next topic was the basis of his allegation that I was a Communist. He said he was told this by a Mr. Peters,

whom he identified as "the head of the entire underground
. . . of the Communist Party in the United States." (An individual identified by the Committee as the "Mr. Peters"
Chambers had referred to refused to testify when summoned
before the Committee on August 30; the following spring, a
few weeks before my first trial began, he was deported. An appendix to the Committee's Hearings for August 28 and 31 and
September 1 and 15, 1950, concludes its section on Peters: "In
April 1949, J. Peters was ordered deported from the United
States.")

Chambers's testimony of August 7 referred to Peters as
his source of accusations about me in this way:

MR. NIXON: I understood you to say that Mr. Hiss was a member
of the party.

MR. CHAMBERS: Mr. Hiss was a member of the Communist Party.

MR. NIXON: How do you know that?

MR. CHAMBERS: I was told by Mr. Peters.

MR. NIXON: You were told that by Mr. Peters?

MR. CHAMBERS: Yes.

MR. NIXON: On what facts did Mr. Peters give you?

MR. CHAMBERS: Mr. Peters was the head of the entire underground,
as far as I know.

MR. NIXON: The entire underground of the Communist Party?

MR. CHAMBERS: Of the Communist Party in the United States.

MR. NIXON: Do you have any other evidence, any factual evidence,
to bear out your claim that Mr. Hiss was a member of the
Communist Party?

MR. CHAMBERS: Nothing beyond the fact that he submitted himself for the 2 or 3 years that I knew him [later he was to claim
that he had known me for four years] as a dedicated and
disciplined Communist.

MR. NIXON: Did you obtain his party dues from him?

MR. CHAMBERS: Yes, I did.

MR. NIXON: Over what period of time?

MR. CHAMBERS: Two or three years, as long as I knew him.

MR. NIXON: Party dues from him and his wife?

MR. CHAMBERS: I assume his wife's dues were there; I understood
it to be.

MR. NIXON: You understood it to be?

MR. CHAMBERS: Mr. Hiss would simply give me an envelope containing party dues which I transferred to Peters. I didn't handle the money.

MR. NIXON: How often?

MR. CHAMBERS: Once a month.

MR. NIXON: What did he say?

MR. CHAMBERS: That was one point it wasn't necessary to say anything. At first he said, "Here are my dues."

MR. NIXON: And once a month over a period of 2 years, approximately, he gave you an envelope which contained the dues?

MR. CHAMBERS: That is right.

MR. NIXON: What did you do with that envelope?

MR. CHAMBERS: I gave it to Peters.

MR. NIXON: In New York?

MR. CHAMBERS: Or Washington.

MR. NIXON: This envelope contained dues of Hiss and other members of the group?

MR. CHAMBERS: Only Hiss.

MR. NIXON: You collected dues from the other members of the group individually?

MR. CHAMBERS: All dues were collected individually.

To make his point more vividly Chambers added a little later:

. . . he was rather pious about paying his dues promptly.

Nixon pressed the general question again:

MR. NIXON: Is there any other circumstance which would substantiate your allegation that he was a member of the party? . . .

MR. CHAMBERS: I must also interpolate there that all Communists in the group in which I originally knew him accepted him as a member of the Communist Party.

MR. NIXON: Referred to him as a member of the party?

MR. CHAMBERS: That doesn't come up in conversation, but this was a Communist group.

Interestingly, Chambers did not repeat his story about dues at the trials. Yet, apart from the story of espionage he pro-

duced in mid-November, payment of dues was the one unequivocally Communist activity he ever alleged. Perhaps he did
not talk of dues at the trials because in his first testimony, only
four days earlier than the testimony just quoted, he had told a
different story:

MR. STRIPLING: Mr. Chambers, when you met with these people
[Chambers had earlier said that I was one of those here referred to] at Mr. Collins' apartment, did you collect Communist Party dues from them?

MR. CHAMBERS: I did not, but the Communist Party dues were
handed over to me by Collins, who was the treasurer of that
group.

The Committee heard him swear to these directly inconsistent statements in the very testimony which they sought to
persuade the public came from a credible witness whose statements "checked" in every detail.

In his book, written after the trials, Chambers employs
the stock phrase "dues-paying members of the Communist
Party," and says it is his recollection that dues were fixed at ten
per cent of salary, added to which were special assessments. He
writes: "Alger Hiss continued devoutly to pay exorbitant dues
to the party." My monthly salary check was deposited regularly.
A large regular monthly payment to Chambers would have
been reflected in my withdrawals, which prior to the trials were
carefully scrutinized—as is shown by the later emphasis upon
a single withdrawal of mine that bore a mere time relation to a
financial transaction by Mrs. Chambers.

The third topic of Chambers's testimony of August 7 became the chief subject of the long public hearing of August 25.
The issue of "checking" those assertions that would really have
demonstrated whether Chambers in fact knew me well was lost
in that hearing, buried under the details of the disposal of my
old Ford roadster, which I had given to Chambers rather than
have it treated as so much junk. The subject, therefore, is also
discussed in the chapter on the August 25 hearing.

Chambers's ability on August 7 to describe the car was one

of the "close relation" items. Stripling lists as one of the "great store of detail" that Chambers added: "Hiss owned a battered Ford roadster [though old, it was not battered], with manual windshield wipers." For completeness I should add that Chambers also recalled that when he knew me I acquired a Plymouth sedan, though he missed the date by a year. (I, too, was inaccurate in my recollection of this date, as appears subsequently.) One would expect him to be able to describe a car that had been given to him and to recall the event that prompted the gift.

Chambers asserted that I had given the Ford to the Communist Party "so it could be of use to some poor organizer in the West or somewhere." This, he said, was accomplished through a Communist who owned a service station or car lot in Washington. Chambers concluded by saying: "I should think the records of that transfer would be traceable."

The records (which, as recounted in Chapter V, I was not able to see until during the course of the August 25 hearing) demonstrate, as I had recalled, that there had been no written sale or assignment of the car to Crosley. When I gave him the car I assumed that he would keep it as long as it was capable of being used. I took no thought then of his wishing to sell it. Consequently, when I handed over the certificate of title to him, its sole function was to establish his right to possession. It never occurred to me to fill out on the back of the certificate the form printed there for use in sale.

The records also show that in July 1936 I signed the car over to the Cherner Motor Company, the largest Ford agency in Washington. Chambers's invention of a Communist owner of a service station or parking lot collapsed. My assignment was notarized by an attorney of many years' service in the Department of Justice who was at that time a colleague of mine in the office of the Solicitor General. This was hardly the place or the notary one would choose for executing a transfer for the benefit of "some poor organizer in the West or somewhere." Evidently this transaction had meant to me only that someone had come to my office to have me complete technically my

prior disposal of the Ford. My ownership of the old car had
ended months before. It was too late to be any concern of mine
that Crosley should have decided to get what he could for it.

The records also show a prompt resale by the Cherner
Company. New title papers in the name of the new owner
were delivered to the Cherner Company subject to a lien of $25,
which would enable it to insist on collection of that amount
from the new owner. This lien, evidencing a monetary incentive
for the transfer, negates the remaining part of Chambers's story
—namely, that the transfer was a gift for a poor organizer. Its
amount also bears out my statement of the value of the car.
The dramatic story shrinks to the small proportions it had in
my mind when the incident of the gift of the car was recalled
on August 16 as part of my recollection of Crosley.

In preparation for the August 25 hearing I sought to trace
whatever records were available to settle clearly the dates and
the order of the various incidents of 1935 and 1936 connected
with Crosley which had seemed minor matters to me at the
time and hadn't been part of my active memory for years. I
sought leases, and records relating to the old Ford and the new
Plymouth.

Not remembering the incident of the execution in my office of the assignment to the Cherner Company, I had no recollection of what Crosley had ultimately done with the Ford
and thus had no way of knowing whether there were records in
Washington of any transfer after I had turned it over to Crosley.
The inquiries in Washington were made on my behalf
by a friend, John F. Davis, who lived in Washington and who
was a lawyer. On our first inquiry at the department that han-
dles car registrations we were told that all old records relating
to transfers were so filed as to be inaccessible without the number of the certificate of title or the engine number. We were
also told that the Committee had made a similar inquiry and
had received the same answer. According to its issue of August 19, *The New York Times* had been told the same thing:

. . . A spokesman for the District of Columbia Department
of Vehicles and Traffic said today that it would be impossible, in

such transactions so long ago, to supply evidence unless the engine number or the number of the title transfer were known.

Later, we were told by a clerk, the Committee's investigators supplied one or the other of these numbers for the Ford and thus obtained the records of the sale to the Cherner Company. (Though the clerk at that time had jotted down the number and later gave it to us, the records, as a result of the Committee's subpœna, were no longer available for our inspection, so that I did not see them until the Committee disclosed them to me piecemeal on August 25.) Having himself disposed of the car, Chambers had, of course, been in position to say that records of its transfer should be available in the District of Columbia.

Two factors enabled the Committee temporarily to construct a prominent role for the Ford roadster. First, I failed to recall—and still do—my signing, in the midst of a day at the office, the routine assignment to the Cherner Company, and I was confused after the lapse of thirteen years as to exactly when in 1935 I had bought a Plymouth, after which I no longer had need of the Ford.

Second, the Cherner Motor Company resold the Ford to one William Rosen, and no invoices have ever been found for the transaction. Not unnaturally, the Cherner officials who had certified to various details of the purchase and resale could not, after a dozen years, remember the car or remember who had brought it in or remember its new purchaser. I have no way of knowing what happened to the car, or the records relating to it, after I executed the assignment to a reputable Ford agency, a requested action not calculated to raise any suspicions on my part. Rosen testified that he did not know me and had never even seen me, but he declined, on the ground of the Fifth Amendment, to answer any questions about the car or to say whether he himself was a Communist. Rosen's refusal to tes-

---

[¹] The Committee's inquiry indicated that Rosen's name on the retransfer papers was not signed by him, so there is actually no evidence that he got the

tify about the car [7] and the absence of other records, which prevented our being able still further to discredit Chambers's
story, were treated by the Committee as positive support for
that story. As was so often the case during the hearings and
the trials, Chambers was not requested to prove his assertions.
I was expected to disprove them. The fear of Communism had
become so great, so unreasoning, that charges made before the
Committee, when once spread across the newspapers of the nation, were widely accepted until completely discredited. Where
a potential witness's death, or another's silence, or the failure
of memory or loss of records after the lapse of many years,
prevented full and positive disproof, the charge stood in the
public mind as if unchallenged. This was a turning-inside-out
of the traditional principle that all those accused are presumed
to be innocent until proved guilty.

With complete inconsistency the Committee's attitude
toward the Ford at this stage in the hearings was both (1) that
my "admission" that I had given it to Crosley was evidence of
a close relationship, and (2) that I hadn't given it to him at
all, but instead had given it to the Communist Party, as Chambers asserted.

After familiarizing myself with the records relating to the
Ford, to the Plymouth, and to my overlapping leases of the
spring of 1935, I was able to reconstruct the correct sequence
of events. The Ford roadster then lost much of its sensational
value to the Committee, although the prosecutor in the second
trial still offered Rosen's silence as if it were evidence rather
than the absence thereof. By the time Stripling wrote his account of these occurrences, he no longer echoed the Committee's August thesis that Chambers's dramatic story about the
disposition of the Ford had been supported. Instead, Stripling
said merely that the ultimate destination of the car remained
"something of a mystery," and he was reduced to emphasizing

---

car. It was also brought out that Rosen had been expelled from the Communist Party in 1929, the year that Chambers, according to his testimony, withdrew for a period of time.

the sad but totally unrelated death (in the autumn of 1948) of
the Department of Justice notary:

> . . . We endeavored then to trace the path of the Ford
> (which Chambers said he never received from Hiss) without too
> much success. It remains something of a mystery, deepened by
> the awful fact that the man who notarized the papers on the car's
> transfer either leaped or fell to a ghastly death from the top floor
> of the Justice Department in Washington.

CHAPTER FOUR

CONFRONTATION AT
THE COMMODORE, AUGUST 17

THE COMMITTEE Hearings from July 31 to September 9, 1948, have been published in a volume of 877 pages. It is evident from those hearings that something not contained in them changed the Committee's plans between 5:30 p.m. on Monday, August 16, and 5:35 p.m. on Tuesday, August 17.

The August 16 hearing, as I have already pointed out, concludes with these remarks addressed to me:

THE CHAIRMAN: Thank you for coming and we will see you August 25.

(Whereupon, at 5:30 p.m., the executive session was concluded.)

The next entry is for August 17. It records another executive session and begins:

The subcommitte met, pursuant to notice, at 5:35 p.m., in room 1400 Hotel Commodore, New York City, Hon. John McDowell presiding.

The preliminary details state in addition that Representatives J. Parnell Thomas and Richard M. Nixon were also present, as were five members of the Committee's staff. The Chairman then stated:

The first witness will be Mr. Alger Hiss.

What had happened in the meantime? Why should the Committee "see" me more than a week earlier than they had decided the day before? Why were they seeing me in a New York hotel room and not in Washington?

As I sat there, I thought I knew why. On the preceding Friday, Harry Dexter White had been a voluntary witness before the Committee in a highly publicized hearing. He had publicly denied charges that both Chambers and Miss Elizabeth Bentley had made against him. His initial statement, as the hearings record, had been greeted by applause. This was not the only expression of sympathy shown by the audience. Early in the hearing the following appears:

MR. WHITE: . . . I fancied myself a little as a ping-pong player, and we played a few times.

THE CHAIRMAN [1]: Just a minute, right there. Let me see that note. [This request was presumably an aside to a staff member.] One thing I cannot reconcile, Mr. White, you send me a note and you say that:

I am recovering from a severe heart attack. I would appreciate it if the chairman would give me 5 or 10 minutes rest after each hour.

For a person who had a severe heart condition, you certainly can play a lot of sports.

MR. WHITE: I did not intend that this note should be read aloud. I do not know any reason why it should be public that I am ill, but I think probably one of the reasons why I suffered a heart attack was because I played so many sports, and so well. The heart attack which I suffered was last year. I am speaking of playing ping-pong, and I was a fair tennis player, and a pretty good ball player, many years prior to that. I hope that clears that up, Mr. Chairman.

THE CHAIRMAN: Yes, sir. [Applause.]

[1] Mr. Thomas.

White answered all questions. There are indications that he retained the sympathy of the audience throughout the hearing. Well along in the session he felt called upon to apologize for applause not noted by the reporter. White said he was sorry for it, that it was not his fault. Toward the end of White's testimony the Chairman admonished the audience directly (although again the reporter omitted to record that there had been applause):

. . . You are the guests of the committee. . . . The Chair would appreciate it if you would not applaud. . . .

Flying back from Washington after my testimony of the afternoon before, I had had time to read the fully reported accounts of White's appearance and had been impressed by his courage in voluntarily facing, despite his illness, the ordeal of a public grilling in the circus-arena atmosphere of klieg lights and flash-bulbs. I had found unpalatable the Committee's badgering of a sick man and its implication that he was malingering in privately asking for an occasional intermission.

The very next morning, Tuesday the 17th, while at my uptown office, I received a telephone call from Appell of the Committee's staff. He said that Mr. McDowell was to be in New York late that afternoon and hoped to be able to see me for ten or fifteen minutes. As McDowell happened to be the only member of the Committee whom I had had occasion to meet before these hearings began, I asked whether he wished to see me on Committee business or on matters of personal interest to him. Appell, in reply, said he didn't know. I said I would be at my midtown office (which was at Fifth Avenue and 44th Street) in the afternoon so as to be available to the Congressman when he reached the city. Subsequently, McDowell wired that he would call me about 5:30.

In the course of the day I learned from the press that Harry Dexter White had died the day before, having over the week end suffered a further heart attack, presumably brought on by his exertions before the Committee. The afternoon papers prominently displayed the news of White's death, but I did not then link this with McDowell's ambiguous message.

When it was nearly 5:30, McDowell called. Instead of saying that he would be along soon, he rather surprised me by inviting me to come to the Commodore Hotel, just a few blocks away, and then added that Nixon "and one other" were with him. At this point I felt quite sure that something more than a casual conversation was planned and that the manner in which the arrangements had been made had been deliberately less than frank. A colleague, Charles Dollard of the Carnegie Corporation, was still in his office, and I took the precaution of asking him if he would walk over to the Commodore with me to see what lay behind this slightly mysterious maneuvering. I was by now highly suspicious of the good faith of various members of the Committee. Biased accounts in the morning papers of my testimony of the day before were a plain and prompt repudiation of the protestations of secrecy by some members of the Committee. I wanted at least one friend present who would be able to give his version of any further relations I might have with the Committee.

We went to McDowell's hotel room and, as we entered, found that it was still in the process of being hastily converted into an improvised hearing room. McDowell and Nixon were there; Thomas arrived a good deal later. Among the staff members I recognized the clerk who had called me that morning and who had said he didn't know the purpose of McDowell's proposed call on me. A stenographic reporter was also present.

Suddenly the connection between White's death and the hastily summoned hearing struck me. The impact of the press accounts of White's fatal heart attack was hardly favorable to the Committee. Their assumption that White was spuriously seeking sympathy or was malingering had been promptly disproved in a tragic and dramatic manner. My experience with the Committee up to this point led me to conclude that they had decided to meet the crisis of a bad press by a sudden and sensational move. Evidently part of the planned sensation, I was glad of the instinct which had led me to ask a friend to come along. Executive sessions, I knew now, were dangerous territory for any witness except one the Committee was itself supporting. To have a friend present was comforting. I felt a little less at the mercy of tendentious leaks by some members of the Committee or its staff. I wished then that I had had someone with me the day before who would have been available to counter unfair leaks by his own account of the session.

Nixon immediately announced that the purpose of this hastily arranged hearing was to bring Chambers and me together. He made no reference to White's death, nor did he attempt to explain why the Committee had suddenly changed its timetable. He said only that it was apparent "that the case is dependent upon the question of identity," but he failed to add that this had been evident for two whole weeks, from the day of Chambers's first testimony and my telegram to the Committee of the same day saying that I did not know Chambers. In particular, no mention was made of why the obvious step of a personal meeting between me and Chambers had not been arranged long before. Yet it was Nixon himself who, when I first appeared, led me to assume that if the matter were to be further gone into at all, a confrontation would be the immediate next step:

Mr. Chairman [he had said on August 5 in the statement partly quoted on pages 10–11], I think in justice to both of these witnesses and in order to avoid what might be a useless appearance on the part of Mr. Chambers, when arrangements are made for his being here, that the witnesses be allowed to confront each other so that any possibility of a mistake in identity may be cleared up. . . .

The conclusion seemed to me warranted at this, the very beginning of the August 17 hearing, that the Committee was subordinating objective inquiry to its political aims. I was indignant at what I considered the Committee's ruthless baiting of White and its callous attempt to divert public attention from his death. I resented the hypocrisy of the elaborate assurances of secrecy that had been given me the day before only to be cynically violated by immediate leaks slanted to injure me. In addition, the disingenuous manner in which McDowell summoned me was displeasing.

First I pointed out that this was likely to take more than the ten or fifteen minutes I had been led to expect, and asked that word be sent calling off a six-o'clock appointment I had made on the assumption that I was simply to have a brief chat with McDowell.

Next I asked permission to make a statement before the hearing began, and said with a good deal of heat:

I would like the record to show that on my way downtown from my uptown office, I learned from the press of the death of Harry White, which came as a great shock to me, and I am not sure that I feel in the best possible mood for testimony. I do not for a moment want to miss the opportunity of seeing Mr. Chambers. I merely wanted the record to show that.

It was not until years later that I received confirmation of my instinctive hunch that the Committee's sudden change in plans was to distract public attention from White's death. Ironically, it was Chambers's book that recounted what had motivated the Committee's sudden improvisation. He says that on the morning of the 17th he was on his way to New York from his farm at Westminster, Maryland, when he "felt a curious need to go and see the Committee, as if its members were the only people left in the world with whom I could communicate." So on reaching Baltimore he went to Washington instead of to New York. As he reached the door of the Old House Office Building, members of the Committee's staff emerged:

. . . They were astonished to see me [he writes] and greeted me with wild relief. They had been frantically trying to reach me at home, in New York and Washington. . . .

No one would tell me why I was wanted. Instead, the subcommittee bundled me into a car crammed with its staff. As we rolled to the Union Station, Appell wrestled a newspaper out of his pocket and pointed to a headline: Harry Dexter White had died of a heart attack. . . .

At the session at the Commodore on the 17th, I continued with the protests I wanted to make a matter of record, adding:

I would like to make one further comment. Yesterday, I think I witnessed—in any event, I was told that those in the room were going to take an oath of secrecy. I made some comments before I answered certain questions of Mr. Nixon which I had not intended as a reflection on the committee, but which some members of the committee thought implied that. I was referring merely to the possibility of leakage of information. . . .

I would also like the record to show at this point that on my way down from my uptown office to keep this appointment after I got Mr. McDowell's telegram, I read in the papers that it was understood that in the course of my testimony yesterday the committee asked me, the subcommittee asked me, if I could arrange to have Mrs. Hiss be examined privately. You will recall, and I hope the record will show, that Mr. Nixon assured me with great consideration that you desired to talk to Mrs. Hiss without any publicity. This was less than 24 hours after you had been so considerate.

There were other statements in the press which I read coming down which referred to other bits of my testimony which could only have come from the committee. They did not come from me.

I would like the record to show that is why I asked if I could bring Mr. Dollard, a personal friend, to be with me at this particular time.

McDowell remarked bluntly: "Obviously, there was a leak, because the story that appeared in the various papers I read was part of the activities of yesterday afternoon." He added: "As a Member of Congress, there is nothing I can do about that. It is a regrettable thing, and I join you in feeling rather rotten about the whole thing."

Nixon then asked an aide to bring Chambers in. The transcript at this point reads:

(Mr. Russell leaves room and returns accompanied by Mr. Chambers.)

MR. NIXON: Sit over here, Mr. Chambers. [Chambers was conducted to a sofa along one side of the room, where he sat beside Mandel of the Committee staff.]
> Mr. Chambers, will you please stand?
> And will you please stand, Mr. Hiss?
> Mr. Hiss, the man standing here is Mr. Whittaker Chambers. I ask you now if you have ever known that man before.

Chambers was short, plump, perspiring, and very pale. His appearance was certainly familiar, and I thought I saw Crosley in the added pounds and rumpled suit. But there was no expression, no spark of individuality as yet. I wanted to hear his voice and to see if he had Crosley's bad teeth before expressing my feeling that this was George Crosley.

MR. HISS: May I ask him to speak?
> Will you ask him to say something?
MR. NIXON: Yes.
> Mr. Chambers, will you tell us your name and your business?
MR. CHAMBERS: My name is Whittaker Chambers.
> (At this point, Mr. Hiss walked in the direction of Mr. Chambers.)
MR. HISS: Would you mind opening your mouth wider?

Chambers did not meet my eye, but stared fixedly before him or up to the ceiling. He had given his name in a tight, rather high-pitched, constrained voice, barely opening his mouth. This seemed evidently not the man's normal voice, nor could I see whether his front teeth were decayed. In response to my request that in speaking he open his mouth wider, he was able only to repeat his name, again in a strangled voice, through almost closed lips. I repeated my request:

> I said, would you open your mouth?
> You know what I am referring to, Mr. Nixon.
> Will you go on talking?

Chambers, still in a tight tone, said: "I am senior editor of Time magazine," and stopped again.

Here I asked the Committee whether his voice had been like this when he testified or whether he had spoken in a lower key. One of the clear recollections I had of Crosley was, as I had told the Committee the day before, that his voice had "a deepness, a lowness" of tone. McDowell thought the voice about the same. I requested that he be asked to talk a little more—he had said only a few words. Nixon, apparently hoping to make it easier for Chambers to find his voice, suggested that he read something and handed him a copy of *Newsweek*, opened by appropriate coincidence to flippant comments on President Truman's search for a Secretary of Labor. Though Chambers had been in the room little more than a minute, I interrupted even before he could begin his reading, without waiting for more indication of the man's personality:

I think he is George Crosley, but I would like to hear him talk a little longer.

McDowell, doubtless to put him at his ease, told Chambers he might sit down. I asked him directly: "Are you George Crosley?"

Chambers replied: "Not to my knowledge." Again I hesitated to make a positive identification in view of this denial.

He then added: "You are Alger Hiss, I believe." I assured him that I certainly was. He in turn said that was his recollection and began reading.

At this point Nixon interposed to suggest that Chambers be sworn, a routine procedure the neglect of which had added to the appearance of Chambers's being part of the Committee's retinue, an appearance that came from his having been produced from another room in the suite and from his having taken his place on entering with members of the Committee's staff instead of in the separate area, opposite the Committee, where my friend Charles Dollard and I had been placed.

I remarked with sarcasm that this was a good idea, drawing a heated retort from Nixon to which I replied in kind:

MR. NIXON: Mr. Hiss, may I say something? I suggested that he be sworn, and when I say something like that I want no interruptions from you.

MR. HISS: Mr. Nixon, in view of what happened yesterday [I was referring to White's death, for which I considered the Committee responsible], I think there is no occasion for you to use that tone of voice in speaking to me, and I hope the record will show what I have just said.

Chambers began again to read and finished the first sentence: "Since June, Harry S. Truman had been peddling the labor secretaryship . . . in hope of gaining the maximum political advantage from the appointment." I needed no more surface indications of personality, but I wished to question Chambers about his refusal to admit he was Crosley. Thereupon I asked if I might interrupt, and with the Chairman's permission said:

The voice sounds a little less resonant than the voice that I recall of the man I knew as George Crosley. The teeth look to me as though either they have been improved upon or that there has been considerable dental work done since I knew George Crosley, which was some years ago.

I believe [,] I am not prepared without further checking to take an absolute oath [,] that he must be George Crosley.

I wanted to question Chambers directly about Crosley. Perhaps he had meant only to deny that his real name was Crosley but would admit that he had used that name in 1934 and 1935. Before I could put my questions, Nixon intervened again:

MR. NIXON: May I ask a question of Mr. Chambers?

MR. HISS: I would like to ask Mr. Chambers, if I may.

MR. NIXON: I will ask the questions at this time.

     Mr. Chambers, have you had any dental work since 1934 of a substantial nature?

MR. CHAMBERS: Yes; I have.

MR. NIXON: What type of dental work?

MR. CHAMBERS: I have had some extractions and a plate.

MR. NIXON: Have you had any dental work in the front of your mouth?
MR. CHAMBERS: Yes.
MR. NIXON: What is the nature of that work?
MR. CHAMBERS: That is a plate in place of some of the upper dentures.

I asked for the name of the dentist and then said that these statements of Chambers, if true, substantiated my feeling that he had represented himself to me as George Crosley, a free-lance writer. I pointed out that "one of my main recollections of Crosley was the poor condition of his teeth." To an inquiry of Nixon's, Chambers said his front teeth had been "in very bad shape" in 1934.

Nixon then asked if I would have to learn from the dentist just what he had done "before you could tell anything about this man." Chambers's refusal to admit that he had called himself Crosley, which I found inexplicable if he were Crosley, made me want to ask him about the circumstances under which Crosley and I had known each other. I therefore replied evenly to Nixon's question, despite its sarcastic overtones, that I would like a few more questions to be asked of Chambers, adding:

. . . I feel very strongly that he is Crosley, but he looks very different in girth and in other appearances—hair, forehead, and so on, particularly the jowls.

But instead of letting me put further questions, Nixon chose to go over again with me my account of when and how I had met Crosley and of the course of our acquaintance. When this rather lengthy interlude had been completed, Stripling interjected an argumentative question as to whether I was relying only on "this denture" in identifying a man whom I had known "so well that he was a guest in your home." I answered Stripling's insinuation at some length:

From the time on Wednesday, August 4, 1948, when I was able to get hold of newspapers containing photographs of one Whittaker Chambers, I was struck by a certain familiarity in features. When I testified on August 5 and was shown a photograph by you, Mr. Stripling, there was again some familiarity [of] features. I could not be sure that I had never seen the person whose photograph you showed me. I said I would want to see the person.

The photographs are rather good photographs of Whittaker Chambers as I see Whittaker Chambers today. I am not given on important occasions to snap judgments or simple, easy statements. I am confident that George Crosley had notably bad teeth. I would not call George Crosley a guest in my house. I have explained the circumstances. If you choose to call him a guest, that is your affair.

Stripling interrupted to withdraw the word "guest," and I went on to my main point: why I needed to ask more questions.

MR. HISS: I saw him at the time I was seeing hundreds of people. Since then I have seen thousands of people. He meant nothing to me except as one I saw under the circumstances I have described.

My recollection of George Crosley, if this man had said he was George Crosley, I would have no difficulty in identification. He denied it right here.

I would like and asked earlier in this hearing if I could ask some further questions to help in identification. I was denied that.

MR. STRIPLING: I think you should be permitted——

MR. HISS: I was denied that right. I am not, therefore, able to take an oath that this man is George Crosley. I have been testifying about George Crosley. Whether he and this man are the same or whether he has means of getting information from George Crosley about my house, I do not know. . . .

Stripling then recommended that I be permitted to question Chambers, and I was finally allowed to go on with the topics that puzzled me. My first question was:

Did you ever go under the name of George Crosley?

Again came the reply: "Not to my knowledge." (Later Chambers was to admit in court and in his book that he "may" have used the name George Crosley when he lived at the 28th

Street apartment. When asked on cross-examination during the second trial what name he had used while living on 28th Street, he replied: "I have never been able to remember." When then asked if it might have been Crosley, he answered: "It may have been." Mrs. Chambers said she, too, had forgotten.)

I then asked if he had subleased my apartment. He replied that he had not. I tried once more by rephrasing this question, too. I asked if he with his family had spent any time in the apartment while my family and I were living on P Street. His answer was in the affirmative, and I asked:

Would you tell me how you reconcile your negative answers with this affirmative answer?

He replied:

Very easily, Alger. I was a Communist and you were a Communist.

This oracular statement revived my earlier sense of fantasy or dream. I asked him to be responsive to my questions and to continue with his answer. He replied: "I do not think it is needed." I commented wonderingly: "That is the answer."

Here Nixon offered to help and asked Chambers to explain how he could deny being George Crosley and yet admit that he spent time in my apartment.

Chambers then said that he came to Washington as a Communist functionary, that he and I became friends, and that "to the best of [his] knowledge" I had suggested he go to the apartment, a proposal he accepted gratefully.

Of course this was Crosley—as I had felt from his entrance—though he chose not to admit the name. The Crosleys, and only the Crosleys, had taken over the apartment when we moved to P Street. Chambers's admission that he and his family had done just this definitely settled the question of identity. He was simply claiming that he had been there not as a tenant but as a fellow conspirator. Any puzzlement as to identity was completely over, and I felt a vast sense of relief, though my irritation with the Committee was heightened by the needless delay, the public furor, and the mystery created by their procedures.

I promptly addressed the Chairman to gain the floor in order to make the identification positive, but Nixon, persisting with a further question, asked Chambers how long he had stayed in the apartment. The reply was: "My recollection was about 3 weeks. It may have been longer. I brought no furniture, I might add." (In his book Chambers more accurately fixes the duration of their stay as "about two months." By that time, records of the utilities services brought out at the trials had made it clear that the length of their stay, from just after mid-April until the end of June, was of a nature sufficient to constitute a family move to new quarters rather than being merely, as he had contended, a few weeks' stay, a contention designed to bolster his assertion that he had not subleased the apartment but had been invited by me to use it. He never explained why an underground "functionary" obsessed with pseudonymous security precautions should, as he asserted, casually accept an invitation to stay for a number of weeks in the apartment of a fellow conspirator with whom he would presumably wish to have as few routine and unnecessary links as possible.)

I now obtained the Chairman's attention and stated:

Mr. Chairman, I don't need to ask Mr. Whittaker Chambers any more questions. I am now perfectly prepared to identify this man as George Crosley.

After discussion of the spelling of "Crosley," the following colloquy occurred:

MR. STRIPLING: You will identify him positively now?
MR. HISS: I will on the basis of what he has just said positively identify him without further questioning as George Crosley.
MR. STRIPLING: Will you produce for the committee three people who will testify that they knew him as George Crosley?
MR. HISS: I will if it is possible. Why is that a question to ask me? . . . This occurred in 1935. The only people that I can think of who would have known him as George Crosley with

certainty would have been the people who were associated with me in the Nye committee.

I mentioned the Secretary of the Nye Committee, one of the principal staff members who was then employed in the Department of Justice, and Miss Elsie Gullender, the committee's chief clerical employee, who acted as receptionist at the Secretary's office. Chambers might have introduced himself to any one of these as Crosley, just as he had in my case.

Nixon went on to ask whether I had had any idea that Chambers was a Communist when I knew him. I replied that I had not, and expanded this to point out that it wasn't the habit in Washington in those days to ask a member of the press who had called upon one whether or not he was a Communist before one would talk with him. "It was a quite different atmosphere in Washington then than today." I went on: "I had no reason to suspect George Crosley of being a Communist. It never occurred to me that he might be or whether that was of any significance to me if he was. He was a press representative and it was my duty to give him information, as I did any other member of the press."

I then expressed my irritation at the Committee's delay in bringing about the confrontation and their constant play for publicity:

I would like to say that to come here and discover that the ass under the lion's skin is Crosley, I don't know why your committee didn't pursue this careful method of interrogation at an earlier date before all the publicity. You told me yesterday you didn't know he was going to mention my name, although a lot of people now tell me that the press did know it in advance. They were apparently more effective in getting information than the committee itself. That is all I have to say now.

McDowell as Chairman then formally asked both Chambers and me for positive identification. When this was concluded I challenged Chambers to make the same statements about me in public where they would not be privileged from a suit for libel. Having lost all confidence in the objectivity of the Committee, I felt that the sooner Chambers's charges could be tested in a court, the sooner they would be demonstrated as false.

After a brief recess I requested the Chairman to ask Chambers his response to my challenge. McDowell demurred, whereupon I made the observation:

I thought the committee was interested in ascertaining truth.

Stripling, too, said that he didn't think Chambers had to reply to my challenge, arguing that he had made similar statements to government agencies and these, Stripling contended, were not privileged. I replied that I had been advised that such statements were probably privileged. Nixon thought voluntary statements to an investigative officer would not be privileged, which led me to ask how evidence of such statements could be obtained. Nixon went on to say that Chambers had made accusations about me to Isaac Don Levine. Here Chambers interrupted to say that he had not made any statements about me to Levine; he had spoken to Adolf A. Berle, Jr. (in 1939, when Mr. Berle was an Assistant Secretary of State), and Levine had been present on that occasion.

Stripling, changing the subject abruptly, said:

You are fully aware that the public was led to believe that you had never seen, heard, or laid eyes upon an individual who is this individual, and now you do know him.

I was astonished at his boldness in thus charging me to my face with the very impression that I knew was being deliberately created by the Committee's procedure of delaying a confrontation while Chambers's secret testimony was being improperly disclosed out of context and while his admission that I had not known him as Chambers was being withheld from the public. I replied vigorously that he was stating his impression of the public impression, and added pointedly:

And you may have helped the public impression if it is anywhere near what you describe it as.

Stripling was implying that I had taken nearly two weeks to identify Chambers as Crosley. In fact, as Stripling of course knew, Crosley had been recalled to my mind only the preceding day, the day of my second appearance before the Committee, when I told them fully of my acquaintance with Crosley. Stripling knew, too, that from the time of Chambers's first testimony I had wanted to see him; I had asked for him on both of my previous appearances. The Committee had stated on the occasion of my first appearance that they would arrange a confrontation, leading me to conclude that I should await their action rather than seek him out on my own. The delay in my identifying Chambers as Crosley was certainly not of my making. Stripling was also charging me with having initially denied that I had ever seen Chambers. Because of the sense of familiarity of the man's press photographs I was not prepared to say, and did not at any time say, that I had never seen him. The Committee, not I, had fostered whatever public impression there was that I had claimed never to have seen the "individual who is this individual."

A few minutes later the Committee returned to its preoccupation with Chambers's knowledge that I was interested in bird watching:

MR. NIXON: Did you ever discuss your hobby, ornithology, with this man?

MR. HISS: I may very likely have. My house has pictures very similar to that [indicating picture on wall]. This is an appropriate hearing room.

MR. MC DOWELL: It was a complete coincidence.

MR. HISS: Anyone who had ever been in my house would remark that I had an interest in birds.

A few moments after this, McDowell asked if I had eaten with Crosley. I replied that I thought we had fed him when he stayed in our house, as would have been our custom with people staying under our roof, and added:

I know I have had lunch with him, because it was my practice, and still is, that if someone wants to talk to me about a matter that requires relatively lengthy discussion, a luncheon discussion has a termination. If they come to see you in your office, it is not quite so easy to terminate it at your own convenience.

After another question or two from McDowell about my relations with Crosley, the Chairman of the full Committee, J. Parnell Thomas, arrived and was informed of the progress of the hearing to date. As McDowell again picked up his questioning I referred to Crosley's tale of having helped lay the first street railway tracks in Washington. Somewhat to my surprise, Chambers blandly reaffirmed his improbable story, saying:

I would be happy to testify that that is the truth, and the company I worked for was the Engel & Hevenor Co.

I suggested, with sarcastic intent, that we might ask him the approximate date when the first street railway was laid in Washington. Here Chambers backed away:

MR. CHAMBERS: Excuse me. I never told him the first street railway.
MR. HISS: A street railway?
MR. CHAMBERS: No. As a matter of fact, I think it was the W. B. & A. Lines.

A bit later I took the opportunity to record my distaste for the lack of candor in the arrangements for the meeting, remarking that I had not been notified by McDowell that this would be the occasion for my meeting Chambers. I pointed out that only the day before, I had been told that the meeting would be in Washington on the 25th "and that my opinion as to whether it should be public or not was of some interest to the committee, whether it would be a public confrontation."

The Chairman then volunteered that he thought I had known the day before that I would probably be called before the Committee at a very early date. His deliberate disregarding of the arrangements he had made a day earlier angered me and led me to say:

That is a statement of your opinion for the record.

This brought on a brief interchange:

THE CHAIRMAN: Yes; naturally, for the record. You made your statement for the record.

MR. HISS: Would you like me to say what my impression actually was?

THE CHAIRMAN: I am not interested in your impression. I am asking you if you didn't believe that you would be called much earlier than the 25th when you built up this Mr. Crosley? [It seemed to me clear from this remark that all pretense of objectivity was gone.]

MR. HISS: I certainly did not. We talked about the 25th, Mr. Chairman, at the very conclusion of our meeting yesterday, and I think the record will so show.

THE CHAIRMAN: Before that time you talked about Mr. Crosley.

MR. HISS: Well before that time.[2] That is the whole point.

Here Nixon moved in to observe that I had wanted a confrontation at the earliest possible time. I said that I had, but had not asked for an earlier meeting once the Committee had fixed the date of the 25th. Nixon then changed his approach and asked if I wanted the record to show that I objected to having had a confrontation. I replied that all I wanted was that the record show the nature of the preliminary to this particular meeting.

Once again came a repetition of questions as to whether I had met Chambers in the presence of various individuals who had been named again and again, and as to whether I had paid dues to Chambers. The session seemed to be running down. I wanted to raise the question of relations with the press after this executive hearing:

MR. HISS: . . . What is the committee's present intention about publicity with respect to this afternoon's session? I know what your intention was with respect to yesterday's session.

MR. MC DOWELL: Mr. Hiss, I can only answer for one member of the committee, the chairman of the subcommittee, that I don't know, I don't know.

MR. HISS: Are you going to decide any time soon, because I am interested in my own protection?

[2] In the editing of the printed hearings a comma has erroneously been placed after "Well."

MR. MC DOWELL: Of course. We appreciate that, sir. I would judge in view of the presence of the chairman of the full committee here, that we will have an executive session shortly after this one is over.

MR. HISS: Is there anyone I can telephone to find out the nature of your decision promptly?

Without answering my question, the Committee then withdrew for a private meeting. On their return the Chairman (Thomas had assumed the chair earlier) announced that "as a result of this testimony the committee has decided to bring about a meeting of the full committee in public session Wednesday, August 25, at 10:30 in the caucus room of the Old House Office Building, at which time both Mr. Hiss and Mr. Chambers, whom Mr. Hiss identified as the person whom he knew as Mr. Crosley, will appear as witnesses."

When Stripling asked if the witnesses were to be given subpœnas, the Chairman went on:

Completing my statement, I instruct the chief investigator to serve a subpena on both Mr. Hiss and Mr. Chambers to appear on that date.

It wasn't clear whether the Committee had, at this point, adjourned. I tried to get the Chairman's attention to say I needed no subpœna any more than I had when, the day before, they had fixed the same date without mention of subpœnas. But the hearing was in confused disorder. The Chairman asked me to wait until he and his colleagues had finished conferring about some unstated issue. When he interrupted his consultation to repeat his instruction to Stripling to make out the subpœnas, I made my point without waiting for recognition and then went on to another matter on which I hoped to get some ruling:

MR. HISS: . . . I was asked yesterday also by the committee—and since the committee seems to change its mind so quickly and frequently, I would like to get it clear—I was asked yesterday to make arrangements for Mrs. Hiss to come down from Vermont to meet in executive session with a subcommittee.

As I mentioned earlier, I was told it would be without publicity. That was volunteered by the committee, although I read about it in the papers this morning. Does the committee still desire to hear Mrs. Hiss in executive session or have you changed your mind?

THE CHAIRMAN: There is no decision on that.

MR. HISS: Yes; there was a decision. I have asked her to start down from Vermont.

THE CHAIRMAN: Well, you asked her to start down from Vermont.

MR. HISS: At your request.

THE CHAIRMAN: Believing she would appear on what date?

MR. HISS: As early as possible was the request you made of me, considering her own convenience and whether she could get somebody to stay with our child.

THE CHAIRMAN: Is she on the way from Vermont?

MR. HISS: I hope she is on her way by now.

It was arranged that my wife would testify the next day in the same room if she had managed to catch that day's train. Nixon said that I could reach him at the hotel that night to let him know if she could appear any time the next day. I warned him that Vermont trains are unpredictable, and the hearing ended.

The Chairman, whose attitude had become increasingly offensive to me, closed the session by thanking me very much. His insincerity of phrase and tone was apparent. Indignantly I made it plain that I did not thank him. The Chairman directed that my remark be italicized, and, so far as I have noted in my examination of the record, my three heartfelt words are the only passage that appears in italics in the lengthy printed record of hearings:

I don't reciprocate.

I had followed the traditional forms long enough out of respect for the office of Congressman and out of habit. I had tried to get the Committee to follow the orderly procedures with which I was familiar. Now at the end of this hearing I wanted to make it quite plain that I resented the Committee's callous and ruthless procedures. It helped, I felt, to clear the air in this fashion. As I told Mr. Dulles that evening in a telephone conversation, it was evident that the Committee and I were now at war.

CHAPTER FIVE

FINAL HEARING, AUGUST 25

MY WIFE had been able to make the necessary arrangements with friends and neighbors and was on the slow day train from northern Vermont. It was sufficiently on time for us to have a very late dinner after she reached New York. I then tried to telephone Nixon at Room 1400 of the Commodore to let him know that she would be available for a Committee hearing the following day, but his phone was continuously busy in response to a succession of calls I made from our apartment.

The Committee had given me no reply to my inquiry about the policy they intended to follow with the press. In view of the day's developments I was confident that in order to blanket the adverse effects of White's death the Committee would seek to make some kind of sensation out of my identification of Chambers as Crosley. But as I had received no answer about their plans, I felt bound to remain silent on the secret hearing of that afternoon.

Near midnight I received the answer to my inquiry. The reply was indirect and also told me why I had not been able to reach Nixon. The press called and gave me the Committee's version of the confrontation. I learned that Nixon had been on the wire all evening giving the press, including members of the Washington corps, the Committee's story of the hearing.

With this information, I summoned a midnight press conference of my own in a one-man attempt to clear up the confusion resulting from the Committee's selective account. The minutes, of course, remained secret and so were not available. In consequence, my belated and singlehanded efforts were not very effective. The Committee's thesis that I had "built up this Mr. Crosley" and that I had belatedly identified Chambers as Crosley was already firmly entrenched in the public mind.

When I finally reached Nixon he fixed eleven o'clock the next morning, Wednesday the 18th, for my wife to come to the Commodore. I had received permission to accompany her, and I again asked Mr. Dollard to come with me. Nixon was the sole representative of the Committee, and the hearing lasted but ten minutes—yet it had taken my wife a full day on a local train to comply with the Committee's request that she come to New York immediately.

I now concerned myself with the well-advertised public show that the Committee had refixed for the next Wednesday, just a week off, which Stripling had forecast would be "bally-hooed into a circus." My friend John Davis, the Washington lawyer whom I have mentioned earlier, volunteered to help me go over the topics that might be expected to arise, and to attend the hearing with me.

The open hostility of the Committee members present at the Commodore made it obvious to me that my next encounter with the Committee was to be what lawyers call an adversary proceeding. Consequently, I felt that the presence of counsel would be helpful. However, I was to find that because of the Committee's intent to discredit me counsel could be of little assistance. For example, at one point Mr. Davis suggested that Stripling identify for the record various photographs of Chambers. The record is still unclear as to

what photographs were being discussed; Mr. Davis, continuing
with his suggestion, got only as far as "Mr. Chairman, I
suggest——" when he was abruptly silenced by the direction
"Never mind, you keep quiet." I had to meet unaided the
full attack of the Committee.

But in attempting to prepare for the hearing, Mr. Davis
was of real help. Together we prepared a letter to the Chairman
of the Committee. In this I attempted, first, to bring into
the open the political motivations which, I was now convinced,
had led some members of the Committee to seek to attack
the New Deal, Yalta, and the United Nations (with all of
which I could be associated) by unwarranted and sensational
attacks on me. In that letter I asserted:

This charge [that I was or had been a Communist] goes
beyond the personal. Attempts will be made to use it, and the
resulting publicity, to discredit recent great achievements of this
country in which I was privileged to participate.

Certain members of your committee have already demonstrated that this use of your hearings and the ensuing publicity is
not a mere possibility, it is a reality. Your acting chairman, Mr.
Mundt, himself, was trigger quick to cast such discredit. Before I
had a chance to testify, even before the press had a chance to
reach me for comment, before you had sought one single fact to
support the charge made by a self-confessed liar, spy, and traitor,
your acting chairman pronounced judgment that I am guilty as
charged by stating that the country should beware the peace work
with which I have been connected.

I urge that these committee members abandon such verdict-
first-and-testimony-later tactics, along with dramatic confrontations
in secret sessions, and get down to business.

In an attempt to restore perspective, which the Committee's attitude had upset, I cited my official record and
listed those under whom I had served who could testify as to
the loyalty and effectiveness of my government service. I
pointed out that Chambers had demonstrated his own lack
of consistent reliability, truthfulness, and honor, and I added
that it was already evident that it would be difficult for me

to get the facts about Chambers which I implied the Committee had ignored.

I went on to repeat suggestions as to procedure that I had made spontaneously in the course of the prior hearings:

At this point I should like to repeat suggestions made by me at preceding hearings with respect to the most effective method of getting facts so far as I can supply them. The suggestions I made, beginning with the very first time I appeared before your committee, were not then accepted, and the result has only been confusion and delay. Let me illustrate by recalling to your minds what I said when you asked me to identify the accuser, not by producing him under your subpena power but by producing only a newspaper photograph taken many years after the time when, by his own statements, I had last seen him. I said to you on the occasion on [sic] my first appearance:

"I would much rather see the individual—I would not want to take oath that I have never seen that man. I would like to see him, and I would be better able to tell whether I had ever seen him. Is he here today—I hoped he would be."

Let me add one further example of how the procedures followed have caused confusion and delay. In your secret sessions you asked me housekeeping and minor details of years ago that few if any busy men could possibly retain in their memories with accuracy. I told you, and one of your own members acknowledged, that you or I should consult the records. I warned you that I had not checked them and that I doubted if I could be helpful under those circumstances.

In conclusion I made a point that it seemed to me any objective inquiry would have long since taken into account:

One personal word. My action in being kind to Crosley years ago was one of humaneness, with results which surely some members of the committee have experienced. You do a favor for a man, he comes for another, he gets a third favor from you. When you finally realize he is an inveterate repeater, you get rid of him. If your loss is only a loss of time and money, you are lucky. You may find yourself calumniated in a degree depending on whether the man is unbalanced or worse.

John Davis's office in Washington attempted to ascertain dates and places of long-past events from real-estate agencies, the motor-vehicles bureau, and various individuals located in Washington. I had not got round to any of this, and now tried to find time to undertake what preparation might be feasible. We found that the Committee was ahead of us, and that its action had closed off access to much of what we needed. Perhaps most important, as it was to turn out, the Washington department of motor vehicles reported that the papers connected with the transfer of title to the Ford had been turned over to the Committee and were not available to us. We, therefore, had no way to ascertain, by reference to the official records, dates which in the intervening years had slipped my mind. Armed with these records, the Committee was to make the details of my turning over the Ford the major topic of the long hearing.

This impounding of public records suggested to me that the Committee had found my memory to be inaccurate in some of the details about the Ford and would probably use this material to my disadvantage in the forthcoming hearing. I now consider that before testifying again, I should perhaps have insisted on seeing the official records, which were, as a matter of course, available to me by law. Instead, knowing that the sequence of minor personal events in my life was in itself unimportant, I decided that I would continue to rely on my unaided memory, but would not permit the Committee to lead me into committing myself to specific dates or to a particular sequence of these long-past occurrences.

My position vis-à-vis the Committee at my final appearance was not an enviable one. The Committee was armed with records that I had been unable to obtain. In contrast, I had only a fallible and unaided memory. The initiative in choosing topics and in making extensive comments lay with the Committee. They were many against one, and they had on their side the prestige of high public office. These advantages, coupled with the open hostility displayed at the meeting at the Commodore, caused me to adopt an attitude of caution. I no longer felt warranted, as I had at my first two appearances, in simply giving my recollection regardless of its quite likely fallibility.

My testimony was, therefore, carefully qualified by the frequent reminder that it was necessarily based on mere recollection. The questioning was lengthy, repetitious, and unfriendly. My attempts to protect myself from likely errors of memory were openly treated as evasiveness and legal fencing. In contrast, Chambers's brief repetition of his charges, given that same day in response to friendly leading questions, was made to sound assured.

The Committee exploited three mistakes in my recollection of the dates of my leases and of my acquisition of one car and disposition of another. As these dates were all linked in point of time, one misdating led to another in my memory. My recollection of the events themselves was accurate enough; my memory—I think an average one—misplaced them in time by only a few months.

My first mistake was in recalling the date of my lease on the 28th Street apartment as having lasted until September 1935. In fact it was until July 1. It followed that I misdated my talk with Crosley about subleasing. In my testimony of August 17, repeating what I had said the day before, I stated:

> I don't remember how long the lease ran. I think to September. Maybe it ran to October. I think this conversation [about the sublease] probably took place in June.

This mistake led me to place Crosley's tenancy as from June to September, instead of from the latter part of April to July 1.

Secondly, I incorrectly recalled that my purchase of a new car had occurred during Crosley's tenancy. In fact it occurred on September 7, 1935, about two months after his tenancy. The new car, the first my wife and I had jointly acquired, had been the subject of much discussion and shopping tours over a number of months. What had still been only a family plan when Crosley was my tenant became in memory an accomplished event.

My third error of recollection was in misdating the time when I turned over the Ford to Crosley. My impression was that this also had taken place during his occupancy of the apartment. Anticipating the new car, I had told him at that time that he could have the old one when I should no longer need it. He also borrowed the Ford once or twice that spring. Thus, my association of his tenancy, the acquisition of the new car, and giving him the old one was basically correct, although I confused intentions with their fulfillment. In fact Crosley did not take possession of the Ford until the winter of 1935 or the early spring of 1936.[1]

Actually, my clearest recollection of the Ford during the period was the inconvenience I had had in parking both cars on the streets of Georgetown. I stated this to the Committee on the 16th:

. . . This is a car which had been sitting on the streets in snows for a year or two. . . . We were using the other car. [In fact the period of responsibility for both cars was only a matter of months in the winter of 1935–6, however long—because of the nuisance involved—it may have seemed in memory.]

On the 17th I had in effect repeated this:

. . . We had had it sitting on the city streets because we had a new one.

If the point had seemed of importance to me, reflection would have shown me that I was confused as to dates. If I had turned over the Ford to Crosley in the spring of 1935, I obviously could not have had it on the streets of Georgetown the *following* winter (nor the preceding winter, since I didn't move to Georgetown until the spring of 1935). Since the picture of the Ford in the snow was so clear in my mind, I

[1] A passport produced for the first time at the second trial showed that during the summer of 1935 Chambers was planning a trip to Europe (see pp. 305–6). This may be the reason he did not take the car that fall.

should have realized that my transfer of the car to Crosley must have been at least as late as the winter of 1935.

The large hearing room was crowded with press and public. The Chairman, J. Parnell Thomas, in opening the session, said: "We are glad to have as many representatives of the American public as is possible to crowd in this room today." Newsreel and TV cameras, microphones and flashbulbs took command. It began at 10:30 of a hot morning; it ended at 8:00 p.m. of a hot night. Most of that time I was the witness. There were a few interruptions as staff members were put on to introduce the records that I had not been able to obtain, and Chambers was the witness for perhaps the last fifth of the session. The Committee's questions to me concerned my full prior testimony, with special emphasis on those topics for which the Committee had documentary records I had not been able to consult. For these reasons, the seeking of information from me could hardly have been the primary purpose of this long public performance. A bench of six members and Stripling took turns in asking questions, as if a relay team were competing against a single runner. My forebodings were justified. As I answered again and again that I was simply relying on the best recollection I had, it was evident that the Committee was seeking to trip me and to lead me into committing myself to specific dates.

The hearing was opened by the Chairman with a summation of prior hearings. This, I was no longer surprised to notice, was not distinguished by its impartiality. Chambers's testimony of August 7, then still unpublished and thus unavailable to me for challenge and correction—or to the press—was again characterized as containing "such detailed information concerning his associations with Mr. Hiss and his family during the period in question that the committee came to the conclusion that it was impossible for the two persons not to have been closely associated."

The Chairman did not hesitate to dramatize the occasion:

As a result of this hearing, certainly one of these witnesses will be tried for perjury. . . .

Nor did he hesitate to emphasize the Committee's special concept of its function as something more than a body intent on investigating for purposes of legislation:

. . . The Congress and the American people are entitled to the truth on this important matter. . . .

The Committee's image of itself was stated formally two days later in the Interim Report unanimously approved August 27. There the Committee quite frankly described its "very special responsibility" as being that of a prosecuting agency which tries its cases before the public. It seems to have considered that it had been established for the very purpose of conducting trial by newspaper, radio, TV, newsreel, and its own crowded hearing room.

The Interim Report began:

It has been the established policy of the House Committee on Un-American Activities since its inception that in a great, virile, free republic like the United States, one of the most effective weapons against un-American activities is their continuous exposure to the spotlight of publicity. . . .

The current investigations and hearings dealing with past and present Communist espionage [2] activities in Government are therefore strictly in conformity with what the members of the House Committee on Un-American Activities conceive to be their duty and responsibility to undertake. . . .

. . . the House Committee on Un-American Activities has . . . a very special responsibility. It functions to permit the greatest court in the world—the court of American public opinion—to have an undirected, uncensored, and unprejudiced opportunity to render a continuing verdict on all of its public officials and to evaluate the merit of many in private life who either openly as-

[2] One would hardly judge from this that Chambers had at this time made no charges of espionage; on the contrary, he had in his very first appearance emphasized: "I should perhaps make the point that these people were specifically not wanted to act as sources of information," and in October, six weeks after this report, he was to tell the grand jury that he knew of no espionage activities.

sociate and assist disloyal groups or covertly operate as members
or fellow travelers of such organizations. . . .

The Committee did not appear to realize that no prosecutor is impartial. For the Chairman's opening statement on
August 25 emphasized: "These hearings will be fair and impartial."

Immediately after the Chairman's summation, Stripling
struck the note of espionage, despite the absence of evidence.
The Committee was hunting spies, and it saw to it that its
hearings were held in a spy-laden atmosphere, whether or not
those hearings dealt with evidence of espionage. Stripling read
the statutory provision under which the Committee was established, and added:

Pursuant to this mandate the committee has been conducting
an investigation in the past several months into alleged Communist infiltration by Communist agents in the Federal Government and *the operation within the Government of certain persons
who were collecting information to be turned over to a foreign
government. The hearing this morning is for the purpose of pur-
suing this investigation.*[3] . . .

I asked permission to read the letter that my counsel and
I had prepared in advance, but my request was refused. Instead,
Chambers and I were asked to stand, as the cameras increased
their activity. I was asked if I had "ever seen this individual,"
and I identified him as George Crosley. From this overly dramatic and anticlimactic confrontation I concluded that the
Committee was not going to overlook opportunities for drama.

At this point, the very beginning of the long day of questioning, I made it plain that I was still unable to testify except
from unaided recollection because I had not been able to
consult various records. Stripling asked me when I had first
met Crosley, and I replied:

According to my best recollection—and I would like to repeat
what I have said to the committee before, that I have not had

[3] Italics added.

the opportunity to consult records of the time—I first knew him sometime in the winter of 1934 or 1935.

Chambers was then sworn, and he identified me. After this, my testimony was resumed with Stripling's going over previous testimony of mine about photographs of Chambers. In my reply I said:

Incidentally, Mr. Stripling is referring to certain testimony of mine taken in executive session, Mr. Chairman. I wonder if there is any reason why all of the testimony thus far taken in this case should not be made public. A good deal of it has reached the press by one means or another. There is a considerable amount of distortion and misunderstanding.

I have no reason to want any of that testimony—mine or Mr. Chambers', which I have never seen—to remain secret. It seems to me the public and the press would like to have full access to all of the testimony that has been taken to this date.

The Chairman ordered that this be done, and the press was able to examine the many pages of typed transcript in the Committee's files. The process of printing the transcript, however, was to delay easy access for a number of weeks to come, by which time interest in the lengthy record had greatly lessened. Distorted impressions erroneously created by selective release of partial testimony and by unfair characterization of the record could not then effectively be corrected.

Stripling went on to ask me once more for the circumstances under which I had met Chambers as Crosley. I reminded him that I had already, on August 16, given the Committee my best recollection of this, and spoke of my problem of getting the records:

. . . According to my best recollection, without checking the records—and I do think it would be more helpful if the committee would go by records; I would like to know what the records say; some of the records I find are not available to me; I believe they are in the custody of the committee. I have attempted through counsel in the last few days to have access to the records.

This precipitated an interruption that led to my counsel, Mr. Davis, being sworn as a witness and badgered as if he had insulted the Committee. An associate of his had been informed, he said, by the department of motor vehicles that the original certificate of title to the Ford, after being photostated by the Committee, was no longer in the files. He was not sure, and said so, which one of two Washington attorneys who had been assisting him had received this information. Though this was Mr. Davis's first appearance before the Committee and he had said but a few sentences, Mundt burst out:

I would just like to register a protest at this continuous evasion on the part of these witnesses. I am getting tired of flying half-way across the country to get evasive answers. If the gentleman doesn't know who told him, let him say, "I don't know." If he knows, let him say "I do know." Let's not say "I believe" or "I think."

The Committee still made no offer to let me examine the copy of the document which they had obtained.

In answer to a question from Nixon, I told him that I found in preparing for the hearing that I had not retained copies of my leases. I had had to try to recall the real-estate agents I had employed and to consult their records as to leases:

I still have not been able to get hold of all the leases. Some of the leases have been consulted, there have been some telephone conversations with the real-estate people. I have asked counsel to prepare as rapidly as possible a collection of all the available record evidence—photostats, originals, or copies—of all the record evidence on these matters, which it is apparent the committee considers of importance. That has not been completed yet.

Stripling read from my testimony of the 16th about subletting the 28th Street apartment to Crosley and asked if that was as I recalled it. I replied:

That was the best recollection I had on the day I testified and that is why I so testified.

I have since learned that my lease on the house began earlier than I thought and my lease on the apartment terminated somewhat earlier than I thought. The overlap which I remembered, and which was the main thing in my memory, was, according to the best records I have so far been able to check, accurate.

Stripling asked when I rented particular premises, and after each reply that, considering the lapse of time, I could not be sure of the exact day or even month, he read into the record a statement from the landlord giving the record date. It seemed to me plain that in asking me about facts he had before him he was not seeking information from me but errors of recollection, as would a prosecutor bent on discrediting a defendant. I made the comment:

May I say it is apparent that the committee has been better staffed with people to inquire into records than I have been. . . .

Nixon then, it seemed to me, sought to give the impression that Chambers had occupied the apartment for only a few weeks, a period not worth charging rent for. The real-estate agent who had handled the P Street house had written to the Committee that my lease was dated May 1, 1935. I had said that as I had now learned of the actual date of the apartment lease (it ran only until July 1, 1935), I felt that I must have moved into the P Street house a little earlier than May 1. I felt sure of my recollection that the actual overlap was longer than just two months. It seemed to me that Nixon was not seeking all relevant facts but only those that fitted a preconceived pattern inimical to me. I had suggested that I might have been permitted, in accordance with Georgetown custom, to move in a little before the formal date fixed in the lease. (In fact it was later established from the public-utility records that we had moved to the P Street house on April 19.) I did not think I should be expected to give final answers on such questions until I had had the chance to examine all relevant records, not just those the Committee selected to make public. I had put it this way:

MR. HISS: . . . I would have thought in view of information I have received as to the date during which my tenancy of the apartment on Twenty-eighth Street lasted, that I must have moved into the P Street house a little earlier than the date just read, which I understood to be May 1.

(Mr. Stripling hands letter to Mr. Hiss.)

MR. HISS (continuing): And again I would like to check all possible records to see whether I moved in before the date of the lease, according to their records, which is sometimes the custom, to be given a month or so in addition to your regular lease, earlier or later, at the beginning preceding the lease or after its termination; so that again I can't testify with any exactness without an opportunity to refresh my recollection by trying to refer to various records which are not easy to get hold of after all this lapse of time.

After a long interchange between Nixon and me on the subject of how long Crosley occupied the apartment, Stripling resumed his questioning. He asked if I knew of anyone in Washington who had known Chambers as George Crosley.

MR. HISS: In answer to that question, Mr. Stripling, I have naturally among the very many other things that I have been trying to check in the few days since Monday of last week, I have been trying to run down the list of staff members of the Senate Committee Investigating the Munitions Industry.

As far as I can find out, there is no one single official list anywhere now available. . . .

Reminding Stripling that I had offhand mentioned the Secretary, his clerk-receptionist, and one of the chief investigators, I gave the results of my inquiries. The Secretary was away on vacation. The investigator was working in New York, where arrangements were being made for friends to see if he recalled Crosley after all these years. I had been told that Miss Elsie Gullender, the receptionist, had died, but I was not yet sure that this was correct. (The information as to Miss Gullender's death unfortunately proved to be correct.) I was trying to recall the names of other staff members and to locate them.

In fact only one person outside of my household was ever found who recalled Chambers's use of the name Crosley. This man, Samuel Roth by name, was the publisher of an erotic

poem written by Chambers. He said that Chambers had used
the name George Crosley as a pen name for some other poems
he had submitted.[4] (Our maid Cleide Catlett remembered a
call by Chambers at the P Street house and his making himself known to her as "Crosby" or "something like that.")
Members of the Nye Committee's staff who may have met
Chambers only once or twice, briefly and casually, did not
recall him or the name he had used fourteen years earlier.
Neighboring tenants of his while he was at the 28th Street
apartment, some of whom had moved to other cities, had no
recollection at all of him or his family. Tradesmen in the neighborhood had, not surprisingly, long since forgotten a temporary
customer of the mid-1930's.

Mrs. Jeffries, the resident manager, with whom I had had
to make arrangements for Chambers to take over the rest of
my lease, had been interviewed by the Committee before I
was able to see her. She may, quite naturally, have reacted to
the fear of being involved in a sensational hearing by saying
she remembered nothing. When I did see her she expressed
regret that she had misunderstood the Committee's representative and hadn't even realized he was talking about me! But
she continued to be unable to recall the family who had taken
over my apartment, much less to recall their names. I did my
best to remind her of the house rules against baby carriages
in the front hall and the arrangement that had been made
with the janitor to keep Mrs. Crosley's baby carriage in the
basement. But I was too late. And the janitor had since died.
On August 25, I could say only:

I received a telephone call—rather, one of my counsel did—
from someone, a woman, who said she had known George Crosley
at this time, that she was fearful of getting her employer in Dutch
or something by publicity. We were not able to trace the call. She
may have been imagining.

[4] Roth had been convicted under the obscenity laws—a fact which sup-
ports the credibility of his information, for he would hardly have dared to in-
vite further trouble for himself by making a false statement in a highly publicized case.

So far, the answer to your question is: I have not been able to find any witness other than my wife who remembers him as George Crosley.

Stripling put in evidence, as if it were at variance with my testimony, a communication from the Library of Congress that no periodical articles by George Crosley had been located, although a book of poems published in 1905 had been found under the name of G. Crosley.

We then moved to the subject of my having given the Ford to Crosley, and we not only stayed on that topic all the rest of the morning, but began again with it as soon as we returned from lunch. This was a subject on which, as I have already pointed out in this chapter (and had already demonstrated to the Committee in my prior testimony), my memory of dates was quite uncertain. It was, too, a subject on which the Committee knew that I had been unable to obtain the clarifying records they had obtained.

Here was a topic, they seemed to feel, with which they could play at cat-and-mouse with me, one on which they could lead me to give an impression of evasiveness or lack of candor that could then by implication be used to cast doubt on my denials of Chambers's basic charges. Indeed, Nixon had early in the day been quite express about the implication the Committee sought to create, at the same time indicating that the Committee was filling the role of prosecutor and judge:

Mr. Hiss, you are an attorney. I think you are aware probably of the standard instruction which is given to the jury on cases of credibility of witnesses.

That instruction, as I recall it, is that if any matter a witness is found to be telling an untruth on any question which is material and which is raised during the course of the court's proceedings, his credibility on other questions is also suspect.

Now, as far as this matter is concerned, you, yourself, have made an issue of the fact as to (1) whether you knew Chambers at all—that issue has now been resolved; and (2) how well you knew Chambers and whether you knew him as a Communist.

That is the purpose of this questioning now.

Stripling, armed with record facts, began by asking me to tell again of the circumstances under which I had turned the Ford over to Crosley. I did so in a brief reply:

My best recollection is that at the time, or shortly after we first talked about Crosley's subletting my apartment, he said that he wished to get a car because his family would be with him while he was in Washington. I think he asked if you could rent a car, and my best recollection is that I told him that I had an old car which I would let him have, a car which had practically no financial value. That is the best recollection I have on the car transaction after all these years.

I repeated also, in answer to questions by Mundt, that I definitely remembered having two cars at once, but, aware of my uncertainty as to the sequence of events, I emphasized that "as to the particular time [when I had the two automobiles], without consulting records, I am not able to testify with positiveness."

The question of when I had both cars was repeated by Hébert in several forms and was then pressed by Stripling. As so often that day, I felt that I was ringed by questioners who, because they took turns, made the same question sound to the onlookers like different questions. In these circumstances the repetition of a frank inability to recall the details of this particular transfer was made to seem a failure of memory with respect to a number of topics.

A few minutes later Stripling asked what Crosley had done with the car. I replied that I did not recall. Here the memory of having had the Ford *after* Crosley had used it, and my uncertainty as to when I had had both cars at the same time, led me to remark that Crosley might have returned it to me after using it. As my recollection was that I had not made any written transfer to him, but had merely given him the certificate of title, I realized (even though I had no actual recollection of the assignment) that I might later have been asked to complete a formal assignment. I said that "if the records show that it bounced back to me" (in the sense of legal title still being technically mine), I would not be surprised.

Here Stripling asked whether in fact I had not "sold" the car a year later than the time when I had given it to Crosley. This seemed to confirm my hypothesis as to the history of the technical title, and, unable to examine the certificate, I resolved to be on my guard in committing myself on this point. Stripling next brought out that I had not registered the Plymouth until early September, and Nixon asked if my recollection still was that I had given the car to Crosley as "part of the apartment deal." Definitely recalling Crosley's use of the car during his tenancy, I stuck to what was clear in my memory and said I recalled that, just as I had been able to give Crosley the *use* of the apartment, I had then, or possibly a little later, given him the *use* of the Ford.

Nixon hastened to remark that on eighteen occasions I had on August 16 and 17 answered "Yes" to questions as to whether the disposal of the car to Chambers "was part of the apartment deal." He said I had not qualified my answers by saying that it was to the best of my recollection. This kind of harassment, which is what it seemed to me, was continuous throughout the remainder of the hearing. In this instance I replied by reminding Nixon that I had on both the 16th and the 17th informed the Committee that I had not been able to check my records. I went on to point out that I had been urged by the Committee, against my reluctance, to give them my best memory. Nixon's use of my former answers, which I had thought were understood to be subject to this plainly stated general qualification, naturally led me thereafter to qualify my answers even more. He then drew a laugh from the audience by the prosecutor's sally: ". . . you certainly can testify, 'Yes' or 'No' as to whether you gave Crosley a car. How many cars have you given away in your life, Mr. Hiss?" I replied:

I have only had one old car of a financial value of $25 in my life. That is the car I let Crosley have the use of.

Nixon followed this with a different approach:

This was a car that had a certain sentimental meaning to you,
I think you said.

To which I replied:

MR. HISS: And that is why I had not been prepared previously to
   accept merely $25 for it.
MR. NIXON: That is right.
MR. HISS: I was more interested in having it used than in merely
   getting $25 for it.

At about this point Mundt took over. He read from my
prior testimony my statement that I had sold the car to
Crosley. He did not continue with the statement, which added
that I had let Crosley have the car as part of the transaction
of renting the apartment because I had kept it for sentimental
reasons when it no longer was worth trading in, but commented
instead in a hectoring tone:

Now, Mr. Hiss, I am trying to get at the truth of this, and I
wish you would make a statement and stand by it. . . .

He went on to say that in 1934 and 1935 we were in a
depression, that "automobiles were not so numerous and so
plentiful that a Government employee would forget what
happened to the cars that he had in his possession. You certainly know whether or not you gave Crosley an automobile;
you know whether or not Crosley gave that car back, and we
want the truth. . . ."

I answered rather warmly that I was as interested in getting at the truth as any member of the Committee could be,
and I asked what his specific question was. He inquired
whether I had testified, as the record reported, that I sold
Crosley an automobile. I assured him that I was not challenging the record. He resorted again to what I felt to be bullying
tactics:

MR. MUNDT: You also know whether or not Mr. Crosley gave
   you back the automobile you sold him. You said this car had

a good sentimental value to you, you had kept it a long time. You certainly know, and we know that you know, whether you got that car back. We want you to tell us the truth, that is all.

MR. HISS: You know a great deal, Mr. Mundt.

MR. MUNDT: It is very hard to know very much about this evasive type of testimony, but I am trying to get at the truth.

MR. HISS: Mr. Mundt, you referred to the depression. It is also a fact that old second-hand cars had a not considerable value during the depression. If the depression is relevant to our question, it seems to me that an additional fact is also relevant. Now, what is the exact question you are asking me?

MR. MUNDT: You have answered it. I have asked it, and you have answered it.

Here Nixon interposed to assert that 1935 want ads showed $59 as the lowest cash value for 1929 Ford roadsters and to assert further that dealers had told the Committee that for trade-in purposes the value would be more than $59. I replied:

Mr. Nixon, as I have testified before, my recollection is that I was at no time ever told that that car, during this period, had a value of more than $25 or $30 or $35.

I did not then know that the day before, Nixon had in executive session asked the head of Cherner Motor Company these questions and had received the following replies:

MR. NIXON: Now, as cars go, Mr. Cherner, you, as a used-car dealer, and a very big one, you probably can help the committee on this point. Do you know approximately what the value, shall we say, what you might term the junk value, of a '29 Ford car would have been in 1936, a roadster? What is the lowest value that you might put upon it?

MR. CHERNER: Probably about $25, and sometimes even $15. We have sold them for junk.

MR. NIXON: $15?

MR. CHERNER: Yes.

MR. NIXON: In other words, they were worth even that for junk.

MR. CHERNER: $15, $25.

MR. NIXON: Even if the car could not run, you could get that out of it just for parts.

MR. CHERNER: Yes; I think so.

MR. NIXON: Suppose the car was in running condition, that is, would it still be worth about that if you were buying it?

MR. CHERNER: Well, in those days, of course, we were selling a lot of cars.

MR. NIXON: I understand.

MR. CHERNER: The '29 car was practically worthless, $25, $50. It depends on the condition of the car, of course.

MR. NIXON: It is worth at least $25.

MR. CHERNER: Yes; it would be worth $25.

MR. STRIPLING: If it were running.

MR. CHERNER: Yes; it would be worth $25.

MR. NIXON: All right.

Nor did I then know that the certificate of title with the assignment transferring the Ford to the Cherner Motor Company, which I had signed in my office at the Department of Justice, recited that the Cherner Company in reassigning the car the same day had imposed a chattel mortgage for $25. This was the certificate of which the Committee then had a copy and I did not.

The long and repetitive questioning about the car continued. Nixon proceeded to read aloud from my testimony of August 16 and August 17. He went on to summarize, in what I resented as an argumentative and distorted fashion, the testimony I had just given. He said, inaccurately, that I now said that I could only "testify to the best of [my] recollection as to whether [I] ever gave Crosley a car at all, that [I was] not sure as to whether or not [I] transferred the car to Crosley, that [I] might have given it to him for his use only, and that [I was] not even sure when the transaction occurred. . . ." He next suggested that I might want to change my testimony, twitted me about having relied on my best recollection, and asked for a "Yes" or "No" answer to whether I had given "Crosley a car."

I prefaced my reply by referring to the Committee's practice of using information that was not available to me:

Mr. Nixon, it is evident that the committee has had access to far more record information than I have had.

We got into an altercation in which I said that in reading over the record (of August 17) I had noticed that whereas I spoke of the apartment as on 29th Street, Nixon had correctly spoken of it as on 28th Street. I said that I thought he had even then had access to records that I had not. He answered shortly: "Certainly."

He continued to press, evidently—as it seemed to me—seeking to trap me into some statement which he could imply was contradicted by the records he had and I did not have. In turn, I refused to be harassed into going beyond what I could be sure I recalled:

MR. NIXON: My point on the car is, is your testimony now that you gave Crosley a car, or is it that you did not give him a car?

MR. HISS: Mr. Nixon, my testimony, I believe from the beginning, based upon the best recollection I have, is that I gave Crosley the use of the car, as I gave him the use of the apartment.

Now, whether I transferred title to him in a legal, formal sense, whether he returned the car to me in connection with my upbraiding him for not having repaid various small loans, and the loans stick in my memory as of more significance than the rental of the house itself, because that rental did not involve anything I was going to get from any other source in any event, a couple of months left over, a couple of months in the summertime, for an apartment in Washington—that was not a very great financial asset in those days.

MR. NIXON: Well, now, is your testimony this morning then that you did not give Crosley the car, that you gave him the use of the car?

MR. HISS: Mr. Nixon, I have testified, and I repeat it, that my best recollection is that I gave Crosley the use of the car. Whether I gave him the car outright, whether the car came back, I don't know.

MR. NIXON: You do not know whether you had the possession of this car after Crosley left you?

MR. HISS: That, I am afraid, I cannot recall. I do recall having a

Plymouth and a Ford at the same time for some months, not
just a few days. I do recall the Ford sitting around because
it was not being used, the tires going down because it was
just sitting on the street.

I told him once again that my best recollection was that
my having the two cars was the reason I had given the Ford
to Crosley.

This sort of thrust and parry went on for some time. I
made clear my uncertainty as to the actual dates and even to
the sequence of events, and for that reason refused to be
stampeded into flat assertions which I could not be certain
of and which I felt sure would be turned against me if the
Committee could do so. I had within the past few days
learned that I had been off in my recollection of the dates of
my leases for the 28th Street apartment and the P Street
house. I reasoned that I could be similarly incorrect as to my
impressions of dates with respect to letting Crosley have the
Ford. This seeming attempt at entrapment was very different
from the atmosphere I had assumed was present at the outset
of the hearing on the 16th, when I was urged to give my
uncertain and unchecked memory on details, details now being held up to me as if they were important matters of the
day before yesterday that must be unclouded in my memory.
The lengthy cross-questioning went on:

MR. NIXON: And your testimony then is that the car—that you
are not sure that the car was tied in to the rental transaction;
you think it might not have been.

MR. HISS: It could have been tied in toward the end, it could have
been tied in toward the beginning. My best recollection is that
there is a connection between the two transactions.

MR. NIXON: Could it have taken place several months after the
rental transaction?

MR. HISS: Mr. Nixon, it could have.

MR. NIXON: You mean several months after he had refused to pay
the rent?

MR. HISS: After he failed to pay the rent.

MR. NIXON: Well, didn't you ask him for the rent?

MR. HISS: Mr. Nixon, I don't recall at any time his ever refusing, ever saying, "I just am not going to pay." Quite the contrary, he was always going to pay at some time.

MR. NIXON: How long after he moved out of his apartment did you decide he was a dead beat?

MR. HISS: Mr. Nixon, I am not able to testify with exactness on that.

MR. NIXON: But you think it is possible that you loaned him a car or gave him a car after he failed to pay the rent?

MR. HISS: I may very well have given him the use of the car even though he had not paid the rent at that particular time.

MR. NIXON: And your testimony is that this man was simply a casual acquaintance.

MR. HISS: This man was an acquaintance. Under the circumstances this man was an acquaintance, under the circumstances to which I have testified.[5]

Here Mundt took over, with the opening remark that "it is certainly inconceivable, Mr. Hiss, that you would not know some of the details of this automobile in the manner in which you have described it." He went on to express the "hope" that I would not have to use the phrase "to the best of my recollection," which he asserted I had used seventy-five times in my appearances before the Committee, as if frank admission of uncertain memory about details of thirteen or fourteen years earlier was undesirable and as if many of the most recent instances were not the repetition of the same answer to an oft-repeated question. I had shortly before this asked Nixon if he had "ever had occasion to have people ask you continuously and over and over again what you did on the night of June 5, 1934 or 1935."

Mundt, using the prosecutor's phrase of "would you like to have this committee believe," wanted to know if I did not remember how I had finally disposed of the Ford. I pointed out:

[5] This appears to be another instance of incorrect editing. With corrected punctuation, the passage reads: "This man was an acquaintance under the circumstances—this man was an acquaintance under the circumstances to which I have testified."

Mr. Mundt, I have already testified that my recollection is that
I let Crosley have the use of it; I may have let him have complete
disposition. He may be the person who disposed of it.

Representative Vail, who had not participated previously,
took over after Mundt. For the moment the subject changed.

MR. VAIL: Mr. Hiss, as a lawyer, don't you think it is a rather peculiar procedure for a tenant who is signatory to a written lease
to sublease an apartment containing valuable furniture to a
comparative stranger?

MR. HISS: Mr. Vail, it so happens that I did exactly that same thing
3 or 4 years before. I sublet, without any formal arrangement,
a house I then had as the tenant in Georgetown on Thirtieth
Street to a man who then was a casual acquaintance in Washington.

I had his name recalled to me this winter through other
circumstances. I have asked him or had him asked whether his
recollection of that transaction of the summer of 1930, I think
it was, is the same as mine, that it was done at the cost to
me of my lease, that it was done informally and without writing, and he said to the best of his recollection it was done exactly the same way then. [This had been a *summer* rental,
when our lease ran to the *fall,* to another couple with a small
daughter and may have led me to make the same assumptions
as to duration in the case of the Crosleys.]

Last summer and this summer, the two places that I have
taken for the summer, I have also taken without a formal lease
from the owners of the premises, simply an informal understanding.

Now, to me, Mr. Vail, it is not an unusual procedure, because I have done it on a number of occasions. It may be unusual to other people; it has not seemed so to me.

After another few questions as to whether I wasn't running a risk unless the Ford was covered by liability insurance,
Stripling produced the photostat of the certificate of title for
the Ford and stated that it showed my assignment of title
to the Cherner Motor Company on July 23, 1936. A staff
member then testified that the Cherner Company's existing
records did not cover the resale of the car, listed on the cer-

tificate as having been to a William Rosen, although the records of other sales of the same day were found and for the period July 21 to July 24 no sales invoices (which were consecutively numbered) were missing. Rosen had not yet been located.

I was then returned to the stand and said that, despite the production of the certificate with its assignment of title, I still had no further recollection of the disposition of the Ford. As the Committee had recited bits of the records of landlords and the motor-vehicles bureau, some details in my memory became clearer. But the hurly-burly of a hostile hearing, with its tension from harassing questions and the physical strain of klieg lights, was not conducive to clarifying a fallible memory. Certain topics remained tightly locked in confusion and forgetfulness until I could consider them in a calmer atmosphere with full and orderly reference to the records. My act of signing the transfer in my office, before the colleague who notarized it, is one item I have never been able to recall. My colleague was equally unable to recall the incident. I can only assume that on July 23, 1936, someone came to my office in the Department of Justice, presented the assignment which the Cherner Company had accepted, and asked me to fill out the form and have it notarized. This I must have done as a routine and unremembered act, recognizing that if Crosley had chosen to turn in the old Ford, that was his privilege.

Soon after, we adjourned for lunch.

When we reconvened, Stripling presented a certificate of inspection executed July 23, 1936, by various officials of the Cherner Motor Company, who attested that they had individually checked lights, brakes, horn, and other items and verified the serial number of the motor. No comment was made that this routine personal examination by several named officials of the company tended to make the company's disposal of the old car less mysterious than had the pre-recess emphasis on "missing" invoices—a topic, I noted, that was presented just in time for the afternoon papers.

I was promptly asked whether I recalled anything of the details of the transfer to the Cherner Company, and I replied:

As I testified before lunch, Mr. Stripling, I do not have any present recollection of the transfer of title, a photostat of the certificate of which you showed me before lunch.

In reply to a question by Nixon, I repeated what I had already said so often—that I had given the car to Crosley, but that I could not recall the details of technical transfer of legal title:

MR. HISS: My best recollection, Mr. Nixon, as I believe I have testified previously on several occasions, is that I made the car available to Crosley. Whether I gave it to him outright, whether it came back to me from him, whether at some later stage he or someone else came to me and said "You disposed of a car, there remains a technical transfer to be completed," I have no present recollection.

MR. NIXON: As I understand your answer then, you are sure that you gave the car to Crosley either for a loan or by transfer.

MR. HISS: I am. That is my best present recollection.

MR. NIXON: On that point. But you do not remember whether or not Mr. Crosley gave the car back to you and whether or not you transferred it later to the Cherner Motor Co.?

MR. HISS: No; I do not.

MR. NIXON: You don't recall that incident at all?

MR. HISS: No; I do not.

MR. NIXON: You don't deny, however, that the notarization of your signature on the transfer to Cherner Motor Co. in July of 1936 is your signature?

MR. HISS: I certainly do not.

MR. NIXON: I see. But you don't recall that transaction?

MR. HISS: I do not recall it. I would want to talk to Mr. Marvin Smith [my colleague in the Department of Justice who had notarized my signature] to see what his recollection is. I have no recollection.

MR. NIXON: The committee took the testimony of Mr. Smith, who testified that he did notarize your signature, that he knew you, and that had you not come before him for notarizing the signature, he would not have notarized the signature.

MR. HISS: I would have had the same impression, because I know Mr. Smith.

Again came further repetition of the same question and the necessary repetition of answer. In this exchange I told Nixon that the July 23, 1936, date certainly did not mean that I had had possession of the car until then, and again I repeated flatly that I had given the car to Crosley:

MR. NIXON: You mean the person that had possession of the car at that time might have asked you to complete this transaction?

MR. HISS: That is quite possible, and someone may have come into my office in the Department of Justice—Mr. Marvin Smith was in the same office where I worked in the Department of Justice—and may have said to me, "You disposed of a car some time ago. There is a technical legal step that needs to be taken. Would you simply sign a statement?" That I have no present recollection of, Mr. Nixon, but I am doing my best to recall[,] to get the evidence.

MR. NIXON: Did Mr. Crosley come in there and ask you to do that?

MR. HISS: I have no recollection of seeing Mr. Crosley after 1935.

MR. NIXON: He is the man you gave the car to?

MR. HISS: That is correct.

MR. NIXON: He is the man who would have had possession?

MR. HISS: That doesn't necessarily follow, Mr. Nixon.

MR. NIXON: Did you give the car to anybody else?

MR. HISS: You are leaving out some possible steps. He may have given the car to somebody else.

A little later Nixon made a summary for the record (and for the press and TV and radio) of what he called "the facts" relating to the car. It put together in a continuous statement of about 1,200 words the unwarranted inferences of fact and argumentative thrusts which had been made by the Committee throughout the day's questioning. He restated his thesis about credibility, making it quite plain that if I was incorrect in my recollection of mere dates about the car, he wanted the conclusion to be drawn that I was also incorrect in denying the charges of Communism.

I asked for the right to comment, and said:

I would like to say that the record which Mr. Nixon has attempted to summarize will, of course, speak for itself. I am glad that the record is now being made public by the committee so that others may make their own summary of it.

I do not accept the summarization that Mr. Nixon has just made. But, of course, that is his privilege. It is the privilege of anyone to summarize the record.

Mundt then proceeded to show me photographs of Chambers, including the two snapshots said to have been taken in 1934, in each of which he was holding his infant up beside his face in such a way as to cover the lower left cheek and side of the face. The right side of the face was largely in shadow, particularly marked in one case. Mundt wanted to know if the snapshots and a 1948 press photograph that he produced showed any marked differences. My reply was:

I am afraid I wouldn't be able to recognize—you can only see part of the face there. Again you can only see part of the face. It would be very hard to say. I have no distinct recollection at this time of the facial appearance of George Crosley, and I have so testified.

My strongest recollection is of the bad teeth. When I saw him for the first time after these hearing[s] began, I asked, as the record will show, if he would please open his mouth so I could look at his teeth.

Here Nixon intervened, ending his remarks with a query, which drew more laughter from the audience, as to whether I hadn't ever seen Crosley with his mouth closed. I restated my position with reference to Nixon's jibe:

The striking thing in my recollection about Crosley was not when he had his mouth shut, but when he had his mouth open.

Nixon persisted with his provocative remarks:

As far as you are concerned, the only way you can identify a person is when he has his mouth open? Is that correct?

Mundt again took up his photographs, and this time the implication of his question became a flat assertion:

MR. MUNDT: Now, going on, I have shown these two pictures of Mr. Chambers taken in 1934, together with a picture of Mr. Chambers taken a few hours before your testimony, to a great many objective people, members of this committee and others, and you are the only one up to now who has said he wouldn't be able to see the striking similarity between the pictures taken in 1934 and the picture now.[6]

MR. HISS: I said, Mr. Mundt——

MR. MUNDT: There is a little portion of the baby's clothing cutting off one portion of the ear and part of the teeth of Mr. Chambers, but his eyes are both evident, his hair is evident, the general facial characteristics are evident, and what is hard for me to understand is why a man whom you now recognize, you say, as being Mr. Crosley, and looks as much as he does like the gentleman whose picture was taken here in 1934, why you should have told us on that first day that you never laid eyes on the man.

MR. HISS: Mr. Mundt, I told you on that first day that I, as far as I knew, had never laid eyes on Whittaker Chambers. I have also said—and the record will show I said it to the committee on the 16th and I said it to others before that—that there was a certain familiarity about the pictures I had seen in the press of the man who calls himself Chambers. There is still a certain familiarity. That is all I am able to say about his present appearance.

In a few moments Mundt said:

Let me change now to another topic.

But his introductory remarks indicated that basically his topic remained that of casting doubt on my veracity:

Since the question has come up so often, the thing we are really trying to get to, Mr. Hiss, is the credibility of your testimony versus the credibility of the testimony of Mr. Chambers and

[6] The statements of the unidentified "objective people" referred to by Mundt are not available, but only the day before, Martha Pope had evidently not found the similarity so great (see pp. 63–4).

whether you have been completely forthright with this committee or whether you have been concealing some of the details which you cannot remember. . . .

He soon asked whether, before I became its president, I had notified the Carnegie Endowment of the interview with the FBI men who had come to see me. I reminded him that that interview had occurred after, not before, I joined the Endowment.

Nixon asked if I had told them of the interview with the FBI in 1946 (which I had sought after James F. Byrnes, then Secretary of State, had told me that members of Congress were going to make speeches attacking me). I replied:

My recollection on that point, Mr. Nixon, is that shortly after I had been elected but before I had assumed office I had a conversation with Mr. John Foster Dulles in which he said that he had heard reports that people had called me a Communist. We discussed those reports at that time.

Mundt asked substantially the same question, and I repeated my answer with some amplification, assuming that he had not understood my first reply. He then asked whether it had been Mr. Dulles or I who had brought up the subject. I replied:

Mr. Dulles called me and said he had had a report. I said, "I thought that had been laid to rest," and I discussed it with him then.

Mundt, in the manner of a prosecutor, commented:

So, it still stands for the record, whether it has any pertinency or not, that you of your own volition did not bring this matter up with your prospective employers?

Soon Hébert stated that I had told Mundt that I had never heard of Chambers's accusation until the hearings began, starting the following interchange:

MR. HISS: Mr. Hébert, I testified that I had never heard until August 3 that when [apparent misprint for "one"] Whittaker

Chambers had been to Mr. Berle with accusations about me. I had heard earlier than that date that a man named Chambers had said I was a Communist. I think I testified to that in the record.

MR. HÉBERT: You heard that a man named Chambers had said you were a Communist. What did you do about it?

MR. HISS: May I again tell you the circumstances under which I heard about it?

Sometime in the past winter I learned indirectly, not from the individual friend involved, that a friend of mine attending a dinner party had heard a fellow guest at the dinner party say that Alger Hiss was a Communist and had been when he was in Government service.

This friend of mine had challenged this fellow guest and the fellow guest said, "I know it, because a man named Chambers said so."

The friend, according to the report as I got it, had followed it up, and had been told several days later by that same person that the person had checked back, and the person had been told that Chambers had been talking too much and was not saying [that] now; so that I paid no further attention to it.

A lot of people, Mr. Hébert, have been called Communists in recent years.

Here Mundt, again in the role of prosecutor, moved in:

MR. MUNDT: Mr. Hiss, is it then your testimony that the first time you ever heard of Whittaker Chambers in connection with allegations that you are a Communist was during the past winter?

MR. HISS: That is correct.

MR. MUNDT: That would be the winter of 19——

MR. HISS: 1948.

MR. MUNDT: You never heard about it before?

MR. HISS: I did not.

MR. MUNDT: You are sure of that?

MR. HISS: I am confident of it. That is my very best recollection.

MR. MUNDT: Let me read this, Mr. Hiss, because this is one of the disturbing parts of your testimony.

He then read my testimony of August 5 that the first time I had heard the *name* Whittaker Chambers was in 1947 when the FBI representatives who called on me asked me if I knew him and various others.

Now, what do you expect this committee to do with a fabric of contradictory evidence like that, Mr. Hiss?

I told Mundt I was shocked by his characterization of my testimony, pointing out that I had said, in what he had just read, that it was in 1947 that I first heard Chambers's *name:*

MR. HISS: . . . They [the FBI agents] in no way indicated that Chambers or any one of the other names I had or had not heard of was making any charge against me. It was merely one of a number of names, some of which I knew and a considerable number of which I had never heard of before.

There is no contradiction, and I resent and protest your saying it was contradictory testimony.

MR. MUNDT: There is a contradiction because you just testified to Mr. Hébert that the first time you ever heard of Mr. Whittaker Chambers was last winter.

MR. HISS: I do not——

MR. MUNDT: Now you say you heard about him in 1947. If that isn't a contradiction, I don't recognize it.

MR. HISS: Mr. Mundt, I do not think I testified to Mr. Hébert that the first time I ever heard of Chambers was last winter. I understood Mr. Hébert to ask me when I first heard that Chambers had said I was a Communist, and those are two very different statements.

Mundt refused to admit the inaccuracy or injustice of his remarks. No other member intervened to clear up his error. He concluded the point by saying:

We will have to let the record speak for that.

The audience in the hearing room and over the airwaves, hardly likely to follow this interchange clearly, was again left with an unwithdrawn charge by a supposedly impartial member of the national legislature that I had presented a "fabric of contradictory" testimony.

Hébert remarked that I had that day said that I had told the Committee that I had recognized "some familiarity in the photograph."

MR. HISS: I did not testify today that I told the committee that on the 5th. It was in my mind. I do not find it in the record. I do recall having said that to a number of individuals on the 4th, the day before I testified. I did testify to it on the 16th.

The particular photograph shown me on the 5th was a poor one for identification purposes because of the distortion caused by the angle at which the photograph had been taken. Some other pictures, had they been shown to me on the 5th, might have made the sense of familiarity momentarily more acute and have led to my expressing it unasked.

Hébert, too, now seemed argumentative in his approach:

MR. HÉBERT: You told somebody before you appeared before the committee that there was a familiarity?

MR. HISS: I told several people.

MR. HÉBERT: Several people?

MR. HISS: Yes, I did.

MR. HÉBERT: Why didn't you tell the committee that?

MR. HISS: The committee did not specifically ask me. I was shown a photograph. I was asked if I could identify it.

Testimony, unlike ordinary conversation, is given in response to specific questions. The pattern and tradition discourage volunteered statements, as they can lead the questioner away from his subject. I had had to concentrate on the pending question and naturally had dealt with it quite literally. But I had been so conscious of the familiarity (though the person of Crosley did not come to mind) that I thought I had mentioned it on my first appearance on the 5th. I had told Stripling at the Commodore, on the 17th, that I had done so, and was surprised to find on examining the record that on the 5th the subject had been changed before the point was reached. I did mention it at my second appearance, on August 16, when more time was given to the identification point, which by that time had grown into major importance.

On the 5th the subject was changed abruptly after my saying that, from the picture shown me, Chambers looked like a lot of people and might even be mistaken for Mundt, that I wouldn't want to take oath I had never seen him, that I would like to see him and had hoped he would be present. There had been a jocular interruption when I said the picture might be taken for one of Mundt. The only other reference to Chambers's identification was the later statement by Nixon, not in the form of a question, that Chambers and I would "be allowed to confront each other so that any possibility of a mistake in identity may be cleared up."

But Hébert persisted, reading aloud the testimony I had given when shown the photograph on the 5th. I pointed out that what he read indicated that there had been an interruption and that the "committee did not proceed with much more about the photograph." (In fact on August 5 there had been *no* more; only a single question had been asked about the photograph. Stripling, who had asked the question, changed the subject away from photographs by bringing up the topic of when I had first heard of Chambers's accusations.) I went on to say to Hébert:

MR. HISS: . . . I have no way of knowing why I did not happen to mention everything that was in my mind on that particular occasion. I have told you—and it is the truth—that I did notice a certain familiarity in the pictures. I was not sure that that familiarity was significant.

    I could be imagining it. It was not an unusual face as I saw it in the pictures.

MR. HÉBERT: But you did think it of importance to tell other people before you appeared before this committee that there was some familiarity about the man's pictures?

MR. HISS: People with whom I was discussing this strange occurrence and proceeding.

MR. HÉBERT: But you didn't think it of importance to tell this committee that?

MR. HISS: It [apparent misprint for "I"] did not at the moment that I was testifying on the particular subject of recognition. I don't remember how many other passages there were in the record about recognition. [As noted earlier, there are none, except Nixon's statement that there would be a confrontation.] It didn't seem of sufficient importance for me to mention; that seems obvious.

Hébert insisted on expressing an opinion:

. . . you left the committee with this impression, and I am sure everybody else that heard it, that you had never seen this man Chambers or anyone who even remotely looked like him.

Nixon joined in:

Now, the impression that was left with me—and I must join Mr. Hébert in this—I think the committee left with the press and I have read most of the stories that appeared in the newspapers the following day—was that you testified you had never seen [t]his man.

Hébert continued with his statement. He twice called me "a very agile young man" and summarized the record as demonstrating that I am an individual who "gives to casual people his apartment, who tosses in an automobile, who doesn't know the laws of liability, who lends money to an individual just casually." This, he said, contrasted with my caution in insisting on seeing Chambers in person and not wishing to testify as to his identity from a photograph.

I replied:

Now, your specific question of me, I understand, again relates to the question of why I was unable to identify a picture, a single picture that was shown to me, and I think it would be wise if the record showed the particular picture which was shown to me.

My recollection is it was a picture taken at a candid-camera angle from under the chin. I don't know whether Mr. Stripling still has or marked as an exhibit the particular picture shown to me. I think it is relevant.

Although Mundt immediately asked that the photograph I had been shown be put in the record, this was never in fact done. I then went on:

MR. HISS: Mr. Hébert, the name Crosley was not in my mind at all when I was testifying before this committee. There was not [apparent misprint for "no"] remote connection in my mind between that man, the transactions I had had with him, and the charges that a man named Chambers was now making against me.

Why should I have connected the two people at that time? . . .

Now, all the confusion might very well have been avoided if you had had him here the first day. I hoped he would be. I remarked on the fact that he was not here the first day.

MR. HÉBERT: Of course, that is mere speculation on what you would have done the first day.

MR. HISS: You said I could continue after you had finished, Mr. Hébert.

MR. HÉBERT: Certainly. I apologize.

MR. HISS: Thank you. You have compared what you term my caution in testifying on what to me was a very important fact: Who was my accuser on such a serious charge? You have compared that in importance to trivial transactions of 14 years earlier. I do not think that is a fair comparison. . . .

J. Parnell Thomas, in his turn, took up the subject of the two 1934 snapshots of Chambers and the baby. I replied as before:

. . . the face is partly in the shadow, the hair is tousled, a child's clothing obscures more than the ear, which one of the committee members mentioned.

He persisted:

THE CHAIRMAN: You have chin, nose, and mouth left. Does it look like this man?

MR. HISS: It obscures a good deal more than an ear. I would not be able to say this is the picture of Whittaker Chambers.

. . . . .

. . . I don't think it is a particularly clear photograph for purposes of identification.

He put his question in various forms. He asked if the 1934 photographs were photographs of George Crosley. I said I had no clear visual recollection of Crosley's appearance. That was why, I pointed out, I had been so careful before identifying

Chambers as Crosley in New York. I added the very obvious consideration that, in addition to other factors, I had been reluctant to bring the names of others into the hearing. I didn't know what damage would be done to Crosley by dragging his name in. I repeated that there was a certain familiarity about the snapshots, as there was about recent photographs. I said there certainly was also some similarity between the 1934 photographs and the current one then being discussed by the Committee.

Stripling next recited that several of those alleged by Chambers to have been in a Communist group with me had claimed the protection of the Fifth Amendment as a reason for not testifying as to whether or not they knew me. (He did not bring out the fact that my brother, one of those accused by Chambers, had not claimed the Fifth Amendment but had, on the contrary, at his own request appeared as a witness before the Committee and had denied the charges.) Stripling had me again testify as to which of these men I had known. (I had known all but one and in varying degrees of casualness or closeness. One was a friend of long standing; the others whom I had known were professional associates.) In answer to his questions I repeated that I had no basis for knowing whether these men were or were not Communists.

Mundt then read into the record quotations from the Associated Press account and from the reports of several newspapers of my initial testimony, which he asserted indicated that the "general public gathered from [my] testimony that [I] had never seen Chambers, had never known him by any name. . . ." Actually the A.P. report that he read aloud said simply that I was unable to identify the picture of Chambers. Three of the individual papers he quoted said that I had denied knowing or meeting *Chambers*. Only the *Washington Evening Star* reported that I had said I had never laid eyes on him. The New York *Daily News*, the *Christian Science Monitor*, and the *Baltimore Evening Sun* all accurately quoted or paraphrased my statement that *so far as I knew* I had never laid eyes on him.

Mundt prefaced his quotations with the statement that I had "concealed" from the Committee the familiarity of "that picture." (As I have already pointed out, it was *not* the picture shown me on the 5th that I had mentioned to friends as having a certain familiarity, but other photographs I had seen in the press after Chambers's testimony.) He concluded:

I regret that you were not more forthright in your testimony before the committee on that occasion so that this that you now say is a false impression went out to the country generally.

I answered:

Mr. Mundt, you used the word "concealed." I came before this committee voluntarily and I appreciate your letting me appear. I came on the 16th and on the 17th in response to a request. I said on the 16th I would be glad to be here on the 25th, today. I have concealed nothing from this committee. I have sought no privilege against answering any question.

Nixon said he had just a few more questions and went once again over the topics of the car and the apartment and my contacts with Crosley in general. The few questions stretched into more than a few. He brought out that the Committee had now learned that the rent, which I had recalled as less than $75 a month, was in fact $60. He emphasized that Chambers owed me at least $120, or two months' rent. I repeated what I had said before:

. . . the apartment did not seem to me then and does not seem to me now to have been a [of?] very significant financial value on the market, on the market at the time. I had some more time to go after I moved out [of] there.
It was not a . . . readily disposable asset at the time.

Mundt followed by delivering a summation of some 2,500 words which he called a review of "the reactions of just one member of this committee" to my testimony and which, he announced, "I shall make without interruption." He, too, began with the by now familiar reference to "espionage," despite the absence of any testimony of espionage by Chambers.

Mundt took the position that the Committee had followed the very procedural suggestions I had made:

You suggested when you first came before the committee that
in an effort to get at the facts that we take certain steps, one of
which was to go to the records, wherever the records are available.
We have done that, and we have spread those records wherever
available into this testimony.

You suggested that you be confronted with your accuser. We
have done that, both in executive session and in open session.

You suggested that we check all the verifiable details, which
we have done.

He said, incorrectly, that I had testified that the photograph shown me "did not bring back the memory of anybody
whom [I] had seen."

Mundt also said that in my testimony of August 16 I had
"verified" the "many details" that Chambers had given on the
7th, "intimate details about your family, about your hobby,
about your pets, about the decorations in the room." The
Committee, he said, could find no one who knew or had seen
George Crosley and I had produced no one. He again asserted
without justification that I had initially said I knew no one
looking like Chambers, and he added that it had been established "that you did know him and that you do know him."

He equated my small loans to Chambers with the latter's
charge that I had paid Communist dues to him. He asserted
that "The points in agreement . . . are these: You knew this
man; you knew him very well. You knew him so well that you
even trusted him with your apartment . . ." and so on with
a considerably less than objective summary of the undisputed
items in my acquaintance with Chambers as George Crosley.

Mundt continued that the points of disagreement were
whether I was a Communist and a member of a Communist
group. He here displayed the classic attitude which in a period
of public tension so effectively undercuts all denials:

. . . This committee never had any illusions that we would be
able to prove definitely whether or not you are a Communist be-

cause, in dealing with people charged with being Communists over a period of years, we have found that those who are guilty, refused to admit it and dodged the question, or deliberately lied.

My denials, he was here telling the public, should be discounted in advance. This was the attitude which in earlier times had ignored the denials of those accused of witchcraft. Of course a witch could be expected to deny her calling! I was reminded of the confused and fearful England of the end of the seventeenth century when Titus Oates and other professional informers aroused public horror with their stories of the "Horrid Popish Plot." In a famous trial of that period the Chief Justice of England, himself affected by the atmosphere, used closely similar words to brush aside the denials of two men who were convicted of political murder in behalf of Catholicism, but who are regarded by modern scholarship as innocent:

We do not expect much from you, and it is no great matter; . . . and we know you have either downright denials, or evasions, or equivocating terms for everything. . . ."

Mundt added that there was one other point in dispute: whether I had known Chambers as Carl or as Crosley. This he considered "not a very important distinction." He went on, in a few moments, to say:

. . . The important thing to me, Mr. Hiss, is that he was living in your home, that you were associating with him, that you were taking him out in the car, that you were letting him use your car, that you were letting him use your apartment, and making him loans and having associations with him of that nature.

In an endeavor to determine the credibility of two witnesses whose testimony conflicts on so many of these points, which are still in dispute, we endeavored to establish that by checking, first, Mr. Chambers' testimony to see . . . whether or not you were an ornithologist, to see whether or not you had a car which had a hand windshield wiper, to see whether or not he had this rather intimate association with you, which the testimony of both of you now conclusively proves did exist.

We also endeavored to check the fact as to whether he lived in your home or spent time in your home, as he said he did. Now, both of you testify to the fact that that actually took place.

We endeavored to verify other aspects of his testimony, about transfers that your son made in school, about certain intimate details of the furniture and material in your home, and on every point on which we have been able to verify, on which we have had verifiable evidence before us, the testimony of Mr. Chambers has stood up. It stands unchallenged. Most of it you admit. . . .

There was more of the same. My testimony as to the car, he asserted, was "clearly refuted by the tangible evidence," and on other items was "clouded by a strangely deficient memory." These attacks on me he followed by a renewed misapplication of the prosecutor's thesis:

We proceed on the conclusion that if either one of you is telling the truth on the verifiable data, that you are telling the truth on all of it. And if either one of you is concealing the truth from the committee on verifiable data, it points out that you are concealing from us the truth on obviously the points that we cannot prove.

He concluded by saying he wanted me "to have that reaction . . . from one member of the committee . . . who, after [I] first testified, was very frankly inclined to accept it at its face value." He then offered me the opportunity to "refute" or "challenge" or "correct" his statement. The Chairman added that I might have "all the time you will require" to answer Mundt, and that I could also now read the letter I had sent him the night before, "and just take as much time as you want."

I had not yet seen Chambers's testimony of August 7. I had no way of knowing what Mundt had characterized as "unchallenged" or admitted by me, as verified by the Committee's checking. The public knew no more than I did of the basis or lack of basis for Mundt's sweeping attack on my testimony. It was plain to me from my own vivid experiences of the preceding three weeks that some members of the Committee were politically motivated to tailor testimony to preconceived conclusions. And I knew the real truth in my own case. Those listening to Mundt over the radio or TV, those reading press accounts of his summary had, however, no way of judging for themselves the fairness or unfairness of his statements and of the other similar statements by Committee members made that day.

The opportunity to reply extemporaneously under these circumstances at the end of a long and tiring day was hardly a mark of great favor by the Committee. Obviously I did not have available the material with which to reply effectively. But, equally obviously, a failure to reply would have been used by the Committee as an implied acceptance of the adequacy of Mundt's summary. I was put once more where either alternative was injurious.

Mundt refused to allow me even a brief consultation with counsel:

(At this point, Mr. Hiss attempts to consult with Mr. Davis.)
MR. MUNDT: No; I want Mr. Hiss to talk now, and you may talk later. I want Mr. Hiss to talk now.

I began:

Commenting on Mr. Mundt's so-called summation, I would like to point out that the man who calls himself Chambers has, by his own testimony, been peddling to various Government agencies for 10 years or so stories about me.

During that time he has had an opportunity to check on all sorts of details about my personality.

You referred to my interest in ornithology. I am only an amateur ornithologist, but that fact, that [it] is one of my hobbies, appears in Who's Who.

I have had no chance to see Chambers' testimony which you have characterized as standing up in verifiable details.

I am very anxious to see that testimony to see how verifiable they are.

From the questions asked me on the 16th, I got the impression that he had testified [,[7]] also from some newspaper reports,

[7] The editor of the printed text has omitted this comma, which seems necessary for clarity.

that I had transferred my stepson from one school to another in order to save money, which I could donate to the Communist Party.

The facts are, the personal facts are, that my stepson's educational expenses were paid by his own father. I could not possibly have saved any money by sending him to any cheaper school. At no time did I transfer him from one school to another for any purpose [8] except to benefit his education.

As a matter of fact, while he was in Washington, he went, after only 1 year at the Friends School, to another more expensive school and, when I concluded that he should go to a boarding school, his own father was not then in a position to meet the full expenses and I paid part of the expenses.

I am anxious to examine other points. I may be erroneously informed as to what he has testified about on this particular point.

I notice that the committee did not ask me questions about my stepson's education today, only about certain other points. . . .

The time has been very short. If this man actually was a Communist at the time, as he testifies—and, so far as I know, you have only his unsupported testimony for that particular allegation—it is not surprising that [if?] that is true, that he was secretive. It is not surprising that it is difficult to get information about him. . . .

I would want to read Mr. Mundt's summation carefully against the record. I do not, for a minute, want to make this impromptu response to what Mr. Mundt has said my final answer to Mr. Mundt.

As part of my reply I then asked and was at last permitted to read my letter into the record. Its suggestions as to proper procedure were, at this hour, somewhat anticlimactic.

I repeated publicly my challenge to Chambers to make his charges where they would not be privileged from suit, and I went on to request the Committee to ask Chambers some questions about himself, a topic the Committee had ignored. I wanted to know where he was living then, where he had lived since 1930, the names he had used at those various places, his name at birth and other names he had used, his record of employment and the names used in that employment, a list

[8] Here the editor inserted an unhelpful comma.

of his writings and pen names. None of these matters was
ever adequately developed by the Committee. They came out
only as a result of my efforts to defend myself in the trials for
which these hearings so unfairly prepared the public. I wanted
him asked if he had been charged with any crime or had ever
been treated for a mental illness.

Hébert interrupted to say I could eliminate the last question, as he had already asked Chambers that. The Committee,
too, he said, had heard reports asserted to come from Chambers's own associates on *Time* magazine that he was a mental
case. Hébert called this "a typical Communist smear."

Nixon asked if, in view of my "charge," I had evidence
to present that Chambers had been in a mental institution. I
said I had made no charge, to which Nixon replied rather
irrelevantly:

The charge has appeared in the newspapers.

Nixon pressed me as to whether I had any evidence of
Chambers's having been in a mental institution, and I replied
that various reports to that effect had been made to me.
Here Hébert obtained the floor. Perversely, he turned
Chambers's fabrication about my stepson's educational expenses into confirmation of Chambers's veracity. Ignoring the
falsity and malice of the charge that I had transferred Timothy
to cheaper schools to get funds for the Communist Party at
his father's expense, Hébert said Chambers's knowledge that
my stepson's education was being paid for by his father proved
Chambers knew me and proved this at a time when the Committee was trying to find out if he knew me. Hébert went on
to say that Chambers knew "all about [my] private life" and
had "unhesitatingly answered every question in the minutest
of details which, as Mr. Mundt has indicated, comes back and
checks, even down to the automobile sale."

Here again, as neither the radio and TV public nor I had
seen Chambers's secret testimony, we could not know what
these "minutest of details" were. I knew only that if Chambers had accurately given numerous details about my private

life, most of them could have come only from inquiry and investigation, others from remembered conversations with me, none from a long and close friendship as he and the Committee asserted. From what Mundt and Hébert said, I had to assume (as, of course, the public did, too) the existence of a record of accurate testimony rather than the one that actually existed:

MR. HISS: Who would remember—how would any man remember all those details about any other man after 14 years?
MR. HÉBERT: Unless he knew him extremely well.
MR. HISS: Unless he was studying up on it.

Hébert insisted on repeating the Committee's major thesis of close association:

Unless he knew him extremely well. . . .

To illustrate his point, Hébert used the Committee's favorite incident, that Chambers knew I had seen a prothonotary warbler. "Now, that," he observed, "is not from Who's Who." I made the obvious reply:

I have told many, many people that I have seen a prothonotary warbler, and I am very, very proud [of having done so]. If Mr. McDowell has seen it, he has told very, very many people about it.

Hébert turned to the list of people I had known, some only casually, who had refused to testify before the Committee. His strong implication was that they were all Communists. In addition to the Committee's usual use of such associations to imply that birds of a feather flock together, Hébert said that if I didn't know whether these people were Communists, how could the officials for whom I had worked say whether I was or not? This twisting of my purpose in citing (in my letter to the Chairman of the Committee) those officials who were most familiar with the quality of my work in government tended—for those who failed to note its distortion of my purpose—to deprive me of all credit for fifteen years of government service. It was a tactic the prosecutor was

to adopt, and čarry even further, in the trials (see pages 341–3).
I protested this confusion of issues:

Mr. Hébert, I did not cite their names on that issue. I cited
their names on my record, because I think my record is relevant to
this inquiry.

Once again Nixon took up the topic of my relations with
Crosley, asking when I had last seen him. I did not then believe I had seen him in 1936, but could not be positive. I was
confident I had not seen him in 1937 or 1938. Once more he
asked if I had seen Crosley under any name in the apartment
of Henry Collins (one of those accused by Chambers) when
no more than a few others were present. I testified positively
that I had not.

Nixon, who on occasion had magnified the sums that
Crosley had owed me for rent and small loans, now emphasized that they could not have totaled more than $150. He
asked whether the implication was that because of this (small)
sum Chambers was circulating false charges against me. I said,
as I had before, that I was not prepared to say that I understood or even had "any inkling" as to what could have led
him to make such charges.

At this point Nixon attempted to picture me, rather than
Chambers, as making irresponsible charges. He asserted that
the inference from my *question* about Chambers's mental
condition was itself a "serious charge." (I did not then know
that just a week earlier Nixon himself in an executive hearing
had asked the same question of Isaac Don Levine: "Has he
[Chambers] ever, to your knowledge, since you have known
him, been in a mental sanitarium?") At Nixon's insistence I
explained the basis for my question—namely, that a news-
paperman at the hearings had told a friend of mine, whose
name I gave when asked, that ever since Chambers had testified, the press had received reports that Chambers had spent a
considerable part of the last four or five years in mental institutions. I also gave the name of a former *Time* employee who
was reported to have said that Chambers had been in a mental

institution in 1946. (My lawyers and I never established in our subsequent investigation of Chambers during our preparation for the trials that he had been a mental patient. The reports to that effect may have originated from a lengthy absence from his *Time* office when he had a breakdown which he believed to be a heart attack but which, according to records produced at the trials, his doctor attributed to nervous exhaustion.)

My long testimony and last appearance before the Committee ended with Mundt bringing in, as he had at the first of these hearings, political issues with which it was possible to link my name and which were to become standard themes for partisan attacks in many later political campaigns. On August 5 he had brought out the facts that I had attended the Yalta Conference and had played some part in the creation of the United Nations. Chambers in his prepared initial statement on August 3 had identified me only by my connection with these two symbols of wartime unity, Yalta and the UN, both of which became the targets of violent, inaccurate vituperation. On that day Mundt had also sought to link me with another partisan political target, our country's policy toward China during the period of Chiang's collapse and the accession to power of the Communists. Now, at the close of my testimony, my counsel, in view of Mundt's tendentious summation, sought to indicate Mundt's initial bias by reading his statement of August 3 that "there is reason to believe that [I] organized within the Department [of State] one of the Communist cells, which endeavored to influence our Chinese policy, and bring about the condemnation of Chiang Kai-shek. . . ."

Mundt thereupon said:

I am glad you read that, Mr. Counsel, because I was just going to make that statement now, and I won't have to do it. . . .

As far as I am concerned, Mr. Hiss, our policy toward China, the political agreement at Yalta, which you said you helped to write, and the Morgenthau plan,[9] you mentioned three of them, are hopelessly bad, and I shall continue to consider them hope-

[9] So far as I can ascertain from the records, this is the only reference in the hearings in which I took part to the Morgenthau plan. Mundt may have

lessly bad even though you prove yourself to be president of the American Daughters of the Revolution.

The fact that you were connected with them may or may not, when these hearings have terminated, increase my skepticism about their wisdom.

Mundt's statement that I had said I "helped to write" the "political agreement at Yalta" is an exaggeration of the testimony I had given on August 5, when I said, in answer to his question about my participation in the drawing up of the UN "veto provisions" agreed to at Yalta:

My best recollection without consulting the actual records is that the text of what is now article 27 of the Charter was drafted in the Department of State in the early winter of 1944 before the Yalta Conference, as part of the negotiations preceding that Conference [1] [it] was dispatched by the President of the United States to the Prime Minister of Great Britain and to Marshal Stalin for their agreement and represented the proposal made by the United States at the Yalta Conference and was accepted by the other two after some discussion. I did participate in the Department of State in the drafting of the messages I have referred to that President Roosevelt sent in, I think, December 1944 prior to the Yalta Conference.

Mundt had also asked if I had favored the veto provision and I had replied:

I did. That was practically the unanimous position of the American Government, I might add.

Mundt's final remark to me at the hearing of August 25 was an allusion to still another of the false, partisan slogans of the time. He implied, erroneously, that the State Department had admitted having had 134 Communists in its employ. Basing his last remarks on this unfounded assumption, he

---

meant the UN or may have said UN and been misunderstood by the reporter. In my letter I had referred to my UN work and to my presence at Yalta. His further instraint that *I* had mentioned "three of them" is not clear. It was he who had brought in China, the third topic.

[1] At this point in the original there is an unhelpful comma.

spoke the Committee's final word to me—one more innuendo.
I had said in my letter that it was inconceivable that there
could have been in my conduct any departure from the
highest rectitude while I was with the government without its
being known to some of my associates, whose names I had
proceeded to list. Mundt, after referring to my letter and to
the mythical 134 Communists in the State Department, implied
that I had been a Communist, by saying: "So it is not at all
inconceivable that the number could just as well have been
135 as 134."

My day-long testimony had ended. The hearing, my fourth
and last, had begun with Chairman J. Parnell Thomas's opening assurance that it would be "fair and impartial." My appearance had ended with Mundt's expression of the view
that I could "just as well" be a Communist, an unmistakable
expression of support for Chambers's charges. The Committee's conduct in the interval between these two statements
seemed to me to have been anything but fair or impartial.

Though this was my last appearance, the Committee's
preoccupation with my affairs did not lessen in the succeeding
months. On the contrary, the Committee increased its efforts
to create an impression with the public that I had been inconsistent and contradictory while Chambers had been uniformly consistent and accurate. My testimony continued to
be adversely characterized, and selected passages were taken
out of context. I did not find that the Committee's attitude
toward me became either fairer or more impartial.

CHAPTER SIX

INDICTMENT BY COMMITTEE

ON THE very day after the hearing of August 25, while the papers were still full of that well-publicized event, the Committee continued its efforts to make me the leading figure in its activities. That was the day when William Rosen, a sixty-four-year-old Washington tailor, refused to answer questions about the Ford.

The record of Rosen's testimony contains one more casual indication of how wedded the Committee was to its preconceived mission of exposing "espionage." Nixon said the transfer of the Ford car in 1936 was material to the inquiry by the Committee into Communist activities in the government "and into espionage activities during that period." (And a few days later, on August 30, McDowell opened a public session by announcing, as Chairman, that the purpose of the session was "to further the investigation into espionage in the United States Government.")

Chambers's book reveals that before this he felt that Nixon was applying strong pressure on him to support the Committee's preconception of espionage. To do so Chambers would have to make false charges of espionage against me, as I had obviously become the Committee's main target. Up to this time Chambers had most definitely not made any such charge, and he was not to do so until it appeared likely that he was in danger of losing the $75,000 libel suit I brought against him.

Chambers describes the Nixon pressure in telling of his reluctance to go through with the August 25 hearing. Before the August 25 hearing, Chambers writes, he felt he "could not go through another public hearing. Another public hearing, especially another confrontation with Hiss in front of hundreds of strange people, was more than I could endure. . . . Another great circus under eager, avid eyes, under batteries of news cameras and the hard stares of a prevailingly hostile press was too much." But when he protested against the ordeal, he was told by Nixon, whom he purports to quote:

"It is for your own sake that the Committee is holding a public hearing. The Department of Justice is all set to move in on you in order to save Hiss.[1] They are planning to indict you at once. The only way to head them off is to let the public judge for itself which one of you is telling the truth. . . ."

Chambers's statement, never disavowed by the Committee, is further indication that he was the Committee's witness and that the public was evidently to be assisted by the Committee in judging "for itself" as between my credibility and Chambers's. Without the benefit of Chambers's privy relationship to the Committee, James Reston of *The New York Times* in an article that was dated August 25 noted that there had been comments upon the "marked difference between the attitude of leading members of the committee toward Mr. Chambers when he finally took the stand tonight than toward Mr. Hiss."

I am also interested in this story for what it reveals as to Chambers's motivation in charging me with espionage, as he was to do about two months later. The hope of leniency sup-

[1] Whatever the intention of the Department of Justice with respect to Chambers may have been at this time, there is, of course, nothing to support the motivation Chambers recites. Chambers himself apparently felt it necessary to weaken the imputation. He adds in a footnote: "Regardless of whether or not Richard Nixon was mistaken—and there are many who would claim that he was—I believed him, and his words weighed heavily upon me."

plies a potent motive for an accused person to implicate falsely
another who, he believes, is considered by the prosecuting authorities to be a more desirable target. Such a motive for
bearing false witness against a neighbor or acquaintance is so
notorious that it has led to the almost universal rule in our
courts and in England that the accusatory testimony of one
who claims to be an accomplice in wrongdoing is suspect and
must be scrutinized with special care. Chambers asserts that
after Nixon warned him that the Department of Justice was
planning to indict him "at once," the Congressman added:

> "If there is anything else that you have not told us about Hiss,
> now is the time to tell us. Think hard about it. If there is anything
> else, for your own sake, tell us now."

Chambers comments that he liked and trusted Nixon. He
then adds revealingly how much he felt at the command of
the Committee:

> I left Nixon, feeling . . . like a very small creature, skirting
> the shadows of encircling powers that would not hesitate to crush
> me as impersonally as a steam roller crushes a bug.

The implication was plain that to save himself Chambers
should attack me still further. Equally evident was the Committee's choice of me as their target. Whatever had led Chambers to accuse me of Communist membership in the first place,
here as incitement for his later charges of espionage were the
classic elements of motivation for false witness. The danger
to himself was, however, not yet quite strong enough to cause
him to assume this further extension of the role which the
Committee so evidently pressed upon him.

As the weeks passed after August 25 the Committee's desire for more sensational "disclosures" did not abate. It seems
likely that its pressures on Chambers, who looked to it as
sponsor and protector, to add to his charges against me also
did not abate. The Democratic victories in the Presidential and
Congressional campaigns gave the Committee no cause for
elation over the public reception of its efforts. Stripling de-

scribes in one brief paragraph the Committee's mood by early November:

> In the meanwhile, the Committee was dealt a series of blows. Chairman J. Parnell Thomas was indicted on a "kickback" charge after a hearing that came to a boil in record time—compared to the leisurely indifference the Justice Department has shown in prosecuting many of those subversives whose names and records we have delivered. Reps. McDowell and Vail were defeated in the November elections. Rep. Mundt ran for and was elected to the Senate. The sweeping Democratic victory presaged an end to the Committee as I knew it.

My own thoughts after the August 25 hearing were concerned almost wholly with getting Chambers's charges before the courts. I wanted the partisan, circuslike setting of the Committee to be replaced promptly by the calm and thorough procedure which—on the basis of my experience as a lawyer— I identified with courts of law. At that time I had actually never seen a jury. The trials in which I had participated as a lawyer were civil cases involving corporate issues and had been decided by a master or a referee, a man trained in the law. The pace in these cases had been unhurried, the procedure thorough and impartial; no part of the dignified proceeding was calculated with an eye to press reactions. I hoped that my challenges would force Chambers to repeat his charges away from the protection of the Committee so that I could sue him.

I did not then know that several days before August 24, when I released to the press my letter to the Committee, Chambers had accepted an invitation from Lawrence E. Spivak (whom Chambers says he considered "friendly") to appear August 27 on *Meet the Press*, a radio program of which Spivak was the director. Chambers writes that after the August 25 hearing he had a change of heart about his acceptance:

> Alger Hiss's challenge to me to repeat my charge of Communism where he could sue me for libel made me hesitate. He had first challenged me at the Hotel Commodore confrontation [August 17]. His challenge had been repeated in the press on August 24th and was repeated at the August 25th hearing. Clearly, one of

the first questions that I would be asked on the air was whether or not I was prepared to repeat my charge. Hiss would then be free to sue me. I did not want to be sued. . . .

Chambers says that on the 24th or the 25th he notified Spivak that he "would not appear after all on his radio program." However, Chambers relates, Spivak's promptly expressed embarrassment at the cancelation led to reconsideration and his decision to appear on the program after all. The opening question forced Chambers to repeat his charge that I "was a Communist," to which he added, though he had admittedly not even seen me for years: "and may be now." This was a plain instance of the contrast between Chambers's readiness to make or imply charges and his evident lack of knowledge on which to base them, but it caused him no embarrassment when it was challenged a few minutes later by a member of the panel who commented that he thought Chambers had in that statement "left it a little unclear as to whether you are certain in your mind if Alger Hiss is now a member of the Communist Party or not." Chambers, checked, replied with no admission of any change in his emphasis:

I would not presume to say whether Mr. Hiss now is or is not a member of the Party.

One series of questions that evening is relevant to the fortunes of the Committee at the end of August and to the mounting pressure on Chambers to add to his charges:

[EDWARD] FOLLIARD [*Washington Post*]: Mr. Chambers, to go back to that opening question, you accepted Alger Hiss' challenge and publicly said that he had been at least a member of the Communist Party. Does that mean that you are now prepared to go into Court and answer to a suit for slander or libel?

CHAMBERS: I do not think Mr. Hiss will sue me for slander or libel.

[TOM] REYNOLDS [Chicago *Sun-Times*]: Would you charge Alger Hiss with an overt act as a Communist, as you said he was? Did Alger Hiss at any time, to your knowledge, do anything that was treasonable or beyond the law of the United States? That, I believe, brings you the opportunity to accept the Hiss challenge.

CHAMBERS: Whether or not it brings me the opportunity to accept the Hiss challenge, I am quite unprepared to say whether he did or did not. I am not familiar with the laws of treason.

. . . .

REYNOLDS: Are you prepared at this time to say that Alger Hiss was anything more than, in your opinion, a Communist? Did he do anything wrong? Did he commit any overt act? Has he been disloyal to his country?

CHAMBERS: I am only prepared at this time to say he was a Communist.

REYNOLDS: It seems to me, then, sir, if I may say so, that in some respects this may be a tempest in a teapot. You say that he was a Communist, but you will not accuse him of any act that is disloyal to the United States.

CHAMBERS: I am not prepared legally to make that charge. My whole interest in this business has been to show that Mr. Hiss was a Communist.

REYNOLDS: Would you be prepared, for instance, to put on the record the testimony that you gave during the three or four or five interrogations by the FBI?

CHAMBERS: The gist of that testimony is already on the record in the Un-American Committee.

REYNOLDS: I am not interested in the gist. But I presume that there were assertions that overt acts were committed. Are you willing to put on the record, so that it can be tested in Courts under the laws of evidence, that this man did something wrong?

CHAMBERS: I think that what needs clarification is the purpose for which that group was set up to which Mr. Hiss belonged. That was a group, not, as I think is in the back of your mind, for the purpose of espionage, but for the purpose of infiltrating the government and influencing government policy by getting Communists in key places.

[NAT] FINNEY [Cowles Publications]: It was not, then, by definition, conspiracy?

CHAMBERS: No, it was not.[2]

A little later, Chambers asserted that influencing policy is "very much more important than spying."

[2] Text of the *Meet the Press* broadcast as reproduced in the February 1949 issue of *The American Mercury*.

At this point he was asked by a member of the panel if he had any idea whether in any of the jobs I had held, I had had any real influence on our policy. For example, did Chambers "know specifically or exactly" what I did at Yalta? When his answer was negative, he was asked if American policy had not changed to a firm policy against the Soviet Union at just the time when I was in charge of the United Nations section of the State Department. He replied that he did not know.

The skeptical reaction implied by the phrase "tempest in a teapot" came only two days after the widely publicized hearings which had themselves been the culmination of three weeks of secret hearings combined with sensational items in the press. The results were not commensurate with the Committee's efforts. One of the reporters asked Chambers early in the session whether he was surprised that his charges, which he had made to the FBI "some time" before, "are now sensationalized." He also asked whether Chambers had become a Democrat or Republican and, upon being told: "I am not affiliated officially with any party," bluntly stated the political realities of the moment:

Are you aware of the possibility that the material you gave the FBI some time ago is now going to be quite useful, presumably, to the Republicans?

What had been a temporary sensation in the August of a Presidential campaign was likely, on calmer examination, to be found to be an overpublicized stunt. Stale charges are suspect at best. They are not enhanced when they come from a man with an obvious flair for the dramatic and a demonstrable talent for invention and when they boil down to such a person's having called another a dirty name but not more. Certainly Chambers must have realized that such charges would, on investigation, be found to be without support. In particular he must have known that his assertion that I had been meant to influence policy (presumably in a pro-Communist direction) could not be confirmed.

Within a few days (August 30) Adolf A. Berle, Jr., former

Assistant Secretary of State, to whom Chambers had been taken by Isaac Don Levine in September 1939, was to tell the Committee that Chambers had on that occasion told him quite a different story—that it had been Communist Party policy in 1934–7 to "try to develop a group of sympathizers who might be of use to them later in the United States Government. . . . With that in mind apparently a study group of some sort had been formed of men who were interested in knowing something about Russia and Russian policy and the general Communist theory of life, and so on." Mr. Berle said that Chambers had told him that I was a member of such a group and had not said to him that I was a member of the Communist Party. Mr. Berle's recollection was that Chambers had said that the group, "it was hoped, would go, as they called it, 'underground'; that is to say, that they would not appear as part of the well-known or open Communist group, but that they would simply be there and be sympathetic." Had Chambers alleged before the Committee that from 1935 to 1937 it was the Communist *hope* to enlist the sympathy of various named people and that I had participated in some kind of "study group," it is not likely that he could have created a stir even in the election climate of August 1948. It did seem, if looked at from the Committee's point of view, as though the "startling" revelations would, indeed, after further inquiry and on reflection appear to most people as irresponsible and insubstantial.

But Chambers's charges mattered to me. When he said over the air that I had been a Communist, I asked my counsel to see if that would support a libel action and, if so, to decide where Chambers should be sued. Their investigation of the law led them to conclude that an action for libel could be brought and that Chambers should be sued in Maryland, where he resided. I chose as my Baltimore attorney for the suit my long-time friend William L. Marbury, who was then in Europe on government business but was due to return soon. On September 27, just a month after the radio talk and soon after Mr. Marbury's return from Europe, suit was filed for $50,000.

When he was served with legal process, Chambers spoke of the "ferocity" and "ingenuity" of the "forces" that were "working through" me. This led my lawyers to file a supplemental complaint increasing the total damages claimed to $75,000.

We lost no time in pushing ahead with the suit. On November 4 my counsel began interrogating Chambers in the first of a series of pre-trial examinations. I now know that my bringing suit added heavily to the pressures on Chambers to pile charge upon charge by accusing me of espionage. In an effort to escape the consequences of his initial charges about me, he responded to the libel suit by adding this new and more vicious charge. The step was dangerous for him: to make his accusation against me, he had to assert that he had himself been engaged in spying. It later turned out that in the 1930's he had in fact received State Department documents from Henry Julian Wadleigh, an employee of the Department. At the same time or later Chambers must have received additional papers from persons whose identity he has never made public. The documents he had received from others were used by him as the basis for his charges against me. In the Committee he had a powerful ally in his venture. They could, and did, create a climate of public opinion not inclined to examine his charges critically; they could, and did, save him from prosecution. With such an ally he could hope for success in his efforts to defeat my suit for libel.

As Chambers recites in his book, in the course of his interrogation in Baltimore by my lawyers he foresaw defeat:

I saw that I might well lose the libel suit, though it was not in my nature to lose it without a fight.

He also has written that "the sum of $75,000 [was] fantastic as compared with any ability [he] had to pay it."

It became clear on the second day of Chambers's examination that he had no evidence that I had been a Communist. As a Committee witness he had not been subjected to skeptical questioning. His only assertion of activity by me that bespoke Communism was the standardized bit about paying dues.

When faced with critical examination by my lawyers his story had a hollow ring. Supported by his wife, he attempted to expand the close-association pose which, temporarily at least, had been so successful before the Committee. With scant regard for consistency with his Committee testimony, Mr. and Mrs. Chambers invented frequent visits between their family and mine and "remembered" details of houses they had never been in. Despite sharp internal contradictions in the Chamberses' statements and inconsistencies between them, the very volume of their stories and the interweaving of fantasy with facts that one or the other of the Chamberses had learned (when we were in fact in their company or after we had ceased to know them) seem to have weighed with some members of the juries in the trials. These stories will, therefore, be described in the account of the trials.

Here it is sufficient to say that it is evident from Chambers's book that they did not impress his own attorneys to the same extent. Chambers had on November 4, the first day of his examination, been asked by my counsel to produce the following day letters or papers, if he had any, from me or members of my family. On the 5th, Mr. Marbury said at the opening of the session:

Yesterday, at the close of the hearing, I asked you if you would produce any papers or notes or correspondence from any member of the Hiss family this morning. Have you got any such papers with you, Mr. Chambers?

Chambers replied: "No, I do not," and his counsel added: ". . . Mr. Chambers has advised us that he has not explored all of the sources where some conceivable data might be." Chambers says in his book that when, after his examination had proceeded for a while, the subject of letters and papers again came up, his lawyer "this time . . . warned me that if I did have anything of Hiss's I had better get it."

Chambers has made various statements about the documents, some of which he was to produce on November 17, two weeks after the Baltimore examinations had begun, and others of which he withheld from his own counsel to turn over to the Committee on December 2, a month after the beginning of those examinations. These documents are of three categories: four small slips of paper with penciled notes of a kind I made regularly in my office routine; sixty-five typewritten pages which I have consistently denounced as ingenious forgeries; and two strips (totaling fifty-eight frames) of developed microfilm containing photographs of eight State Department documents. The handwritten and typed papers Chambers presented in Baltimore on November 17. When on the next day my attorneys showed me photostats of the typewritten pages, I immediately directed that the papers be turned over to the Department of Justice, as it was evident that they were copies and summaries of State Department documents which warranted inquiry as to how they came into Chambers's possession. The microfilm was presented by Chambers at his farm to representatives of the Committee on the evening of December 2 after he had, in their presence, removed it from a hollowed-out pumpkin in which he says he had that morning hidden it.

Chambers on December 2 also delivered to the Committee investigators three rolls of undeveloped microfilm. These proved to be, in part, light-struck. Some frames appear to contain pictures of documents of the Bureau of Standards. It has been Chambers's contention that the documents so photographed came to him via an employee of the Bureau of Standards. The legible portions have not apparently been of any significance. The only comment of the Committee is this declaration in its report of December 31, 1948:

> The committee wishes to emphasize that this film received expert technical attention from the time it was received by the committee from Mr. Chambers to the present time, and that none was destroyed or light-struck after it was surrendered to the committee.

One more item was produced by Chambers. This was an informal handwritten memorandum on long yellow paper which is said to be in the handwriting of Harry Dexter White. Chambers says that he gave it to his attorneys with the typed pages and my handwritten notes. It has been reprinted in the *Congressional Record*[3] and in Lord Jowitt's book,[4] where it may be read by those interested to see whether in their own judgment it reads like an espionage document, as Chambers asserts, or a personal memorandum of office jottings—"some sort of diary" or letters intended for a Treasury colleague absent from Washington, as Lord Jowitt suggests they appear to be.

Chambers has said that he "put by" these papers when he broke with Communism. He has given various explanations of why they were "put by." His most recent one is that contained in his book. There he says that he regarded them as "a life preserver" which, "should the party move against [his] life, [he] might have an outside chance of using as a dissuader." On this basis, one would think that these documents on which he says he believed his life depended would bulk large in his consciousness. Instead, he writes, he remembered only the four slips bearing office notes of mine. He had remembered, he says, only a "small" envelope and was surprised to receive a bulky one from his wife's nephew, Nathan Levine, who had kept it for him. On opening it, his first reaction was "a reflex of amazement." He felt that "an act of God" had happened to him. When asked by Levine if he had found what he was looking for, he says of his reply:

My answer was more to myself than to him. "Good God," I said, "I did not know that this still existed."

And he says that when he telephoned to his wife to be sure to be on time in meeting his train, he told her:

"I have found something."

We were to find only after the trials evidence that the papers he produced had not all been stored, as his story runs, in

[3] January 30, 1950.
[4] The Earl Jowitt: *The Strange Case Of Alger Hiss* (Doubleday, 1953).

one place, much less in one envelope. That and the further
evidence (also obtained too late for the trials) that the typed
pages were forgeries are discussed in Chapter XI. But it is appropriate to emphasize here that the nephew says he never saw
the contents of the envelope when Chambers gave it to him
for safekeeping or what came out of it in November 1948 when
Chambers reclaimed it. The story of the "life preserver" stands
on Chambers's unsupported word.

Chambers writes that he simply forgot what he had hidden:

> . . . This much is certain: if during the last six or seven years
> of that decade [from 1938, when he claims to have given the en-
> velope to his nephew, until 1948, when he reclaimed it], anyone
> had asked me, "What is your wife's nephew hiding for you?" I
> should have answered, "Two or three scraps of Alger Hiss's hand-
> writing and perhaps something of Harry White's." The heap of
> copied State Department documents, the spools of microfilm, had
> sunk from my memory as completely as the Russian regiments in
> World War I sank into the Masurian swamps.

According to Chambers's account, he had not gone to
look for my handwritten notes until mid-November because
he "did not believe that they were of much importance."
Later he says of his talks with his lawyers: "What I might
have had seemed to me of so little importance that we had
scarcely touched on it."

Isaac Don Levine, who had tried to help Chambers find
a market for a manuscript that Chambers had prepared as
early as May 1939, gives a different version. According to
Levine, it would appear that Chambers "forgot" only the
typewritten documents, the most effective "evidence" he was
to produce in support of his charges against me. Did Chambers
fail to mention to Levine a bulky file of typed material, while
emphasizing microfilm (a few rolls, mostly undeveloped), because he had "forgotten" the typed pages, because he then
feared to put these false documents to the test, or perhaps
because they had not then been created?

In his attempts to employ the typed material against me,

Chambers asserted that I gave him typed copies of official documents every week or ten days. His failure to mention to Levine a regular practice of receiving typed material further suggests that this was an invention concocted in the fall of 1948.

Levine testified on December 8, *after* Chambers had produced penciled notes, typed pages, and microfilm:

MR. STRIPLING: Now, Mr. Levine, I am interested in one particular thing. In your conferences and conversations with Whittaker Chambers, did he ever at any time tell you that he had any documentary evidence to substantiate his allegations?

MR. LEVINE: Yes, sir.

MR. STRIPLING: When did he tell you that?

MR. LEVINE: In the course of the summer of 1939, when we discussed the marketability of his articles, I asked him if he had any evidence, and he told me that there was such evidence. He mentioned microfilm and he also mentioned in a general way documentary evidence, without going into detail.

MR. STRIPLING: Well; did he say that that evidence was available?

MR. LEVINE: Yes, sir.

MR. MCDOWELL: Did he show them to you?

MR. LEVINE: No, no.

MR. STRIPLING: Did you ask him for the evidence?

MR. LEVINE: I understood when I was going to Washington in an effort to bring him to President Roosevelt, that that is exactly what would transpire, that Mr. Chambers would leave certain evidence which he wouldn't show to me before the President of the United States, and something or another would happen, and the whole matter would be clinched right there and then.

MR. STRIPLING: But when you took him to see Mr. Berle, did he have with him any documentary evidence?

MR. LEVINE: No, sir; he did not.

Later that same day Levine added:

. . . I believe that some time in 1940 I asked Mr. Chambers about them, and he intimated to me, in such a way that I could not quite put my finger on it, that he had perhaps destroyed them. . . .

Levine seems to have been, unintentionally, one of the
factors influencing Chambers to make ever wider and more
dramatic charges. Levine had collaborated in the writing of
articles on Soviet espionage. He knew from experience that this
was a marketable topic. At an earlier session (August 18) he
described how Chambers first came to see him in 1939:

In consequence of the exposures by Gen. Walter Krivitsky,
formerly chief of the Soviet military espionage in western Europe,
exposures which were published in the Saturday Evening Post with
my collaboration, various ex-Communists contacted me.

The editor of a monthly magazine told me of Mr. Whittaker
Chambers who had a manuscript of his experiences and his exposures. I agreed to see him and indicated an interest in his story. . . .

He told me he had a wife and two children, that he slept
with a rifle at his side, behind drawn curtains, to protect them; that
he had broken with the Communist underground a year or two before, and that he had a manuscript which he thought I might be
able to place with a big and reputable magazine like the Saturday
Evening Post, for he was in very bad need of money.

It turned out that the manuscript was well written but contained a lot of round-about information, and description, dates,
and names were carefully avoided. . . .

I kept in touch with Mr. Chambers subsequently, as he had
been impressed by the Krivitsky revelations. I thought perhaps I
could do something with his manuscript, but there seemed little
chance of enticing him at that time to tell his full story in print.

Levine soon introduced Chambers to Krivitsky, and the
two men exchanged information. I shall return later to some
of the information supplied by Krivitsky to Chambers—information which Chambers repeated in the trials as based on his
own experiences, perhaps an early instance of his being unable
to distinguish what he had heard from what he once knew.
But the Krivitsky meetings apparently did not advance the
"marketability" of Chambers's manuscript, for no article was
published. Levine on December 8 explained why:

. . . Mr. Chambers found that his articles could not be published because he was not prepared at that time to incorporate in

them the material which I thought was essential to their market-ability. . . .

Levine said that it was the impact of the Hitler-Stalin pact later in 1939 which let him overcome Chambers's previous reluctance to talk to any official. The meeting with Mr. Berle in September 1939 was thereupon arranged.

Levine also mentioned Chambers's espionage *before* Chambers produced the documents. On August 18, when the Committee was so hopefully hunting spies despite Chambers's disclaimers of knowledge of espionage, Levine's secret testimony fitted the Committee's preconception. His account (on this occasion) of the Krivitsky-Chambers talks was full of talk of espionage. "Krivitsky," he said, "knew considerable about the Soviet espionage operations in the United States." Chambers, he said, recognized some of Krivitsky's "intimate collaborators." Levine himself "got a tremendous education into the Soviet espionage workings everywhere as well as in the United States" from hearing them talk.

At one point he even implied, without expressly saying so, that Chambers had told Mr. Berle of espionage activities in the State Department, and he said expressly that Chambers had had in "the State Department and various other departments in Washington . . . underground contacts who supplied him with documentary and confidential information for transmission to the Soviet Government."

The morning papers of August 31 carried an account by Mr. Berle of his secret testimony of the day before [5] that Chambers, in talking to him in 1939, had not claimed that I was a Communist. Mr. Berle, whose testimony was not released by the Committee for another six weeks, had testified:

This was not, as he put it, any question of espionage. There was no espionage involved in it. He stated that their hope merely was to get some people who would be sympathetic to their point of view. With that in mind apparently a study group of some sort had been formed. . . .

[5] See pp. 156–7.

In one respect, what he told me omitted something that he has told you: He did not make the direct statement that any of these men were members of the Communist Party. . . .

That very day (August 31) Levine called his own press conference and gave a directly contrary version of the Chambers-Berle meeting. This time his statements were considerably more colorful than those he had made when under oath on August 18. He asserted, according to *The New York Times*, that Chambers in 1939 had told Berle of twenty or twenty-one government officials whom he accused of espionage for Soviet Russia. Levine went on to assert to the press that Chambers had asserted in the meeting with Berle that I had belonged to "underground groups which knowingly supplied information to Soviet Russia." There is nothing to support this contradiction of Mr. Berle's sworn testimony. Mr. Berle's position as Assistant Secretary of State would have made him alert to any such grave charge. His contemporaneous notes of his talk with Chambers make no reference to the subject.[6] Chambers admitted when he produced the documents in November 1948 that he had never before made any such accusation to any one.

Quite apart from the question of the inaccuracy of Levine's press statement of August 31 as to what Chambers said about me to Berle in September 1939, that statement demonstrates once again that Chambers had never told Levine any story of Chambers's having received copies of State Department documents that had been typed for him. Levine made no reference to typing copies of State Department papers as part of the procedures employed. The *Times* account of Levine's press conference reports Levine as saying that Chambers had told Berle "how confidential papers were taken from State Depart-

[6] Chambers's testimony of October 14 and 15 to the grand jury (see pp. 170–1), *after* Levine's press conference, also demonstrates that Chambers said nothing of the kind to Berle, for he felt free on October 14 and 15 to ignore Levine's statement. The grand jury had just been reconvened as a direct result of Chambers's charges against me before the Committee. When asked if he had knowledge of any acts of espionage, he made a flat denial, as he would hardly have felt safe in doing had he accused me of espionage in his talk with Berle, by then a much publicized conversation.

ment files, microfilmed and returned, copies being then delivered by Mr. Chambers to New York for shipment to Russia. . . ."

The primary effect of Levine's statement was to assist the Committee by refurbishing and expanding Chambers's story, which had lost luster through Mr. Berle's disclosure that it had grown greatly from its original relatively innocuous form in 1939. But by its reference to Chambers's espionage, Levine's statement, like the Committee's desire for greater sensations and like the warning from Chambers's attorney, also increased the forces at work on Chambers to assume the role urged upon him by the Committee and charge me with espionage.

It is here relevant to bring out a fact we did not learn until later which indicates that Chambers may long since have considered using material in his possession (or to which he might have access) to give seeming support to charges he might make. On December 13, 1940, Chambers had told another writer, Malcolm Cowley, that Francis B. Sayre, who had recently resigned as Assistant Secretary of State to accept the post of High Commissioner to the Philippines, had been "the head of a Communist apparatus in the State Department." To this false charge, Cowley had expressed his complete incredulity. Chambers had in addition mentioned others in government, but had not mentioned me. With a writer's appreciation for the spectacular incident, Cowley promptly wrote and preserved an account of Chambers's strange demeanor and charges.

Was this a rehearsal by Chambers of a possible use of his hoarded material? Mr. Sayre had been my immediate superior during the months in which the originals of the Chambers papers are dated. The microfilmed State Department documents (three of which bore my initials) all had some actual or apparent connection with Mr. Sayre's office, where I was quartered during those months. It was this combination of facts which permitted Chambers, with some plausibility at first glance, to offer the microfilm strips in support of his charges against me. With no greater stretch of logic they could have been offered in support of his 1940 charge against Mr. Sayre. And copies of most of the original documents summarized or copied in the typewritten pages had been routed (among other places) to Mr. Sayre's office, a point made much of by the prosecution in my trials. Moreover, Mrs. Chambers had once worked for an organization in which Mr. Sayre's brother was prominent. Perhaps the Chamberses could give a seemingly knowing account of some of Mr. Sayre's personal affairs.[7] Did Cowley's discouraging reception lead to the abandonment of this possible use of whatever material Chambers had hidden, so that it remained available for use in answer to Chambers's needs in mid-November 1948?

Chambers has written that when I sued him *"Time,* with its usual generosity, came to [his] aid." He says that his legal costs were largely borne by *Time,* which "had a direct concern in [his] vindication" because I had "impugned [Chambers's] veracity, not merely as an individual man, but as an editor of *Time."* Chambers says also that when he resigned in December it was simply because "Worried stockholders and furious subscribers were deluging the [*Time*] company with angry pleas to get rid of [him]." He says that no other course was possible. "Time, Inc. is a business, and, like any other business, it exists for the purpose of making and marketing a product." But he adds:

Time, Inc. made upon me a settlement so generous that, with what I had accumulated over the years in its trust funds, I did not have to worry about money again during the Case.[8]

[7] Chambers's penchant for collecting dossiers of personal information about people he did not even know or knew but slightly was illustrated by another incident. Wadleigh, an admitted source of State Department documents for Chambers, testified that he had had a conversation with Chambers about Charles Darlington, a superior of Wadleigh's and his office mate: ". . . he started telling me a lot of details about Charles Darlington, his background and career and all the rest, and I said 'How come you know so much about Charlie Darlington?' And he said, 'Well, we naturally like to know about a person who is your roommate so we have made inquiries from our friends in the State Department and that is how I got the information.'"

[8] Chambers in his book almost always capitalizes the initial letter in "case" when referring to the hearings devoted to his charges or to my trials. On

Later he states that *Time* had insured his life for $20,000. *Time*'s aid to Chambers's cause was more than financial. Whatever the basis of its "direct concern" in supporting Chambers, its coverage of the case was, I think, clearly partisan.

A passage in Chambers's book indicates that it was the fear of losing the libel suit (in which he felt that he represented *Time* as well as himself) that precipitated his decision to yield to the Committee's importunings and to paint me as a fellow purloiner of documents. The charge of an underground group formed to influence policy was bound to be discredited soon by thoughtful people. Chambers says that as he spent "day after day" with his attorneys, he found that they were dissatisfied; as he puts it, "they were probing for something that they could not put their finger upon, but which they sensed should be there, and which was not there."

It is not surprising that Chambers's testimony in August, which had momentarily pleased the Committee, should not seem satisfactory to his attorneys as a basis for defense in court. Chambers had actually obtained documents from State Department employees. Were he to implicate me in that activity, he could be more convincing. Instead of talking of people who were of "service" to the Communist Party because they "were going places in the Government" and for whom "power and influence were the paramount objectives," he could talk with actual knowledge of microfilming activities and even point to an actual photographer.[9] At least there would be the diversion of a new sensation. And he could at the same time gratify his sponsors, the Committee, whose fortunes were low and getting steadily lower. Chambers writes that one day when he had once more gone over parts of his story with his attorney, the latter "paused and gazed off toward Druid Hill Park." Chambers says he then spoke up and asked his inattentive lawyer:

You feel, don't you, that there is something missing?

the second page he establishes an even larger frame of reference at the outset of his story by twice calling it the "Great Case."

[9] See pp. 327-8.

His attorney agreed, and Chambers writes that he then said that the missing element was "Espionage" and that he had been "shielding" me. Initially Chambers seems to have hoped that a mere assertion of espionage without attempted support would suffice to enable his lawyers to meet my suit. For apparently even *after* his assertion of espionage to his lawyers he still did not believe that the only papers of mine he said he remembered—my handwritten notes—"were of much importance." "What I might have had," he put it again, "seemed to me of so little importance that we had scarcely touched on it." But once again he was faced with the need to add lie to lie. He had to come up with something that seemed to back up his new charge. And, as the progress of the case was to show, it had to be something other than the slips of handwritten notes that were quite truly "of so little importance." The stage was set for the use of the material which I denounced as forgery by typewriter.

Whatever the total number of pressures, their combined weight seems to have been just sufficient to overcome Chambers's fear of the consequences of adding the charge of espionage. As late as October 14 and 15, Chambers was not ready to take this course. The grand jury had been reconvened, in response to Committee demands, and was obviously primarily intent, as had been the journalists on *Meet the Press*, on probing fully Chambers's charges against me. He was asked on the 14th:

JUROR: Could you give one name of anybody who, in your opinion, was positively guilty of espionage against the United States? Yes or no.

[MR. CHAMBERS:] Let me think a moment and I will try to answer that. I don't think so but I would like to have the opportunity to answer you tomorrow more definitely. Let me think it over overnight.

When he returned the next day he gave his answer:

A: . . . I assume that espionage means in this case the turning over of secret or confidential documents.

Q: Or information—oral information.
A: Or oral information. I do not believe I do know such a
name.

His caution was not easily overcome in the course of the
succeeding month. He says that even when, a month later, he
had finally turned over the typed pages to his lawyers, he had
not decided to let them be used and he seriously contemplated
killing himself instead. This was his attitude even after the
typed papers had passed the first test of scrutiny by his own
counsel. Chambers writes that he obtained the "forgotten" papers on a Sunday, presumably November 13, and showed them
to his lawyers the next day:

> Cleveland [one of Chambers's attorneys] had at once said em-
> phatically that he hoped that it was my intention to introduce the
> documents into the pre-trial examination. . . . This had happened
> on a Monday. On Tuesday I still had not reached a decision and
> said that I must have a day in which to think things through. . . .
>
>   .   .   .   .
>
> . . . Should I destroy the microfilm [which he had not given
> to his attorneys but saved for the Committee, whose support he
> was careful to retain] and destroy myself? . . .
>
>   .   .   .   .
>
> My family would be better off without me, not simply because
> my act would liberate them from their only connection with the
> Case, which would, in fact, cease to exist. Living, I could be noth-
> ing to them but a dishonored man. . . .
>
> My gun was upstairs. It had the merciful merit of being in-
> stantaneous. But I shrank from the physical aspects of using it, es-
> pecially the horror that it must leave for my wife. There is a gas-
> producing substance of which a cyanide compound is one com-
> ponent. It is in common use on farms. . . . I decided that, if I
> chose death, I would use that gas whose action I then supposed to
> be much quicker than is the case.

He was right to fear the risk of proof that the typed documents were forgeries. Were that to occur, he would lose all
that his action in producing these papers was designed to
achieve. Within the month, when the outcome of his venture

was in doubt, Chambers was, he says, actually to try suicide. This was after an expert for the Eastman Kodak Company had reported to the Committee early in December that some of the film produced by Chambers had not been manufactured until 1945 or 1946. (Chambers gives the former date and Stripling the latter.) Chambers reports that on this occasion Nixon's voice was "harsh." Stripling reports that even he "felt like taking a dry dive out the nearest window," and that he got "downright mad at Whittaker Chambers." He says he was too mad to trust himself on the phone in calling Chambers for an explanation of the Eastman report. Stripling records Chambers's reply to Nixon, who did the calling, as:

"I have nothing to say except that Fate is against us."

Chambers's version is that he thought: "God is against me."

The incident reveals once again the Committee's preconceptions for which it sought "proof." (Mr. McDowell as far back as August 30 had, in interrogating Mr. Berle about Chambers's charges that I had belonged to an "underground" group, used the very phrase "if we can finally prove this.") Stripling says:

Our case lay in ruins around our feet.

The Committee had, indeed, regarded this as *their* case. Stripling adds a revelation of the investment the Committee had in "proving" their case:

. . . I knew full well the tremendous (and deserved) blast we'd get, and the jubilation of anti-Committee forces. . . .

Nixon and Stripling were spared the collapse of their case at that time. The Eastman representative changed his opinion of the date of manufacture to 1937. (Some of the film was made by the du Pont Company. Their expert's opinion was that the du Pont film was made either in December 1936 or in June 1944. He said expressly that there was no way of telling in which of the two years it had been manufactured.) But in

Chambers's case the change of the Eastman Kodak opinion did not restore his nerve. He bought two cans of cyanide poison that same day, and after an evening session with the Committee he took them to his mother's house.

He says that "almost from the time that [he] had disclosed the copied State Department documents" he had felt "a drought of the soul, a sense of estrangement and of being discarded. . . . There was nothing. I was not only alone among men. I was alone in an absolute sense." He writes of the "repugnance" he felt for what he had done, an "organic revulsion," a "self-revulsion . . . whipped to torment under the mounting sense of the futility of everything that [he] had done."

Chambers does not specify which night he attempted suicide. His delivery of the microfilm to the Committee resulted in another reconvening of the grand jury in early December; he relates only that his attempt was during the inquiry by the grand jury. These were days during which he could not be sure that he would escape indictment by having me substituted in his stead. How narrow his escape was I learned long after the event.[1]

According to his account, his escape from death was equally narrow. He ascribes his failure in the attempt to his inability to read the small type in which the instructions were printed. He had thought he "understood the principles involved" but had made "a mistake in moistening the chemical." Had he been able to read the instructions, he says, he would not have made the mistake. Once he had made the attempt, "it was never possible to make it again." He could "scarcely think of it again, or see such a can of chemical, or smell similar fumes, without a shudder of organic horror."

Chambers's delay of four or five days after he obtained the "forgotten" papers before producing them at the Baltimore libel proceedings may also have been necessary to him for putting in order the story he would have to tell—*for the first time*—to "authenticate" those documents.

[1] See pp. 192, 197.

It was at this point that Chambers again turned to the Committee for help and received it in full measure. It will be remembered that when he gave the typed pages and handwritten notes to his attorneys for use in defending himself against my libel suit, Chambers withheld the microfilm. According to Stripling, another of Chambers's attorneys, Nicholas Vazzana, let the Committee know that something had occurred in the libel suit, adding: "and it concerns documents." From the Committee's point of view, Chambers's action was well timed. Stripling says that at this very time "the Committee . . . appeared to be going down the drain." In Stripling's account, Chambers's lawyer refused to tell them more:

> "Can't talk," he said, "or I might be held in contempt of court."

On December 1,[2] Stripling says, he saw a Washington columnist's reference, evidently a planned leak by Chambers, to "new and sensational" information in the libel suit. He continues:

> All I had to go on was Vazzana's hint and the item about "new and sensational" evidence in the Washington column. But I had an overpowering feeling that I must see Chambers again. . . .
>
> I found myself developing a slight frenzy to question Chambers further, and that frenzy proved contagious. Though he had precious little time before his [cruise] ship sailed from New York, Nixon hopped in the car with me and we drove—faster than the law allowed—to Chambers's Maryland farm. . . .
>
> It was Chambers who brought us to the point.
>
> "I know why you're here," he said, suddenly. He looked at me for a time and added, "You were right, Mr. Stripling. I was withholding information." He could add no more at this time, he said, because his lawyers had warned him he might be held in contempt of court.

    [2] Stripling's book contains the misprint "December 11" for "December 1" as the date of the item in the *Washington Post* to which he refers. Succeeding passages make it clear that the error is typographical: "Early the next morning, December 2 . . ." and, referring to two days after the date of the columnist's comment, "The next morning, December 3. . . ."

"You don't have to go into details," Nixon said. "Just answer this: did you drop a bombshell in Baltimore not long ago?"

Chambers smiled slightly. "Yes, I did," he reflected. "But the first one was nothing compared to the second."

"I'm here for that second one," Nixon said. Chambers shook his head, but not in an unfriendly manner. . . .

This conversation took place two weeks after I had directed that the papers Chambers had produced in Baltimore be turned over to the Department of Justice for examination and for inquiry as to how they came to be in his possession. Stripling says that before going to see Chambers he had had newspaper friends inquire at the Department of Justice whether there had been any new developments in the case. The uniform reply had been that the case was "dead" and on the same day that the columnist had written of "new and sensational" evidence Stripling quotes the press as saying "that the Department was ready to drop the whole Hiss-Chambers case." Stripling adds to his account of Chambers's informing him and Nixon of his second "bombshell":

. . . It was my subsequent belief that he [Chambers] was relieved by the Committee's continuing interest in the case, especially in view of the Justice Department's reported indifference to the papers he had turned over [the reference here is to Chambers having produced them in the Baltimore libel suit—he did *not* turn them over to the Department of Justice]. That indifference was an ominous sign, so far as Alger Hiss's slander suits against him were concerned.

As a result of the information Chambers had given, the Committee the next day issued a subpœna to Chambers, who that night (December 2) delivered the microfilm which he had hidden in what Stripling calls, and did his best to make, "the most famous pumpkin in history."

Stripling then sent a radio message to Nixon:

SECOND BOMBSHELL OBTAINED. CONTENTS AMAZING. CAN YOU GET OFF BOAT?

The Committee launched a prodigious publicity campaign which made impossible any careful, objective, official examination of the papers Chambers had produced. Such an examination would have taken many months—as my counsel and I were soon to discover. Instead, the public was bombarded with faulty conclusions supported by biased use of the documents and constant iteration of Chambers's new story. The grand jury's legal mandate had less than two weeks more to run. Forced into reconvening again by the Committee's tactics, they considered Chambers's charges under constant pressure from the Committee and with scant time for their deliberations.

The Committee took little or no time to analyze the Chambers documents or to test his new assertions. On December 3, Mundt, who had just been elected a Senator, said "a final conclusion is imminent" in the "Hiss-Chambers espionage case" and announced that the film was proof of espionage. The press reproduced cables from the microfilm bearing my initials. There were daily headlines. On December 6, Nixon, who flew back from his vacation cruise, released Chambers's statements in his Baltimore testimony (which Nixon had somehow obtained) that I had given him the documents. Nixon added that the Committee had three documents said by a handwriting expert to be in my hand. A new "prosecution" of me by the Committee had begun, this time openly and directly for espionage. Stripling, announcing new hearings, had said on the 4th:

We expect to show conclusively the source of these documents from the State Department to Chambers.

On December 6, Nixon also indicated that the Committee wished to protect Chambers and have the Department of Justice concern itself only with me:

The committee is concerned over the apparent lack of interest by the Department of Justice in getting to the crux of this case. It seems to be trying frantically to find a method which will place the blame of possession of these documents on Mr. Chambers. . . . The real issue which concerns the committee, and should con-

cern the Department of Justice, is to determine who in the State
Department furnished this information to Mr. Chambers.

Chambers had correctly gauged the assistance he would
receive from the Committee. They could not afford to have
him discredited. Chambers devotes a chapter to the subject of
why he did not turn over the microfilm to his attorneys and
why he instead saved it for the Committee. Here he re-empha-
sizes that one of the pressures upon him in the days preceding
his decision to turn over the typed and handwritten papers to
his lawyers was his fear of being indicted for perjury for the
testimony he had given against me before the Committee:

The climate of 1948 was set by a report that forces within the
Government were determined to stifle the Hiss Case by indicting
me and thereby removing the one witness who could make the
case possible. Congressman Nixon believed that the Government
had already taken the preliminary steps necessary to indict me. A
special night session of members of the House Committee on Un-
American Activities was called to discuss ways to counteract the effort to indict me—not because the Committee felt any personal
fondness for me or wished to save me from indictment as an individual man, but because my indictment must clearly smother the
Hiss Case.

Events demonstrated the accuracy of Chambers's estimate
that he would enhance his own safety by giving the Committee, unsuccessful in its attempt to have me indicted for my
August testimony before it, another chance—and one openly
based at last on their predetermined charge of espionage. He
concludes his explanation of his turning the microfilm over
to the Committee by calling this his "decisive act in the
Case":

No act of mine was more effective in forcing into the open
the long-smothered Hiss Case than my act in dividing the documentary evidence against Hiss, introducing the copied State Department documents into the pre-trial examination (which, in effect, meant turning them over to the Justice Department), and
placing the microfilm, separately, in the pumpkin. It was my decisive act in the Case. For when the second part of the divided evi-

dence, the microfilm, fell into the hands of the Committee, it became impossible ever again to suppress the Hiss Case. . . .

. . . I like to trust that I was moved by an intuition, if only from my reading of military history, that, in general, battles are won by the reserves. The microfilm stands for the reserves.

I knew nothing of Chambers's pressures and problems. I did not know of a night session of the Committee held to prevent Chambers from being indicted. I knew only that the evil menace of the August hearings, which I had thought my libel suit was dispelling, had suddenly turned into a grosser nightmare.

Reports from my lawyers of the progress of the examinations in Baltimore had augured well for the vindication I so desired. As I have already mentioned, all that Chambers and his wife did was to add to his Committee testimony demonstrably flimsy statements of other occasions when, they asserted, my wife or I had seen one or the other of them. While claiming a close friendship and asserting that he had advised me to enter the Department of Justice (where I worked from August 1935 until September 1936), he admitted he had no idea of my duties there.

He had also spun palpably false stories of being permitted by me to read State Department documents. One document, he testified, concerned the "Phantom Red Cosmetics Company," which he asserted was a "front" for a Communist "apparatus" located in England. He testified that I had also told him of a Bulgarian rug dealer who was engaged in espionage in Moscow for the British Government. No State Department documents of this nature have ever been produced to give even seeming support to these stories.

On November 5, the same day that he made his assertions about the Phantom Red Company and the Bulgarian, he had expressly said:

. . . I never transmitted a State Department document from Mr. Hiss to the Communist Party.

There had followed two sessions in the Baltimore testimony, on November 16 and the morning of November 17, at which Mrs. Chambers fared no better, and then, on the afternoon of the 17th, had come the astounding charge of systematic delivery of documents and copies of documents.

Chambers was, I believe, quite truthful that day in one respect. He said when he produced the typed material:

I have never informed any one of this activity.

As we have seen, it appears from Isaac Don Levine's statements that, after his efforts at "enticing" Chambers to improve the "marketability" of his reminiscences (by incorporating "in them material which [Levine] thought was essential" for that purpose), Chambers had told Levine that he had received papers for microfilming.[3] But even his desire to market his writings had never led him, it also seems evident, to pretend to Levine or anyone else that he had engaged in espionage activity that involved the typing of copies of government documents. Of this subsequently invented activity he had indeed "never informed any one." In an apparent effort to explain this silence he says in his book, it will be remembered, that the typed papers "had sunk from my memory . . . completely." On November 17, 1948, his explanation had been:

. . . I forgot I had put [them] by. I thought I had destroyed them. I supposed that the documents I had put away were the handwriting specimens of Mr. Hiss. . . .

(This statement, as implausible as his later version, has a special interest of its own with reference to the four handwritten notes. Would one think of espionage transmissions, which is what Chambers asserts they were, as "handwriting specimens"? Or does that suggest a different category in the mind of the hoarder

---

[3] Whatever Chambers told Levine about his espionage activities, Chambers has made it plain that he did not accuse *me* of anything in his private talks with Levine. Chambers testified that he had made no accusations about me in Levine's presence except in his conversation with Mr. Berle in September 1939 (see p. 93)—and on that occasion, Mr. Berle says, no charge of Communism or of espionage was made against me by Chambers.

—samples for forgery of my handwriting, rather than the forgery by typewriter actually practiced here?)

In any event, we have in this instance more than Chambers's word to go on in concluding that never before had he
contended that I (or, indeed, anyone else) had given him
typed copies of State Department material.

The internal weaknesses and the external disproof of his
brand-new testimony will be described in the chapters on the
trials and the motion for a new trial. Chambers's pride of
accomplishment is evident in the boast, so far still justified,
that he chose to incorporate in his book (attributing it to a
youthful companion of his young son's):

> . . . both boys always called me "Papa." During the Hiss
> Case, when it seemed as if my enemies must destroy me by mass
> of power and weight of numbers, I overheard Donald comforting
> my son. "They'll never get Papa," he said. "He's too smart for
> them." . . .

Chambers *has* proved "too smart" to pay for his admitted
crimes of espionage and perjury and to be adjudged guilty of
having slandered me. But for this avoidance of his proper de-
serts he can thank Committee members even more than his
own smartness, for their efforts saved him. Their witness must
not be indicted (it is evident that Chambers's public admission of his crimes was *not* regarded as destroying his usefulness
as a witness against me, whereas his formal indictment, to
which he could have had no defense, *would* have done so).
Their quarry must be indicted.

The Committee's means for achieving success were considerable at any time, but in the temper of fear and conformity
of that period they proved irresistible. It had ready access to the
press and radio, by which the thesis of my guilt and Chambers's public service in recanting could be one-sidedly blanketed
across the nation. As the embodiment of anti-Communism, the
Committee had greater influence than its official status naturally gave it. The public obloquy that was attached to any
position that could be labeled obstructive to the anti-Com-

munist crusade was intimidating to government officials and jurors concerned with any case involving the charge of Communism.

The launching of the Committee's new "prosecution" of me was described earlier.[4] As a result, on December 3 the New York grand jury was again ordered reconvened. By law the grand jury's authority expired at midnight on December 15. During the two-week period ending on that day the Committee pressed its objectives without ceasing.

On December 5, Stripling called it a "grave question" whether all of the microfilm documents could even then be released to the public. Nixon called the new evidence "shocking" and said he would have former Under Secretary of State Sumner Welles testify as to exactly what international repercussions would come from release of the documents.

On the 6th, Nixon, who had come to New York, where he conferred with the United States Attorney, said the Committee was co-operating with Federal attorneys and the grand jury to bring to justice those responsible for passing out the documents. At the same time Nixon issued his first statement openly protecting Chambers and by implication centering the attention of the public, the grand jury, and the U.S. Attorney's staff solely on me.[5]

On December 7 the Committee held public hearings at which Mundt presided, the former Chairman, J. Parnell Thomas, being under indictment. The Acting Chairman said:

These hearings are a resumption of hearings which started on August 3 . . . what came to be called generally in the newspapers as the Hiss-Chambers situation.

The calling of the hearing at this particular time was necessitated by the rather startling development and disclosures of December 2, and the finding of some missing files and documents from

[4] See pp. 175–7.
[5] This is the statement quoted earlier which (1) expressed the Committee's concern that the Department of Justice was not interested in the "crux" of the case—namely, who furnished the information to Chambers—and (2) criticized the Department for "trying frantically to find a method which will place the blame of possession of these documents on Mr. Chambers."

the State Department which were located in an entirely unofficial and unwarranted location. [Laughter]

The purpose of the hearing is to determine who took these secret documents from the State Department and delivered them to Mr. Chambers.

Enlarged prints of the developed microfilm were presented by a member of the staff, William Wheeler, who testified that he had submitted another set to the New York grand jury the day before.

Welles and Assistant Secretary of State Peurifoy both testified. Peurifoy said that he thought publication of two of the documents (though ten years old) would not be "in the national interest." (This added to the sensational aspects of the hearing. At the trials all the documents were made public, without visible repercussions to the national interest.)

Welles was regarded by the press as having testified that purloining of the documents had broken confidential codes. (In fact Mr. Welles said this would be the case if the same person had the encoded telegraphic message and its decoded counterpart. If Chambers's activities had involved attempts at code-breaking for the Russians, he would for this reason obviously have sought decoded copies of cables sent to or from our embassy in Russia, as the related encoded messages would be in the hands of Soviet officials, readily available for comparison with the decoded texts. As none of the microfilmed or typed messages in confidential code produced by Chambers was from or to any point in Russia, there was no indication that the codes had been broken.)

On that same day I appeared before the grand jury,[6] as I was to do for each of the next eight days except Sunday the 12th. Among other things, I was asked on December 7 if I had ever made loans to others similar to those I had made to Chambers. I answered that only a year or two before I met

---

[6] According to statements by the prosecutor at the first trial, the grand-jury records indicate that I also appeared on December 6. Memoranda which I made after each of my appearances include no reference to my having been before the jury until December 7.

Chambers I had made larger loans amounting to about $200 to a man I did not know very well who was badly strapped by the Depression. (These were later paid in full.) I was also asked about my relations with Julian Wadleigh, a State Department employee, and noted that considerable importance seemed to be attached to him.

On December 8, the Committee again held public hearings. They met at the unusual hour of eight p.m. Isaac Don Levine was the sole witness. He expanded considerably his previous accounts of Chambers's meeting with Mr. Berle. He said that Chambers had given Berle the names of people in the State Department who were "transmitting them [government files], photostating them, and transmitting them to Soviet agents. . . ." Levine said that he preferred to give the names in executive session, but proceeded to assert that my name and my brother's were among those he had recorded that evening as having been mentioned. (Chambers has never contended that he received any documents from my brother and has, quite to the contrary, consistently testified that he did not.) Levine gave no other names in his public testimony. The effect on the grand jury, sitting simultaneously, was obviously highly prejudicial to me.

Levine was permitted to volunteer an encomium for Chambers, in the course of which he said:

> I feel that there is altogether too much preoccupation and speculation as to why Chambers did not produce the documents in time, and that there is not enough concern about the persons who stole the papers. . . .
> The question before the country is not why Mr. Chambers committed or did not commit an error of judgment, but what are we going to do in order to ferret out in all its enormity, this horrible monstrosity?

He was told by Mundt that "insofar as this committee is concerned, we are going to continue to try to disclose the identity of the man or people who did steal these documents in the State Department. . . ."

McDowell read a resolution in praise of Chambers which he hoped would be adopted by the Committee. The resolution recited that "as a direct result of [Chambers's] cooperation [the Committee] has been enabled to reveal to the Nation a vast network of Communist espionage involving high officials of our Government. . . ." There was obviously nothing left for the grand jury but to indict. McDowell's proposed resolution expressed "in behalf of the American people [the Committee's] appreciation and gratitude for the service Mr. Chambers has rendered."

In a few moments Representative Rankin accused the Department of Justice of "shadow-boxing between Alger Hiss and Chambers in New York. . . ."

Mundt soon added "that if we are ever going to get at the people who have stolen these documents and given them to Chambers, and get a conviction, the American public is going to have to rely upon this committee, and not the Department of Justice, because on the basis of the record up to now, certainly there isn't much to hope for from the standpoint of the public."

Rankin spoke again, concluding:

. . . So what this committee is trying to do is to save this country.

Nixon then made a series of statements which included the following:

Mr. Chairman, I for one, as a member of this committee, am stating now publicly that I do not intend to entrust to the Department of Justice or to the present administration, which for 10 years has had these facts and done nothing about it, the responsibility which is ours, as well as theirs, of putting the spotlight on these activities, whether or not a technical crime has been committed.

Now, in that connection I wish to make one other observation. The Department of Justice has indicated, as they should—and I may disagree with some of my colleagues on this point—has indicated an interest in indicting Mr. Chambers for technical violations of law, particularly technical perjury, which he may be guilty of by reason of the fact that he testified before this committee in one connection in one way, and a later connection in another way. . . .

. . . . .

. . . The indication is at the present time that Mr. Chambers will certainly be indicted for perjury. The indications are also that Mr. Chambers will be indicted for perjury probably before any of the other people involved in this particular conspiracy are indicted.

I wish to point out to the Department of Justice [that] to proceed along that line, and I am making public this statement tonight, in the event this occurs, that they will thereby have probably destroyed their only opportunity to obtain an indictment of the other individuals involved, because the star witness against the other individuals will have been an indicted and convicted perjurer.

I should also like to state in that connection that as Mr. Levine so well pointed out tonight . . . the way to give the greatest encouragement to the Communist conspiracy in this country is to stop this particular investigation by simply indicting the man who turned over the information to the committee and made it available to the country. . . .

Again Levine voluntarily took the floor, saying:

. . . I think there is one aspect of the matter which should be stressed in connection with the statement of Representative Nixon, namely, the indictment of Chambers in the cold war being waged today will negate and nullify most of the money and propaganda which the Voice of America is spending abroad in defense of this country.

Outside of the United States, the proposed shocking indictment of Mr. Chambers will mean that we punish the people who help us in the fight against communism and we reward the people who are serving as Stalin's agents in our midst today.

I can imagine nothing more calamitous as a pre-Pearl Harbor move for the third world war, than this particular strategy in somebody's immature mind, if that be the case.

Somewhat later Hébert struck a similar note:

And don't let us lose sight of the fact, and again to reiterate, that the main culprit, the main offender against the American people is not the messenger boy Chambers, but the trigger man in the State Department.

Vail soon interjected several questions that emphasized the same contentions. He asked Levine if there were other potential informers and if they were "watching the operation of the grand jury investigation closely in New York at this time." He then proceeded:

In the event of the indictment, subsequent conviction and imprisonment of Chambers, what effect, in your opinion will that have on the possibility of obtaining information from such sources, at any future date?

Levine's reply was an even more inflammatory warning to the grand jury and the Department of Justice, a warning that obviously had the enthusiastic backing of the Committee:

I think it will make espionage safe. It will be a postwar bonus to Stalin which he never expected, and which he will greatly appreciate. I think it will speed up the process of putrefying this country from within, which Stalin is tremendously interested in. . . .

No further questions were asked. Mundt, the Acting Chairman, told Levine that he had been "very helpful and very stimulating." His closing remarks ended on a note that linked up quite openly with the political tone of the initial hearings in August:

I would like to add as one who has listened somewhat monotonously to the repetition of a phrase rather recently, that this is a "do-nothing" Congress, that from the standpoint of punishing and disclosing espionage in Government, we certainly have had a "do-nothing" administration.

On that same December 8, as I sat in the waiting room of the grand jury, I had a conversation of startling interest. Julian Wadleigh, who had been an economist in the Trade Agreements Division of the Department of State, was also in attendance, and we greeted each other. I had not known Wadleigh well, but had frequently seen him in the Department at conferences on trade-agreement problems, for my chief, Mr. Sayre, was the Assistant Secretary of State who (among other duties) reviewed recommendations of the Trade Agreements Division. I remembered Wadleigh as nervous and eccentric. He seemed much the same this day, though his nervousness was more pronounced than ever.

Some of the things he said to me were so strikingly important that I immediately made notes of them and that afternoon dictated a memorandum of them. It is from that memorandum that I am able to quote what I believe to be the actual words he used. Having greeted me, he went on:

My lawyer tells me I am not supposed to recognize you because I am going to have to refuse to answer on grounds that it might incriminate me whether I know you or not.

This statement ended further conversation, as I assumed it was intended to. But later he took the initiative in speaking to me again, saying that he thought it was silly for him not to talk to my brother, who was also present, and to me. He quickly went on to astound us by saying:

The F.B.I. came to see me and I got sort of panicky and told them that I had given some documents to Chambers. However, my lawyer tells me this may not be too bad to have said because I did not tell them whether the documents were restricted or not. . . .

My brother and I, uncomfortable at this unsolicited confidence—the first information I had that Wadleigh had given papers to Chambers—immediately warned him that we were waiting to testify and that we would have to repeat what he had told us if we were asked about it. He asked:

Couldn't you forget what I said so that it could be as if it hadn't been said?

We told him that this would be impossible, and he walked away to another part of the room and sat down disconsolately. Subsequently he went before the grand jury, returning soon and saying:

Now they want to talk to my lawyer but perhaps I shouldn't have told you even that. I don't know what to say and what not to say.

The next day, December 9, Wadleigh testified in Washington before the Committee at a public hearing. He refused, on the ground that it might incriminate him, to say whether or not he knew me or Chambers, whether or not he had ever seen one of the microfilmed "pumpkin" papers that had originated in the Trade Agreements Division, and whether or not he had ever turned over any restricted information to an unauthorized person. He similarly refused to answer all related questions, except that he denied that he had ever been a Communist.

The Committee then informed Wadleigh that on Monday (December 6) of that week Chambers had told the Committee in an executive session that Wadleigh had been an "active source" and that "it is possible some of these documents [the microfilmed papers] were from him."

This information resulted in no change in Wadleigh's position. He subsequently gave as the reason for his attitude:

. . . I was advised by counsel not to answer any question which might have any connection, however remote, with the accusations that have been made against me by Mr. Chambers.

On December 9, according to the *Times*, Nixon again attacked the Department of Justice for seeking Chambers's indictment for perjury. He repeated his thesis that if the grand jury should indict Chambers it would imperil the case against those accused by Chambers, as it would forfeit the chief witness against them.

On December 10 the Committee had still another public hearing. This time Nathan Levine, Mrs. Chambers's nephew, recited his story of having received a sealed envelope from Chambers some ten years earlier, which he hid in his mother's house in Brooklyn in a dumb-waiter shaft reached from the bathroom. He said that he had returned the envelope to Chambers a few weeks before without ever having opened it. He also said that after he had cleaned up the dust spilled from the dumb-waiter shaft he had gone to the kitchen, where Chambers had taken the envelope (which Levine had not seen Chambers open), and had found him with some papers in his hands. Chambers had then exclaimed: "I didn't think that this still existed" or "was still in existence"; Nathan Levine couldn't remember the exact words.

Levine testified that in all the time he had known Chambers (since just before Chambers's marriage) he did not know what business Chambers was in "other than I remember something about the word 'accounting' or he was translating books."

MR. HÉBERT: He was a writer?

MR. LEVINE: He was either a writer or translator. He translated for other writers.

Levine also testified that he had no indication that Chambers was a member of the Communist Party until Chambers told him that he had broken with Communism and was in danger of his life.

During the course of the hearing Nixon made a statement that concluded:

I am not making this statement for the purpose of making a defense of Mr. Chambers, but I think the record should show the factors which enter in at this time, and I for one wish to say that Mr. Chambers, apart from the disservice that was rendered to the country and a disservice that was rendered only because there were people in this Government who gave him the information that he was able to turn over to the Communists and which he couldn't have rendered without the cooperation of those people, that apart from that, that Mr. Chambers has willingly and voluntarily, with no necessity at all upon his part to do so, rendered a great service to the country by bringing these facts before the American people at this time.

Hébert then made a statement, the last paragraph of which was:

I appreciate what Mr. Chambers has done, and I don't appreciate the fact that he may be used as the goat of this situation,

and all these expressions of gratitude to Mr. Chambers and condemnation of others should not allow this committee to lose sight
of the fact that the man, men, woman, or women in the State
Department who stole those documents have not been appre-
hended by the proper agency of this Government after 10 years.
That is the important thing. Chambers and Hiss are incidents to
me. I want the real criminals and I want the people who are
supposed to know how to do their business to get them and stop
issuing statements in criticism of a committee which is trying to
do its job.

On Saturday, December 11, the Committee, having obtained copies of the typewritten papers and handwritten notes,
released photostatic copies of more of the papers that Chambers had produced, including one of my handwritten notes.
These were prominently reproduced in Sunday's papers.

Nixon announced this same day that he would personally
take the pumpkin films to New York for the grand jury. He
said that he would answer any questions that "will assist them
in bringing to justice those who fed this information to Chambers."

There seems to have been a lull on Sunday the 12th, except for the reproduction in the press of various of the documents with a full repetition of Chambers's story that they
came to him from me.

On Monday the 13th, Mundt announced (his information was entirely inaccurate, as appeared at the trials) that
inquiry in the State Department had narrowed to four persons
—Mr. Sayre, myself, and Mr. Sayre's two clerical assistants—
those with "ready access," as the *Times* put it, to the microfilmed documents.

Also on the 13th, Nixon appeared before the grand jury.
I do not know what he told the jury. Certainly his views as to
what the jury should do (indict me) and should not do (indict
Chambers) were by this time well known. His mere appearance powerfully reinforced these exhortations, and I do know
that for good measure, just before testifying, he repeated his
views to the press, saying that "the indictment of Chambers

for perjury without anybody else would constitute a whitewash because it would be impossible to bring out the truth regarding other people."

Chambers had this to say about Nixon's appearance and his later efforts:

Senator Nixon's role did not end with his dash back to the United States to rally the House Committee when the microfilm was in its hands. His testimony before the Grand Jury that indicted Alger Hiss is a significant part of the Hiss Case. Throughout the most trying phases of the Case, Nixon and his family, and sometimes his parents, were at our farm, encouraging me and comforting my family. My children have caught him lovingly in a nickname. To them, he is always "Nixie," the kind and the good, about whom they will tolerate no nonsense. His somewhat martial Quakerism sometimes amused and always heartened me. I have a vivid picture of him, in the blackest hour of the Hiss Case, standing by the barn and saying in his quietly savage way (he is the kindest of men): "If the American people understood the real character of Alger Hiss, they would boil him in oil."

I know, in addition, that the very next day Mr. Alexander Campbell, Assistant Attorney General in charge of the Criminal Division, who had for some days been conferring with members of the Committee and who had in the preceding few days come to New York from Washington, asked for the first time to speak to me. He said flatly that I was going to be indicted and that my wife would be, too. Indictment is the function of the grand jury alone. I had been before the grand jury daily for a week. I felt certain that they had reached no such decision. Either Nixon's appearance had closed their minds or Campbell was telling me that he had decided to obtain an indictment if he could. Perhaps Nixon's public statements had closed Campbell's mind, if not the minds of the jurors.

This same day Campbell, in a casual conversation with my New York lawyer, Edward C. McLean, said that he realized that Chambers was unstable and abnormal. Campbell continued, according to Mr. McLean's record of the conversation which he has put in an affidavit:

I have expected for several days to pick up the paper in the morning and read that Mr. Chambers has jumped out the window.

Chambers's confirmation of the suicidal intent of which Campbell was aware has already been mentioned. This was no figure of speech. For the chief of the Criminal Division to decide to *press* for an indictment (as I later learned he had), though convinced that the sole witness to the alleged espionage was unstable and abnormal, bespeaks the political and press influences then current.

Campbell's apparent admission of Chambers's unreliability came a few days after an FBI man seeking support for Chambers's charges had told William Marbury, my Baltimore attorney, that the Bureau had file drawers of transcripts of my telephone conversations for years—taken without my knowledge sometime following Chambers's meeting with Mr. Berle. This disclosure carried the plain implication that the wiretapping failed to support Chambers.

Much later I came to know that the next day (the last of the grand jury's legal life) Campbell exhorted the jurors to indict me.[7] He pointed out to them, in an effort to win over those who did not wish to indict me, that under our law an indictment means only that a trial should be held, not that the grand jury has itself determined guilt or innocence. But when he had obtained my indictment by a narrow majority, he was opposed to an indictment of Chambers, which would have put the prosecution in the position of attacking their sole witness to the charge of espionage and so would have nullified the decision that I should be tried.

[7] The proper functions of a Federal attorney in presenting material to a grand jury were stated by the late Augustus N. Hand, when he was a Federal District Judge: ". . . I think the true rule is that he may question the witnesses, advise as to the law, and explain the relation of the testimony to the law of the case. In doing this, he may review the evidence. He must refrain from the slightest coercion of the grand jury and take every pains to have a fair inquest. . . ." (United States *v.* Rintelen, 235 Fed. 787, 794.)

On December 14, I continued, as I had on previous days, to be questioned by the jurors. I knew no better than they did how Chambers had obtained State Department documents and my handwritten notes, how he had come by typed pages that the Federal attorney said had been typed on an old machine we had once owned. I assumed that they knew (from the FBI) as much as I did—and no doubt more—of Wadleigh's admission of having given some papers to Chambers. Had Wadleigh also on the occasion of a visit to my office in the course of his duties picked up the handwritten notes and the three telegrams that bore Mr. Sayre's office stamp of January 14, 1938, and my penciled initials? Or, as these would have been available to others (officials other than Wadleigh, charwomen in the case of the handwritten notes if thrown into the wastebasket, messengers in the case of the telegrams), had someone else passed these on to Chambers? Had Chambers himself come into my office in my absence and picked them up? [8] I had already told the grand jury that I did not know how he obtained them, but that it must have been in some such fashion.

As to the typed documents, assuming that they had been typed on our old Woodstock, as the Federal attorney insisted, then Chambers must have got access to the typewriter while we still had it—we would certainly not have missed it for a few days—or after we had disposed of it.

In my appearance that day before the grand jury I was not conscious of any marked change in the jury's attitude. Some members, I knew, were hostile to me, but others continued to ask their questions with objectivity.

[8] From October 1937 until the end of January 1938 (as I learned only in the fall of 1948) Chambers had a government job and worked within a few blocks of the State Department. Any member of the public was free in those days to enter the State Department building unchallenged. The three initialed copies of cables, which were all in my office at the same time, are stamped as having been received there on January 14, 1938. Judge Charles Wyzanski testified that in 1937 or 1938, when he was in private law practice, he had called on me at my office: ". . . I went into his office and he was not there and I waited. While I waited no secretary was there, no messenger, no one except myself. He came there after I waited for, I would say, 15 minutes." (The quotation is from the record of the second trial.)

On this next-to-last day of the grand jury's session the Committee was not idle. It held its final public hearing on the case. The witness, Mrs. Marion Bachrach, testified that she was employed in the national office of the Communist Party, where she had been working about three years. (I had known Mrs. Bachrach as the wife of a colleague of mine in the Department of Agriculture, in which I worked from 1933 until 1935.) The Committee brought out that her attorney had represented Steve Nelson, a Communist official, who, Stripling asserted, "was called before the committee in connection with the espionage investigation regarding the theft of atomic secrets." She claimed her constitutional privilege in refusing to answer a number of questions. When she was asked if she knew several individuals, including me and my wife, she declined to answer. She was asked, but declined to answer, whether she had ever been in our house in Washington and whether she had ever seen a typewriter in our house. She denied that she had copied documents removed from the State Department, the Bureau of Standards, or the Navy Department, that she had lent a typewriter to my wife, and that my wife had ever delivered a typewriter to her.

As the hearing neared its end, Mr. Mundt announced:

The chairman would like to state that the crime involved here is very definitely a capital crime. It is either treason in wartime or treason in peacetime.

The Committee had constantly expanded beyond the charges made before it the scope of its own charges. On October 14 the hearings of the summer had finally appeared in printed form. This was the day before Chambers denied to the grand jury (reconvened as a result of his charges against me) that he made any charge of espionage. Yet the volume bore the unqualified title: "Hearings Regarding Communist Espionage in the United States Government." Now that Chambers had at last gratified their desire that he charge me with espionage, the Committee charged "capital crime" and "treason."

The timing of these latest inflammatory statements can-

not have been accidental. The grand jury's authority was to
expire next day. December 14 was the last day on which proceedings in Washington could be reported in New York papers and read by members of the jury before they decided
whether or not to bring in any indictments. There had been a
steady crescendo of Committee statements and hearings. The
last public hearing relating even indirectly to the Hiss-Chambers case for more than a year was this hearing of December
14, which ended on the note of capital crimes and treason.
There was, however, no cessation by Committee members, during that period, of other activity prejudicial to my fight to
clear my name. Subsequent reports and statements in Congress
and to the press before both trials undoubtedly influenced the
jurors at the trials. But the crude method of a competing
presentation of "evidence" as the platform for prejudicial statements stopped on December 14, after which it could no longer
influence the grand jury, and no further public hearings were
held until after my trials.

On this same day the Committee also issued a long
further statement reviewing the case, and openly expressed its
hope for indictments by the grand jury of "all guilty parties."
It again made plain that it did not include Chambers in this
category by saying:

The committee deems it its obligation, however, to point out
the fact to the American public that the most important thing is
the discovery, apprehension, indictment and conviction of the individual or individuals who stole the secret Government documents
from Government departments. . . .

The Committee had thus insured last-minute items for
the jurors' morning papers of December 15 as they prepared
for their final day. For two weeks the jurors had been kept
similarly well advised of the views of this powerful and feared
Committee as to whom they should indict and whom they
should not, as to who was guilty of espionage and treason and
who of mere "technical perjury" and "disservice . . . to the
country." The Committee had throughout that period made it

plain that it agreed with Nixon that an indictment of Chambers would "give the greatest encouragement to the Communist conspiracy in this country." The jurors had equal reason to believe that the Committee would consider them responsible for just as dire results if I were not indicted.

On this final day of the jury's tenure of office there was a marked change in the attitude of the member of the United States Attorney's staff who was presenting information to the grand jury. Had he received directions from Mr. Campbell? I commented on the change in attitude in the memorandum that I wrote in Mr. McLean's office at the end of the day's session while the jury was still deliberating as to what, if any, action they would take. I noted that for the first time the questions asked me by the Federal attorney were apparently designed to minimize the effect of my answers to other questions. I had the impression that he was no longer simply eliciting information for the jury to pass on. Instead, it seemed to me that by implication he was adversely characterizing and belittling my testimony. I said to Mr. McLean that I thought he had tried to influence the jury to indict me.

At an earlier session I had been asked whether I had made gifts to other people comparable to my gift of the Ford to Chambers. I had not immediately recalled any from that period, but after talking to my wife and son I was now able to say that we had given our old upright piano to Timothy's music teacher when we moved to P Street and at some time in that period we had given a used radio to Perry Catlett, our maid's son, when he took a radio course.

I had the day before told the grand jury that I did not pretend to understand fully why Chambers was trying to destroy me and had deliberately framed me. On this last day I added that Chambers's use of our typewriter was simply a form of forgery less easily detected than an attempted forgery of my handwriting would have been.

Later I was recalled for a few minutes and, to my surprise, was again asked, now in perfunctory form, questions that had been fully covered and had been gone over more than once and at great length. I was then excused after eight days' attendance.

This grand jury had had an unusually long life. It had served for eighteen months, from June 16, 1947. Its primary area of investigation had been violation of the espionage laws, and it had been known as a do-nothing grand jury because of its prior failure to produce a single indictment in this field. Now it had heard an admitted violator, Chambers. Under these circumstances the urge to do something was great. There was strong pressure by the Committee, and by those elements of the press that gloried in the Committee's "disclosures" and point of view, that this "something" be an indictment of me, not of Chambers. On this last day the influence of Mr. Campbell and that of the Federal attorney who had been associated with the jury for months were evidently added to the urgings of the Committee and to the opinion of that portion of the public inflamed by the sensational press and by the fears of the time.

The last act of the grand jury was to indict me on the charge of perjury. They acted by a divided vote, only one more than a bare majority. They wished to indict Chambers, but were persuaded not to. But all the various influences on them did not obtain the indictment of my wife. There was at least this one victory for sanity at this crucial stage of the case.

The indictment was based not on any of my answers given in any of the previous long sessions. Instead, the charge was based upon the last-minute repetition of questions (the answers to which were already well known to the grand jury) repeated, it seems obvious, only because Mr. Campbell had decided in advance to obtain an indictment based on my answers:

COUNT I

Q. Mr. Hiss, you have probably been asked this question before, but I'd like to ask the question again. At any time did you, or Mrs. Hiss in your presence, turn any documents of the State Department or any other Government organization, or copies of any documents of the State Department or any other Government organization, over to Whittaker Chambers? A. Never. Excepting, I assume, the title certificate to the Ford.

COUNT II

Q. Can you say definitely that you did not see him after January 1, 1937? A. Yes, I think I can definitely say that.

CHAPTER SEVEN

THE JURY THAT
COULD NOT AGREE

NEARLY six months passed after the indictment before the first trial began on May 31, 1949. Initially set for January 24, the trial was postponed several times. Preparation was necessarily lengthy for a case that involved happenings and non-happenings of from eleven to fourteen years before. Witnesses had died, had scattered, or had forgotten what they once knew; others were afraid to say what they still recalled; records were often in storage, were missing, or had been destroyed in the ordinary course of business. Document experts had to be consulted.

There was also a series of motions involving my counsel's request for clarification as to the meaning of the indictment and for access to the grand-jury minutes.

The second count of the indictment charged that my statement that I did not see Chambers after January 1, 1937, was "untrue in that [I] did in fact see and converse with the said Mr. Chambers in or about the months of February and March, 1938." We were officially informed, by a bill of partic-

ulars in response to our request for clarification, that this was
a charge only that I had seen Chambers in or about February
and March 1938 at Volta Place for the alleged purpose of
giving him documents. The conclusion seemed clear that the
prosecution itself had no confidence in obtaining credence for
the Chamberses' ever growing stories of a close relationship
and recognized that without the documents produced by
Chambers they had no case at all.

The Committee, whose members had been named by the
80th Congress, in which the Republicans had a majority, had
to await fresh action by the new Congress for reincarnation under a Democratic Chairman. Some of its members had not
been re-elected to Congress, and Mundt had become a Senator.
Then, too, its efforts had not been universally acclaimed even
in the emotionally charged climate of opinion that then invested the topics with which the Committee dealt. The reor-
ganization of its personnel was almost complete. Only Nixon [1]
retained his place on the newly created Committee. Even Stripling resigned from his position as chief assistant. (Other members of the staff, however, remained, including Chambers's
former Communist friend Mandel. Continuity of the staff's
attitude was thus preserved.)

But during the remaining weeks of its life the old Committee managed to continue its attacks on me, not content
with the indictment it had so effectively urged. In addition, it
pursued me well beyond its grave—its final reports, though
dated December 31 and released to the press about that time,
were not made available to the public in printed form until
several months after the new year and the new Congress
had begun. [2]

Nixon greeted the indictment with a statement that same
evening (December 15) that it was a "vindication" of the

[1] The Republican caucus also named Thomas, then under indictment.
His trial was delayed until November 1949 because of frequent hospitalization
from January to May, but he apparently took no part in the Committee's
activities.

[2] They were first listed in the March 1949 catalogue of the Superintendent
of Documents.

Committee, a frank admission of the Committee's investment in the result.

In its final plea of December 14 to the grand jury for "indictments of all guilty parties" the Committee had also emphasized the importance it attached to "conviction" as well. This same statement announced that the Committee would continue to release further installments of the Chambers papers. It said dramatically that it would make public all those "which the State Department has said may be released at this time without detriment to our present national security." It announced that the releases would be "daily in such numbers as to make possible a comprehensive understanding of their contents." The Committee's activities, which had played such a part in bringing about the indictment, were thus to continue—and did continue long after the indictment.

On December 16 the date of January 24 was tentatively set for my trial. For three days after the 16th the press described at length, or reproduced, additional documents released by the Committee from Chambers's hoard. To the ordinary reader these appeared to be proof of Chambers's accusations against me, restated by the press as each new batch of papers was reported.

Then on December 20, just five days after the indictment, the Committee capitalized upon the tragic death of Laurence Duggan, the gifted president of the Institute of International Education and a former official of the State Department, who fell from his office window. Duggan had been one of those accused by Chambers. His name appears in the notes Mr. Berle made of his 1939 talk with Chambers, but Mr. Berle did not even mention Duggan in his testimony about his talk with Chambers. Duggan had not been named in any of the Committee's published testimony. However, Isaac Don Levine had asserted to the Committee in executive session on December 8 that Chambers had given Duggan's name to Mr. Berle as a man who had "passed confidential information." (Was Duggan perhaps, like Mr. Sayre, an alternate target that Chambers had simply tried out on Mr. Berle? With microfilms of State Department documents in his possession, Chambers could have fabricated a case against Duggan or any other officer of the Department.)

Mundt and Nixon chose to adopt an asserted accusation by Chambers as if it were fact. When they learned of Duggan's death they immediately, that same night, released Levine's testimony, and Mundt was reported to have said that the Committee would release the names of others "as they jump out of windows."

The resulting public protests at this smearing by hearsay quickly led to backtracking. Nixon said two days later that a statement made by Chambers that Duggan had never given him documents "clears" Duggan of espionage. On Christmas Eve, Mundt added that, as far as he was concerned, Duggan had been "cleared." The Attorney General on the same day announced that "Mr. Duggan was a loyal employee of the United States Government." One, at least, of Chambers's intended victims had been vindicated, though only posthumously.

On December 29 the press reported that the preceding day Nixon and Mundt had had a five-hour interview with Chambers at his farm, at which he gave still more "information" about various individuals, whose names were not made public.

Most damaging to me were the two reports dated December 31, one of the last days of the Committee's life. The briefer of the two (twenty-five pages), a general report of the Committee's activities over the preceding two years, purported to survey "the most active and productive period in the history" of the Committee. Under the heading "Soviet Espionage Within the United States Government" appeared the following:

The most startling disclosures ever confronted by the committee, disclosures which should rock our national complacence to its foundations, have been developed in connection with the testimony of Elizabeth Terrill Bentley and Whittaker Chambers, both confessed former members of Communist espionage rings, operating within the Government of the United States. . . . These groups . . . have no visible Communist Party ties and disclaim membership or affiliation of any kind. According to the testimony presented, these agents maintain a steady flow of secret and confidential Government documents to special couriers, which are quickly microfilmed for transmission to Soviet intelligence officers, after which the originals are returned to Government files. These conspirators also seek to and indeed have influenced major decisions of Government policy.

These activities are described more fully in the interim report on hearings regarding Communist espionage in the United States Government dated August 28, 1948,[3] hearings regarding Communist espionage in the United States Government dated July 21 through September 9, 1948 [in which chief place is given to the hearings dealing with Chambers's charges], and the committee report on Soviet espionage within the United States Government, dated December 31, 1948.[4] It is not our purpose to recapitulate these reports here which go to the very roots of the Communist conspiracy. . . .

The inadequacy of our present legislative and prosecuting machinery is alarmingly demonstrated by the fact that not one of these individuals has been prosecuted to date on these grave charges, with the single notable exception of Alger Hiss, indicted for perjury on two counts by a New York Federal grand jury on December 15, 1948.

Earlier in the report the Committee noted eleven of its publications and said that "The intense interest of the country in these publications is demonstrated by the fact that our supply of these publications is almost exhausted at this time." It added:

In a number of instances committee reports were reprinted in full or in major part by newspapers throughout the country.

The papers of New York City were no exception. Prospective jurors in my case had ample opportunity not only to know the Committee's "startling disclosures" but its opinion of their meaning.

[3] This is the report, referred to on pp. 26–7, which was issued just after the August 25 hearing.

[4] This is the other of the two reports of that date. It is taken up next in the text of this book.

The longer report of December 31, "Soviet Espionage Within the United States Government," totaled 129 pages. Pages 13–129 were devoted to photostatic reproductions of papers Chambers had produced in Baltimore and from the pumpkin, including my handwritten notes. Indeed, the entire report was devoted to Chambers's story, as "just ONE such Communist apparatus set up in Washington, D.C., for the benefit of world communism." The report said that it "should be read as a supplement to the committee report of August 28, 1948. . . ." Extensive parts relating to me were quoted from that earlier report, including the bald statement that the testimony taken by the Committee "has definitely shifted the burden of proof from Chambers to Hiss, in the opinion of this committee." Other reprinted passages characterized various portions of my testimony as "conflicting," "vague," "evasive," "badly shaken," "refuted." In contrast, the "verifiable" parts of Chambers's testimony were said to have "stood up strongly." He was, the report said, "for the most part forthright, and emphatic in his answers to questions."

The report again featured the charge, as "perhaps the most significant and disturbing feature," that the documents had caused the breaking of "the most secret diplomatic codes of the United States" with the result that "the government which received these identified documents . . . without question, also had complete access to all of the secret and confidential messages transmitted by the State Department during the period involved. . . ." This false charge was now expanded to cover the years after the dates in early 1938 of Chambers's papers, thus tapping not only the extreme fear of Communism but the public animus against Nazi Germany and Japan:

. . . Since this was in the general historical era of the Stalin-Hitler pact, it is also likely that Nazi Germany and subsequently Japan may have known our State Department secret codes and communications, before and during the war.

The Committee stated that the most important of the microfilmed documents came from Mr. Sayre's office and added

erroneously that only I, Mr. Sayre, and his two clerical assistants had access to them. The testimony of the latter was
summarized as saying that it was my practice and Mr. Sayre's
to take papers home for study and that neither the handwritten
nor the typed papers could have been "prepared for the
purpose of transmitting information in the regular course of
State Department business." The Committee also reported
that Mr. Sayre had said that neither the typed nor the handwritten papers had been brought to his attention. The Committee's final word concerning the typed papers was that it
had been "conclusively established where and on what machine
these documents were typed."

Here, as near the eve of my trial as the defunct Committee
could voice its views, was an announcement, widely available to
all prospective jurors, their friends, acquaintances, employers,
and neighbors, that a Congressional committee claiming special knowledge of my case was of the opinion that the traditional burden of proof had been shifted to me and that I was
not worthy of belief (the one issue in a perjury trial), whereas
the Committee vouched for the credibility of my traducer.
Coupled with this were a wholly one-sided summary of the
evidence against me and the plainest inference that the Committee had conclusively established my guilt.

Just a month after my indictment the enormously publicized trial of the Communist leaders began in the same
courthouse to which my prospective jurors were later summoned for selection and where, day after day for six weeks,
these jurors and I were to attend my trial. The Communist
trial began January 16, 1949. It continued without interruption
throughout my first trial and until October 14, just a month
before my second trial began. The press featured daily sensational testimony and charges as the two trials were day after
day reported side by side as front-page news. Often during
my trial the courthouse was ringed with Communist pickets
protesting the trial of their leaders. The jurors in my case
threaded their way through these lines, through policemen
watching over them, and through throngs of curious spectators.

The courthouse was invested by the largest force of uniformed policemen, according to *The New York Times*, ever to be assigned to a New York trial. They were stationed outside the building, in the lobby, and in the corridors. The courthouse, inside and out, was heavy with an atmosphere of tension and uniformed force, far more so than had been the case even during the war.

On January 28 the newly constituted Committee achieved front-page prominence with its announcement that the purposes of the Communist Party were espionage and treason, an indication to the public that the Committee's change of members had not changed its preoccupation with Communist espionage.

On January 30 the *New York Journal-American* began a series of articles by Stripling, summarizing his Committee experiences, which appeared in book form about the time of my second trial.[5] The articles continued until February 26. The biased and prejudicial nature of Stripling's account of Chambers's testimony and mine before the Committee has been described earlier.[6] It retold in like manner a good deal of Chambers's story about the documents. Here was still another version, this one in popular form, of Chambers's and the Committee's point of view, which was widely distributed in the city where my trial was pending.

Soon the press gave wide prominence to another case that emphasized and still further heightened the official and public obsession with Communism and espionage. On March 4, Judith Coplon, a government employee, and V. A. Gubitchev, a citizen of the U.S.S.R. employed by the United Nations, were arrested in New York City on the charge of espionage. It was announced that when Miss Coplon was arrested she had in her possession copies of confidential material she was planning to deliver to the Russian. Six days later the two were indicted, and six days after that Miss Coplon was indicted in Washington also.

[5] See p. 302.
[6] See pp. 39–40, 44–6.

Her Washington trial began on April 25 and resulted in her conviction on June 30. From her arrest on March 4 until the end of her Washington trial, just eight days before the conclusion of my first trial, there were few days when the press did not contain lurid stories about her case.

On July 1, *The New York Times* expressly noted in a featured article the impact on my case of this simultaneous trial, an impact the prosecution did nothing to discourage. Under the headline "Coplon Verdict Spreads Fast in Hiss Trial Room," the *Times* commented in part:

High up on the thirteenth floor of the United States Courthouse on Foley Square a bailiff entered the Alger Hiss perjury trial at 3:47 yesterday afternoon and whispered the words "Coplon guilty."

In less than thirty seconds the news had flashed through the courtroom, passing rapidly by low whispers from the press section to the spectators' benches.

Thomas F. Murphy, Assistant United States Attorney [the prosecutor in my case], and Thomas J. Donegan, special assistant to the Attorney General [his chief assistant], were pleased with the news. They regard the case they are now prosecuting as parallel in many respects to that of Judith Coplon.

Nor was this all. On May 12 the press reported that Gerhart Eisler had stowed away on a Polish ship. For the preceding two years he had been a target of the Committee, which in its general report of December 31, 1948, had called him "an important international Communist and responsible representative of the Communist International," "a notorious international terrorist, and operative of the GPU, the Soviet secret terrorist organization." The report stated that he had been sentenced to a year in jail for contempt of Congress and, in a separate case, to one to three years for passport fraud. At the time he fled the country he was free, pending his appeals.

Eisler's dramatic flight and the subsequent unsuccessful attempts by the Federal authorities to have him arrested at a British port and extradited were a sensation of the time. Throughout the remainder of May and during the entire period of my trial there were frequent, almost daily, references to him in the press. Toward the end of the trial the press played up the prosecutor's attempt to use Eisler's ex-wife (Mrs. Massing) as a "mystery" witness in my case. (While the trial was still in progress the *New York World-Telegram* published a summary of what the former Mrs. Eisler said she would have said against me had she been permitted to testify. Her testimony at the second trial is discussed at pages 307–11.)

The influence of the Committee was again felt in the early days of the trial. At the end of the first week, on June 4, the *New York World-Telegram* obtained access to the secret and unpublished testimony that Chambers had given in December and published this repetition of his accusations against me.

The publication of this story and the one in the same newspaper about the former Mrs. Eisler were not the only instances in which the protection of cross-examination and orderly court procedure was to be impaired during the course of the trial by press reports of statements made outside the courtroom. After Malcom Cowley had testified for the defense about Chambers's attack on Mr. Sayre in 1940, Chambers, who was not recalled to testify about the incident, issued a contradictory statement to the press.

The Committee, in a new publication, also made available outside the court the substance of Chambers's Committee testimony. About the time my trial began, there became available publicly a pamphlet of the Committee's, in question-and-answer form, entitled *Spotlight on Spies*.[7] My name was not mentioned, but there were numerous references to the most publicized items in Chambers's accusations against me. Chambers and I were described in all but name. Chambers

---

[7] This was the latest of a "series of reports on various phases of the Communist problem [published by the Committee] in the interest of public enlightenment. . . ," to quote the Committee's December 31 report to Congress. It was first listed in the May 1949 catalogue of the Superintendent of Documents.

was thus again vouched for officially at the time of the trial based on his charges.

The first sentence of the new pamphlet was:

This is the story of Communist spying in the United States.

A few sentences later the official nature of the report was emphasized and the impression given that its contents were factually undisputed "information":

The information we are setting before you is based on many long hours of investigation . . . and many hundreds of pages of testimony by witnesses, some of them former spies for the Soviet Union in the United States.

The style was popular, even inflammatory. There was the unsettling suggestion that anyone might be guilty:

Who serve as the actual thieves for these spy rings?
Self-styled "loyal" AMERICANS, believe it or not.

Later this insidious theme was expanded:

Soviet spy rings contain well-educated and able Americans who are looked up to by their fellow men. They may be scientists, lawyers, professors, writers, Government career workers, and even successful business men who have been filled with Communist poison.

. . . .

. . . They never hold Party membership cards or attend regular Party meetings. In fact, they're not allowed even to discuss their real political view with anybody.

Support for Chambers's charges against me was implied in this concept; the spy is a secret Communist whose affiliation can't be and therefore need not be proved except by the mere accusation of an informer.

Even Mr. Berle's account of Chambers's imaginary placing of me in a "study group" seemed to have been included —but with sinister trimmings:

If inexperienced Communists are in a spot to help the spy rings, they might be given "special treatment."

What is this "special treatment"?

They are invited to join small Communist "study groups" which to outsiders appear to be harmless social gatherings or discussion groups.

Actually, these gatherings are used to teach the "students" blind loyalty to the Soviet Union and to get them into a conspiratorial frame of mind against the American Government.

Weeks after I had told the Committee of Chambers's giving me a rug which I regarded as partial payment for his unpaid rent, he mentioned the rug to the Committee, but claimed that he had delivered it to me as a Soviet presentation for my "services." His story was widely circulated and was repeated in Stripling's articles and book. At the trials Chambers contended that the date of the gift was later than I had said, attempting to back up his version of the length of time he had known me by saying it was one of four rugs purchased at a much later time, of which transaction there was a record in the rug dealer's books. The rug and the Committee's verdict, if not the names, appeared in the pamphlet:

There are "good will" presents such as expensive rugs, which four American spies in high U.S. Government jobs received from the Soviet Government.

The acceptance as fact of Chambers's well-ventilated charges continued:

Committee investigations have shown that the spy turns his information over to a "go-between" or "courier." Sometimes he tells the courier what he has heard; sometimes he gives him notes, and copies of letters or other papers revealing secret plans. Sometimes he even steals original records. . . .

. . . . .

They make a date to meet—maybe at a restaurant, a drug store, or the home of a Communist. Maybe even in a park or on a street corner. . . . The spy knows the courier only by some alias such as "Carl" or "Helen."

. . . . .

Several spies had such important jobs that it was their duty to handle confidential State Department papers.

. . . .

Your Committee has copies of more than 60 secret State Department papers . . . which were stolen by a spy. We can't tell you what some of them say because even now it would endanger the safety of our country.

In concluding, the Committee reaffirmed its predecessor's position as to its functions and re-emphasized its predecessor's position that its charges were exposures, revelation of fact:

The Committee is doing everything it can to run down the Communist spy rings in this country and has already succeeded in exposing many of the spies. . . .

The final peroration was hortatory:

What can I do to help
Do some deep thinking about what the Soviet spy system and the American Communist mean to the safety of our country.
Then let your Government and your Congress know that you want to see REAL ACTION to rid our country of these menaces.

There was little new evidence in the trial except the defense's demonstration of the falsity of some of Chambers's expanding stories of visits and trips, of the discrepancies in his tale about the documents, and of the internal evidence of the documents themselves in contradiction of his charges. But for the very reason that Chambers's charges had so largely monopolized the press—new charges replacing old ones before there was time for refutation—many people, though themselves less vulnerable than the jurors to the pressures of the times to follow the Committee's exhortations, had made up their minds in his favor without waiting for the defense's case. It is difficult to believe that some of the jurors had not done the same.

James Reston of *The New York Times* commented on the extent to which opinions had already been formed by the second week of the trial—that is, before the defense had begun its case. At this stage it was known only that I denied Chambers's accusations and that my testimony before the Committee had been directly contrary to his on the question of the nature of our relationship in the 1930's. Reston wrote in an article that appeared on June 9:

It seldom happens that in the presence of such conflicting testimony men and women take a positive position for and against the accused. Yet this has happened in the case of Alger Hiss.

Repeatedly in the last few days, counsel on both sides have asked for a recess, and the audience at the trial has retired to the outer hall on the thirteenth floor of the Federal Court building.

There, the conversation has disclosed that, despite the gap between the two sides, few men are saying they do not know whether Mr. Hiss is guilty or innocent. Though Mr. Hiss has not gone on the stand, men and women do not hesitate to pronounce their personal verdicts.

The reason for this apparently is that Mr. Hiss has become elevated by partisan minds into a symbol of the controversial group of young New Dealers who came to Washington in the 1930s and remained to administer a revolution in the nation's domestic and foreign policy.

He went on to emphasize the barriers to objectivity:

. . . so different are the two stories of the accused and the accuser, and so fundamental are the issues to the central political conflict of our time, that the quality of patient objectivity among the spectators seems remarkably small. . . .

Meanwhile, Mr. Hiss himself will undoubtedly continue to be portrayed as the man who sat at Franklin Roosevelt's right hand at Yalta, a great power in the direction of the nation's policy. This, of course, was not true. He did not make policy at Yalta. He was one of many technicians who did small jobs when he was told.

. . . most popular impressions of the case were gained from Congressional hearings that did not disclose the discrepancies in the accuser's case. . . .

Certainly the air of partisanship, pro and con, was palpable beneath the decorum of the courtroom. There was a large press corps at each session, some of whose members reflected the sensational outlook of their employers. During recesses and before and after sessions the prosecutor seemed to have a regular claque of certain journalists, whose accounts of the trial seemed to my counsel and me strongly bent in his direction. Opposed to trial by newspaper, my counsel sought no special contacts with the press, and I had no discussions of the case with any journalist. William Marshall Bullitt, an elderly former Solicitor General (and a relative of former Ambassador William C. Bullitt, to whom Isaac Don Levine had relayed in expanded form the statements Chambers had made to Mr. Berle), distributed during the trial a pamphlet, which he had prepared and had had privately printed, analyzing my testimony before the Committee along lines already marked out by members of the Committee.

The spectators seemed to me sharply divided. I certainly did not feel without supporters, and on frequent occasions as I stood in the hallway during a recess in the proceedings some friendly stranger would express sympathy or support for my position. Others, doubtless a majority, of those who came and went struck me as already committed to an adverse position or idly drawn to a publicized spectacle.

I shall not attempt to give a day-by-day description of the trial, with its elements of color and drama, nor to summarize all of the evidence. This would take a book in itself, and can more appropriately be done by others. I shall, instead, set forth and discuss the gist of the prosecution's case, referring to the numerous witnesses and exhibits only where they bear most directly on Chambers's charges. For convenience of presentation I shall deal separately with Chambers's charges involving the papers he produced (these are considered in the next chapter) and the testimony he and his wife gave on their relations with me.[8] This latter testimony, the subject of most

---

[8] I shall include in this chapter related material from both trials, leaving for the account of the second trial only those subjects which first appeared there.

of the rest of this chapter, incorporated much of what Chambers had previously asserted at Committee hearings and at the Baltimore libel proceedings, but other incidents were added as the imaginations of the Chamberses continued to work.

In his opening remarks, in which he outlined the views that he hoped to persuade the jury to adopt, the prosecutor accurately told the members of the jury:

> . . . if you don't believe Chambers then we have no case under the federal perjury rule, as Judge Kaufman will tell you, where you need one witness plus corroboration, and if one of the props goes out goes the case.

This was, of course, as it always had been, the only real issue: Chambers's veracity against mine. The sensational publicity, political prejudices heightened during the national election, the public anxieties and tensions of those days constantly obscured this issue. The prosecutor came to regard this simple accurate statement of his as a tactical lapse. He refrained from again uttering this plain statement of the essence of the case, and vigorously and successfully objected to my counsel telling the jury in the next trial that the prosecutor had thus initially recognized that "if you don't believe Chambers then we have no case."

After Chambers had begun to testify, we asked to examine the grand-jury minutes of his testimony on the general ground that his testimony there differed from his story at the trial. As the prosecutor objected to our request, the judge who presided at the trial, Judge Samuel H. Kaufman, examined the minutes to see if our contentions were warranted, and he reported:

> . . . I have noted 19 very substantial discrepancies between the testimony he has given before the Grand Jury on his first appearance and the testimony that he has given on this trial. . . .

Portions of Chambers's testimony before the grand jury were then made available to us on the Judge's orders. Questioned about this testimony, Chambers stated that he had perjured himself—he, the sole essential witness in a perjury case, thus publicly asserted at the trial that he had committed a series of perjuries before the very grand jury that had been induced to indict me because my testimony was in conflict with his. He also said that he had committed perjury before the Committee which had fostered and supported him from the outset. The undisputed evidence of his own espionage and Wadleigh's made it clear that when Chambers had denied knowledge of espionage he had committed perjury.

The prosecution's entire position depended upon Chambers's story, by then thoroughly familiar to the public, that he had seen me every week or ten days from early 1935 until mid-April 1938, and that from 1937 on he had every week or ten days come to my house at night to receive from me State Department documents in their original form or in typewritten copies. Mrs. Chambers, in attempted support of her husband's story of a close relationship, went beyond him in assertions of an interfamily friendship. But she did not assert that her husband was away from home at night once a week or every ten days, nor did she (or anyone else) in any other way corroborate her husband's assertions that he received documents from me.

Many witnesses were called by both sides, and literally hundreds of exhibits were introduced. Analysis of the papers Chambers had produced required the placing in evidence of their counterparts from the official records of the State Department. Various letters that had been typed by my wife or other members of our family were made exhibits for comparison of their typescript with that of the typed papers which Chambers had produced. A great number of transactions, asserted to have some possible bearing on the issues, were brought into the case. These topics involved further exhibits: bank records, leases, contracts, the registry book of an inn, official motor-vehicle records, memoranda of Chambers's statements made to the FBI, to Raymond Murphy, and to Mr. Berle, and many other items. The source and nature of each piece of paper introduced had to be explained by a witness.

The prosecution even chose to prove by records, photographs, and witnesses the uncontested facts of dates and places of my residence. There was testimony and there were further exhibits on the practices of the State Department in the 1930's and fixing the location of my office and that of the Trade Agreements Division (located on a different floor). More testimony and exhibits dealt with Chambers's suspension by Columbia University and his later discharge from the New York Public Library. My colleagues and friends testified as to my habits at home and at the office, and to my general reputation. But all the necessary related or tangential issues, standard ingredients of a court trial, were of significance only as they tended to support or disprove Chambers's and Mrs. Chambers's allegations.

At the trials my counsel brought out in cross-examining Chambers and Mrs. Chambers numerous variants of their stories as told at different times before the trials. In Chapter III I have already given an account of the contradictions and inconsistencies in Chambers's version of our relationship as he told it to the Committee at the August 7 hearings. (On August 27 he had added a new embellishment. He said that he thought my wife and I—who had in fact met on shipboard—had met at "Rand School in New York City," which he described as "a Socialist institution." Though neither of us had ever been in the place, he said he thought we had both been students there. Mrs. Chambers testified that *she* had once studied at the Rand School, but never claimed that my wife or I had ever done so.)

Until the August 25 hearing he had not attempted to name the street (Volta Place) to which we moved on December 29, 1937, and where we lived until 1943. On his first appearance on August 3 he had told his story of coming to see me to try to "break [me] away from the party" and chose a 1937 date. (His story had come in answer to a question as to whether, "when [he] left the Communist Party in 1937," he had tried to get others to "break with" him.) On August 7 he placed the locale of this alleged meeting "in the house

[I] later moved to, which was on the other side of Wisconsin Avenue." On August 25 he chose a new date. He said that he saw me "once again toward the end of 1938." Later that day he added to this: "About 1938, toward the end of 1938, I tried to break away from the Communist Party a number of people." His testimony states that I "was then living on Dent Place" (a street near Volta Place, and on the same "side of Wisconsin Avenue," but one on which I have never lived). In the first trial, the prosecutor, in an attempt to repair the mistake in street names, called as a witness the stenographer who had recorded this testimony. The stenographer testified that Chambers had said "Balt Place" and that he (the stenographer) had asked someone connected with the Committee (he thought it was a member of the Committee staff) for confirmation of this address and had been told that it should be "Dent." As Chambers had talked to various Committee members and the staff several times by August 25, it seems likely that he had previously told them I had lived on "Dent" Place and on the 25th still had not learned the correct address of my residence after I left 30th Street. (When Chambers first told the story he said he had found my wife at home; on August 25 he said that only a maid was at home and that he waited near by until my wife returned home.)

By the time he repeated the story on November 5 in the Baltimore libel proceedings he picked December 1938 as the date and he was still unsure of where I was living at that time:

A: I saw him at the house, which I believe is in Volta Place. I think that is the address. I am not exactly sure.

He went on to misplace my house, putting it at the wrong end of the little Place, which runs three blocks from Wisconsin Avenue to 35th Street. The house is, as the number (3415) discloses, between 34th and 35th streets. It is, indeed, the last house before the street ends at 35th Street. He said: "It is about I should think two or three houses down Volta Place. I have forgotten." He was asked if he meant two or three houses down from Wisconsin Avenue, and he said: "I think so." Even by the time of the first trial, prior to which he had, he admitted, been to all of the houses with the FBI, he still thought it was "about a block" from Wisconsin Avenue, a two-block miss. Yet this was a house that, in attempted support of his story of espionage, he said he visited every week or ten days in the first three and a half months of 1938, returning a second time on each occasion, and in addition paying "social" visits.

In 1945 and 1946, Raymond Murphy, a State Department employee, interviewed Chambers. Murphy's notes record that Chambers said (in 1945) that he remembered *several* conversations with me "in the *early* [9] part of 1938" during which I was "adamant" against "breaking," and (in 1946) that he "personally" asked me "to break . . . in *early* [9] 1938" but I had refused "with tears in [my] eyes." On these occasions it would appear that Chambers was not asked if he knew where I was living in early 1938.

His pre-November 1948 versions of a last meeting were inconsistent with his later testimony that I had given him the papers he produced the afternoon of November 17. All of the State Department documents copied or summarized in those papers are dated in January, February, March, and April of 1938. If he had stuck to either of his earlier stories (that he saw me in early 1938 to urge me to "break" from Communism or that after he broke with Communism in 1937 or early 1938 [1] he saw me once more, in December 1938) he could hardly, at the same time, contend that he was receiving typed papers from me every ten days or so during the first three and a half months of 1938.

In the Baltimore libel proceedings, on the morning of November 17, a few hours before Chambers produced the typed papers, Mrs. Chambers, presumably in preparation for her husband's afternoon effort, alleged that on one occasion she had been to Volta "Street" with him. She was quite vivid

---

[9] Italics added.
[1] See pp. 243–8.

in her details. The occasion, she said, was my "wedding anniversary"; they had been served "champagne" (she did not
attempt to be consistent with her husband's assertion to the
Committee that he never drank with me), and as a result
Chambers had become ill "on the way home." This was,
however, too carelessly contrived to be helpful to her husband's new position, for our wedding anniversary is December
11 and we did not move to Volta Place until December 29,
1937. Indeed, an anniversary party in December 1938 (the first
time we could have celebrated an anniversary at Volta Place)
wasn't within the bounds of any of Chambers's changing testimony.

Seven months later, on June 10, 1949, Mrs. Chambers
was testifying at the trial. By then she apparently had been
told that such a wedding-anniversary party couldn't have occurred at Volta Place, but she still did not know *when* we
had lived there. Attempting to repair the blunder she had
made in Baltimore, she fell into a new one, telling the prosecutor, whose witness she was, that she had been to Volta Place
for a *New Year's Eve* party on *January 1, 1937.* She said in a
moment "New Year's Day" and then corrected this to New
Year's Eve, "which would be of course December 31st." The
Judge asked if she meant New Year's Eve 1936, and she said:
"1936, yes." Murphy, the prosecutor, asked her twice if she
meant 1936. Each time she repeated the date. She added for
emphasis:

. . . and furthermore, my recollection is more distinctly made
because Mr. Chambers was given some port at the time and——

Here she was interrupted, and she failed to finish her
train of thought. Murphy finally told her that we had not
moved to Volta Place until December 29, 1937. She said:

Well, then, it must be the New Year's Eve of that year that
they were there—1937?

Within a few minutes the wedding anniversary appeared
in a new version:

Q: Now, you said that was not the only time that you had seen Mr. and Mrs. Hiss, is that correct? A: That is right.

Q: When was the next time, or were there times prior to this you told us about? A: This was a wedding anniversary which we celebrated at Mount Royal Terrace in Baltimore at our house, at which time Mr. and Mrs. Hiss brought a bottle of champagne.

Q: You are not allowed to tell us about——

THE COURT: When was that?

Q: Can you recall when that was, Mrs. Chambers?

A: I would say 1937.

Q: The address was Mount Royal? A: Mount Royal Terrace, in Baltimore.

Thus Mrs. Chambers attempted to salvage her story of a Volta Place wedding-anniversary celebration by using the location in one new story (of a New Year's Eve party at Volta Place) and the occasion in another (of a wedding-anniversary party at Mount Royal Terrace). But both new stories were contradicted by her testimony in the Baltimore libel proceedings. There she had been asked carefully about every period of time during which her husband claimed to know us, including 1937 and 1938:

Q: . . . Now, while you were living at Mt. Royal Terrace [the Chamberses lived there from October or November 1937 until March 1938], did you see anything of the Hisses during that period?

A: I cannot remember a specific instance at this minute. It is rather vague in my mind at this minute.

To fix the period of time in terms of her own activities she had then been reminded that this was the time when her daughter attended the Park School. Still she did not mention a New Year's Eve party, or a wedding anniversary, whether with champagne or with port, either in Baltimore or in Washington, during that winter. Instead, she persisted in her negative reply:

A: I believe not. That was shortly before we broke with the party. I don't remember any time this minute that I did see them at Mt. Royal.

Q: How about Mrs. Hiss?

A: Either—I mean I don't visualize it. It may come to me later on.

Q: Now, did you go to Washington to visit them?

A: Now, I don't remember that either.

Q: Well, would you say you did or you did not?

A: Well, I cannot say—it may come back to me any moment. I don't know.

June 10, 1949, was a Friday. The trial session adjourned for the week end not long after Mrs. Chambers had testified that she went to a "New Year's Eve party" at Volta Place and that we had come to Mount Royal Terrace for our "wedding anniversary" in December 1937. On the following Monday my counsel, Lloyd Paul Stryker, cross-examined her. He reminded her of her story on Friday of the New Year's Eve party which she had changed to December 31, 1937, and asked her if she had been living at Mount Royal Terrace at the time. Her answer was "Yes."

After brief remarks by counsel and the court, the following appears:

THE WITNESS: Unfortunately, your Honor, my memory is the kind that is not good on dates, but associates things, and if it appears that I cannot remember dates it is quite true, but I do know the events that occur at the time and by associating with them I am trying to give you the best of my ability to remember.

THE COURT: That is what counsel is attempting to do at the present time. He is attempting to associate the end of 1937 with the place that you were living at and you testified a few moments ago that you moved to Mount Royal Terrace in October of 1937?

THE WITNESS: I would say that was correct.

Mr. Stryker proceeded to read to her the statements quoted above from her Baltimore deposition and asked her if she still stuck to her testimony of Friday:

Q: Please, Mrs. Chambers. Do you wish to change the testimony you gave on Friday?

A: I wish to put a question in there as to whether it was a New Year's party, or simply a housewarming party. I am not sure about that. But that I was there at a party of just the four of us that is certain.

Q: Now I would like to go back once more: Do you or not wish to change the testimony you gave on Friday?

A: No, I don't want to change it. I would like to say that it might not have been a New Year's party but simply a housewarming party. In talking it over with my husband over the week-end we thought that the second time that I had been at 30th Street might have been the New Year's party instead of the Volta Place. . . . Now it may be, as my husband said, that that was the time we went for a New Year's party at which time he had port. The other time at Volta Place, somehow in my memory is connected with a housewarming party that the Hisses had for their new home. We had sandwiches, which I understood had been served at the cocktail party that afternoon, and then we came on in the evening. Now I may have mistaken that. I am willing to say I might have been mistaken about it, but that I was there that is true.

Chambers in his Baltimore testimony had given still another version of these imaginary celebratory doings:

Q: What can you recall about visits to you at Mt. Royal Terrace?

A: As near as I can recall, they came there for a kind of impromptu New Year's celebration.

Q: This is the one you mentioned yesterday?

A: Did I? I thought there was.

Q: Was that New Year's Eve or New Year's Day?

A: I think it was New Year's night.

Q: It was New Year's Eve, January, 1939? [2]

A: Yes.

Q: That is the time you had the champagne?

A: That is right.

The confusion of stories had become extreme. In her Baltimore testimony Mrs. Chambers had not made the slightest claim of having ever been to our 30th Street house, where

[2] Evidently a stenographic error for "1938."

we lived from July 1, 1936, until the move to Volta Place
on December 29, 1937. (Our tenancy at 30th Street thus included New Year's Eve only in 1936.) At the first trial, however, she for the first time said that she had been there during
the summer of 1937 and that she recalled the occasion because she had brought her baby and it had "wet the floor."
My wife, Mrs. Chambers said in her new story, had given her
for use as a diaper a "lovely old linen towel" which she had
"unfortunately . . . lost" since then. She added to this at the
second trial that she recalled seeing Timothy standing on the
stairs in "long pepper and salt trousers." (Later evidence proved
that Timothy had been away at camp the entire summer of
1937 except for a single trip to the city on August 15 at the
end of my vacation, when he paid a Sunday visit to see his
doctor. He has never had pepper-and-salt trousers—rather
strange garb, certainly, for Washington in summer.)

Cleide Catlett (who had started working for us after the
Crosleys' two-day visit at P Street in 1935) testified that the
FBI had shown her pictures of a woman and of a baby, and
then continued:

Q: Now, at either 2905 P Street or the 30th Street house or
Volta Place house, did you ever see the woman whose picture they
showed you? A: I never did.

Q: Or the baby? A: I never did; never was no baby there.

The sudden addition of new assertions stretched out the
process of positive disproof in those cases where the Chamberses were incautious enough to include specific dates and
other details that could be checked. It was not until after the
first trial that we unearthed a letter from me mailed in Washington on December 30, 1936, to my wife, who was still in
Chappaqua, where we had spent the holidays. The letter made
it clear that as Timothy, who was with her in Chappaqua, had
just come down with chicken pox, my wife was not available
for a New Year's Eve party that year at 30th Street, Mrs. Chambers's final locale for her New Year's Eve story.

In Baltimore, to support her November 17 testimony of
a "wedding anniversary" celebration at Volta Place, Mrs.
Chambers had that day given a brief description of the exterior of the house. She made no mention of the interior or
any furnishings. She had said that the "entrance was to the
left as you went in, on a little stone porch, I believe." This
she repeated at the first trial ("You . . . turned to the left
on a stoned-in porch . . .") and later added: "there was a
white wall." At that trial she was shown a recent photograph
of the building, which she said was "in general the same" as
when she claimed to have been there. Her description tallied
with the appearance of the house after 1947 but not when we
had lived there. Teunis Collier, the contractor for the house,
testified for the defense that the "stone porch" had been built
beginning in late 1946 and replaced a large tree (and several
tons of earth) which had marked the entrance before that time.
At the second trial Mr. Collier testified that the brick wall
had been brick color and unpainted in our time. And in another respect the building was not "in general the same": the
windows in that wall, as shown in the recent photograph produced at the first trial, had been cut through at the time of
the 1946–7 remodeling.

At the first trial when Mrs. Chambers first claimed to
have visited 30th Street also, she had proceeded to give color
to her account by saying that the house was "white" and that
the living room was "pink." At the second trial Mr. Collier,
who had been the contractor for that house, too, testified
that his company had in 1942 painted the 30th Street house
gray, but that when we lived there it was "yellow with blue
blinds" and that he had recently taken wall patches from the
living room which disclosed that at no time had that room
ever been pink. (Chambers, too, in Baltimore had thought
that the 30th Street house was white with green shutters.)

The contractor also testified that between the first trial
and the second trial he had prepared for the FBI, at their
request, plans of Volta Place showing the exterior and interior
of the house as it was when I lived there, and a separate set

showing the house as it was after the remodeling.[3] (He also drew plans of the 30th Street house for the FBI.) At the second trial Mrs. Chambers's description of the entrance, following as it did Collier's first-trial testimony and his drawing of plans for the FBI, was very brief and closer to the realities of 1938. She added at the second trial, for the first time, that trained against the wall "was . . . the usual forsythias cascading." (The espaliered forsythia was still there in 1949, and that spring its blossoms may have appeared to be "cascading," but its bare branches would hardly have given that effect in the winter of 1938 when Mrs. Chambers said she came to Volta Place.) She proceeded to give an accurate description of the 1938 floor plan. At both trials she furnished the house with imaginary wallpaper, bedspread, and curtains.

Mrs. Chambers's reference to the forsythia was a part of her story of a second "visit" to Volta Place which she first recounted during her second-trial testimony. (It is a sample of the strange unreality encouraged by the atmosphere of a publicized trial that overwhelming incredulity was not aroused by a witness pretending to remember wallpaper, curtains, and a bedspread as supporting a claim to have twice been briefly in a house eleven years earlier.) Her account of a "further visit" reads:

Q: How many times were you there [Volta Place], Mrs. Chambers? A: Well, I have heretofore described only one, I believe, but I have a recollection of a further visit there but I can't tell you what the occasion was except that it was later.

. . . .

And, Mr. Murphy, . . . I have a distinct picture of Alger and Priscilla and my husband and myself standing in the hallway of that house and Priscilla reaching out with her left hand and switching on the light. It was about four o'clock or so in the afternoon. Alger had been out all day doing some [sic] something which I have not been able to recall, and therefore is rather bad, perhaps to

---

[3] Mrs. Olivia Tesone, an architect friend of ours, testified that the FBI had asked her "a good many detail questions about the various houses the Hisses had occupied."

tell, but he was dressed in formal clothes with a swallowtail, and we had a kind of a discussion there, just simply jocularly, of the formal clothes that a person in his place would have to have, dating way back from his Boston [4] days where things had to be kept in mothballs, but I am awfully sorry that I can't remember what the occasion was that made him have to be out that whole day, having just come back, quite weary and worn from some duties which were relative to his position, you see.

I only remember this discussion and I remember just standing there in the hallway talking about this just as he was about to go out again.

Later, my counsel in that trial, Claude Cross, bringing out that this was among the new stories of the second trial, received a further comment from her:

Q: That is new? A: Yes. That was my first—I have as a matter of fact remembered that but have never brought it up because it was never very clear in my mind, and I still want you to understand that I cannot remember what the occasion was and therefore have not felt it was wise to bring it in.

Q: My only question, Mrs. Chambers, is, you have testified to it here for the first time? A: That is right.

A significant aspect of both trials was that in their attempts to stretch the period of my acquaintanceship beyond the time when I had actually known Chambers, Chambers's stories and those of Mrs. Chambers never tallied. No one of the "meetings" which they said came after January 1, 1937 (the date chosen by the indictment), and which they pretended to describe, was mentioned by both. And no other witness ever has testified to any such meeting—indeed, no other witness has testified to any meeting that I denied with the exception of a "surprise" witness at the end of the second trial, whose appearance will be discussed later.

In 1937 and 1938 Chambers was living in Baltimore under his own name (previously he had used the name Cantwell

[4] Neither in Boston nor in the State Department (whatever popular notions as to State Department attire may be) did I ever wear formal "swallowtail" clothes.

in Baltimore). Both he and his wife admitted that we had never known them by their real name. He has made it clear that he had been very anxious that I should not learn his name. In telling the Committee on August 27 that a farm he purchased was one he had heard of from me when I was interested in it in 1935, he said:

> . . . Hiss did not know that I was in the picture then. I did not want him to know it, because I bought the house under my name, and didn't want him to know my real name. . . .

Later that day he was even more emphatic. As he had contended that he knew me well, he was asked if I had not visited him at his farm after he acquired it. He replied that it was "utterly impossible" and repeated that I never knew he had it:

MR. NIXON: You didn't let him know?
MR. CHAMBERS: I was very eager that he should not know.
MR. STRIPLING: Why?
MR. CHAMBERS: It was in the name of Chambers.

Yet he and his wife, trying to create a pattern of a long-continued friendship, asserted that my wife and I had visited them in Baltimore a number of times during the period when they rented houses in their own name. (In fact, we never visited the Chamberses anywhere.)

At both trials the Chamberses did describe some of our furniture correctly, although at the Committee hearings of the previous August Chambers was able to recall only a red leather cigarette box (in his Baltimore testimony this became a box "covered probably with a brownish leather"). None of the furniture they described was acquired after we had moved from P Street. Perhaps Mrs. Chambers remembered some pieces from her stay there. Whatever recollection the Chamberses had was refreshed and added to by various means. In February 1949, some months before the first trial, the FBI brought Cleide Catlett and Martha Pope, the maids we had had from 1935 through 1938, to FBI headquarters for Chambers to interview. Chambers was asked at the second trial if on this occasion he had talked to the maids about "the interior of those houses" (30th Street and Volta Place), and he replied:

It would be more correct to say I asked questions about the interior.

Before the Committee, Chambers had claimed that he frequently spent the night at my house during the time that I was living on 30th Street (I lived there from July 1, 1936, to December 29, 1937):

MR. NIXON: You saw him once a week?

MR. CHAMBERS: Yes.

MR. NIXON: After 1935?

MR. CHAMBERS: Certainly.

MR. NIXON: You saw Mr. Hiss—during 1936 you saw him, and through the whole year?

MR. CHAMBERS: I saw him through 1936, 1937, up until the time I broke with the Communist Party.

MR. NIXON: Where did you see him on these occasions?

MR. CHAMBERS: After our first meeting together, I saw him nearly always at his home.

MR. NIXON: Nearly always in his home?

MR. CHAMBERS: Nearly always in his home.

MR. NIXON: Did you ever stay overnight in his home?

MR. CHAMBERS: I stayed overnight frequently in his home.

MR. NIXON: When you say "frequently," do you mean twice or more than that?

MR. CHAMBERS: I mean that I made his home a kind of headquarters.

MR. NIXON: Mr. Hiss' home was a kind of a headquarters?

MR. CHAMBERS: That is true.

MR. NIXON: And you stayed in his home overnight on several occasions in 1936, did you?

MR. CHAMBERS: Certainly, and also in 1937.

A few questions later Chambers indicated his then (August 1948) lack of familiarity with the house in which I was living during half of 1936 and all of 1937 and in which he claimed glibly he had frequently spent the night. He was asked what house of mine he had been in since the P Street house (which we left in June 1936) and replied:

The house on the street which crosses P Street, which I have never identified by its correct name.

On that day he didn't once refer to it as being on a numbered street, though surely once-a-week visits and overnight visits would have left that much recollection.

Cleide testified at the second trial about her FBI-sponsored interview with Chambers:

Q: Will you tell us what was said? A: Well, Mr. Chambers asked me the questions. He asked me about furniture and asked me was it a red rug on the floor at 30th Street, and I told him it wasn't; I told him they had gray rugs on the floor.

Q: What else? A: And he asked me about different pieces of furniture; he asked me about a table which was at P Street and it was broke—he said it was an old broken table. I said no, that wasn't Mrs. Hiss's table; and he asked me about some chairs, and I told him yes, that was Mrs. Hiss's chairs because she moved them, and I told them there was a red rug, and it was in the closet but it wasn't on the floor; they had gray rugs on the floor. He said no, they were yellow, and I said no, no yellow rugs on the floor.

Q: What else, if anything, was said about 30th Street?
A: He asked me didn't I serve dinner for them on 30th Street, and I told him no, that I never did. He said, "Yes, you are the woman who used to mash potatoes." I said, "No, it wasn't me. Of course, anybody can mash potatoes," just like that. I said, "You was never to dinner on 30th Street," and he never was at P Street for dinner.

Q: How about Volta Place? A: No indeed, he never was at Volta Place.

Q: Have you told us all that you recall about the meeting? A: Yes.

Q: Was anything said about his sleeping at 30th Street? A: Oh yes, he said he slept at 30th Street, he stayed there all night, and I told him no, he didn't because they only had two bedrooms, and I asked him where would he sleep; and he said, "I stayed there"; and I said, "No, you didn't, because there wasn't but two bedrooms, and there was a bed in each room," so he couldn't have stayed there.

Q: Will you tell his Honor and the jury just how the rooms were located on 30th Street?

A: On 30th Street? There was a back bedroom and a very small front room, just big enough to get a single bed in, and that is all, and put a table, something small.

Q: Who slept in the front—I mean, was this small room toward the street? A: Yes, sir, right in the front of the street taking up the whole front of the house.

Q: And who slept in there? A: Their son.

Q: Is that Timmy? A: Timmy, yes, sir.

Q: And how old was he when he had the accident, would you say? A: I don't know if he was 10 or 11 years old, I don't know which.

Q: Where did Mr. and Mrs. Hiss sleep? A: In the back bedroom.

Q: Was that with two beds in there or just one?
A: One bed.

Q: One bed? A: Yes.

Q: Was there ever an occasion when you made up any other beds at 30th Street? A: Never did in my life, and I have taken care of everything like that.

After his February 1949 interview with Cleide, Chambers was asked in his Baltimore testimony (which continued into March) if he had ever spent the night at 30th Street. He replied:

That is the point which I was not clear about. I may have on several occasions, but as I cannot recall that lay-out, I cannot be quite sure.

At the first trial he was asked by Mr. Stryker if he had stayed overnight at 30th Street on several occasions, and he replied:

I am not sure.

At the second trial, by which time Collier, the contractor, had drawn plans of the house for the FBI, Chambers put it this way:

A: . . . I have no clear recollection of spending a night there.
Q: Well, do you have a vague one? A: I have no vague recollection either.

In her Baltimore testimony Mrs. Chambers said that in August 1935 my wife had visited her for ten days at a summer cottage along the Delaware River to take care of the Chambers baby so that Mrs. Chambers, who had studied art, could "do a little painting along the Canal there." Mrs. Chambers said that the landlord was a Mr. Boucot, whom she had come to know quite well and who was in and out of the cottage a good deal. At the second trial Mr. Cross asked if Mr. Boucot had met my wife. Mrs. Chambers said he had and that she herself had introduced my wife to Boucot. Mr. Cross went on:

Q: And was he present when Mrs. Hiss was there on more than one occasion? A: Oh yes. He would come in for coffee quite frequently.
Q: He would come for coffee quite frequently while Mrs. Hiss was there? A: Yes, of course.
Q: As many as a half a dozen times would you say?
A: Well, perhaps.

Joseph R. Boucot testified for the defense that he had rented a cottage to a man named Breen in the summer of 1935. (Before the trials we had learned that one of Chambers's aliases had been Breen.) He had seen Mrs. Chambers, as Mrs. Breen, a number of times, for he was occupying another cottage only about a hundred feet away. He said that he had never seen my wife or me there. The FBI had interviewed him and shown him pictures of the Chamberses. He testified that Chambers "is much changed" from 1935, "much fatter, stouter in the face," and he could not recognize him as Breen. The FBI had also shown him pictures of me and my wife, and he had told them he had never seen us before. He testified that he had, indeed, never seen any other woman besides Mrs. Chambers at the cottage.

At the first trial Chambers said that my wife and I had

driven him in early August 1937 from Washington to Peterboro, New Hampshire, to see Harry Dexter White. At the
second trial he said that he first recalled this trip during his
"recollections to the FBI some time in the spring" (of 1949)
before the first trial. In his testimony to the Committee on
August 7, 1948, when he was first attempting to give the impression of a close association with me, he had said, as noted
in Chapter III, that he had once been driving with us "beyond Paoli." The testimony then reads:

MR. NIXON: You drove with them?
MR. CHAMBERS: Yes.
MR. NIXON: Did you ever go on a trip with them other than by
    automobile?
MR. CHAMBERS: No.
MR. NIXON: Did you stay overnight on any of these trips?
MR. CHAMBERS: No.

Yet his story of a long drive to Peterboro included two overnight stops. The first, he said, had been at a "tourist home"
in Thomaston, Connecticut, which he had since been unable
to locate even with the help of the FBI. (The Thomaston
embroidery appeared only in the second trial, when Mr. Cross
was emphasizing the distance between Washington and Peterboro.) Chambers testified that the second night was August 10,
1937, and was spent at a place in Peterboro called "Bleak
House" which was then operated as an inn. He dated the trip
from a performance of *She Stoops to Conquer* at a summer
theater in the town, which he said we had attended.

We proved that during the first two weeks of August
1937 my wife and I were at Chestertown, on the Eastern
Shore of Maryland (from which one would hardly return to
Washington to meet someone living in Baltimore, in order to
begin a long drive north). We proved also that my brother-
in-law, who had just returned from Europe, spent the week
end of Friday, August 6, to Monday, August 9, with us in
Chestertown, and that we drove him to Wilmington, Delaware, on the 9th to catch his train back to New York. (This

was the morning Chambers said we started from Washington for Peterboro.) Mrs. Lucy Elliott Davis testified that she operated "Bleak House" and opened it on August 1, 1937. The following is her testimony at the second trial:

Q: Did you live there? A: Yes.
Q: Were you on the premises 24 hours a day?
A: Yes, sir.
Q: What was the rule or the practice with reference to guests registering? A: It was my practice to have them register on arrival.

Mrs. Davis produced her guest book, which was marked as a defense exhibit and showed no entries throughout August which could possibly have been those of Chambers, under any name, or of myself or my wife. She said she had never seen my wife or me before the trials and had never seen Chambers. She remembered, individually, all the guests who had registered before August 13, 1937—there were only three (one before the official opening date, another on the 3rd, and another on the 6th).

At the second trial Chambers told for the first time of two other alleged trips. One of these, too, he said had required stopping overnight at a "tourist home," this one in Pennsylvania run by a man with "a Polish name." Chambers "no longer remember[ed] the object of that trip" but believed the trip was in 1935. He said he had first told the story, about a month before the second trial, to the FBI. The other new testimony had it that in 1935 we also made a lengthy trip to Long Eddy, New York, "expecting to find a pleasant place to spend the summer" but instead "found a very wretched kind of a shack after the end of a long trip."

Mrs. Chambers testified on various occasions that she saw my wife a number of times for lunch or to go to the movies or to take short automobile drives in the environs of Baltimore or Washington. As far as I can determine from examination of her testimony, Mrs. Chambers came up with another sudden first edition of a story during cross-examination by my lawyer in the second trial. From early summer of 1936 until the spring of 1937 the Chamberses lived at New Hope, Pennsylvania, under the name Breen, with little chance for Mrs. Chambers to be in Baltimore or Washington for social visits. In her Baltimore testimony Mrs. Chambers had testified about New Hope unequivocally:

Q: Did they [my wife and I] ever visit at New Hope?
A: No.

Perhaps she subsequently felt that such a long gap in her recital of meetings and visits was inartistic. At any event, when asked a similar question by Mr. Cross about a year later, she replied:

Yes. I recall one instance of Mrs. Hiss returning from some trip—Mr. and Mrs. Hiss returning from some trip with my husband and bringing me a little rocker, an antique Austin rocker from Westchester. They had bought it at a little shop which my husband later took me to.

One final example may be given of Mrs. Chambers's contradictions, confusions, and evident flights of newly stimulated testimony. This example suggests imaginative building upon some incident she faintly recalled or had later learned of. My wife had as a young girl wanted to study medicine. As Timothy grew older she thought seriously of becoming a medical technician. This was a subject very much in her mind and in her conversation during our first years in Washington. She made inquiries and learned early in the 1930's that Mercy Hospital in Baltimore was the nearest institution at which a course in medical technology was given.

It is not unlikely that during the two days Mrs. Chambers was at P Street in the spring of 1935 my wife in Mrs. Chambers's hearing spoke of her objective of eventually studying medical technology at Mercy Hospital. In her Baltimore testimony, when Mrs. Chambers was attempting to create the impression of having known my wife well and of having seen her frequently, she said that my wife was studying "nursing" at Mercy Hospital while the Chamberses were living on Eutaw Place in Baltimore (this was their address from the fall of 1935 until the spring of 1936):

Q: . . . Did you see her at any other time?

A: I believe it was at that time that Mrs. Hiss was enrolled at Mercy Hospital to learn nursing. She did not stay there very long. It was rather a task. And what with the housekeeping and having to dash back and forth from Washington, it was a little more than she needed to continue with. And it was at that time while she was making inquiries about the nursing business that I did see quite a good deal of her. I probably met her at the Fountain Shop, as I say, at Hutzler's, and she came to the house to stay with the baby one night. And she came to the house several times during that period, mainly through the afternoon, the early afternoon, that she would have to get home in time to have dinner for Alger.

Q: Now, this was while you were at Eutaw Place?

A: This is while we were at Eutaw Place, that is right.

Q: You are perfectly sure of that?

A: Yes, I am sure of that. That is right.

Q: All right. She came to see you while she was studying at Merch [sic] Hospital, is that right?

A: I believe that was the combination. At any rate, I saw more of her there than I did at the previous places. I believe that was true, that she was going to Mercy Hospital at that time.

The undisputed facts, as developed at the trials, are: My wife never contemplated a nursing course. She never so much as started the contemplated medical-technology course. She never took any course at Mercy Hospital—or anywhere else in 1935 or 1936. She did in fact take a chemistry course in Baltimore at the University of Maryland in the summer of 1937, a year after I had last seen Chambers and when the Chamberses, it was shown at the trials, having just returned from nearly a year's stay at New Hope, Pennsylvania, were no longer living on Eutaw Place but at Auchentoroly Terrace in another section of the city.

In the winter of 1937–8 my wife took a further chemistry course in Washington at George Washington University and, returning to her first goal of becoming a doctor, took up with the University the question of entering their pre-medical course. Of my wife's real studies and her real hopes Mrs. Chambers said nothing, because—unlike our friends—she knew nothing of them.

The first trial had one other new story by Chambers. As part of his effort to extend beyond mid-1936 the time I had known him, he testified that in the fall of 1937 I had lent him $400, which he did not repay, for the purchase of an automobile.

Evidence was produced that on November 23, 1937, Mrs. Chambers did in fact pay $486.75 in cash for a 1937 Ford and was given $325 credit for a 1934 Ford traded in. In her Baltimore deposition Mrs. Chambers had been queried about family finances. The source of the funds for the new car (which she bought, which was registered in her name, and for which she took out her first driver's license) was specifically asked about:

Q: How about the automobile?

A: Mother comes in there some place. I don't know. Mother did help us out at various times. She probably gave us the money for that.

Q: Well, now, how many times did your mother give you money? That is your husband's mother, is it not?

A: Yes. That I cannot tell exactly. Mother helped us out in many ways very often.

Q: Well, now, can you give us some idea? Up to this point I have had the impression that you lived off entirely, from June '34 until your husband got this Government job, that you lived off entirely what he was paid by the Communist Party?

A: Yes.

Q: Now, you tell me that his mother helped him out. Now, to what extent did she help him out financially?

A: I cannot tell you that. I don't know. But in the instance of the car, for instance, she did help on that.

Q: You think she gave him the money to pay for that?

A: I think so. I am not certain. These things were taken care of by him, and I don't know. I can only tell you what I know.

In the second trial we put in evidence the contract of March 12, 1937, by which the Chamberses had bought their farm near Westminster, Maryland, making a down payment of $40; a receipt showing that Mrs. Chambers had made a payment of $285 to the real-estate agent on April 10, 1937; and her check of June 25, 1937, on the Westminster Savings Bank to the local tax collector. (The Chamberses paid a total of $650 in the spring and fall of 1937 for the farm.[5]) In addition to that bank account in their own name, the prosecutor brought out in the second trial that in 1936 and 1937 the Chamberses, under the name Breen, also had bank accounts in Pennsylvania, two at Newtown and one at New Hope. The bank books are not clear as to just when these accounts were closed. One of the Newtown books has as its last entry a deposit for $45 on January 14, 1937. The New Hope bank book shows deposits totalling $994 from May 1936 until March 1937. No withdrawals appear here either. When asked by the prosecutor what these sums were, Chambers answered casually:

I do not know. I imagine they were partly apparatus funds.

In June of 1938, Chambers bought a house in Baltimore on St. Paul Street for which he made a down payment of $500. As in the case of the final payment of $325 made in 1937 on the Westminster farm, Chambers testified that this $500 came: "From my mother."

In addition, Chambers had taken a government job in Washington in October 1937.

It is thus evident that during the fall of 1937 Chambers was not without adequate funds to buy a new Ford.

The prosecution made much of the fact that on November 19, 1937, my wife withdrew $400 from our savings account, leaving a balance of $40.46. This sum was used in making purchases for the larger Volta Place house (over a third again as many square feet), the rental of which we then were assured of (though the lease itself was not signed until

[5] Chambers testified that he received the funds for the final payment of $325 (due by October 12, 1937): "From my mother."

some days later) and into which we moved at the end of the next month. Our financial position was certainly not one that permitted lending anyone $400—particularly someone who already had a car and wanted simply to buy a new one. At that time we had just (September 20, 1937) bought on credit a car of our own (paying only $3 in cash) on which we were paying off a $433 note in monthly installments of $36, needing the money for furnishing our contemplated new house. More, our expenses in moving to the new house were such that on December 8, 1937, we borrowed an additional $300 from the bank.

Chambers was asked on cross-examination whether he had ever told the loan story to the Committee or in his lengthy Baltimore testimony and admitted that he had not. Mr. Stryker went on:

Q: Then that was a brand new statement, wasn't it?
A: That is right.
Q: Now let's see. In 1939 you got a job, didn't you?
A: Yes.
Q: With Time? A: That is right.
Q: Then you began [6] working for honest people at regular pay, is that right? A: That is right.

. . . .

Q: Did you repay that loan to Mr. Hiss? A: I did not.

His original account of this fantasy in his testimony to the prosecutor, Murphy, was:

Q: Where did you get the money to pay for that car? A: Part of the money was given to me by Alger Hiss.
Q: How much? A: $400.
Q: And did you ask Mr. Hiss for the money? A: I told him that I was very eager to buy a new car.
THE COURT: Did you ask him for the money? That is the question.
THE WITNESS: No, I did not ask him directly for the money.
Q: What did you tell him? A: I told him that I was eager to

[6] The record here contains a typographical error, reading "became."

buy a new car and that Colonel Bykov [7] was objecting to it.

Q: And what did he say? A: And he offered to loan me some money toward buying it.

We brought out that since the end of January 1949 the prosecution by subpœna had had photostatic copies of my bank records.

Chambers admitted on cross-examination during the second trial that he had spent the period from early December, 1948, during the grand-jury proceedings, until "sometime in March" 1949 "talking with the F.B.I.":

I think I had been in New York talking with the F.B.I. every day except weekends for a matter of some months. . . .

Q: You say you were staying in New York and spending practically the entire time with the F.B.I. for a matter of months except for weekends? A: I believe that is correct.

Q: Beginning when? A: Beginning during the grand jury proceedings.

Q: Beg your pardon? A: Beginning during the grand jury proceedings of last—I think it is December 1948.

Q: And extending down to what period?

A: Extending to about sometime in March,[8] I believe, of 1949.

Q: And, of course, you have spent considerable time with them since? A: I have seen them from time to time.

Q: During that time would it be fair to say that you were spending some five or six days a week with them?

A: Five I believe would be a liberal estimate.

Q: The entire day? A: From about 10:30 in the morning until 4 or 4:30 in the evening.

Q: Over a period of three or three and a half months?

A: Yes, with time out for lunch.

[7] This legendary figure will be discussed in the next chapter. When Chambers produced the papers, "Bykov" came to the center of Chambers's stage as his fearsome Russian superior. Before that time Chambers had told the FBI that he had met him only once and hadn't known who he was until, years later, Krivitsky had identified him as Bykov.

[8] In the first trial Chambers put the period of his preparatory work with the FBI as lasting into May. On June 8 he testified that he went over "the whole story with the F.B.I. . . . from December until about a month ago, I believe."

We showed from our bank records other examples of withdrawals of comparable sums from the same savings account
to meet non-recurring family needs; for example, the following
June (1938) we drew out $150, in September 1940 we with-
drew another $400, and in January 1942 the amount of $200.
We had before this made it a practice to build up a savings
account of several hundred dollars for such purposes. When
we moved to Washington, the records showed, our New York
savings account was $652, which we transferred to our Wash-
ington checking account in the fall of 1935 in anticipation of
larger-than-usual expenditures that fall.

It seems clear that among the things Chambers learned
in the course of his three and a half months or more of daily
conferring with the FBI during the prosecution's preparation
for the trial was the fact that our savings account showed a
withdrawal of $400 during the period of time that he claimed
to have known me. Chambers was asked by the prosecutor
when he remembered the supposed loan for the first time, and
he replied:

A: When I was going over this whole history with the F.B.I.,
which was sometime in the spring of this year.

Q: 1949? A: 1949.

It was during this same period that he visited with the
FBI the various Georgetown houses in which we had lived,
and which he described at the trials, and interviewed Cleide
Catlett and Martha Pope. It is pertinent to quote here Chambers's reply to a question he was asked on cross-examination in
the second trial about a landmark on Volta Place—the police
station he had not mentioned:

Q: Don't you know that the police station is between Wisconsin Avenue and 33rd Street? A: I have been told there is one
there and I am no longer sure whether I recollected that independently or whether I have picked it up in the course of this
investigation.

Apart from the documents themselves, which are discussed in the next chapter, this was the nature of the chief

testimony presented to sustain Chambers's assertion that I had known him well from 1935 to mid-April 1938 and had given him State Department papers dated in the first months of 1938.

The jury began their consideration at 4:20 p.m. on July 7, 1949. They remained out all night, all the next day, and on into the night of July 8, when they did not even recess for dinner.

The long six weeks of trial had ended. The courtroom emptied except for the lawyers, a few newspapermen, my wife and me, and some of our friends. We waited for the jury's verdict, remaining within call of the courtroom.

At 10:30 p.m. that first night the foreman said he foresaw no immediate verdict and the jurors were sent to a hotel.

Just before noon the next day the jury asked that the Judge repeat the part of his charge which dealt with corroborative and circumstantial evidence. They then went on with their deliberations, going out to lunch at one o'clock.

At 3:25 that afternoon the jury returned to the courtroom and the Judge read a communication from them:

The jury feels that it cannot arrive at a verdict.

Judge Kaufman reminded them of their duty "to listen patiently" to each other "with a disposition to be convinced," and he sent them back "to make one further attempt to arrive at a verdict."

At 4:55 the Judge read another note from the jury:

The jury is unable to arrive at [a] verdict.

The Judge asked the prosecutor what suggestion he had as to what should be done. Murphy replied:

Well, your Honor, I think that we should take the jury at their word and discharge them. They say they have been unable to agree and they have had it now for over a day. . . .

I was confident of acquittal, convinced that, despite all the prejudice and fear of the times, no reasonably objective juror could seriously doubt my innocence. I urged Mr. Stryker not to oppose the Judge's evident desire to ask the jury to try again. Accordingly, when asked what he had to say, Mr. Stryker said:

I would prefer to leave it up to your Honor.

Once more the Judge asked them to try again.

At 6:39 p.m. the Judge called the jury in to see if they wanted to go to dinner and was told they did not but wanted additional time.

Finally at 8:55 the Judge read a last communication from them:

The jury find it impossible to reach a verdict.

He said that the new note "seems to be more peremptory and more definite than the others," and called them in. He then asked if any useful purpose would be served by their going to a hotel and trying again the next day. When the foreman said that he believed he reflected the opinion of the jury in saying no, the Judge announced:

Well, that leaves me no alternative but to discharge the jury.

The United States Attorney announced immediately that he would demand another trial. The whole long, costly, wearing procedure had to be gone through again. I was astonished to learn from the press that the jury had divided eight to four against me. Only then did I begin to appreciate the degree of public confusion and bias.

CHAPTER EIGHT

PUMPKIN AND OTHER PAPERS

AMONG the striking discrepancies in Chambers's story of the documents was the contrast between their dates (all the documents were evidently removed from the State Department sometime after January 5, 1938; some bear dates as late as April 1, 1938) and his statements over a period of many years—beginning with his meeting with Mr. Berle in 1939—that he had left the Communist Party in 1937.

On August 3, 1948, one of the first questions asked him was:

How long did you remain a member of the Communist Party?

He answered without qualification:

Until 1937.

And in the statement he had prepared, with time for reflection, in advance of that hearing he wrote:

In 1937 I repudiated Marx' doctrines and Lenin's tactics.

This date was repeated that same day when Representative Rankin asked:

MR. RANKIN: When did you cease to be a Communist because of
   your convictions?
MR. CHAMBERS: 1937.

On August 7, when he was seeking to give the impression
of having known me well, and to stretch the period out as a
lengthy one, he was asked at what period he had known me
and he replied:

I knew Mr. Hiss, roughly, between the years 1935 to 1937.

There is no doubt that in all his contacts with the Committee, up until the August 25 hearing, he had been explicit
in saying he ceased to be a Communist in 1937. There are
numerous references to this effect, of which I shall cite only
a few as examples. On August 3, Stripling prefaced a question
to Chambers with the words "When you left the Communist
Party in 1937." During my testimony of August 5, Stripling
said to me:

We are not referring to recent years. We are referring back
to the period 1934 through 1937.

On August 16, Nixon said during my testimony:

If as much as possible we can limit our testimony to the years
1934 to 1937, it will be helpful because there is nothing else at
issue.

One would think that such an important event in Chambers's life would remain fixed in his memory. Apart from that
consideration, 1937 is the date he consistently gave on occasions much nearer to the event, when faulty memory could
not be involved. Indeed, this terminal date is the one consistent aspect of his otherwise fluctuating story until August 25,
1948.

He saw Mr. Berle in September of 1939. Mr. Berle's
notes of that talk mention no dates later than 1936 and 1937,
and Mr. Berle testified:

   . . . He related a story to me that he had been a member
of the [Washington] undercover Communist group from 1934 to
end of 1937, as nearly as I can recall; that at that time, and ap-

parently as a result of the purge activities which had been going on, he had decided to cut clear of the whole thing. . . .

Malcolm Cowley's memorandum of his talk with Chambers of December 13, 1940, records Chambers's assertion as to his break with Communism:

He resigned about 1937. . . .

Of Chambers's interviews with FBI agents before 1948 we were able to have submitted for the examination of the Judges at both trials only two reports, dated May 14, 1942, and June 26, 1945. According to both reports, as read to the jury at the second trial, "Chambers stated that he was a member of the Communist Party from 1924 until the spring of 1937."

Chambers's interviews with Raymond Murphy of the State Department are recorded in memoranda dated March 20, 1945, and August 28, 1946. The earlier memorandum contains this statement:

The informant dealt with these people from 1934 to the end of 1937 when he broke with the Party. . . .

The second memorandum is more explicit as to the terminal date:

My informant entered into the Washington picture in the summer of 1935 and left it and the Party at the end of December, 1937. . . .

I have already mentioned the following instance in which Chambers, by association of events, as opposed to merely reciting dates, put his break with the Communist Party sometime before the end of 1937. I lived on 30th Street only until December 29, 1937. I do not know why or how Chambers was aware of my continued residence there in 1937, for I had ceased to see him prior to my moving there on July 1, 1936. In any event, he told the Committee on August 7, 1948, when he was referring to the 30th Street house: [1]

[1] On this occasion, as later on August 25, he did not name the street or state even that it was a numbered street, but said it was the house "on an up-and-down street" to which I moved after P Street.

I think he was there when I broke with the Communist Party.

As late as the first trial, Mrs. Chambers, who prided herself on her association of events (and might have been expected to remember correctly where she was living when her husband broke with Communism, as contrasted with imaginary associations with invented visits to or from us), also fixed 1937 as the time by association. She had just emphasized the importance of the event in their lives: "It was a long time in coming and thought out very thoroughly and suffered through, and he finally broke." The record continues:

Q: [2] Now, regardless of the processes, could you tell these ladies and gentlemen of the jury as this man's wife when the end came, now [sic] matter how long the process was, and when did he stop being a criminal Communist conspirator?
    THE COURT: Will you answer that question?
    THE WITNESS: I am trying to, sir.
    THE COURT: If you can't answer it, just say so.
    THE WITNESS: It was while we were living at Auchentoroly Terrace; Auchentoroly Terrace, isn't it?
    Q: When was that, Mrs. Chambers? A: Well, that is what I can't remember. '38 or '37. I have forgotten.[3]

The Chamberses moved from Auchentoroly Terrace to Mount Royal Terrace sometime between October 4 and November 23, 1937. Thus, by association of the event with their residence at the time, she was saying that Chambers's break with Communism occurred in 1937.

On August 25, 1948, Chambers first extended the date of his break to "early 1938," but in the context of his testimony the impression was clear that "early 1938" was in terms of days or at most a few weeks of that year. This first reference to early 1938 was:

[2] The questioning was by Mr. Stryker.
[3] This testimony was given on Friday, June 10, 1949. On the following Monday, June 13, Mrs. Chambers (who in the meantime had been home for the week end and said she had conferred with her husband) changed her answer to fit Chambers's then current account that he broke from the Party in mid-April of 1938.

I was a member of the Communist Party from 1924 until about 1937 or 1938, early '38.

A few minutes later, when he was asked how long he had been a member of the underground of the Communist Party, he replied:

From 1932, roughly, through 1937.

After being asked to repeat his story about meeting me, he was also asked to repeat his claim of how long he had known me. Here again he used the phrase "early 1938" with no indication that this meant any date substantially later than "through 1937":

. . . I then continued to know Mr. Hiss until I broke with the Communist Party in early 1938, and I saw him once again toward the end of 1938.

The known activities of the Chambers family in 1937, as they were proved at the trials, support his statements that he broke from the party in 1937 or very early in 1938. The family in 1937, for the first time, ceased to use false names. In 1937, Chambers had a telephone in Baltimore under his own name and Mrs. Chambers obtained her driver's license in her own name. The new Ford was purchased by Mrs. Chambers in her own name, and she used her own name that same fall in writing to the Park School in Baltimore for a scholarship for her daughter, Ellen.

Chambers also took a government job that fall in his own name. Chambers's testimony to the Committee about this job is inconsistent with the mid-April 1938 date he was forced to select for his break once he had decided to claim that he had received from me papers dated April 1, 1938. His government job, the official records of which were produced at the trials, ended on January 31, 1938. His August 30, 1948, testimony includes the following:

MR. NIXON: After you left the job, what happened then?
Did you leave the party immediately?
MR. CHAMBERS: I think there may have been 2 or 3 weeks in be-

tween. I have no longer a recollection, but I left very shortly thereafter.

MR. NIXON: In other words, you severed your relationship with the party completely a few weeks afterward?

MR. CHAMBERS: I disappeared.

MR. NIXON: Completely disappeared?

MR. CHAMBERS: Yes, sir.

By June of 1938 he had reappeared, for he bought the St. Paul Street house in Baltimore in his own name, dealing directly with the agent in charge of the house.[4] In between he had completed the translation of a book, *Henri Dunant—The Story of the Red Cross,* by Martin Gumpert, which was published by the Oxford University Press in the fall of 1938. This, he said, he undertook *after* his break with the Party, going to Florida "as soon as [he] had the translation and the advance. . . ."[5]

On May 3, 1938, Chambers wrote to the Oxford University Press from St. Augustine, Florida (in a letter discovered by my lawyers only after the trials), that he had not been in Baltimore "for more than a month," still further contradiction of his concocted story at the trials of the date of his "break":

I believe it was April 15.

Wadleigh's testimony gave no support to the April 15 date forced on Chambers by the dates of the documents [6] but, rather,

[4] Certainly not much is left, except the terminal date, of his dramatic prepared statement of August 3, 1948—with which his public attack on me began—that after he repudiated "Marx' doctrines and Lenin's tactics" in 1937: "For a year I lived in hiding, sleeping by day and watching through the night with gun or revolver within easy reach. That was what underground communism could do to one man in the peaceful United States in the year 1938."

[5] Only after the trials were we able to discover from the records of the Oxford University Press and Dr. Gumpert's literary agent in London that Chambers's negotiations for this work began probably in December 1937 and that by early March 1938 at the latest he had received an advance and the bulk of the manuscript. This and other evidence showing that Chambers had broken with his Communist activities, and had perhaps left the neighborhood of Washington, before some of the documents were received in the State Department is discussed more fully in the last chapter, which deals with evidence discovered after the trials.

[6] Because one of the copied documents was received in the State Department as late as 7:45 p.m., April 1, 1938, a Friday, Chambers's story of having

confirms the evidence found after the trials that Chambers had given up his Communist activity by early March at the latest. Wadleigh said that he last saw Chambers that winter "some weeks" before March 11, 1938, the date Wadleigh left for Turkey. He testified at the first trial that "there was an interval, there was a period of some weeks prior to my leaving for Turkey in which I was instructed by Chambers or Carpenter [Wadleigh said that he had given documents to a man named Carpenter as well as to Chambers], I forget which now, not to deliver any documents for the time being." During this period he was notified by the State Department that he was being sent to Turkey. In turn, he wished to notify Chambers and Carpenter that he was leaving. He said that he sent word by the one person through whom he had met and could communicate with them, one Eleanor Nelson. As a result he saw Carpenter, but did not see Chambers.

From his original statements that he left the Communist Party in 1937 and from his August 25, 1948, extension of this date to early 1938, Chambers moved the date forward to mid-April 1938 by continually adjusting his story until the first trial. As late as February 17, 1949, in his Baltimore testimony he said that he was sure he received the typewritten documents within a few days of the dates they bore. (This would have permitted him to fix his break—which he had moved to mid-February 1938 in his account of August 30, 1948—as occurring a few days after April 1, 1938, the last date of any of the documents.) But at the end of the day's hearing Mr. Whearty, who attended these sessions for the government, remarked that Chambers wasn't allowing enough time (that is, for alleged delivery). Whereupon, first thing the next morning Chambers said that "after discussing it with counsel" he "should make it perfectly explicit" that the documents "may have been delivered as much as a week or ten days after." At the first trial, where

---

received the typewritten copy of it from me necessitated his fixing a date late enough to allow for distribution within the State Department over the week end, and its subsequent abstraction from the Department, copying, and transmittal to him.

he finally chose the date of April 15, he was asked by the prosecutor on June 8, 1949, when he had realized that he had broken in 1938 and not in 1937. He answered:

> When I began to go over the whole story with the F.B.I. and in relation to the documents.

THE COURT: What date was that?

THE WITNESS: That was from December until about a month ago, I believe.

At the trials we did not have the records of the Oxford University Press and the author, Dr. Gumpert, so that we could not show that the dates of Chambers's undertaking the translation (which he said occurred after his break) and of his leaving Baltimore contradicted essential elements of his story about the documents. We could only point out the unreliability of so shifting an account of a basic event and the fundamental contradiction between his charge that he received documents from me in mid-April 1938 and his long-continued prior account of when he broke with the Communist Party.

Judge Kaufman, who presided at the first trial, considered this change in Chambers's story so important that he made special mention of it in his charge to the jury:

> In considering the credibility of Mr. Chambers as a witness, you must consider his testimony that he was a member of the Communist Party from about 1926 until the spring of 1938, whereas in his sworn testimony previously given and in some previous statements made by him, he stated that he left the Communist Party in the spring of 1937. The time of his leaving the Party is an important factor in connection with the validity of the testimony that he has given here.

But even at the first trial we were able to show that Chambers's story was flatly contradicted by the internal evidence of the documents themselves. This required painstaking, lengthy, and unavoidably complex analysis of the many documents by my counsel. They compared the papers produced by Chambers with the related original documents still in the files of the State Department. It was difficult in the extreme for a jury (forbidden by established practice to take notes) to follow this analysis. The difficulty of following the analysis was greatly increased by the necessity of presenting it, in the question-and-answer form of court procedure, through the words of numerous witnesses who appeared over a period of many days.

THE PUMPKIN MICROFILMS

The two microfilm strips which Chambers produced from a pumpkin for the Committee, and which were used so extensively by the Committee as "proof" that I had given the papers there photographed to him, contained pictures of fifty-eight pages. These comprised a group of five memoranda dealing with trade-agreement negotiations with Germany, and three mimeographed copies of cables (totaling eight pages) stamped with Mr. Sayre's office stamp on January 14, 1938, and initialed by me. In accordance with Department practice, I had initialed the cables to show that I had seen them and had finished with them.

Chambers testified that all eight documents were given to him at the same time, by the same person:

Q:[7] And they also represent the papers delivered to you from one delivery, don't they? A: That is right.

Q: So that if you know who gave you any one of the papers marked from 1 to 58, you know who gave you all the others, don't you? A: That is right.

Q: There is no question about that? A: Not the slightest in the world.

The photographs were of papers in use in the Department of State during the first half of January 1938. The pages bore consecutive numbers apparently added as part of the photographing process. The microfilm thus was shown to have been the result of a single photographic operation.

Chambers also testified that "there is no possible doubt"

[7] The quotation is from the record of the second trial; the questions were asked by Mr. Cross.

that I had handed to him "each particular one of those pieces of paper." It is easy to see why Chambers and the Committee had thought the film would seem to support his charge. Three of the photographed documents had not only clearly been in my office but when photographed bore my initials. Chambers relied on these in his testimony. The fact that all the microfilm was part of one photographic operation and included these cables "convince[d]" him that I had given all the microfilmed documents to him "and leaves no question whatsoever." [8] Murphy then pressed the point further:

Q: In other words, you could not possibly have received any of those from Mr. Wadleigh? A: No.

Q: Although you were frank to say you did receive some papers from Mr. Wadleigh? A: Certainly, and I pointed out in Baltimore that Mr. Wadleigh was an active source. . . . [Chambers's reference is to sessions of the Baltimore libel proceedings after the indictment.]

Careful examination by my counsel of the five trade-agreement memoranda disclosed that the particular pages photographed had not come to Mr. Sayre's office, but instead were working-file copies retained in the Trade Agreements Division, where Wadleigh worked and which was located on a different floor. We demonstrated that Chambers had been tripped by his argument. If I had been bringing out documents to Chambers for microfilming, obviously I would have brought out the original documents that came to my office, not the working-file copies retained in other offices. Once it was shown that I was not the source of the five working-file copies of trade-agreement papers, then Chambers's assertion that all of the microfilmed papers came from one source negated my having given him the three cables.

Chambers's failure to turn over the microfilm to his lawyers when he gave them the typed papers and penciled notes

[8] At the first trial Chambers had confirmed his Baltimore statements that he had no recollection of these papers being handed to him or of where they were given to him. He had also said in Baltimore that he had no recollection of the person who gave them to him "except as I reconstruct the event."

may well have been due to his wishing to take time to examine them carefully, as well as to his desire to insure continued support from the Committee. Unless they could be fitted into his charges against me they might give his whole case away. His initial caution and his uncertainty as to how to use them against me appear from a brief excerpt of testimony he gave to the Committee on December 6, 1948, testimony which has never been published in full. When Wadleigh was before the Committee on Thursday, December 9, Nixon read to him a brief part of what he described as testimony given by Chambers in New York on the preceding Monday—i.e., December 6 (Chambers delivered the microfilm to the Committee's investigators on the evening of Thursday, December 2):

> Mr. Chambers, I hand you herewith photographic copies of documents made from the microfilm which you submitted to the committee in response to a subpena the committee served upon you.
>
> MR. CHAMBERS: Yes, sir.
>
> (Mr. Chambers examined the document[s].)
>
> [MR. NIXON:] The documents you are now examining are all documents from the State Department, they bear the stamp "State Department, Assistant Secretary of State." [This description fits only the three cables, which bear Mr. Sayre's stamp and my initials.]
>
> MR. CHAMBERS: Yes. I should think from the nature of these documents which I have examined they were turned over to me by Alger Hiss, and I should make the point right here, perhaps, that the same procedure that I have described above in the case of other photographers was also followed by Alger Hiss, in addition to the typed documents. There was, however, another active source in the State Department, Mr. Julian Wadleigh, who was in the Trade Agreements Division of the State Department and it is possible some of these documents were from him.
>
> [From the context of the question asked, it seems clear that this admission by Chambers was made with specific reference to the three cables that I had initialed, the very papers that—because they bore my initials—he later tried to

use as "proof" that I had given them to him and had also given him the remaining fifty pages photographed on the microfilm.]

Perhaps Chambers later concluded that his argument about a single photographic operation made it practicable for him to claim without qualification that I had given him these papers. Perhaps the evident desire of some members of the Committee to find a spy and to convict me, which had long been one of the pressures on Chambers to charge me with espionage, forced his hand.

His examination of the microfilm was insufficiently thorough. Certainly at first sight even the five trade-agreement papers seem well tailored to support his false witness against me. For these memoranda (with one exception) were part of a single related group, the original (or ribbon-copy) pages of which were compiled for transmission to Mr. Sayre and were sent to him as a single file. The group of memoranda was topped by a covering memo of January 8, 1938, addressed to Mr. Sayre by Harry C. Hawkins, Chief of the Trade Agreements Division. Superficially, therefore, the pages photographed on the microfilm looked as though they, like the cables, had been sent to Mr. Sayre's office.

But production at the trial, from the official records of the State Department, of the papers that had gone to Mr. Sayre's office in January 1938 made it clear that Chambers's photographs were of entirely different pieces of paper. Mr. Hawkins's covering memorandum of January 8, 1938, as it actually went to Mr. Sayre, was on heavy paper with the printed letterhead of the Division of Trade Agreements, and was signed by Mr. Hawkins. Chambers's photograph was of a *carbon copy* on plain paper without letterhead and unsigned. The *original* bore Mr. Sayre's office stamp, showing receipt by his office on January 11. The photographed carbon had no stamp. In the last paragraph a correction in ink had been made on the *original*, the letter "s" having been added to change a singular to a plural, a change presumably made by Mr. Hawkins before signing. The carbon had no correction. No carbon copy would have accompanied Mr. Hawkins's memorandum any more than one would send a carbon copy with an ordinary letter. Mr. Hawkins testified: "It was not the practice to send along duplicates with action documents of this kind." The situation, then, was like that of any typewritten letter. The signed original on the sender's letterhead is mailed, a carbon copy being kept in the sender's files. Chambers, to prove access to the *receiver's* papers, had produced a photograph of the carbon copy retained in the *sender's* office.

The same demonstration was made at the trials for each of the other items in this collection of trade-agreement papers. Mr. Hawkins's memorandum stated that he was then forwarding to Mr. Sayre a German aide-memoire (which Mr. Sayre had sent to him for comment the preceding November) and a detailed memorandum of comment by Charles F. Darlington, one of Mr. Hawkins's associates. In turn, Mr. Darlington's memorandum stated that it attached a suggested reply to the German Government. The *original* of Mr. Darlington's memorandum, dated December 31, 1937, was also typed on heavy paper with the printed letterhead of the Trade Agreements Division, and was initialed by him and by two other officials of the Division. The Chambers photograph was of a carbon copy on plain paper and did not bear any initials. The first page of the photographed copy was not even an exact carbon copy made at the same time as the original, but was shown by my counsel to be from a subsequently typed copy of that page, further indication of its nature as part of the working files of the Trade Agreements Division.

The official copy of the draft reply to the German Government (which was in fact never sent), produced at the trials from the State Department's permanent records, was itself a carbon copy, the original having been destroyed (in accordance with State Department practice) when it was decided not to send it. This retained carbon was on blue paper and bore the initials of Mr. Darlington, who drafted it, of Mr. Hawkins, who approved it, and of another official of the Divi-

sion. Under Department practice all white carbon copies accompanying the original of the draft reply and its blue carbon
were exact conformed copies typed at the same time as the
original and the official blue file copy. This practice permitted
a clerk to certify, with minimal comparison and conforming,
each attached carbon as an exact copy of the original as soon
as the original was finally approved. The microfilm picture was
of a carbon copy made during an entirely different subsequent
typing, evidently made for purposes of completing the Trade
Agreements Division's working files. It was certainly not in
the file sent to Mr. Sayre.

Two copies of the German aide-memoire which was being
considered were produced at the trials from the official files.
One of these was the original in the German language and
the other was an English translation of it. The practice was
for an embassy to send such a note in duplicate, an original
accompanied by an exact carbon. Upon receipt, the note would
be sent to the Department's Division of Communications and
Records, which, in turn, would arrange to have a translation
made. It would then record the originals of the note and its
translation by placing a coded file number on the margin of
the front page of each document. Accompanying carbons
would *not* be so indexed. The official record copy of the
original German-language aide-memoire and that of its translation both bore the official indexing file number. The microfilm contained no picture of the translation, and the photograph of the aide-memoire itself did not have any file number,
proof that this was not a picture of the original but of the
exact carbon copy which accompanied the original aide-
memoire and which, unindexed, would have been kept in the
working files of the Trade Agreements Division when the master file of papers was sent forward for Mr. Sayre's consideration of the action recommended. And, as Mr. Sayre did not
read German and as the official indexed translation was therefore assuredly among the papers actually sent to him, this
further demonstrates that the microfilm (which contained no

photograph of the translation) was not made from the collection of papers sent to him.

The microfilm, on the other hand, does contain a photograph of one document of which there is no evidence that
either it or any copy ever came to Mr. Sayre's office. This
fifth document photographed on the microfilm was the official
blue carbon copy of a State Department aide-memoire that
had been handed to the German Ambassador the preceding
July (1937). It had been prepared not in the Trade Agreements Division but in the Economic Adviser's office, and
dealt not with trade agreements but with a prior complaint
by the German Ambassador about conversations the United
States was then having with the Brazilian Finance Minister.
This was the only case in which the microfilm pictured an
official copy as opposed to a working-file copy. This memorandum related only indirectly to the question of possible
trade-agreement negotiations with Germany. As such, it would
have been of background use to the Trade Agreements Division experts formulating a proposal as to trade policy vis-à-vis
Germany. They no doubt had obtained it from the central
files for study. It would undoubtedly have remained in the
Trade Agreements Division's working files until the project of
trade negotiations with Germany was dropped, when it would
have been returned to the central files. Here again, therefore,
the evidence of the documents themselves demonstrated that
the microfilm's first five photographed documents came not
from Mr. Sayre's office but from the files of the Trade Agreements Division, where Wadleigh was employed.

As the proposal for trade-agreement negotiations with
Germany was under consideration by Mr. Sayre in the days
following January 11 (when the original of Mr. Hawkins's memorandum with its accompanying papers reached Mr. Sayre's
office and received his office stamp), there was certainly a succession of conferences in Mr. Sayre's office in which members
of the staff of the Trade Agreements Division would have
participated. The three mimeographed copies of cables reached

Mr. Sayre's office on January 14. When he or I had finished with copies of cables, it was our practice to initial them in order to indicate that fact to the office secretaries who then collected them for disposal. Copies were rather widely distributed, hence the practice of mimeographing them. (Copies of one of the three microfilm cables were sent to at least nineteen offices, another to nine, and the other to twelve.) Some offices regularly received more than a single copy of each cable. With many cables arriving daily, and with little or no security arrangements, the practice was for messengers to pick up the discarded piles of cables from the various offices at irregular intervals. As a State Department employee testified, when "enough to take to the basement and burn" had been accumulated at the "telegraph room" of the records division, the messengers so disposed of them, carrying them as so much waste paper in "little pushcarts they had with wire baskets and they just filled them up and took them down there."

Under these circumstances these three cables, once I had initialed them and had put them in my outgoing box, would never have been missed. My door was always open. In my absence, officers of the Department and even callers not connected with the Department sometimes waited there for my return.[9] When I was in, I had frequent meetings and conferences. While the three cables were in my room or were in the anteroom awaiting the arrival of a messenger, some official (Wadleigh denied it was he) may intentionally or inadvertently have placed his own batch of papers on top of them and later have picked up the eight mimeographed sheets with his own, carrying them off to the Trade Agreements Division. Or they may have come to Chambers via a messenger or clerk responsible for some step in the disposal of discarded papers.

Just as Chambers's actual rental of my apartment for two and a half months (as well, of course, as his fanciful accounts of numerous social visits and trips) is patently inconsistent with any joint conspiratorial relationship, so—as we pointed

⁹ See p. 193, footnote 8.

out at the trials—it is absurd for him to assert that it was I who delivered to him, for photographing, documents on which I had first placed my identifying initials.

THE FOUR HANDWRITTEN NOTES

The volume of incoming copies of cables was so heavy, often as many as a hundred in a day, that Mr. Sayre did not have time to read them all in order to determine those of special interest to him. One of my duties, as his assistant, was to go through the batch of incoming cables and to select for him those which I thought he needed to see. Some I would send to him to be read in full. Others, of less interest to him, I would summarize orally, whenever he had time for such reports. Sometimes a day or more would elapse before such an opportunity presented itself; such a delay was, of course, inevitable during his frequent absences on official business. Occasionally the only opportunity to tell Mr. Sayre of these items of moderate interest was at lunch. For these reasons and because of the volume of cables involved, I made hurried notes on small slips of paper of the items of interest as I went through the piles of cables. These notes I left attached to the relevant cables as I went over them so that if Mr. Sayre's interest proved greater than I had anticipated, I would have available the individual cable itself to hand him when reporting. The slips would remain attached in the piles of cables on my desk until I could make my report. When that had been completed, they would be disposed of. At times I would leave the slips in place to be disposed of with the cables themselves. At other times I would take them off as I reported and later throw them into a wastebasket. When I reported at lunch, I would remove the notes and take them with me, disposing of them on my return.

It was four of these little notes to myself that Chambers produced in Baltimore on November 17, 1948, along with the typed pages. They could have come to him in a variety of ways (for instance, from messengers or charwomen), as the earlier discussion of Department practices demonstrates. In the absence of specific knowledge on that score, the important point that we proved is that by their very nature they show they are not what Chambers pretended they were. His first description of them, mentioned earlier, was as "the handwriting specimens of Mr. Hiss," which they certainly were. Even as late as the second trial this characterization was so firmly fixed in Chambers's mind that he said of his stored envelope:

> . . . in which, as I recalled it, were some handwritten specimens from Mr. Hiss.

But he had to turn them into something else if he was to use them to support his new charges. So he said that I made the notes *for him* "about documents which had passed under [my] eyes quickly and which . . . [I] was unable to bring out. . . ."

Mr. Sayre, in addition to testifying about the general practice followed in his office, said that each of the cables summarized in the four notes concerned a subject in which he was interested. One related to a celebrated, widely publicized, and sensational case of an American couple in Russia to whom our officials were at first denied access, the other three to our neutrality policy, on which Mr. Sayre was frequently consulted by his superiors, and disarmament, in which his interest was marked. The cables to which the notes refer were made exhibits at the trials. They were routine in nature and would not, therefore, have passed quickly through my office or have been impossible for me to "bring out," had I in fact been engaged in espionage.

The notes were shown to be in part manifestly not understandable to anyone but me. They were obviously written hastily and carelessly. Two were in part readily legible only to me; one of these also used a personal shorthand and abbreviations. The other two I had expanded from the original almost illegible summary notes, evidently because on going over them I found that I would need more data when reporting to Mr. Sayre on these particular cables. All four showed patently what they were: notes to myself not intended for transmission to anyone else. As with the three microfilmed cables bearing my initials, it is ridiculous to assume that a conspirator would give a fellow conspirator material in his own handwriting.

The substance of the notes also contradicted Chambers's story. The one containing personal shorthand ("M28" meant to me a cable from Moscow on the 28th of January, and "Lib. Cong., Law Div." the Law Division of the Library of Congress) described a cable which set forth in non-confidential code a commercial telegram received by our embassy in Moscow from an American employed in the Library of Congress. Obviously this would be no news for the Russians, who would have seen the original commercial message sent to our embassy.

Another referred to a cable, dated March 3, 1938, which dealt with discussions between our officials and the British on our respective attitudes toward certain clauses of the London Disarmament Treaty of 1936, then under joint consideration. The decisions resulting from these talks, when reached a few weeks later, were immediately made public on April 1, and were thus clearly not deep secrets. The other two referred to cables, dated March 2 and March 11, which contained, so far as my interest on Mr. Sayre's behalf went, facts relevant to our neutrality policy as applied in the Sino-Japanese hostilities. My notes on the first of these cables recorded that France was not applying strict neutrality toward China, and on the second that our consul in Shanghai reported large-scale fighting in China. These two cables arrived while the Department of State was determining whether the hostilities must be considered a war under the Neutrality Act, with the resulting embargo of arms to both countries. As a formal basis of record for the determination of this issue, and only for that special purpose, the consul's official report of publicly known fact was of importance. (His report was in non-confidential code, inasmuch as the information was public property in the press of the world.) The decision not to apply the Act to China was announced on March 15, when Cordell Hull, then Secretary of State, issued the text of a major address stating that decision and explaining his reasons.

The omissions in my notes on the cable of March 2 conclusively demonstrated the falsity of Chambers's story that I made these notes for transmission to him—instead of for myself, to use in reporting to Mr. Sayre. I had limited my notes on this cable to the information relevant to the pending problem of neutrality. But the full cable, an exhibit at the trial, contained the further information that the French Ambassador at Tokyo had reported "that the Japanese may be preparing for a move against the Russian maritime provinces." The cable, we pointed out, went on to report that "other competent observers of the Far East" had the same feeling, and proceeded to set forth their reasoning in detail:

The Japanese army chiefs realize that today the Japanese people are worked up to a pitch where they will accept any sacrifice in prosecution of war; that if this patriotic fervor is allowed to subside it will be extremely difficult to whip it up again; and that therefore advantage should be taken of the situation to strike against Russia. Furthermore these military chiefs are convinced that they will be able to wage a successful war against Russia while holding the Chinese in check on their flank with little difficulty. My informant added that this was also the view of many French military officers.

In all the State Department documents that figured in the trials (the fifty-eight pages of microfilm papers, and the seventy-two documents of many more pages that are copied or summarized in the typed material), this was *the one passage of vital interest to the Russians.* Its omission from my notes, we pointed out, was consistent only with those notes having been prepared as part of my official duties, which included keeping Mr. Sayre advised of information relating to his special responsibilities and interests. Had my notes been prepared for Russian use, obviously this passage would have been emphasized in them rather than omitted.

THE TYPEWRITTEN PAPERS

In passing on now to consider the sheaf of sixty-five type-written pages whose existence Chambers said he had forgotten until he found them just before November 17, 1948, I should point out that his production of the penciled notes contradicted the very basis of his story of the nature and history of the typed pages and of my having participated in espionage.

To make use of the typewritten material as supporting his new charges of espionage by me, Chambers was forced to concoct a reason for the typing. His original unofficial accounts of his own espionage, as recounted by Isaac Don Levine, had no place for the typed papers. Moreover, his one admitted accomplice, Wadleigh, gave only official papers, never copies typed for transmission. The whole operation, in Chambers's early accounts—and in fact in Wadleigh's case—was a microfilming procedure. Typing would obviously have supplied less reliable copies than would microfilming official documents. The concocted story of typing, not unnaturally, bore evidence of fabrication. The inner contradictions and inconsistencies were numerous, but before going into them I want to emphasize that had my wife been engaged in typing material for·Chambers, as he asserted as part of his story of the typing,[1] the cryptic and illegible handwritten notes would not have been passed to him, as he says they were. If the penciled notes had been made for him, they would, according to his story, obviously have been typed out, eliminating undecipherable abbreviations, illegibility, and the inconvenience of handling tiny scraps of paper as separate documents. The notes are on pieces of paper measuring three by five and four by four inches, from official pads of "chit" paper intended (and used, as the evidence showed, throughout

---

[1] When he produced the typewritten documents in Baltimore, Chambers said that my wife "usually typed" the documents. He immediately added: "I. am not sure that she typed all of them. Alger Hiss may have typed some of them himself." I have never learned to type, and I so informed the grand jury. By the time of the trials Chambers had limited his story on this point to the unqualified assertion that my wife was the typist.

the Department) for attachment to larger papers to which their handwritten contents related.

These notes also contradicted Chambers's basic story in an additional way. As I have already said, the cables to which the notes refer were routine in nature. They obviously did not pass under my eyes quickly, as he asserted. Were Chambers correct in his story that I brought out many State Department documents to be photographed, I would have brought out these cables, too, rather than giving him unreadable or fragmentary accounts.

The penciled notes were, therefore, inconsistent with my having taken part in espionage and themselves contradicted his story constructed around the typewritten pages.

Chambers's story at the trials was that I had given him all three types of papers: documents that had actually been taken from the State Department to be microfilmed, my handwritten notes, and the typed pages. It was possible to disprove at the trials his charges with respect to the first two categories almost as fully as if the burden of proof had actually lain upon me. Even allowing for the difficulty the jury faced in a long and complex trial in following and retaining without notes the details of voluminous documentary proof, this demolishment of two of his three categories of "corroborative evidence" should have led any objective observer to refuse credence to the story as a whole. If Chambers was willing to try to palm off two types of bogus documents as genuine, did it not follow that he would do the same with a third in which the disproof was by its very nature more difficult?

It was not, in fact, until after the trials that we were able to find independent evidence of the forgery of the typed papers (see Chapter XI), but even in the overwhelming press of detailed preparation for the two long trials we were able to demonstrate conclusively the internal contradictions that discredited his story about these papers. In calmer times and in a case in which there had been no such advance distortion of the evidence, I do not doubt that the general attitude would have been to reject Chambers's charges as a whole. This was, evidently, the attitude of the four jurors in the first trial who steadfastly voted for acquittal despite the pressures and confusions under which they heard the case. I am confident that this will be the view of a steadily increasing majority of those, the real Court of Public Opinion, who will in the future give their attention to the case.

Chambers's story woven about the sixty-five typed pages changed even after its first telling on November 17, 1948. To support his use of these papers, he imported into his account a figure he called "Colonel Bykov," his "superior," who bore all the earmarks of Chambers's tendency to build fancifully upon a slight incident and upon what he had heard from others. On November 17 in his Baltimore testimony Chambers said:

. . . Sometime in 1937, I think about the middle of the year, J. Peters introduced me to a Russian who identified himself under the pseudonym Peter, I presume for the purposes of confusion between his name and J. Peters. I subsequently learned from Mr. Krivitsky that the Russian Peter was one Colonel Bykov— B-y-k-o-v, I believe it is spelled and I propose to refer to him as Bykov hereafter, to avoid the confusion between his pseydonym [*sic*] and the name J. Peters. . . .

He went on to say:

. . . I should think in August or the early fall of 1937 I arranged a meeting between Alger Hiss and Colonel Bykov. . . .

Chambers said that I came to New York for this purpose, meeting him in a cafeteria on "Chambers Street" and then going on to meet "Bykov" in a movie theater in Brooklyn.

In February 1949, continuing his Baltimore testimony, Chambers asserted that I had begun to turn over typed documents in the summer of 1937. This, he said, had been at Bykov's suggestion in order "to increase the flow of materials from the State Department." This account required Chambers to change his story of November 17, 1948, and to have me meet Bykov sometime before the summer of 1937. In his February 1949 version, therefore, Chambers had me meet

Bykov toward the end of 1936 or very early in 1937, months before Chambers—according to his November 17 story—had himself ever met the man.

Isaac Don Levine, in testimony already mentioned, told of the contribution of Krivitsky to Chambers's information about Bykov. On December 8, 1948, after Chambers's tale of the documents had been published again and again from coast to coast, Levine said, in telling the Committee about the all-night meeting he had arranged between Chambers and Krivitsky:

. . . And the most astonishing thing that developed that night was the identification of the man who is now in the press under the name of Colonel Bykov. That occurred in my presence.
Mr. Chambers, I believe, did not know him under that name. He simply described a very high top-secret officer of the Soviet secret service in this country, under an alias.

Krivitsky not only gave Chambers a name for the character he was later to build into such proportions, he fully described him and his activities, according to Levine:

First, Krivitsky described him as a man with singular, reddish eyes. He was small, had red hair, came from Odessa, and described him as a very dangerous man.

. . . .

I am sure that he stated that Colonel Bykov—that he, Krivitsky, had crossed the path of Colonel Bykov in dozens of different places, probably from Italy to Holland, because Krivitsky had operated, before coming to the United States, in half a dozen western European countries.

We succeeded in having produced at the trials the FBI report of an interview with Chambers which took place on June 26, 1945, years after Chambers's talk with Krivitsky. This disclosed the extent to which Chambers later imaginatively reconstructed the original Colonel Boris Bykov and gave him an imaginary role in my case:

Continuing Chambers related that other people whom he met while in the company of Peter [As appears from the remainder of this interview, Chambers on this occasion was using the name Peter to refer not to Bykov but to some other individual, perhaps J. Peters.] included an individual whom he believed to be connected with the Russian Intelligence System, who was later identified to him as Boris Bykov by Krivitsky. He recalled that during 1936 he met Peter one time in a theatre which he could not recall. Peter was accompanied by a man about 5 feet 7 inches tall, red hair, slightly baldy, Jewish, very shifty appearance, who spoke very little English and poor German, was approximately 36–37 years old in 1937. He explained that Peter introduced him to this man, giving him some first name which he could not recall, and that he had sensed that this man was connected with the OGPU or Russian Intelligence because he had believed that he had been introduced to the man so that he could size up Chambers. In this connection he also stated that on numerous occasions when he entered a restaurant with Peter he would become conscious of someone watching him from across the room who would get up and walk out of the restaurant after having observed closely.[2] He explained that it was his impression that these men may have been secret agents of Peter who were instructed to check up on Chambers' activities and his personal life.

From a man he claimed to have met once in a theater, whose name, details of appearance,[3] personality, and activities he had learned from Krivitsky, Chambers created for the purposes of his charges against me his imaginary superior. From Chambers's having been introduced to a man in a theater he constructed his introducing me to that man in a theater—again the trick of combining the real and the imaginary.

The fabricated nature of Chambers's story about Bykov was shown by another evident invention contained in it. Attempting to give body to his story, Chambers testified that

[2] Chambers's feeling that he was constantly under hostile observation was apparently a fixed one. Malcolm Cowley testified that in his meeting with Chambers on December 13, 1940, Chambers's behavior had been one of "Infinite suspiciousness." Chambers, having said in effect "that we were surrounded by spies and traitors," "kept looking around the room. . . ."

[3] In his testimony Chambers made use of the information supplied by Krivitsky about Bykov's appearance. At the second trial he described Bykov as about Mr. Cross's height (Mr. Cross is short), weighing about 155 pounds, "with reddish brown eyes . . . and a slight reddish tint in his hair. . . ."

Bykov asked me if my brother "could also procure" State Department documents. This was supposed to have occurred, according to Chambers's trial testimony, in January 1937. My brother did not enter the Department until February 1, 1938.

The imaginary nature of the role created by Chambers for the sinister Bykov was further exposed by Wadleigh. For Wadleigh actually met Chambers's "boss in the apparatus." He met him in Washington and did not meet him until sometime in the latter part of 1937. Wadleigh said that Chambers's actual superior had only one arm. And Wadleigh had no recollection of red hair. In addition, the real superior used the pseudonym "Sasha," not "Peter." Chambers, to avoid the anomaly of two bosses, could only contend that nevertheless Sasha was Bykov and had both arms.

Demonstration that his story of Bykov's role is fictitious discredited Chambers's espionage charges against me as a whole. That demonstration has been placed at this point in my account of my experiences because of the special use Chambers made of this dummy figure in his attempt to explain the existence of the typed pages.

According to Chambers, in 1935 on my own initiative I gave him State Department documents obtained through the Nye Committee.[4] I entered the State Department on September 1, 1936. Yet Chambers's story is that four months later, in January 1937, for the first time after I went to the State Department, it was proposed (by Bykov) that I turn over State Department documents. In contrast, Wadleigh, who actually engaged in espionage, began passing out papers a few weeks after he went to the State Department in March 1936.

Chambers's story that Bykov suggested typing to increase the amount of material also contrasts with Wadleigh's actual practice. Wadleigh never turned over copies of papers typed for the purpose of transmission, although he testified that when he met Sasha late in 1937 the latter especially complained that "people in Moscow thought a person who saw—a person

[4] See pp. 284–5.

who received the papers that I [Wadleigh] turned in must also be receiving other papers which they [the Russians] did not get from me." But there was no suggestion that to increase the flow of material Wadleigh should have papers typed for that purpose.

The whole typing story, like that of its essential character, Bykov, we showed to be inherently incredible.

The typed papers included some verbatim copies of official papers, including cables. They also included a number of summaries of documents or brief quoted excerpts. There was no rational classification which would explain why this differing procedure was followed by the typist. A long and dull report of a non-confidential nature on economic conditions in Manchuria was typed verbatim, as were its related memoranda. This one collection of papers took up twenty pages, nearly a third of the total of sixty-five. Lengthy as well as short cables were copied verbatim. On the other hand, short as well as long cables were summarized. In other words, cables of comparable interest and length were summarized or elaborately copied in full quite arbitrarily. At the second trial Chambers apparently tried to gloss over this variation of treatment by saying that he had told me "we wished" (i.e., the mysterious Bykov and Chambers) to have "some of them typed as nearly verbatim as possible and some of them paraphrased." This described the typed pages, but attempted no criteria for the categories. Nowhere did he offer any explanation.

Another arbitrary feature of these papers was that some pages containing several summaries or excerpts were full, while others contained only a few lines of the same kind of material —brief summaries of cables of the same or closely following dates being put on separate pages. Again, some copies placed date, salutation, and signature as in a facsimile reproduction of the original; others had an informal summary of date, place of origin, address, and sender and then quoted exactly the full text of the message. If these pages had in fact been prepared for espionage purposes, surely some uniformity of relationship to the originals would have been maintained. Then, too, the preferring of loose and often partial summaries and hit-or-miss excerpts to full copies was inexplicable unless the typist, with the purpose of incriminating me, was satisfied merely to show access to the official documents concerned. And in content the documents selected and the passages chosen for excerpting were not of a kind likely to have been of special interest to the Russians.

Most significant, the sole attempted explanation given by Chambers for copying, whether in full or by partial summaries, was contradicted by the documents themselves. For example, the original of the bulky file on economic conditions in Manchuria, which accounted for nearly a third of the total number of typed pages, was in Mr. Sayre's office from February 16, 1938, until March 11. Chambers's story is that he collected papers from me once every week or ten days. Here, clearly, there could have been no increase in the "flow" by a laborious typing job. Had I actually been supplying Chambers with documents, this batch of papers would have been available for microfilming at any time for nearly a month.

The same thing is true of a memorandum of February 18, 1938, that Mr. Sayre had written of a conversation he had with the Czechoslovak Minister, copies of which went to the Trade Agreements and other divisions. In the typed papers Chambers produced, this memorandum was copied in full in facsimile form. A copy was of course retained permanently in Mr. Sayre's office files. If I had in fact been seeing Chambers in 1938 and giving him documents, most evidently this, too, was a document I would have taken home on some day that I was to meet him, so that he could have a photograph of an authentic official copy.

Some of the typed pages were based on documents of which no copy ever came to my office at all. Here Chambers slipped clumsily in his assembly of material. As to one of these the slip was especially bad. Not only did I never see the underlying original document, but—as the prosecution admitted— the typed copy was not even typed on a Woodstock machine, the otherwise quite skillful and essential element in the whole procedure of forgery by typewriter.

Before discussing that document, therefore, it is helpful to go into the question of the Woodstock typewriter. When my father-in-law, Mr. Thomas Fansler, retired from business in the early 1930's, he gave my wife a Woodstock office-type machine that had been in use in his office in Philadelphia. At just about that time my wife was engaged in preparing a manuscript, of which she was a joint author, of a book on the teaching of fine arts which was published in 1934. The machine was helpful to her in typing some of the manuscript. She continued to use it for occasional typing into 1937. (The latest instance of her use of the old machine, following our own search for samples of typing and a country-wide search by the FBI, is a letter of May 25, 1937, applying for admission to the University of Maryland's course in inorganic chemistry.) The machine by then was in poor condition and inconvenient to use; some of the keys stuck, and the roller had to be turned directly by hand. In the fall of that year my wife bought a portable.

As part of our move to Volta Place in Georgetown (on December 29, 1937) we gave the heavy old machine to Cleide's teen-aged sons, Perry (Pat) and Raymond (Mike) Catlett, who washed windows and did other odd jobs for us and to whom we often gave items that had outlived their usefulness for us but still had wear left in them. Perry, in particular, was gifted mechanically and interested in mechanical equipment. By 1948 my wife and I had both completely forgotten how we had disposed of the old Woodstock and didn't even recall its make. Timothy was the only one of us who thought it might have gone to the Catlett boys, his own contemporaries. In the end it was Mike who, in the spring of 1949, came to my brother in Washington to solve the mystery with the information that we had given it to him and his brother years before. He and his brother were able to remember the various places other than their mother's house where it had subsequently been taken before it was picked up in 1945 by Ira

Lockey, a trucker, apparently as partial payment for some moving. Lockey, who had found it in a back yard in the rain,
testified:

Well, after I got it it was in such bad condition that I didn't
think it was worthwhile to have it repaired; but I got it for my
daughter to type on because at that particular time she was taking
typing. I gave it to her.

Just six weeks before the first trial began, my attorneys
found the machine still in Lockey's house. As he said, "that
is where it just stayed, because no one ever used it [after his
daughter's initial use], it was in such bad condition, couldn't
even have it repaired at that time."

Perry Catlett testified that we gave him the typewriter
"during the time they were moving; between 30th Street and
Volta Place." On May 28, 1949, three days before the trial
began, Perry had signed a statement prepared for him by the
FBI. In addition to his statement that he had received the
tpyewriter "during the period" of the moving, this statement
contained the further sentences: "I can't remember whether
they gave it to me before they moved or after they had moved
to Volta Place. They could have lived on Volta Place for
several months before they gave it to me." But on the stand
Perry, who was then working at the War Department, said:

I did not tell him [the FBI agent] that they gave it to me
after they moved in Volta Place. . . .

. . . .

That is a mistake. He wrote that hisself.

Mike, the younger brother, also associated receiving the
typewriter with our moving: "I would say it was one of the
moves." (It could not have been during an earlier move, and
Mike was no longer doing odd jobs for us when we left Volta
Place in 1943.) He testified that he also remembered receiving
"some clothes, some books and a tie rack" at the same time.

Apart from the fact that one normally disposes of excess
belongings at the time of preparing to move, my wife and I

have no way of being certain from direct memory, so long after the event, just when we gave the typewriter to the Catlett boys. The boys' account of the gift did, however, remind my wife of the incident, which she, too, then related to the move to Volta Place.

Identification of this as the general period of the gift— whether in anticipation of leaving 30th Street or soon after we arrived at Volta Place but before completely settling in— was supported by the prosecution's evidence, too. They produced at the second trial a Sergeant Roulhac, then on active army duty, who had been a boarder at the Catletts'. He said that he first saw the typewriter "about three months after we lived there" (referring to a house to which the Catletts moved late in 1937 or in January 1938, the lease being dated January 17 —according to Roulhac, they "moved in the same day we signed that lease"). He said that he saw the typewriter "out in the hallway on the washing machine."

Sergeant Roulhac's testimony, "about three months" from January 17, was a bit too close to the needs of Chambers's story to be convincing as a recollection of an event that had occurred more than eleven years before. In any event, he could testify only as to when *he* had first seen it, and the hallway location would indicate that by then the boys were already tired of their first interest in a new toy. Mike said that at first they had kept it in "the den."

The prosecution's whole case with respect to the typewritten pages produced by Chambers, some dated as late as April 1938, was based on their expert's testimony that in his opinion "the same machine" was used to type those pages and to type the various personal letters and statements which my wife had indeed typed on our old Woodstock. Had the case arisen nearer the events involved, we could have firmly established the date we gave the machine to the Catlett boys. With the fact established that the machine was not in our possession after December 29, 1937, or a few days later, the expert's testimony could in no way support Chambers's charges. It would, on the contrary, be evidence that the documents, all dated between January 5, 1938, and April 1, 1938, had been copied or summarized by someone else in an obvious attempt to link me with the documents. The date the Catlett boys remembered as that on which they received the machine was consistent only with forgery by typewriter.

But after the lapse of more than eleven years, exact dates of such events are hard to establish incontrovertibly. Pat said that he had taken the typewriter to the Catletts' new house, to which he was sure they had moved before we moved to Volta Place (I recall the same sequence of the two moves). Roulhac said that they moved in on the day they signed the lease. Mike said that for "a good while" after their move they had used kerosene lamps for light. According to the utility records, the electricity was turned on January 17, and Roulhac said that they were without electricity for only a day. Pat recalled taking the machine to a repair shop, the general location of which he gave, "Shortly after" he got it. There he was told it could not be repaired because the Woodstock people were out of business. The prosecutor showed that on March 29, 1938, the Woodstock Company leased space in the neighborhood Pat had described (a fact which tended to support Pat's recollection that he had received the typewriter about the first of the year, for it proved that at the time when he thought he had gone to get the machine repaired the Woodstock concern was indeed not in business in that neighborhood). With these minor differences or supposed differences and the length of time that had passed, the prosecutor apparently felt that he could argue that we gave the typewriter to the boys "when Chambers broke with the Party" and that we did so to get rid of it as an incriminating item. The spirit of prejudice and the absence of objectivity prevailing at the time apparently made it plausible to some minds that (1) an identifiable old machine would be used for conspiratorial work and (2) that a guilty person would dispose of it by giving it to members of his own household staff.

From evidence of forgery (by the typing of papers on the machine to implicate me), the typewriter—which we, not the prosecution, produced at the trial—was thus turned by the prosecution into a major exhibit in support of Chambers. Logically, of course, the production of pages typed on an identifiable machine is no proof at all as to who used the machine in typing the pages. The prosecution's typewriting expert made no attempt to identify the typist. There was no fingerprint evidence to show that my wife or I had ever touched any of these sixty-five pages. Judge Kaufman in the first trial was, therefore, asked to dismiss the indictment on the ground that the prosecution had "wholly failed to corroborate Chambers" and that therefore the jury should not even be allowed to consider the case. In denying the motion he said:

. . . I am very frank to say that I am deeply troubled by the question in the light (and I think it is a very important legal question that will survive a verdict in this case, if there is an adverse verdict) [5] of the rulings of the Circuit Court of Appeals and the Supreme Court not to dismiss indictments where there is some evidence, even though it is an arguable question. . . .

. . . . .

I have stated the reasons. I think there is a very substantial question of law that will continue in this case for all time.

This was said at a time when my counsel and I accepted uncritically the view, championed by the prosecution and disproved by us only after the trials, that each typewriter—like a fingerprint—is unique, from which it would follow that a duplicate machine capable of reproducing the same idiosyncrasies or flaws was an impossibility. But we knew even then that the papers could have been typed, from microfilmed copies of documents or from documents later brought from the files of the State Department, at any time before November 17, 1948. We knew that Chambers could, without our knowledge, have located the machine and got access to it for the time that would be needed to type sixty-four pages (one page was typed on a different machine), many of them with only a few lines of typing. The Catletts took boarders who, natu-

[5] Parentheses added as clarifying punctuation.

rally, changed from time to time. The house was often full of visitors. One of the boarders or a friend of the house could for a modest payment have let Chambers use the machine without the Catletts' knowing or caring.

As my account of our analysis of the typed pages has shown, we did not stop with the evidence that the machine had been disposed of to the Catletts before the papers had come into existence. We showed that the very papers themselves contradicted Chambers's charge that I had given them to him. As already noted, one of the sixty-five pages was not even typed on a Woodstock. The prosecution's expert thought it had been typed on a Royal machine. The paper had a government watermark; none of the other typed pages had any watermark. The prosecutor, under these circumstances, naturally excepted this one page from most of his attention. But not Chambers.

From November 17, 1948, on he insisted that I had given it to him, until, on November 28, 1949, late in his cross-examination in the second trial, he seemed to realize that in this instance his charge was untenable. For the first time he then said, a year after his production of the documents, that he merely *believed* that I had given it to him, but was not sure. In his Baltimore testimony he had without hesitation or qualification said that he was sure; and he had raised no doubt at the first trial, when his testimony had preceded that of the typewriting expert. He had made no qualification in his direct testimony for the prosecution even at this second trial. But when these contradictions were pointed out to him, he went on to say that this paper might have been given to him by Harry Dexter White. When Mr. Cross inquired if this wasn't the first time Chambers had made that suggestion, Chambers acknowledged that it was. The transcript of the record at this point continues as follows:

Q: And Harry White is dead? A: That is also true.

Q: And when did you tell Mr. Murphy that? Have you told Mr. Murphy that? A: That just crossed my mind now as I looked at the report.

Q: And you have never told the F.B.I., or Mr. Murphy, or anyone representing the Government, that Harry Dexter White may have handed you that paper? A: No, I have not yet had time to.

But the next day Chambers reverted to his attempt to brazen out his position, asserting:

I believe Alger Hiss gave me that paper.

Here again we had an example of clear proof of false witness, this time by a demonstration that one of the typed papers themselves could not be what he had pretended it was. This particular piece of paper indicated also that, in addition to a source, or sources, of material in the Trade Agreements Division, Chambers was receiving papers from someone in the Far Eastern Division. For this paper, known in the trials as Baltimore Exhibit No. 10, was an excerpt from a document which went only to that Division. That document, also an exhibit at the trials, was a report of January 7, 1938, prepared by the Military Intelligence Division of the War Department. It was sent to the Chief of the Far Eastern Division and bore the receiving stamps only of that Division (dated January 18, 1938) and the division of records, which filed it on February 8.

Chambers's story was that "the papers that were brought out were what Mr. Hiss had on his desk that day or a selection therefrom." Therefore, demonstration that any one of the documents copied or summarized on a Woodstock typewriter did not come to my desk would undo Chambers's entire story about the typing. The typing must then have been undertaken, whenever it was done, only to incriminate me.

Despite the wide circulation of copies of cables to many offices, the evidence was that copies of two of the cables summarized on the pages Chambers produced never went to Mr. Sayre's office. One of these, dated January 22, 1938, was summarized on the same page with five other cables ranging in date from January 22 to January 29. We pointed out that as I had not received one item on the page, it followed that I could not have been the source for the page. Three other pages summarized eleven cables dated from January 21 to February 2;

all four pages made up a group so closely related in date and appearance as to indicate that they were removed from the State Department as a group, and that the same conclusion, therefore, applied to them. The other cable shown not to have been designated for circulation to Mr. Sayre was dated March 28. It was summarized on the same page with another cable and was one of twenty-one documents (summarized or copied on eleven of the typewritten pages) that appear to have been removed from the State Department as a group subsequent to April 1. It is *possible* that, though not recorded as having been sent to Mr. Sayre's office, copies of these two were actually sent to him. In that sense we could not *prove* that they were not. The only available evidence was, however, that they did not come to his office.

However, as to one other page, we were able to prove conclusively that the brief memorandum it quoted had at no time been in Mr. Sayre's office. This memorandum was dated February 9 and was known in the trials as State Exhibit No. 13.[6] It was prepared in the Far Eastern Division and referred to a brief dispatch from Japan not copied or summarized in the typewritten pages. From the receiving stamps on the dispatch, to which the memorandum was attached as a summary, it was evident that the dispatch and the memorandum went to only two offices besides the Far Eastern Division before being filed. Neither of these was Mr. Sayre's office.[7] But a carbon copy of the memorandum would have remained in the working files of the Far Eastern Division, where, as Baltimore Exhibit No. 10 shows, Chambers appears to have had a source.

[6] Three other memoranda and twenty-five cables (summarized or copied on thirty of the typewritten pages) range in date from February 7 to February 18 and seem to form with the memorandum of February 9 a group taken from the State Department at the same time. (They include Mr. Sayre's memorandum of February 18 of a talk with the Czechoslovak Minister and the lengthy file on economic conditions in Manchuria.) Here again the conclusion is evident that if one of the copied documents had not come to my desk, I was not the source for the group as a whole.

[7] An initial suggestion by the prosecution that State Exhibit No. 13 might have reached Mr. Sayre's office by being stapled to other documents was demonstrated by my counsel to be untenable. The demonstration, as summarized in my brief on appeal, appears as Appendix B.

Analysis of the official copies of the cables and other documents on which the typewritten pages were based demonstrated that, without exception, a copy of every one of these was available to an employee of the Trade Agreements Division or to an employee of the Far Eastern Division. The Far Eastern Division, we showed, received all four of the documents that were not proved to have gone to Mr. Sayre's office or were positively proved never to have gone there. And each of the other documents went to the Far Eastern Division, to the Trade Agreements Division, or to the Special Assistant to the Secretary, Dr. Pasvolsky, whose office was part of the Trade Agreements Division's suite of offices, and whose work included the field of trade agreements. Papers that went to Dr. Pasvolsky's office were thus available to employees of the Trade Agreements Division.

At the second trial it developed that the FBI and the prosecutor had never shown Wadleigh the typed material. As a result of this disclosure, he was asked at the second trial, for the first time, if he had given Chambers any of the original State Department documents from which the typed pages were copied. He said he "could not be certain" that he hadn't given the long economic report on Manchuria because "the paper could have come to [his] desk." As to one of the related memoranda, he said that he "might conceivably have turned it over to Chambers or Carpenter." On cross-examination he picked out from the exhibits six or seven additional of the original official papers as documents he might have turned over, plus the microfilmed trade-agreement documents. He testified that "anything that I received in connection with my work I may have passed out," and estimated that the number of documents he had turned over was "somewhere in the neighborhood of 400." (Wadleigh testified that he gave only four or five documents each time. Chambers said ten to twenty-five, which would make the total somewhere between one thousand and twenty-five hundred.) On the basis of his testimony, Wadleigh may have been the source from whom Chambers received, for photographing (after which Chambers was in a position to have the typed copies made from the photographs), any of the original documents that went to the Trade Agreements Division or to Dr. Pasvolsky's office up to March 11, 1938, when Wadleigh left the country.

The dates of the documents and Wadleigh's testimony further discredited Chambers's charges against me. The typed pages referred to no document dated between February 18 and March 26 (except for a dispatch that was summarized on the same page with a cable of April 1). Chambers's story about me allowed for no such gap in his receipt of documents as these dates disclosed. He said he came to collect documents "approximately once a week or once in ten days." Asked expressly if the practice continued until "the latter part of March or early April, 1938," he said that he believed so. Wadleigh's testimony offers the explanation for the gap in dates. He testified in the first trial that "there was a period of some weeks prior to my leaving for Turkey in which I was instructed by Chambers or Carpenter, I forget which now, not to deliver any documents for the time being."

Wadleigh may also have been the source of some papers that did not come to his Division. A superior of his, Charles Darlington, testified for the defense:

. . . I think there were times Wadleigh had a well developed curiosity, I might say, in a lot of things that were going on. There were occasions when . . . I would come into my room after lunch and Mr. Wadleigh would be there reading a paper. . . .

. . . .

Well, he would be at my desk maybe reading one of the papers. . . .

. . . .

Official papers.

Wadleigh disclosed that late in 1937 Sasha, Chambers's boss, said "that they suspected [Wadleigh] of holding back some material." He testified that as a result of Sasha's complaints:

. . . I certainly indicated that I was intending to do my best and that I hoped I would have the opportunity to do better.

He said that he picked up around the State Department, and passed on, any oral information that he thought the Communist Party would like to have, and that he took all the papers that he thought would be of interest to Chambers and Carpenter if he could get them out without being caught. We pointed out that it seemed likely that in early 1938 Wadleigh was making special efforts to satisfy the demanding boss Sasha.

Apart from Wadleigh and a source Chambers seems to have had in the Far Eastern Division, Chambers must also have had another source or sources from whom he received State Department documents. Wadleigh testified that "Chambers had made it abundantly clear he had other sources inside of the State Department." The evidence disclosed also that Chambers in his talk with Mr. Berle mentioned, in addition to Wadleigh, another member of the Trade Agreements Division. So far as the individual mentioned is concerned, I am quite prepared to assume that this was simply another false accusation. Nevertheless, it appeared that Chambers had at that time a second source in that Division or obtained, then or later, the group of documents latest in date from someone with access to the general files. For some of these papers, dated after Wadleigh had left for Turkey, were available to members of the Trade Agreements Division and not to those of the Far Eastern Division. In view of the evidence obtained after the trials that Chambers had gone into hiding by mid-March [8] and may even have left for Florida, it seems unlikely that he could have obtained these documents in the spring of 1938. They may have been obtained by him much later, through someone who wished to assist him, for the express purpose of bolstering his charges against me by copying some papers that could not have come from Wadleigh. Typing of the papers Chambers produced in Baltimore could have been done at any time, from microfilms or from originals obtained for that purpose.

In addition to the internal evidence of the documents and the inherent contradictions in Chambers's charges, there was other evidence in disproof of these charges. His story involved

[8] See pp. 387–92, 398–400.

nightly typing, from the middle of 1937 on, in our house on an old and hence noisy office-type machine. It also included his calling at my house at intervals of a week or ten days or two weeks from 1935 on. His story as to the transmission of documents was that he would arrive at my house between 4:30 and 6:00 p.m. to collect the documents (I don't believe I ever left my office at 4:30, the official closing time, in my fifteen years of government service). Having taken the documents with him for photographing, he would then return them, his story had it, after midnight that same night.

According to Chambers, no friend or other caller was ever present or happened to drop in while he was there—impossible, were his story true, in a neighborhood like Georgetown and for a family with a schoolboy son. Timothy never saw him (or his wife) except during their brief stay at P Street while waiting for their goods to arrive. Cleide saw Chambers only once, at P Street, and never saw Mrs. Chambers. Martha, presumably absent due to illness during the Crosleys' brief stay at P Street, testified that she had never seen either of them.

From July 1, 1936, until December 29, 1937, we lived at 1245 30th Street. During that entire time our next-door neighbors were Mr. and Mrs. Geoffrey May. The houses were adjoining frame houses with a very thin connecting wall. Mr. May testified:

A: Well, after the first few months our relations were quite informal and we would drop in when we felt they would be interested in visitors.

. . . .

A: We were very close neighbors, as you can judge from the pictures, and one of our windows overlooked the entrance to their house. We could not help seeing visitors occasionally as they would enter.

. . . .

A: As nearly as I can remember I would probably leave the office at about 5 and get home about 5:30 or quarter to 6.

Q: What did you observe with reference to the time that Mr. Hiss generally got home when you were living there on 30th

Street? A: I would say State Department hours are slightly later than other hours——

. . . .

A: It seems to me he would come home later than I would by 15 minutes or half an hour probably.

He had never seen Chambers. Mr. May, like the contractor, said that when we lived there the houses were "a bright yellow, with vivid blue blinds, shutters." He was also asked about the thin walls and sounds of typing:

Q: Were the walls of the house where you were living, 1243, rather thin so that you could hear noises in the other apartment? A: They were inconveniently thin.

. . . .

Q: Did you ever hear any typewriter being used in the Hisses' apartment when they were living there? A: I don't recall having heard any typewriting in their house while they were living there.

Q: Did you hear such typewriting when a subsequent tenant was living there? A: Yes; a subsequent tenant was a newspaper columnist and he used a typewriter a great deal.

Q: And you could hear the typewriter in your apartment? A: To my own inconvenience; yes.

Georgetown in the 1930's was a quiet residential district of old houses. To anyone who knew the neighborhood, the suggestion is ridiculous that a conspirator receiving stolen documents would call every week or ten days at the house of a co-conspirator and would then return late that night or in the early hours of the next morning. The atmosphere was essentially that of a village, with unannounced neighborly visits throughout the day and early evening. After midnight the quiet of the streets made distinctly audible the sounds of all latecomers. In addition, Chambers's story of a clandestine relationship involved numerous social visits and trips to restaurants and movies, in Baltimore and Washington. The implausibility is increased by the fact that, as I was born in Baltimore and went to school and college there, I was known to many people in both cities. I learned, as a result of Chambers's charges, of a striking example of this hole in his story. At Mount Royal Terrace in Baltimore he lived next door to a former neighbor of my family's who had known me all my life. This neighbor's daughter and son-in-law rented the Chamberses' third floor. To reach their apartment, they had to pass the open living-room area of the Chamberses. (Incidentally, though all three had known him by his own name, none of them recognized Chambers from his newspaper photographs and testimony. They didn't place him until they learned later that he had lived at Mount Royal Terrace.)

Chambers's stories about me are in sharp contrast to the facts of his actual meetings with Wadleigh. When delivering documents, Wadleigh always met Chambers or Carpenter on a street corner and delivered a briefcase, which he would pick up the next morning, again on a street corner. If he met them for discussions, it was in a restaurant or "in all kinds of odd places." He never went to Chambers's house, he never met Chambers's wife, Chambers never came to his house and "may" once have met his wife somewhere else. After Chambers had broken his relationship with Wadleigh, he called Wadleigh in 1939, "desperate" for money, and asked him to meet him in Jackson Place. Wadleigh's reaction indicates the nature of an actual as opposed to an imaginary espionage relationship:

. . . Jackson Place. Was the man completely crazy? Why, that was a mere stone's throw from the State Department. Appointments with my underground contacts had never been anywhere in the neighborhood of the Department.

We demonstrated at the trials that Chambers's story about the documents was inherently incredible, was internally inconsistent, and was contradicted by the documents themselves as well as at every available point at which the story could be checked by outside evidence. This demonstration was made with respect to each category of documents he produced in an effort to bolster his charges. There was one other charge of his as to documents which further illustrated his readiness to fabricate testimony. Without regard for consistency with his story that Bykov (who in no version of the story "met" me before January 1937) had been the first to *propose* that I turn over documents, Chambers said that while I was still with the Nye Committee in 1935 I had myself suggested obtaining State Department documents for him to photograph. He said that at that time I delivered to him *original* State Department papers (*with seals and stamps on them,* he believed) which I had obtained from a Mr. Green in the State Department.

Joseph C. Green of the State Department, who had been in charge of the Department's relations with the Nye Committee, testified that no *original* documents went to the Nye Committee and that he had given *me* no documents of any kind. His testimony also established that the documents of which he had supplied copies to the Committee were all of a non-secret character and, as such, would have had no espionage value. He said that of thousands of documents, copies or paraphrases of which were given to the Nye Committee, permission was given to publish all except about twenty, in which instances refusal was withheld not for "security reasons but for reasons of international courtesy."

One further incident concerning typewriters was established at the trials. It indicated a sense of guilt on Chambers's part and demonstrated his awareness that typewriters can be used to assert an identification. It may indicate much more. Chambers said that from 1934 until 1940 he had a Remington portable. In 1940 "or thereabouts," he said, he wanted to get rid of this machine because it reminded him of his past. He disposed of it by bringing it from his Maryland farm to New York City and leaving it "on a streetcar or on an elevated train." He admitted that he "certainly must have known" that by ridding himself of it in this manner he had made it impossible for it to be traced to him.[9]

[9] We have only Chambers's word that this vanished machine was a portable or a Remington. In the light of evidence collected after the trials that the Woodstock we found before the trials was a fabricated replica of our old machine (see Chapter XI), this bizarre story of Chambers's may well indicate the actual disposition by him of the original Woodstock.

The prosecution's sole witness on the subject of the alleged delivery of documents had been a perjurer. Though one or another of that witness's stories was *proved* false and the others were shown to be false in essential elements, his entire effort was not generally and immediately regarded as discredited. The very number of the stories, the great number of exhibits and the resulting complexity of our disproof seem to have let the prejudices of the times influence the views of many who could have made no independent study of the evidence. The verdict of the second jury prevented others from exercising their own judgment. The jury, a strong safeguard against unpopular officials, is little or no protection in times of public stress. Any jury would find difficulty in following the oral presentation of the necessarily complex details proving the fraudulent nature of the documents.[1] The conclusions on which the first jury could not agree were uncritically adopted by many when a second jury, necessarily subjected to a longer period of prejudicial comment and national tensions (and initially split, as was the first jury), finally announced its acceptance of those conclusions on the same documentary evidence.

---

[1] "But are jurors good fact-finders? . . . It [fact-finding] requires devoted attention, skill in analysis, and, above all, high powers of resistance to a multitude of personal biases. But these qualities are obviously not possessed by juries. . . ." (The late Federal Judge) Jerome N. Frank: *Law and the Modern Mind* (Coward-McCann, 1949), pp. 178–9.

CHAPTER NINE

CONVICTION BY COMMITTEE

ON JULY 9, 1949, the day after the end of the first trial, the press contained interviews with those jurors who had voted for conviction and *The New York Times* reported that the "prosecutors said they were certain they could convict [me] on retrial." The *Times* noted further that the New York "trial of Judith Coplon on espionage charges had been put over until Oct. 15. It was considered likely that the retrial of Mr. Hiss would be scheduled for that time." (In fact my second trial did not begin until November 17. By what may have been pure coincidence, widely publicized hearings and other proceedings in the Coplon case began on November 14 and continued with few interruptions throughout my trial.)

The *New York Journal-American* on July 9 quoted a juror who had voted for conviction as describing, "in a storm of angry words," the four who had voted for acquittal:

The foreman was emotional, two were blockheads and one was a dope.

It appeared that on the initial ballot the vote had been four for acquittal, four for conviction, and four undecided. This juror's comments may indicate in part the considerations that led to the change of view of the undecided four. Speaking further of the four who remained steadfast for acquittal, he said:

Eight of us pounded the hell out of the four since Thursday night but we couldn't get anywhere.

In the absence of expert evidence as to who had typed the typewritten papers, a clear indication that the prosecution experts had no evidence that pointed to my wife, the jurors attempted to supply this absence of evidence on a crucial point by acting as if they were qualified experts. The meaninglessness of the few common typing errors noted by the jurors is discussed on pages 320-1 and 344-5. Thus, to the extent that any juror relied on common typing errors as "evidence" against me, he based his decision on observations that proved nothing. One juror said, according to the *Times*, that the jurors adverse to me had compared the Chambers papers with letters my wife had typed and had found that *a, q, f, g, i,* and *o* had been applied on top of other letters. He was quoted as saying:

I can't understand why the Government overlooked the typing errors, which were similar in both the documents and the letters.

A juror who voted for acquittal found the respective typing errors quite dissimilar.

There was no evidence on this point at the second trial either, but we shall see that Murphy put to effective use this revelation of the willingness of jurors to go beyond the record and to be their own witnesses.

The *Times* also reported that "Five or six jurors remained behind to shake [Murphy's] hand and compliment him. . . . A woman juror told him she had been on juries all her life and that his summing up was the finest she had ever heard. There was no doubt, she added, that it had strongly influenced a majority of the jurors."

There were press articles about the foreman, one of the four standing for acquittal. The first of these appeared in the *Journal-American* and the *New York World-Telegram* on July

8, the final day of the trial, saying that early in the trial Murphy had told the Judge one of the jurors had expressed outside the court an opinion as to my innocence. The *Journal-American* article said that Murphy had suggested substituting an alternate juror, but that the Judge had said "all the prosecutor had at most was hearsay and suspicion." Murphy was quoted as saying: "The article is correct." Without naming him, both articles made it clear that the foreman was meant. On July 9 and 10, the *Journal-American* expressly identified the juror as the foreman. The foreman "categorically" denied the accusation.

The type of prejudice and pressure which those jurors favoring acquittal had to withstand was indicated by the charge of one of the other jurors, published in the *Daily Mirror* on July 10:

Those who voted for acquittal could not be convinced otherwise. . . . There might have been a Communist sympathizer in the group.

The long arm of the Committee appeared prepared to strike at those jurors who had voted for acquittal. Howard Rushmore of the *Journal-American*, reputed to have close relations with the Committee, reported on July 9:

Nixon expressed extreme interest in the fact that Kaufman had refused to disqualify [the foreman] after his alleged bias was brought to the attention of the court, and indicated that members of the jury might be subpoenaed to appear before the House committee.

That pressure on the jurors was recognized appears from a letter sent after the second trial to the *New York Post* (March 21, 1950) which, as published, gave only the signer's initials:

. . . I was one of the jurors picked to serve on the Hiss case and I asked to be excused for the very fact that I was afraid if I found Hiss to be innocent I would be branded a Communist if I said so. Furthermore, my son and husband would be hounded on their jobs here in the city when the fact was known that I voted for acquittal. That was the opinion of quite a few of the jurors who asked to be excused, which this juror well knows. . . .

In addition to the attacks in the press, each of the four jurors who voted for acquittal received anonymous threats by mail and by telephone. These were reported in the press as still continuing two weeks after the trial. One juror was told to "go to Russia." Another received a note saying "We will trap you soon and that will be your end." The wife of still another was told over the telephone: "Tell your husband that he is a Communist, that he is at the top of our list and that we will get him." Her husband said that "for about three weeks, every night, between 12 P.M. and 3 A.M. my telephone rang. When I would lift the receiver and inquire as to who was calling, I would get no answer. The party on the other end would simply hang up."

Soon after the first trial began, Leslie Gould, financial editor of the *Journal-American*, had written an article (on June 4) unfriendly to Judge Kaufman, alleging that his appointment as a judge had been opposed by a New York bar association. In another article on the same day the *Journal-American* said that as a lawyer Judge Kaufman had been retained by Serge Rubenstein, and that he had been "closely aligned for years with the New Deal and Tammany Hall. . . ." My own New Deal service was then commented upon.

On June 30 the same columnist, Gould, implied that Mr. Stryker, as a member of the New York County Lawyers Association, had helped obtain that body's endorsement for the Judge's nomination. On the same day Westbrook Pegler wrote that Judge Kaufman "is exercised over the uncomplimentary press that he has been getting from George Sokolsky and me." He said further that "the trend and present state of affairs in our Federal Courts . . . have unquestionably brought the honor and integrity of our national jurisprudence into question with many of our citizens and into downright disrepute with many others." On July 1, Gould in an article headed "How Did Judge Kaufman Get Hiss Trial Assignment?" said there was a "mystery" about the question which the writer could not solve though he "put in a day of telephone calls."

The facts are, of course, that the defendant is not consulted about the choice of a judge. On the contrary, the prosecution, in consultation with the appropriate judges, had the assignment made. Judge Kaufman was in charge of criminal cases when the date of my trial was set.

After the trial there developed what can only be called a campaign against Judge Kaufman. In this the leadership was taken by my first and continuing prosecutors, the Committee. On July 9, Nixon asserted that "a full investigation should immediately be made of the fitness of Judge Kaufman to serve on the bench." He was quoted by the press as saying:

> His prejudice against the prosecution was so obvious and apparent that the 8-to-4 vote for conviction frankly surprised me.
>
> When the full facts of the conduct of this trial are laid before the nation, the people will be shocked.

On the same day Representative Case of South Dakota, a new Republican member of the Committee, said the Committee should inquire into Judge Kaufman's "fitness to serve on the bench."

On July 10, Representative Velde, a new Republican member of the Committee from Illinois, charged that Judge Kaufman had shown "bias bordering on judicial misconduct" in my favor. Among his charges was "gross impropriety" for shaking hands with the two Supreme Court Justices who had testified for me. He was quoted as saying that "inquiry into the conduct of Judge Kaufman in this trial cannot be sidestepped." He also said he would not ask for impeachment proceedings at that time, adding that the Judiciary Committee was headed by a former law partner of the Judge, "so there would not be much chance of that anyway." Velde gave as his reason for demanding an inquiry:

> I am seeking to get the facts before the public to show that the New Deal has been covering up these facts for the last seventeen years. You know the number of espionage agents turned up

by our committee and in practically every case nothing has been done about it.

Judge Kaufman was, of course, not without stanch defenders, and there is no doubt that all informed and fair-minded people resented these attacks and were not adversely influenced by them. Their effect on prospective jurors, unfamiliar with legal matters, is, however, another matter. And these attacks no doubt had another important result.

On the 12th of July, Congressman Walter, a new Democratic member of the Committee from Pennsylvania, said in a speech on the floor of the House: "Presumably there will be another judge when the case is retried. . . ." Even earlier, on the 9th, the *Journal-American's* Howard Rushmore had predicted:

. . . It was considered highly unlikely that Kaufman would again be assigned or assign himself to the case.

Despite his familiarity with the issues and the evidence in the case, Judge Kaufman did not preside at the second trial. His place was taken by elderly Judge Henry W. Goddard, who has since died. Judge Goddard had been nominated to the bench by President Harding. His conduct of the second trial was well calculated to avoid any criticism, however irresponsible, of having favored the defense. His rulings will be referred to in the next chapter.

The campaign against Judge Kaufman, having thus been supported by members of the Committee, was continued by the more sensational press. The *Journal-American* sent to the jurors lengthy and slanted questionnaires on Judge Kaufman's conduct of the trial. Their views were soon asked by other newspapers. In addition to having acted as typing experts, the jurors were thus encouraged to become jurists. A juror who voted for conviction said frankly to the *New York Herald Tribune* that "if all this hadn't been in the newspapers after the trial, I wouldn't have thought about it at all." But he said that the Judge's "attitude toward the defense witnesses seemed to be different than toward the others." Another said he was "not versed in legal matters" and so had "no opinion now." A third refused to comment, but others expressed the view, some echoing Velde's points, that the Judge had been partial to the defense.

The agitation went full cycle, Congressman Dondero, Republican, of Michigan, rising to say: "When five members of the jury in the New York Herald Tribune this morning say that the judge was prejudiced in favor of the defendant, there is surely some basis for the charge that the trial was unfair."

On July 10 the *Journal-American's* financial editor found "ample evidence that Kaufman's rulings and attitudes during the trial were detrimental to the Government's case." On the 11th the *Daily Mirror* published a cartoon that portrayed the Judge addressing himself in a mirror as he assigned the case to himself.

When former Secretary of War and former Federal Judge Robert P. Patterson spoke up in defense of Judge Kaufman, the *Journal-American* and the *World-Telegram* evidently thought to hurt Mr. Patterson by publishing on July 11 a note he had sent to me, on the day after Chambers's first attack, in which he said "the stories in the press this morning have not made the slightest dent in my trust and confidence in you." The *Journal-American* returned to its attack on Mr. Patterson the next day. On July 12 and July 16, Pegler continued to blacken Judge Kaufman.

The Committee members found other allies in Congress for their assaults on Judge Kaufman. Eugene Cox, Democrat, of Georgia, had denounced the Judge on July 11. He said: "The presiding judge reflected discredit upon the bench," adding that the Judge's name "is this morning throughout the entire country . . . spoken with censure." On July 13, Representative Macy, Republican, of New York, said that the Judge had "tried to intimidate the press."

The Congressman apparently referred to remarks Judge Kaufman made on June 29, after the trial had been in progress nearly a month. William Marshall Bullitt, who attended several sessions of the trial, had distributed to the press his pamphlet attacking me. In his pamphlet Bullitt (who was one of the trustees of the Carnegie Endowment) had said that after the August hearings Mr. Dulles had suggested that I resign as president of the Endowment. On the morning of the 28th the prosecutor asked me in cross-examination if Mr. Dulles had asked me to resign. I replied in the negative. The same day the *World-Telegram* implied that Mr. Dulles had asked me to resign, and on the 29th, after quoting from Bullitt's pamphlet, concluded:

In effect, government sources pointed out, the issue has now become: Who is lying—Mr. Dulles or Mr. Hiss?

My counsel promptly protested this flagrantly prejudicial comment, and Judge Kaufman, in consequence, said to the jury:

. . . It has been called to my attention that there have been various columnists writing about their views of the case, some of whom have been in court and some of whom have not been here. It is unfortunate that that kind of thing can take place with respect to an important case of this kind, but it is taking place. What the Court can do about it I do not know, but after the conclusion of this trial that subject should be considered, either by the Court or through some other method.

He had gone on in a worthy but futile effort to guard the jury against outside comment:

This jury . . . have taken an oath at the commencement of this trial, to try this case on the evidence as it is adduced in the courtroom without regard to what they see or hear on the outside. That is not evidence, and if we are going to get into trials by publicity the function of courts will end. . . .

On July 18, Representative Keefe, Republican, of Wisconsin, also joined the Committee group that was attacking Judge Kaufman. He made a long speech in which, according to the *Herald Tribune*, he urged the Judiciary Committee to make a "minute" examination of "all the facts and circumstances relating to Judge Kaufman, particularly with reference to this important trial." Keefe went so far as to suggest impeachment—he linked the fact that the House of Representatives has the sole Constitutional power of impeachment with his recommendation for a "minute" examination. Representative Celler, the Chairman of the Judiciary Committee, felt called upon to state on the floor of the House that, as a former partner of Judge Kaufman's, he would disqualify himself "if a resolution of impeachment should come before [his] committee. . . ."

Simultaneously there were attacks upon Justice Frankfurter and Justice Reed of the Supreme Court, who had testified as character witnesses on my behalf. These attacks had begun during the trial in offensive articles, on June 28 and July 1, by Pegler. The *Daily Mirror* on June 28 and the *Journal-American* on June 29 editorially attacked the two Justices, the *Mirror* saying "they have further dragged down the high position of the Supreme Court" and the *Journal-American* beginning its comment by calling their appearance as witnesses "an amazing and furthermore a disquieting performance." On July 12 and 16, Pegler returned to vulgar attacks on Justice Frankfurter.

On July 13, Representative Lawrence H. Smith, Republican, of Wisconsin, introduced a bill to prohibit Justices of the Supreme Court or other Federal judges from being subpœnaed to testify as character witnesses. He said that appearances of Federal judges in any litigation is "against the public interest" and "beneath the dignity" of the Federal courts. On the 17th, Smith said their appearance had set "a degrading precedent" and that "the practice is reprehensible." On the 18th a similar bill was introduced by Representative Keating, Republican, of New York.

The topic was widely commented upon in ensuing weeks and months and was brought before bar associations and other bodies. It seemed as though strong forces would attack any step, however justified, that was taken in my behalf—jurors, judge, witnesses, all were vilified. As with the attacks on Judge Kaufman and the jurors, the effect of these attacks was definite. Because we did not wish to cause further unfair attacks on the two Justices who had known me well enough to be qualified to testify as to my character, we did not ask them to testify at the next trial.

Other prejudicial statements were made by members of Congress. Representative Cox, in paying "tribute" to Murphy, asserted that "Almost single-handed and alone he beat down what was apparently a conspiracy to cheat the law and to liberate a traitor."

On July 9, Nixon in a broadcast interview declared that "the entire Truman administration was extremely anxious that nothing bad happen to Mr. Hiss," and asserted that "A new trial should be held just as soon as possible." As a lawyer, he implied strongly that the mistrial had been due to "technicalities" in that the Judge excluded the testimony of Mrs. Massing (Eisler's former wife) and Rosen:

. . . Perhaps the judge has good technical grounds for barring these witnesses. But I think the average American wanted all technicalities waived in this case. . . .

Nixon went on to say that he would ask the Committee to call Mrs. Massing, adding:

In that way, the American people will at least have the knowledge of what she would have sworn to. And they will be able to form their own opinion as to what effect her testimony might have had on the jury.

He said expressly that Rosen should have been allowed to testify, and complimented Murphy for "a great job against great odds in trying to bring out the whole truth." With this endorsement of the prosecutor as on the side of "truth" he coupled an implication that the Judge had suppressed facts:

I think the average layman wished that the judge had let the truth—the whole truth and nothing but the truth—come out so that the jury could have had every single solitary fact before it.

On July 12, Nixon and Velde announced that they would "demand" that the Committee, in the words of the Associated

Press, "reopen its Alger Hiss hearings" and in particular would ask the Committee to hear Mrs. Massing, Eisler's ex-wife. The Committee did not do so because it might "hinder the conduct" of my next trial. It may be noted, however, that Judge Goddard permitted Mrs. Massing and Rosen to testify.

Case, one of the new members of the Committee, continued his predecessors' practice of assuming my guilt as unquestioned and the statements of hostile witnesses as demonstrated fact. In criticizing Judge Kaufman for excluding Mrs. Massing, Case was quoted as saying bluntly:

> Mrs. Massing was understood to be ready to testify as to her knowledge of Alger Hiss' connection with the spy apparatcs [sic] in 1936.

The constant publicity continued. Judge Kaufman had said to the jury at the end of the first trial:

> This case has attracted much public comment. Numerous accounts of this case, including editorials and feature stories, have appeared in the public press, and it has been referred to over the radio and on television, by news commentators, news analysts, and others.

Though they had at the outset of the trial been cautioned to consider the evidence without prejudice, he had realistically continued:

> You would be more than human if you had been able to avoid all contact with some of the articles in the press or to avoid hearing accounts on the radio. . . .

Certainly some of the accounts were examples of "slanting" the news, a topic the Judge went on to mention as having been a subject of evidence in the case. (Chambers had testified that he had slanted the news for the *Daily Worker*.) The day after the first trial ended, the late Don Hollenbeck commented over the Columbia Broadcasting System on the press treatment of that trial. He chose the morning headlines for a single day, June 28, as an example, noting that headlines "'are extremely important in giving quick impressions to readers," and commented:

> . . . In the Herald Tribune, this way: "Hiss on stand four hours, holds to his story. Cross examination leaves him calm.[1] Clears up discrepancies on auto for Chambers and about typewriter." In the Times, it was this way: "Testimony of Hiss conflicts nine times, prosecutor finds. Cross-examination brings out 15 meetings with Chambers—10 or 11 were admitted. Clash on memorandums. Differences on typewriter and car transfer dates also noted by government." In the News, this way: "Gave Chambers a jalopy and brush-off, Hiss claims." In the Mirror, "Hiss says leftist friendship led to Red charges." You might not think it was practically the same story all these headlines were advertising. Our best example of what you can do with actual testimony, though, comes on the afternoon of June 28th. The Journal-American's leading paragraph began as follows: "The government ended its cross-examination of Alger Hiss at 3:01 p.m. today after forcing him to admit he was an associate of Mrs. Carol King, prominent legal defender of Communists, and a friend of Nathan Witt, ex-New Deal lawyer who was fired because of his Communist activities." Now let's compare that with the transcript: ["]Question: Did you know Mrs. Carol King at the time? [Answer:] I think I met her once or twice during that period. Question: So I think your answer is that you knew her? Answer: I said I think I met her once or twice; that is my answer. Question: Was Nathan Witt one of the people in the association? Answer: I'm not sure whether he was or not. If so, that's how I met him. If not, I met him later while I was with the Department of Agriculture.["] Now that question and answer transcript adds up to something rather different than what the Journal-American made of it in the opening paragraph of its story.

The "trial by newspaper" did not consist only of slanted articles, attacks on Judge Kaufman, the minority jurors, and defense witnesses, and the practice of some Committee members of continuously pronouncing me guilty in public statements. After the first trial the press printed a number of summaries of the evidence in the entire trial, which retold once more Chambers's charges. My task had been the difficult and

---

[1] The mimeographed script here contains quotation marks by typographical error.

unsensational one of proving a negative: I had *not* done what Chambers charged. Even objective reporting of the evidence thus tended to emphasize by repetition the old Chambers stories. On July 11, Wadleigh began a series of twelve articles in the *New York Post,* which (except for Saturday, when the *Post* had no issue) ran daily through the 24th. These were titled "Why I Spied for the Communists." The accompanying editorial display and comment again repeated the substance of Chambers's testimony.

The August 1949 issue of Isaac Don Levine's magazine *Plain Talk,* published in New York, reproduced extensive portions of Murphy's summation in the first trial, in which he had repeatedly listed all the evidence from his point of view, attempted to ridicule the defense, and called me "a traitor." He had, in addition, called me "another Benedict Arnold, another Judas Iscariot," both of whom, he said, had also had good reputations.

The volume of the metropolitan press coverage, and the bias of some of it, convinced my lawyers that a fair trial was no longer possible in New York. Announcement of their decision to seek a change of venue produced another flurry of publicity that began as early as September 23, though our motion to have the case transferred to Vermont (where I had spent my summers since 1938) was not filed until October 4. My lawyers stated in that motion "that the publicity which has been given to this case before, during and after the first trial, by the newspapers and periodicals circulating in the Southern District of New York [which includes Manhattan], has been of such unprecedented volume and in some respects of such extraordinary virulence that the defendant cannot obtain a fair and impartial trial in this District before a jury which has not already formed an opinion on the merits of his case." The motion also said:

An extraordinary amount of space has been devoted to this case by the New York newspapers ever since August 1948. The hearings before the House Committee in August 1948 were front-page news in the New York newspapers for many days. Considerable coverage was also given to the institution of the libel suit in September 1948 and to the production of the films from the pumpkin in December 1948.[2] Further extended publicity occurred upon the finding of the indictment.

The trial before Judge Kaufman was reported with a fullness which deponent verily believes to be unprecedented in this District. The case was first-page news in practically every metropolitan paper throughout the six weeks of the trial. . . .

The motion summarized the prejudicial articles from the trial on. In contrast, it was pointed out "that the prejudicial atmosphere which has been created in the Southern District of New York does not obtain in Vermont and that a fair and impartial trial can more readily be had in that District." The Federal District Court for Vermont was then sitting in Rutland. My lawyers submitted a sworn analysis by the president of Cornelius Du Bois & Company, Inc., an opinion-research firm, stating that almost all the New Yorkers interviewed were readers of one or more New York papers whereas in Rutland only about one in five read New York papers. Mr. Du Bois found, on the basis of sampling interviews, that "people in New York City are more likely to have made up their minds about the case than those in Rutland, Vermont." And those Rutland residents who had read New York papers were "more likely to have made up their minds" about the case than those who read only Rutland papers.

Other affidavits showed that, except for Sunday papers, the New York press had little circulation in the Vermont counties from which Rutland jurors are chosen. The *Journal-American* had a daily circulation of less than twenty-five in one county, a daily circulation of thirty-one copies in another, and fifty copies in the third. The circulations of the *Sun, Post,* and *World-Telegram* were less than twenty-five copies in each of the three counties. The two Vermont papers that circulate in Rutland (*Rutland Daily Herald* and *Burlington Free Press*) published regular Associated Press dispatches on less than two thirds of the days that the trial lasted. These articles were for

[2] The motion reads "1938" by typographical error.

the most part concise and unemotional and contained brief recitals of the proceedings which took place at the trial. Most of
the articles were about one column or less in length. Only one
columnist commented on the case during the trial; two of his
three columns of comment appeared in both papers. Pegler
and Sokolsky were not at the time carried by any Vermont
newspaper.

The *Rutland Daily Herald* was the only daily published in
the city and had the largest circulation in the city of any paper published in or out of the state. Its editor, Robert W.
Mitchell, said in an affidavit:

> That I am reasonably familiar with the state of public opinion
> in Vermont in general and in Rutland County in particular; that
> there is no pronounced public sentiment either for or against Alger
> Hiss or for or against the prosecution.
>
> That in my opinion Alger Hiss would have a better chance
> to have a fair trial in Vermont than in any other place in the
> east.

The motion for a change of venue and its disposition resulted in much additional publicity in the New York press,
most of it stressing the threats to the jurors who had voted for
acquittal. Murphy, the prosecutor, opposed the motion, concluding that if prospective jurors are asked as to their bias and
the Judge is satisfied that none exists, "the statute is satisfied
and the defendant protected." He said that "bias is an illusive
[*sic*] condition of the mind, and certainly cannot be gauged by
newspaper stories which, in their essence, merely represent the
views of a particular writer." Widespread press coverage, he
said, "has not been sufficient to cause a change of venue."

On October 14, Judge Coxe denied the motion in a brief
order. He mentioned from the bench that on his vacation in
Manchester, Vermont, he had seen the New York papers at
his hotel.

I had been confident that the motion would be granted.
Vermont is in the same judicial circuit as New York. What
objection could there be to having the case heard in the one

area within the circuit where evidently the sensationalism of
the metropolitan press was not widely prevalent and where I
had been a summer resident for longer than I had been a resident of New York? At the same time that I asked for a change
of venue, I also announced that I had engaged Claude Cross
of Boston as my attorney for the second trial. I felt that I
needed a New England lawyer for a trial in Vermont, and I
had some doubts as to Mr. Stryker's physical ability, in view of
his age, to go through another long and wearing trial so soon.
This change was also news, as were the postponements which
preceded the opening of the trial, again in New York City, on
November 17, 1949.

During the fall Stripling's book appeared, published by a
company that was apparently organized just in time to bring
out the volume.[3] Originally listed for publication on October 1,[4] it seems to have been delayed from that month until
November. Its title, *The Red Plot Against America*, and its
biased recapitulation of the Chambers story and of my testimony before the Committee added further prejudicial material outside the court record. It was edited by Bob Considine
of Hearst's International News Service and had appeared seri-
ally earlier in the year in the *Journal-American*. Frank Conniff's
praise of Stripling was reprinted from that paper as a foreword
to the book. Conniff's "few words in tribute to 'Strip' as he
takes leave of the task he has fulfilled so conspicuously"
characterized Stripling as "the one man who has really put the
finger on the subversives tunnelling under our form of life."

Those who composed the jury in the second trial could,
of course, have been under no caution not to read the press
coverage of the first trial or the continuing publicity that followed it. And they, too, would have been "more than human"
if they hadn't continued to read and hear accounts of the case
after they became jurors. Judge Kaufman had on the first day
instructed the first jury against discussing the case:

[3] It is listed in the November 26, 1949, issue of *Publisher's Weekly*,
which says that it was the first publication of Bell Publishing Company.
[4] *Retail Bookseller*, October 1949.

Oh, yes. One other thing, members of the jury, and that is that you will not discuss this case amongst yourselves. You will not permit anybody to discuss it with you. Your minds are to be kept open until all the evidence in the case is concluded. Nobody under any circumstances should discuss this case with you. If perchance any such thing happens you will promptly report it to the Court.

Judge Goddard did not expressly instruct the members of the second jury not to discuss the case amongst themselves. His caution was more general: that they were not to talk with anybody about the case or to read or listen to any comments on the trial. Perhaps they would have been more than human not to discuss it together. Perhaps they thought that was not forbidden by the Judge. At all events, we learned later that some members of the jury had been hostile to the defense from the very beginning of the trial and in conversation with their fellow jurors "lobbied" strongly for the prosecution, ridiculing the defense's position.

The balloting of the second jury, like the first, started with four for acquittal. The hostile jurors, reminiscent of those in the first trial who "pounded the hell out of the four" then for acquittal, paired off, two to each of the four, in an attempt that was eventually successful to win them to the prosecution's point of view.

Early in the trial we were informed by the Judge that one of the jurors was the wife of Judge Coxe's [5] bailiff. Somehow this disqualification had not been discovered when she was selected for the jury. The Department of Justice is responsible for much of the administration of the Federal courts generally. Where, as at Foley Square, the United States Attorneys are quartered in the same building as the courts, the relation between court attachés and the United States Attorneys is necessarily close. We considered the likelihood of this juror's being biased in favor of the prosecution. But we were faced with the possibility of the delays and expenses incident to a new trial. I could not afford greater expenses. My wife's and my savings

[5] See p. 301.

and much of my family's were already used up. Except for contributions from known and unknown supporters and sacrifices on the part of many friends who were lawyers, I could not have managed as I did. More was not possible. We knew also the pressures that *all* prospective jurors were subject to. It had required the examination of many prospective jurors to get this jury. We had no way of knowing whom we would get on another drawing. Perhaps we were, in general, overconfident. For these reasons we waived the right to dismiss the bailiff's wife from the jury. After the verdict she waved cheerfully to Murphy as she left the courtroom. (As my wife and I had left the courthouse after the first trial we had seen several adverse jurors dancing gaily in the lobby with several of the FBI agents who had worked on the case. This was hardly the attitude of citizens who felt they had completed an onerous and solemn public duty. On the contrary, this was a celebration with co-workers of having prevented an acquittal.)

At the end of the second trial one woman juror, I assume one of the four who had favored acquittal, gave signs of tears, and we learned that the last of the four to give in had finally given in not on the grounds of his own judgment, but because he did not wish to hold out against the others. Two of the men, one of whom had been ill during the trial, looked downcast. To the desire to end a long and burdensome jury service was added the pressure of the other jurors to terminate their deliberation in time to spend Saturday night and Sunday at home. The partisanship of those jurors who were strongly adverse was as great as that of their counterparts of the first jury. One woman, a leader of the hostile "lobby," when the Judge offered her relief from further jury duty because of the length of the trial (more than two full months), rejected the offer cheerfully, indicating that she had enjoyed herself hugely.

The evidence at this second trial was substantially the same as at the first. Chambers and his wife repeated their stories, which have been discussed in Chapter VII. We still had no idea that it was possible to construct a typewriter which duplicated the typographical imperfections of another machine. We still did not know that it was possible for experts to show that the work of individual typists can be distinguished, and that we could therefore (as we later did) produce expert evidence that my wife was definitely not the typist. Consequently, the evidence on the documents was the same, though perhaps our demonstration of the way in which the documents themselves contradicted Chambers was presented more fully and clearly.

My counsel had received reports that Chambers had been out of the country for a lengthy trip during the very time that he claimed to have seen me every week or ten days. In the interval between the two trials we asked the State Department for any passport applications that Chambers might have filed under any of his known pseudonyms. Early in the second trial we finally obtained from the Department, by subpœna, an application filed by Chambers in the spring of 1935 under the name of David Breen. Subsequently the prosecutor produced a passport dated May 31, 1935, in Breen's name, to which was affixed a photograph of Chambers wearing a prominent mustache that was evidently part of the transformation of Chambers into Breen. Chambers said he had given the passport to the FBI early in 1949, before the first trial.

In the application Chambers, as Breen, had said that he intended to visit France, England, and Italy. Chambers's passport, which he said he had saved, contained uncanceled British and French visas, both dated August 26, 1935. Chambers denied that he had ever used this passport. We were, thus, unable to prove that Chambers had gone abroad.

With his usual agility, Chambers said—for the first time —that I had known him with the mustache. As the application was notarized May 28, 1935, the growing of the mustache started at least a few weeks before then. Presumably the mustache, as part of the Breen disguise, was still in existence until sometime after August 26, when the visas were affixed.

It had never before been suggested by Chambers (or anyone else) that he had worn a mustache during this period. No one had suggested before that I had ever seen him with a mustache (as, indeed, I never had). Yet at the Committee hearings, the Baltimore libel proceedings, the investigation of the grand jury, and the first trial there was heavy emphasis on the issue of my identification of him. His appearance during the mid-1930's was constantly referred to. There had obviously been an intensive search by the Committee and others for photographs taken of him during this time. The only photographs produced (the two snapshots of him holding his child), though unclear as to his features, showed him as clean-shaven. Surely had Chambers believed that I had ever seen him during the months that he had a mustache it would have been brought out as one of his identifying features, more striking than his bad teeth. I have always made clear the fact that I saw little of him after he leased the apartment in the spring of 1935, seeing him only once or twice during his tenancy and a few times thereafter up to the spring of 1936. I did not see him when he left the apartment and have never recalled whether he left the keys with the resident manager or forwarded them to me in some other manner. Whether he went to Europe or not, the belated disclosure that from sometime in May 1935 until at least the end of that summer he wore a heavy mustache is thus additional evidence of the falsity of his claim that after he first met me he saw me every week or ten days.

The new judge, Judge Goddard, permitted Rosen to testify despite our notification to the court that Rosen's counsel had said Rosen "would claim the privilege [against self-incrimination] with respect to any questions pertaining to his membership in the Communist Party and with respect to any questions pertaining to his transaction involving the Ford car which at one time belonged to Mr. Hiss." He did claim his privilege on these matters just as forecast. Rosen said only that he did not know J. Peters in 1936 (the year of the transfer) and that he had never seen me or had any dealings with me.

As the prosecutor knew that Rosen would refuse to testify about the car and would also claim the privilege when

asked if he were a Communist, this witness—it seems plain—
was introduced not for the evidence he gave but to lead the
jury to draw speculative inferences without evidence, to assume that Rosen was a Communist and that, as the prosecutor had produced him, his testimony about the car, had he
given it, would have implicated me. Under these circumstances
the Judge's formally correct direction to the jury not to draw
such an inference was not likely to cure the prejudice. Indeed,
why would he so warn them unless they were likely to draw
that inference? And in his summation at the end of the trial,
although there was no evidence that Rosen was a Communist,
Murphy, in disregard of the Judge's statement, plainly implied
to the jury that Rosen's silence meant that he was a Communist
and that I had given the Ford to him as Chambers claimed.
He said that the Ford "ends up with Rosen," adding:

Now, does that corroborate what Mr. Chambers says? "He had a
Ford; he wanted to give it to the CP. . . ."
You saw what happened to it. Corroboration: . . . Ford, dis-
position of the Ford.

Mrs. Hede Massing testified that she had met me once in
1935 at the Noel Fields'. (I had known Field and his wife in
Washington before he went abroad in the 1930's as an official
of the League of Nations. Some years after World War II, Field
was arrested in Poland or Czechoslovakia. He and his wife have
never since returned to this country. His wife was in Geneva
in the summer of 1949. After Mrs. Massing's story had been
published during the first trial, we had Mrs. Field interviewed
by Swiss counsel. She said that Mrs. Massing and I had never
been in the Field apartment at the same time. Then Mrs. Field
also disappeared.) In fact I had never seen Mrs. Massing anywhere before the FBI in December 1948 arranged for me to
see her and asked if I could identify her.

Mrs. Massing's story of her alleged sole meeting with me,
in 1935, was:

I said to Mr. Hiss, "I understand that you are trying to get
Noel Field away from my organization into yours," and he said, "So

you are this famous girl that is trying to get Noel Field away from me," and I said, "Yes." And he said, as far as I can remember, "Well, we will see who is going to win," at which point I said, "Well, Mr. Hiss,"—I did not say, "Mr. Hiss"—"Well, you realize that you are competing with a woman," at which either he or I said, the gist of the sentence was, "Whoever is going to win we are working for the same boss."

Now, as I say, I don't remember whether he or I said that, but this sentence I remember distinctly because it was very important.

Mrs. Massing said that she had been affiliated with the Communist Party from about 1919 until she "broke with the Russians in 1937" (the same date Chambers so consistently put forward until late August of 1948). She also said she had been in "a Russian apparatus" in 1933. With this lurid background, including her marriage to Eisler, her tale of a supposed single meeting with me could take on, like Rosen's silence, all sorts of sinister overtones.

She admitted that it was "probably" a fact that she had never told her story about me to anyone before she went to the FBI with it in December 1948. She admitted also that she planned a series of articles, with Eugene Lyons as ghost writer, to appear after the trial (as they did). Her appearance at the trial would not lessen their commercial value.[6]

[6] The attractions of my case for actual or alleged former participants in Communist activity, which led persons like Mrs. Massing to attach themselves to it in some way, did not end with the trials or even with the denial of the appeal. (For several years charges even more fantastic than those of Chambers figured in political campaigns and in the hearings of various committees. My disappearance behind the walls of Lewisburg Penitentiary was favorable to the continuing growth of a symbol quite removed from the real Alger Hiss.)

On February 19, 1952, after I had been in prison for nearly a year, Nathaniel Weyl, a writer, told the Subcommittee on Internal Security of the Judiciary Committee of the Senate (the subcommittee was popularly known as the McCarran Committee) that in late 1932 or early 1933, at the age of twenty-two, he had become a Communist while in the National Student League. He had, he testified, at the time openly said that he was a Communist and had written (Communist) articles under his own name. In 1933 he joined the Agricultural Adjustment Administration as an economist. There, he said, he was for *six months after late* 1933 in a Communist "unit" with me and some others Chambers had named, including Lee Pressman. He said that he attended meetings with me on "more than two occasions" and he "saw [me]

Mrs. Massing couldn't remember the dates of her marriage to and divorce from Eisler, of which she had at various times given different versions. She couldn't remember testimony she had given in 1942, conceding: "I have a bad memory."

Henrikas Rabinavicius was a defense witness. He had been a Lithuanian diplomat from 1919 until 1940, when "the Bolsheviks gobbled up Lithuania" and he came to this country. During the war he was with the Office of Strategic Services. He had met Mrs. Massing at the Eugene Lyonses' in September 1949, before the second trial. There Mrs. Massing gave still another account of her supposed meeting with me. She said that she was assigned "to endeavor to contact young men

pay dues," that Chambers was not a member of the "unit" nor was my brother, and that it was engaged "purely in study, that is Marxist study."

However, in April 1943 Weyl had testified before the House Committee that as a student he had been active in Communist activities for some months *ending in May* 1933, but he denied that he had ever been a member of the Communist Party and he said that for a year or so before 1943 he had written anti-Communist articles. He was asked in 1952 why he had not told his 1952 story in 1943, and his answer was that he had assumed "that a man like Alger Hiss . . . would not have remained in the Communist organization after or during the alliance with Hitler" and that Hede Massing had told him that she had made the same assumption. But in 1950, after my conviction, Weyl had published a book, *Treason*, that capitalized on the sensational trials, mine included, of the time. In his discussion of my case he made no mention of his story of my being with him in a "unit" engaged in "study" and, indeed, made no claim to personal knowledge of any relevant information.

Between 1950 and Weyl's testimony on February 19, 1952, there had been one new factor. On January 24, 1952, my attorneys had filed a motion for a new trial based on evidence that had become available after the trials. Included in this new evidence was the the testimony of Lee Pressman (see pp. 337–40, 392–5) that although he had been a member of a Communist study group in Washington in 1934 and 1935, I had not been. This statement was in direct contradiction of the core around which Chambers had fashioned his growing charges against me. Chambers had asserted from his first appearance before the Committee that he had met me and Pressman as co-members of a Communist "underground" group to which he (Chambers) was "attached" and with which he met regularly.

I remember Weyl as a young economist in the Agricultural Adjustment Administration. His story of 1952 about my belonging to a Marxist study group, which I did not, does not fit Chambers's more lurid tale, but—like Mrs. Massing's earlier story—it brought its author publicity. Again like her story, it happened to coincide with the prosecution's needs: Weyl supplied an offset, in connection with my motion for a new trial, to Pressman's testimony that contradicts both Weyl and Chambers.

in the Department of State" and that Field [7]—who, according to her, introduced her to me—and I were both in the Department of State at the time of the alleged meeting. (In fact Field left the State Department and went to Europe before I went to the Department.) She also told Rabinavicius that she "carefully concealed" from the young men in the State Department whom she met "that she was either a Communist or a Soviet Russian spy because that would have frightened them away from her." She said that she was successful in getting Field to join an organization to fight fascism, and that he had said I headed just such an organization in the State Department. She made no mention of the "very important" sentence about "working for the same boss." In the middle of her story she turned to Lyons and said: "Gene, what did Alger Hiss say?" To this Lyons replied that she herself should know. She said that she had repeated her story so many times that she was beginning to be confused.

When Rabinavicius had expressed skepticism of her story, she became angry and said: "Look straight into my eyes and tell me that I am lying." Later she had said to him, in substance (Rabinavicius didn't remember the exact words): "You wait and see; I will write articles after this trial is over and I will have one that will be addressed to you. . . . And if I am permitted to testify Hiss will be indicted or put to prison."

It seemed to me plain that Mrs. Massing, like Rosen, was called as a witness less for the content of her testimony than as part of the atmosphere of sinister intrigue which the prosecutor sought to bring into the courtroom. She spoke with a marked foreign accent, was a self-proclaimed courier for the Russians, and had been married to Gerhart Eisler. In his summation Murphy made his purposes clear:

Now, Mrs. Massing said that she was first married to Mr. Eisler. You can see she moved up on the top echelon in that business. . . . So they had this dinner meeting, and she tells Hiss, "This is my guy, leave him alone." And they get into an argument.

[7] Rabinavicius did not get Field's name and called him Mr. X in his testimony.

And she says, "We are both working for the same boss. What is the difference whether you get him or I get him."

Now, doesn't that show an inclination to be a spy? Doesn't that show a probability that he gave these documents to Chambers?

John Foster Dulles testified at both trials. In the first trial Murphy had asked me about my having served as president of the Carnegie Endowment for International Peace, of which Mr. Dulles was then Chairman. Murphy had tried to create an appearance of contradiction between Mr. Dulles and me.[8] There had been no real contradiction in our testimony; at most there were minor differences of recollection. Judge Kaufman had remarked in a colloquy with counsel in the course of Mr. Dulles's testimony that he saw no conflict, and he later said that he had been wrong in allowing Mr. Dulles to testify.

At the second trial Murphy saved Mr. Dulles for his last witness. The jury may have been impressed that a former United States Senator and distinguished public figure was appearing as a prosecution witness and that the prosecutor thought his testimony was adverse to me. Here again the unjustified inference from the appearance of the witness was apparently more valuable to the prosecutor than the testimony given.

I repeated what both of us had in effect said at the first trial. Mr. Dulles emphasized and expanded upon our slight differences of recollection. Those differences concerned four conversations we had had, two of them by telephone.

The first conversation occurred in January 1946 when Mr. Dulles and I were traveling by ship to the first meeting, in London, of the newly created United Nations. I testified that he had then asked me if I would be interested in becoming president of the Carnegie Endowment. Mr. Dulles's recollection was that he had simply asked if I expected to stay on indefinitely in government service; he did not think he had mentioned the Endowment to me until several months later, because he was but one of twenty or more trustees who by January had not definitely taken up the matter of seeking a presi-

[8] See pp. 293–4, 328–9.

dent. He said, however, that he had had the possibility of my
availability for the position in mind when he spoke to me in
January. As the subject was perhaps of more importance to me
than to Mr. Dulles, it had made a stronger impression on my
memory than on his. In any event, my recollection on this point
was borne out when, after the trial, my wife and I came across
a letter I had written to her from shipboard telling her that Mr.
Dulles had asked if I would be interested in considering the
Endowment position.

The second conversation was a telephone talk which I recalled as having occurred in December 1946, shortly after my
election as president of the Endowment, but which Mr. Dulles
put in early January 1947. My recollection was that Mr. Dulles
called me and asked what he should say in answer to a letter
which charged that I was a Communist. I told him that I
thought the subject had been laid to rest and asked if he knew
the background. (I referred to Secretary of State Byrnes's having told me the preceding March that because of FBI statements
several Congressmen were planning to call me a Communist; as
a result, I had gone to see the FBI to answer any questions
that they might have. Having heard nothing further for nine
months, I had naturally assumed that the matter had been
dropped.) Mr. Dulles, in turn, said that he had discussed the
matter fully with Mr. Byrnes—both of them were then in New
York at a United Nations session—but wanted suggestions as
to what to reply to the letter. I said I could only suggest that
he ask for the basis for such a charge. In his testimony Mr.
Dulles indicated that he did not recall the conversation that
way. He said he had not talked to Mr. Byrnes and that he
had seen the author of the letter the same day he had received
it and so had not sent any reply.

The third conversation was in March of 1948 when I told
Mr. Dulles of my having appeared that day before the grand
jury to answer questions about a number of people. I testified
that in that conversation Mr. Dulles told me that the author
of the letter was Alfred Kohlberg (the publisher of *Plain Talk*,
the magazine edited by Isaac Don Levine), that he had replied

to Kohlberg along the lines I had suggested, and that Kohlberg had said he had no facts. Mr. Dulles testified that he did not recall having told me Kohlberg's name.

In his testimony about a fourth conversation Mr. Dulles said that my recollection of it did not "wholly square" with his. When on August 3, 1948, I learned from newspapermen of Chambers's testimony before the Committee, I had called Mr. Dulles by telephone [9] to inform him of what I had learned and to tell him of my intention to appear before the Committee. At that time I had also told him that I was aware that the mere charges might impair my usefulness as president of the Endowment, and that I therefore wanted him to decide if at any time my continuing as president would embarrass the Endowment, and if he did so decide I would of course resign. Mr. Dulles did not recall our discussing my possible resignation until later that month.

Our differences of recollection were thus entirely negligible. For his own purposes, Murphy gave them an importance far beyond their actuality.

Murphy produced at this trial one entirely new witness. Again the witness's appearance was calculated to produce maximum drama. Though she had, unknown to us, been brought to the courthouse on the first day of the trial, not until the last day of the trial was Edith Murray called to the stand. She testified that she had worked as a full-time maid for the Chamberses (then living under the name "Cantwell") at 903 St. Paul Street, Baltimore, from the fall of 1934 to the spring of 1935, and at 1617 Eutaw Place, Baltimore, from the fall of 1935 to the spring of 1936. She said that at Eutaw Place she had once seen me and my wife, and had seen my wife on three other occasions. Her story of seeing me was that she was about to go home one night when she answered the doorbell and let us in; then, after finishing her work, she had "come on to go through where they were, and I bid them all good-night, and I went on home."

Her testimony, in itself insubstantial, was simply that

[9] See p. 5.

my wife and I had visited the Chamberses during the period 1935–6 when I actually knew Chambers. As we testified, we never visited them.

The prosecution claimed that they had located Mrs. Murray for the first time after the first trial, but they gave no excuse for withholding her until the last moments of the second trial instead of calling her as part of the prosecution's regular case. However, on cross-examination we were able to show the flimsy nature of her identification of me and my wife, a weakness that, had she appeared in the regular order, would have robbed her testimony of its dramatic impact. Murphy's withholding her until the last moment gave us no chance to discredit her testimony further, although we later located witnesses who submitted affidavits that the Chamberses had had no colored maid when they lived on Eutaw Place and did not live at 903 St. Paul Street at any time between 1932 and 1938, and that no maid was employed at 903 St. Paul Street during that period. (See Chapter XI.)

Cross-examination brought out that when the FBI agent had approached Mrs. Murray he had told her that "he was working for Mr. Cantwell" and did not say "he was no FBI until the next day." He had shown her a photograph of my wife. She testified about this:

. . . They asked me did I know this lady, and I said it looks like someone that I know. It looked like—I thought maybe it was an actress or something. I say it looks like someone I know, but I just couldn't remember at that time.

Later she added: ". . . I said this looks like someone I have seen, I said to myself, maybe it was in the movies. . . ."

At the time, newsreel pictures of my wife and me, taken throughout the first trial, had been shown frequently in theaters throughout the country and our photographs had appeared so often in the press and in periodicals that we are still recognized by strangers wherever we go.

She had also been shown a photograph of me. Her testimony was that "it looked like I had seen him, but I wasn't sure, I told him I wasn't sure." Later she testified that when the FBI agent had shown her my picture he had asked if she recognized "this man." She continued:

I told him I did not know.

The day after her first interview with the FBI, two or three agents drove her to the Chambers farm. She thought she was going to work again for the "Cantwells." According to her testimony, she stayed at the farm about three hours. Mrs. Chambers and an FBI agent showed her around the house and "a little after four" the Chamberses' daughter, whom she said she had known as a baby, was brought home from school by Chambers. Subsequently she had additional talks with the FBI:

I just can't remember how often I saw them, but they was around there for quite a while there once.

Then on the opening day of the trial she was brought to New York by the FBI and taken to the courthouse for a purpose she described as follows:

. . . all they wanted to do was bring me up here to see if I could recognize the woman that was in the picture and the man on the picture.

This she (along with many others who also did not know us) was able to do as my wife and I entered the courtroom, the center of attention of the bystanders and reporters at that moment at least:

Well, I just stood out in the hall, and it was a crowd of people. They asked me did I see anybody in the crowd that I know, and I looked around, and I didn't see anyone at this time, and stood there and stood there; so, then, after a while, in the back of me where I was standing was an elevator, in the back of me, like, and I looked around, and then I see Mr. and Mrs. Hiss come over, and right away I knew them.

Mrs. Murray may not have been consciously falsifying. It came out on cross-examination that she had had a nervous

breakdown in 1942, had been under a doctor's care for over
a year, and had not worked since then. During the afternoon
at the Chamberses' farm, what with the actual familiarity of
our faces from newsreels, newspapers, and magazines and her
desire to please the Chamberses, who, she thought, wanted her
to work for them, the Chamberses may have brought her
genuinely to confuse us with another couple she had seen
thirteen years before. It appears that she was certainly helped
with the street numbers of the St. Paul Street and Eutaw
Place houses, which she gave without hesitation; she could
not give the street number of the last place she had worked
or that of her doctor. Her inability to recall features or prominent marks of identification is shown by her inability to remember whether she had ever seen Chambers (Cantwell),
for whom she said she had worked for two years, with a mustache.

The process of suggestion is indicated by the following:
In her Baltimore testimony Mrs. Chambers, attempting to
show close friendship and frequent meetings with my wife,
had told a story suggested by questions of the preceding day.
On November 16, 1948, Mrs. Chambers had been asked (in
an effort to establish her whereabouts and activities at various
times) whether she had received pre-natal care before her son
was born. She had testified that she had "a faint recollection
of . . . a flying trip to New York" to visit a Dr. Shields.
The following day she herself revived this topic, evidently for
the purpose of volunteering:

> Priscilla Hiss very kindly came and stayed with the baby so
> that I could go to New York and visit Dr. Shields.

In what seemed an effort to exclude the possibility of this
being checked with others, she had immediately gone on to
say:

> My recollection at this moment is that it was a Wednesday, and
> that Edith, who is our maid, had the afternoon off, and Priscilla
> came to relieve her and stay with the child until I returned, which
> to my best recollection was about 11 o'clock at night.

She was asked what my wife had done then, and replied:

Then she went home.

After Mrs. Murray's visit to the Chamberses' farm, Mrs. Chambers, at the second trial, changed this tale for the first time and testified (in obvious anticipation of Mrs. Murray's coming appearance) that my wife had "stayed overnight with the baby." This change in testimony opened the way for Mrs. Murray to say that two of the three times when she had assertedly seen my wife without me were once briefly in the evening before she (Mrs. Murray) left work and a second time briefly the following morning when she returned to work. She said this was when Mrs. Chambers had gone to New York for pre-natal care. It seems quite possible that Mrs. Chambers did make such a trip, and that Mrs. Murray did work occasionally for the Chamberses at Eutaw Place and did recall that a woman friend had stayed the night. Her statement that she remembered that briefly seen visitor to be my wife could be, then, not conscious fabrication but an instance of what the experience of the courts has disclosed to be "the result of suggestion and subconscious, though innocent, fabrication." [1]

Mrs. Murray testified that she had called my wife "Miss Priscilla" and that my wife had said she lived in Washington and had "one little boy." These touches, too, may have been suggested to her (perhaps when she went to the Chambers farm with the FBI agents) in such a way that she believed them to be her own recollection.

Like Rosen, Mrs. Massing, and Mr. Dulles, she was produced with an eye to dramatic effect. The timing of her appearance left the jury with the impact of a last-minute witness for the prosecution whom we were prevented from countering fully. Judge Goddard seemed to recognize the impropriety of the prosecution's calling Mrs. Murray at the end of the trial instead of earlier, in the presentation of the prosecution's direct

---

[1] Di Carlo v. United States, 6 F. (2d) 364, at p. 366. This is an opinion of the same Court of Appeals that reviewed my appeal.

case, but he refused our motion to strike out her testimony, saying that "it might more properly have been offered in the direct case, but I don't think that it should be excluded because it is offered in rebuttal. . . ."

Two other witnesses also appeared for the first time at the second trial. Dr. Carl A. L. Binger, a psychiatrist, and Dr. Henry A. Murray, a psychologist with psychiatric experience, were qualified as experts for the defense. Their testimony was based on a summary of the evidence, most of it testimony by Chambers himself, and on a study of Chambers's writings and translations, which were put in evidence. Dr. Binger had also observed Chambers on the witness stand in both trials.

These two experts testified that the material available to them was sufficient for valid diagnosis. Their diagnosis was that Chambers suffered from the mental ailment of psychopathic personality of the type characterized by amoral, asocial, and delinquent behavior, which has no regard for the good of society and of individuals and is therefore frequently destructive of both. They noted a history of theft, pathological lying, deceiving, bizarre or eccentric behavior, false accusations, a disposition to smear, degrade, and destroy, abnormal emotionality, instability of attachments, and paranoid ideas.

Dr. Binger defined pathological lying as "a kind of living out of a part, playing a part as if it were true, assuming a role." He said also:

. . . These unfortunate people have a conviction of the truth and validity of their own imaginations, of their own fantasies without respect to outer reality; so that they play a part in life, play a role. . . . and on the basis of such imaginations they will claim friendships where none exist, just as they will make accusations which have no basis in fact. . . .

Dr. Binger pointed out "the extraordinary analogies," of medical significance, between the story of *Class Reunion,* by Franz Werfel, which Chambers translated in 1929, and the evidence in the case as presented to him:

There are two characters, principal characters in the book. One is Sebastian and the other is Adler. The name Adler is very close to the name Alger. . . .

. . . .

Adler is described in the book as . . . the closest friend of the other character Sebastian, [but] later became the enemy whom he is trying to destroy. . . .

. . . .

. . . [Sebastian describes] how he himself committed a forgery and he signed a paper that the other man had done the thing and not he. How he had proposed a suicide pact with him by the use of illuminating gas, which is, as you recall, the way Mr. Chambers' brother committed suicide.

. . . .

. . . Adler is described as having gray eyes, as having a ludicrous walk when seen from behind.

. . . .

. . . Mr. Chambers says that Mr. Hiss's eyes were gray.[2] . . . Mr. Chambers says of Mr. Hiss that he has a mincing gait when seen from behind.[2]

Adler's father is said to have committed suicide when he was a small child. . . . Hiss's father committed suicide when he was a small child. Adler's mother was said to be a domineering woman; that Hiss's mother was described [by Chambers][3] in some such terms. . . .

Mr. Sebastian at the age of 43 describes himself as too fat, as smoking too much, as drinking too much coffee, as working too hard, as fearing a heart attack. He says that his father died of a heart attack.

. . . I have seen the medical record of Mr. Chambers with the same facts in it. . . .

The crime which was actually committed in the book is one of falsification of documents by a man [Sebastian] who says of himself, "I would lie. I would—I have no conscience. I would stop at nothing to gain my end."

The crime was then pinned on to the character of Adler, and Sebastian signed a document saying, "I did not do this, I didn't

2 See p. 48.
3 See p. 51.

falsify the records, I wasn't the forger; Adler was." . . .

. . . And Adler, the character in the book, made fun of him, and because he said something slighting to him, at that moment he sealed his own doom and then started a process in Sebastian which was not completed until he came very near destroying this other man.

Both experts testified that a psychopath has a defect of conscience which renders him insensible to the feelings and sufferings of others and leaves him without restraint against attacking and destroying them.

Dr. Binger and Dr. Murray were subjected to lengthy cross-examination, but maintained their diagnoses.

On Chambers's mental condition there was no conflict of expert evidence. The prosecutor offered no testimony in contradiction of the two doctors, whose opinions remain the sole medical evidence on this important point.

At the very end of the long trial Murphy introduced a totally unwarranted and highly misleading point. As is the usual practice, the prosecutor, in his summation, had the last word before the Judge's charge to the jury. Murphy apparently remembered that some of the first jury had played at being typewriting experts. Near the close of his peroration at the end of the second trial he specifically invited the jury to "look for similarity of mistakes" in typing in the personal letters my wife had typed and the papers Chambers had produced. "When you get these these documents inside," he said—thus proposing that they call for the papers—they were to look for the use of *r* for *i*, *f* for *g*, and *f* for *d* in both the Chambers papers and the personal letters iny wife had typed. It was too late to protest effectively that this was not evidence, that the sole typewriting expert had given no testimony on this subject. The gross prejudice of proposing the use of erroneous criteria outside the record had been implanted and could not be erased by protest. Under the rules we could not make a reply in which we could have pointed out the illogic of Murphy's suggestions. We thus could not point out that in letters admittedly typed by Chambers and in the carelessly typed memorandum of Chambers's interview with Raymond Murphy at Chambers's farm on March 20, 1945 (which looks as though it had been typed on the spot), there were also typing errors in common with the forged papers, errors of the very kind the prosecutor had singled out.[4]

This was perhaps Murphy's most damaging action. The jurors promptly accepted his invitation by asking for the typed papers Chambers had produced and the personal letters my wife had written. If the jurors finally concluded, as a result of Murphy's unjustifiable suggestion of a comparison of common typing errors, that my wife had in fact typed the Chambers papers, their deliberations ended at that moment. For, regardless of all the other evidence in the case, that conclusion could lead only to a verdict of guilty.

As I left the courtroom at the conclusion of the trial that Friday afternoon several of the reporters who had covered both trials spoke to me, saying in a friendly manner that they thought we had this time made our position much clearer. My counsel and I were alike more optimistic than before, though one of my lawyers was disturbed by what he considered the partiality for the prosecution of Judge Goddard's charge. He called it "a hanging charge."

It soon became plain that once again there were uncertainty and dissension among the jury. It had retired just after three o'clock in the afternoon. At five the jury in a note asked for:

[4] After the trial my counsel obtained an expert analysis of the typed papers which further demonstrated the misleading nature of Murphy's reference to three similar typing mistakes and which showed that the typing errors in the papers produced by Chambers not only did not support his story but contradicted it. (See pp. 410–2.) Murphy's invitation to the jury to look for three similar mistakes was made in the face of a formal contention of his, three months earlier, that *even an expert* could not identify a typist from comparison of typing samples. On November 3, 1949—two weeks before the second trial began—my counsel unsuccessfully sought to inspect any material available to the prosecution which had been typed by Chambers or Mrs. Chambers, expressly stating that this might help the defense to identify the typist. Murphy filed an affidavit opposing our request to examine such material, saying that "it strains one's imagination to see how that would tend to prove who the operator of the Woodstock was. It can hardly be claimed that an expert could tell what individual typed a certain instrument by having a specimen of his typing. . . ."

Mrs. Hiss testimony; Wadleigh testimony; Catlett testimony. Chambers testimony Peterboro trip.

Mrs. Hiss's letters written on typewriter.

Papers in evidence 5 to 47, etc. [the exhibit numbers of the typed papers produced by Chambers].

Testimony of date when Hisses moved from 30th Street to Volta Place.

Catletts'—when did they move to [their new house on] P street.

FBI sample typing [done in court on the Woodstock machine].

Soon after the court reporter started reading the testimony requested, the forelady, realizing the time that would be consumed, suggested that the jury reduce their request. At 5:30 the new request was received:

Testimony of Mrs. Hiss giving date of disposal of typewriter to the Catletts. Also date Catlett boy claimed to have received typewriter from the Hisses.

Testimony of disposal of typewriter by the Catletts.

All typewritten material written on the Woodstock typewriter including Mrs. Hiss's personal correspondence and F.B.I. sample.

Above includes all Baltimore exhibits [the name given at the trials to the typed papers produced by Chambers].

After the jury had been to dinner, the requested testimony was read to it (the jury had already received the requested exhibits).

At 10:45 the jury was sent to a hotel for the night.

Early the next morning the jury asked for a redefinition of "reasonable doubt; circumstantial evidence, acceptable corroborative evidence and their relations to each other." The Judge reread portions of his charge, emphasizing passages prejudicial to me (see Chapter X).

My hopes and my counsel's continued high. Murphy, on the other hand, looked discouraged during the long wait. He had been irritated at the jury's request for rereading of the testimony. He was overheard to say that if the jury disagreed again, that would end the case. During lunch a member of the staff of *The New York Times*, who had not attended either trial but had come down to be present at the end of the jury's deliberation, spoke to me. I had met him during my vacation a year or two before and we had established a friendly relation. He said affably that he had been talking to the working press who had covered the trials and that perhaps I might be interested to know the "verdict" of these men. He went on to give their "verdict" as "Acquittal in five minutes."

At 2:47 p.m. on Saturday, January 21, 1950, the jury returned and announced a verdict of guilty. The Judge, confirming the impression of his attitude that I had received in the course of the trial, in thanking the jurors for their long service of well over two months told them that he thought they had rendered "a just verdict."

On January 25, 1950, Judge Goddard imposed the maximum sentence of five years. I had asked for the privilege of making a statement just before sentence, a privilege assured by law. I said merely this:

I would like to thank your Honor for this opportunity again to deny the charges that have been made against me. I want only to add that I am confident that in the future the full facts of how Whittaker Chambers was able to carry out forgery by typewriter will be disclosed.

CHAPTER TEN

CONDUCT OF PROSECUTOR
AND JUDGE—APPEAL

DESPITE my second bitter disappointment with the deliberations of a jury, I was confident of obtaining a new trial. As had been the case from the time of the first public attack by Chambers a year and a half earlier, my spirits and confidence remained high. Knowing my innocence of the charges, I was, as I still am, certain of eventual vindication. My lawyers and I felt that Judge Goddard's charge to the jury at the conclusion of the trial was ground for reversal and that he had made a succession of erroneous rulings against us. We also felt that the conduct of the prosecutor had been such that it, too, vitiated the fairness of the trial.

During the succeeding months I worked with my attorneys [1] in readying the voluminous record for appeal and in selecting the points to be raised on appeal. With a trial of

---

[1] When Mr. Cross came into the case as my trial counsel for the second trial, it was understood that he could afford to leave his Boston practice only for the duration of that trial. To argue the appeal and to write the necessary briefs on appeal, I was fortunate to have an experienced appellate lawyer, Robert M. Benjamin, whom I had known because he, too, had been one of Justice Holmes's secretaries.

such magnitude, the task of sifting the record of approximately 4,000 pages and of reducing the brief on appeal to the 125 pages allowed us was lengthy and onerous.[2] Simultaneously, my lawyers found time, now that the daily demands of preparation for trial and active participation in trial had ended, to search for new evidence as an independent ground for the new trial I sought. This latter topic forms the subject of the next chapter.

The atmosphere of fear and the extraordinary distribution of false and biased accounts of the case continued to be my greatest obstacles.

So soon after the trial that it had obviously been largely written before the trial had ended, there appeared a volume, *Seeds of Treason*, by Victor Lasky, who had covered the trials for the *World-Telegram*, and Ralph de Toledano, who had acted in a similar capacity for *Newsweek*. This book, which uncritically supported Chambers, was promptly summarized in *Reader's Digest*.

The outbreak of the Korean War in June 1950 added greatly to public tension and to the hostility against all accused of Communism. Rigidity of mind and neglect of individual rights almost inevitably characterize wartime attitudes. Who can say how much he is affected by reiterated propaganda, especially in the midst of war and when it carries official sponsorship? During the summer the widely circulated Sunday supplement *The American Weekly* published in two installments an article by Win Brooks entitled "How the FBI Trapped Hiss." This purported to be "the complete, official story" of Mrs. Murray's appearance at the second trial. Though the appeal was then pending and public comment by the parties was questionable, the prosecution had collaborated in the preparation of the article. In addition to lengthy direct quotations from "the FBI account," the article contained the following introductory statements:

[2] As I am not here under so restrictive a limitation, I shall discuss in this chapter some examples of the prosecutor's and the Judge's conduct which were not dealt with in our appeal.

I heard from J. Edgar Hoover in Washington an outline of the story of search for Edith Murray. He described it as "one of the finest examples of FBI investigative procedure." I asked if I might have it in detail for The American Weekly and he agreed.

The considerable research necessary to correlate the reports of all FBI agents engaged in the hunt recently was completed and a 14-page condensation made available. With this account I visited Asst. U.S. Atty. Thomas F. Murphy, prosecutor at both trials, to build up the climax from his records. These he produced and helped screen to stress the importance of Edith Murray to the final conviction.

The new developments in world affairs and prejudicial publicity would, in any event, hardly have made easier the selection of unbiased jurors in the new trial I sought. This "official story" made matters worse and actually exploited anxieties over the Korean War. It spoke of "this nation [I] betrayed" and incorporated the myth of the evil nature of the Yalta Conference (where my actual role was the modest one of a technician on United Nations affairs). The search for Mrs. Murray, it said, had gone on while

Far across the Pacific Russia was arming Communist North Korea to the teeth for the hot war to come and Russia was in North Korea by virtue of the Yalta Agreement at which Roosevelt acted with the guidance of Alger Hiss. . . .

The law is clear that appellate courts practically never pass upon the credibility of witnesses, but leave that issue to the jury. We therefore considered that we were foreclosed from asking the Court of Appeals to re-examine the inherent incredibility of Chambers's charges and our numerous demonstrations of false statements by him. The first point of our brief demonstrated, for reasons discussed in Chapter VIII, the insufficiency of the documentary evidence to support Chambers's charges and its actual disproof of those charges. Consequently, we contended, as we had at the trials, that the case should have been dismissed and a judgment of acquittal ordered without allowing the case to go to the jury. This was the "very substantial question of law" that Judge Kaufman had said "will continue in this case for all time." We pointed out that the applicable rulings of the courts in such cases required that the supporting evidence must be "independent evidence inconsistent with the innocence of the defendant," whereas the documents, far from independently confirming Chambers, contradicted vital aspects of his testimony.

We also contended that Judge Goddard should not have allowed Rosen to take the stand when it was known that he would not testify but would instead claim a privilege against self-incrimination.[3] Shortly after Judge Goddard's ruling, the Court of Appeals had said in another case that it might "be ground for reversal if the party who called a witness connected with a challenged transaction knew, or had reasonable cause to know, before putting the witness on the stand that he would claim his privilege." In my case the prejudice of this evidentially useless maneuver was readily apparent: a "Fifth Amendment Communist" seemed to have received the car and wouldn't tell the prosecutor why or how. Emphasizing Rosen's refusal to answer as to whether in July 1936 he was a Communist, the prosecutor had the court reporter read Rosen's answer claiming the privilege. Thus, the jury heard the full claim twice.

In addition to Rosen, the prosecutor had called still another witness who, we had told the Judge, might claim a privilege and who in fact did so when asked if he knew Chambers in 1937 and whether he had photographed documents in 1937. The prosecutor had then produced records to show that in 1933 the witness, a Felix Inslerman, had registered as a Communist. Inslerman's camera was accepted in evidence, against our objection, and an FBI expert had been permitted to demonstrate with elaborate technical proof that this camera had photographed the pumpkin microfilms.

Murphy had stated before the jury that this proof tended "to corroborate . . . to the nth degree" Chambers's story "that the documents he received from Hiss" were photo-

[3] See pp. 306–7.

graphed by Inslerman. Obviously, it proved nothing as to
where Chambers had got the documents. This maneuver of
pseudo-corroboration resorted to by Murphy was most injurious.
Though the camera and expert evidence corroborated nothing
that related to me, yet there was a specious relevance that could
only confuse the jury into perhaps being persuaded that if
Chambers was telling the truth when he said Inslerman photographed the documents, he was also telling the truth when he
said that I had given him those documents. Murphy's reference
to corroboration "to the nth degree" and the Judge's ruling that
the evidence was relevant heightened the chances of this confusion. The appearance of the camera and of the expert's elaborate "scientific" use of photomicrographs further heightened the
damaging effect of this irrelevant but prejudicial evidence. One
of the great experts on evidence, Dean John H. Wigmore, has
pointed out that there is "a natural tendency to infer from
the mere production of any material object, and without
further evidence, the truth of all that is predicated of it." It is
this tendency which is ridiculed in the popular saying: "George
Washington slept in that bed. If you don't believe it, there's
the bed." But pseudo-corroboration that is carried out solemnly
in a court of law, and is expressly permitted by the Judge over
objection, is likely to be recognized for what it really is only
by the most wary juror.

We also asserted that it was error to allow the appeal to
current inflammatory prejudice that was involved in permitting
Mrs. Massing's testimony to remain in the record. (When
testimony is stricken from the record, the judge directs the
jury to disregard it.) Similarly, we urged that Mrs. Murray's
delayed appearance was a deliberate deprivation of the defense's right to the fullest opportunity, by investigation and
prepared cross-examination, to controvert and impeach her testimony, and that it was injurious error for the Judge to refuse
to strike out her testimony. We also pointed out the error
of the Judge's refusal to strike out the Dulles testimony,
which involved no real contradiction and was on collateral
matters. As press comment inspired by the prosecution had

disclosed, this was a clumsy but perhaps effective attempt to substitute in the jury's mind a prominent personage for Chambers as disputing my testimony.[4] And in his closing remarks to the jury Murphy, misstating Mr. Dulles's attitude, had said: "Mr. Dulles was in there fighting to get him out [of my position as president of the Carnegie Endowment]." The facts were quite to the contrary: as Mr. Dulles had testi- fied, he had, months after our discussion of my possi- ble resignation, voted to extend my leave of absence at the Endowment until the full end of the term of office for which I had been elected.

As the immediately following pages demonstrate, the most pervasive and unfair prejudice in the whole trial came from the conduct of the prosecutor, whom the Judge had done nothing to restrain. In days of popular emotional aberration it is always difficult, if not impossible, to insulate a trial that raises the very issues involved in inflamed public feelings. It is, therefore, a specially grievous departure from proper standards of justice when at such times a prosecutor appeals to the very passions that militate against a fair trial.

My appellate lawyer, Robert M. Benjamin, in his brief put the issue succinctly:

Wherever the bounds of conduct permissible to a prosecutor may be fixed, the prosecutor exceeded them.

In dealing with conduct that permeated the long trial we could only, as Mr. Benjamin said, present

. . . illustrative instances of the prosecutor's inflammatory and prejudicial questioning of witnesses and argument to the jury, and of his direct statements or implications of fact unsupported by, and in many cases directly contrary to, the record.

---

[4] The *World-Telegram* article, referred to on p. 294, had, it will be re- membered, concluded: "In effect, government sources pointed out, the issue has now become: Who is lying—Mr. Dulles or Mr. Hiss?"

As Mr. Benjamin pointed out, the defendant cannot protect himself against tactics of the kind the prosecutor had
adopted:

> . . . The damage done by the question or argument was in-
> curable, and objection would only have aggravated it; the number
> of instances, especially in the summation, rendered effective ob-
> jection impossible and any attempt at objection harmful. . . .

An alert and forceful trial judge, and only he, can mitigate
the injury caused by such conduct. Failing restraint by the
trial judge, there remains only the protection of appellate
judges ready to overturn the unfair results of a case, however
long, sensational, and controversial.

We put our reliance on a searching and independent review by the Court of Appeals. The legal merits of its review
should in their technical aspects more properly be passed upon
by others. Here I shall do no more than describe the issues
we raised, as demonstrating the basis for our confidence that
the conviction should be reversed, and report the reasons given
by Judge Harrie B. Chase, who wrote the opinion, for denying
the appeal. For these topics are germane to this stage of my
effort to refute Chambers's false charges.

To return to the discussion of the prosecutor's conduct
of the second trial—our brief took up many examples of misconduct, though there was insufficient space to list them all.
An indictment serves only to list charges to be tried. Were
its effect greater than this, the whole position of the defendant,
presumed innocent, would be compromised and the prosecution would not be under the burden of submitting proof beyond a reasonable doubt. Nonetheless, Murphy in his opening
statement, before any evidence had been produced, referred
to the grand jury as if its action meant that the issues of the
trial had already been decided against me by that body and
as if its functions were the same as those of the trial jury:

> Finally . . . the grand jury here in this building . . . heard
> . . . the testimony of both Mr. Chambers and the defendant . . .
> over a number of days, until finally on December 15th, 1948 Mr.

Hiss testified and, as they say in their indictment, he lied to them on that day.

So you can see how . . . the grand jury, after listening to both of these men on a number of days—I am just guessing now, but I think ten, I might be wrong, but ten days—and they believed Chambers and not Hiss and they indicted Hiss for perjury for having lied to them under oath.

. . . . .

But when the chips were down in December in the grand jury, when the grand jury, a body like yourself—twice as many—called him and called Mr. Hiss, first one, then the other, first one, then the other—where was the truth here? Where was the truth? Did you or didn't you?

And they indicted Hiss.

This erroneous and damaging insinuation remained with the jury and he repeated his reference to the grand jury in his closing argument. First and last Murphy's arguments planted in the jury's mind the idea, potently reinforcing the Committee's continual assertion of unquestioned guilt, that I had already been found guilty by a body just like themselves:

Now, ladies and gentlemen, the indictment here? . . . You have to find out whether Mr. Hiss lied twice while under oath upstairs here in the grand jury. Did he commit two lies deliberately before a body like yours, larger perhaps, but a group of New York citizens? . . .

Once again his argument included the misleading point:

Now, ladies and gentlemen, the proof, as you can see it, as it was presented to you, has been previously melting into some sort of a form back in 1948. The grand jury was in session in December and they were hearing this story. They heard Mr. Hiss, they heard Mrs. Hiss. They had the documents, they knew about the typewriter. The expert says they are the same. "Get Mr. Hiss back."

"Tell us, did you hand over State Department documents to Mr. Chambers?"

"Never."

"Did you see him after January 1, 1937?"

"Never."

You can see how the lie grew. You can see why he had to lie there. And that is why he is here today. . . . They had to have the documentary proof. And we have it. . . .

The grand jury had already achieved special status in the case due to Judge Goddard's volunteering, quite unnecessarily, that he had himself sworn in that body.

Murphy also brought into the record Nixon's proposal that I take a lie-detector test and his statement that Chambers was willing to take it. I told Murphy that I had not specifically refused, that I had written to the Committee that I would like to consider the matter at some length, and that the Committee had dropped the matter. Murphy repeatedly emphasized the incident as if such a test were reliable and as if I had refused to take it. He said first:

Well, in any event you did not submit to a lie-detector test?

And then a little later:

Well in any event you did not take the test?

To this he added for emphasis:

Well, you didn't come forward and insist upon it?

We pointed out in our brief that every court that has considered the question has shared my doubts of the scientific validity of these tests, a fact obviously known to the prosecutor. "Yet the risk and hope were clear," we concluded, "that the jury, ignorant of the scientific status of such tests, would draw a vitally prejudicial conclusion." The prosecutor's suggestion was that if innocent I would have insisted on taking the test. The whole issue in the trial being veracity, the impression thus deliberately and unwarrantably created was especially improper.

Murphy continuously exploited the fear of Communism and the public loathing of Communists. He went so far as to imply that I and my counsel were following the Communist

Party line. In his opening statement he said of my bringing the libel suit, that "when that lawsuit was started then [Chambers] saw the Communist Party at work, he says." Chambers did not say this at the trial, and Murphy thus did not have even the excuse of "support" in the record for this inflammatory appeal to the hostility toward Communism.

In his final remarks to the jury he repeated this theme:

. . . He had to admit or deny—admit or deny—fish or cut bait. If he admitted—bang. Everything crumbles at once, the job to boot. So you deny, you accuse, accuse the other guy, yell cop. That is standard CP practice, isn't it? Accuse the other guy, accuse me, accuse the Judge, everybody.

Farther along in these remarks he attempted to divert attention from my lawyer's mild censure of certain FBI practices by a further appeal to prejudice:

. . . This is the open season on the FBI; everybody is taking potshots at them. It is the party line to do it. It is the party line.

These remarks came while public memory of the trials of the Communist leaders and of Judith Coplon was still fresh. The "accuse the Judge" phrase, called "standard CP practice," could only suggest to the jury the attacks that had been made on Judge Harold Medina in the former case, and the reference to "potshots" at the FBI recalled the hearings (begun in November just before my trial and continued until the end of December) in the Coplon case that disclosed wiretapping by the FBI of conversations with counsel. The prejudice inseparable from my trial being held in the same building where these recent cases had attracted so much notoriety was thus deliberately increased and made use of.

In view of the notably unhistrionic manner in which Mr. Cross had conducted himself in this trial, Murphy's unprovoked appeals to prejudice were doubly unjustifiable. His reference to the "party line" as involving "potshots" at the FBI was based on the following incident. Mrs. Norma B. Brown (the sister of the Mr. Boucot from whom Chambers,

as Breen, had in 1935 rented a summer cottage) had denied
Mrs. Chambers's testimony that she, Mrs. Brown, had met
my wife. On the witness stand Mrs. Brown disclosed that an
FBI agent had come to see her at a hospital and, showing
her a picture of my wife, had misleadingly asked: "Does this
look like Mrs. Breen?" Assuming that it was a photograph
of Mrs. Breen, she at first said it did because the hair was
combed the same way and the person appeared dark. But she
soon said:

No, that is not Mrs. Breen. The expression is not the same. She
has a more pert look than Mrs. Breen has and it is not the
same nose.

When the agent returned, she told him:

I really wanted to see you because I am sure now after sleeping
on it that that picture was not Mrs. Breen.

Only then did the agent admit that it was a picture not of
Mrs. Breen but of my wife. In his summation Mr. Cross,
commenting on this incident, said only that there were instances "of over-zealousness on the part of some representatives
of the FBI. . . ." In view of the tactics followed in obtaining
Mrs. Murray's "identification" of me and my wife and in
arranging for Chambers's questioning of our maids, to mention
only the most clear-cut other instances of impropriety, Mr.
Cross did not overstate his complaint. Murphy was, therefore,
not provoked to his reply by any misconduct of Mr. Cross,
but sought an excuse to insert his innuendo of similarity between my defense and that of the Coplon case and the case
of the Communist leaders.

Murphy's use of Mr. Cross's reference to the FBI also
subtly intimidated the jury. He equated a vote for acquittal
with condoning an attack on the FBI, a position no juror
could wish to be in. He thundered:

If you think that any bit of evidence in this case, any
bit, material or immaterial, was manufactured, conceived or sub-
orned by the FBI, acquit this man. The FBI ought to be told

by you that they can't tamper with witnesses and evidence, if you believe that to be the fact. And I am telling you, that's for Sweeney, actually for Sweeney. It is the thing to do today—call the FBI conspirators. It sounds good. A lot of the press like it— some of the press. Smart. The intelligentsia like it, love it.

Murphy met our discovery of Chambers's fraudulent pass- port application and the mustachioed photograph by insinuat- ing that my counsel and I had invented an informant. During the first trial John Davis, my Washington counsel, had made informal inquiry at the State Department in investigating re- ports Harold Rosenwald, another of my lawyers, had received that Chambers had made a lengthy trip or trips abroad in the 1930's. In October 1949, Mr. Davis had written to the State Department asking if Chambers had received a passport under his own name or under any of a number of assumed names that we had by then learned that he had employed. The Department replied that it had "been able to identify only one application [for a passport] in one of the names" and that that would be produced at the trial on subpœna. The prosecutor unsuccessfully opposed the subpœna, and my coun- sel saw for the first time this "Breen" application shortly before the second trial, where it was introduced in evidence. We then learned that the FBI had received a copy of the same applica- tion in March 1949, before the first trial, but had kept the subject of the passport secret; no mention of it was made at that trial.

Knowing that we had discovered the application, the pros- ecutor at the second trial drew from Chambers, for the first time, a story that he had informed me of a contemplated trip to England. But even then Chambers said he did not recall ever having told me of the passport. During the trial the prosecutor persistently insinuated that I had known about the application all along and that it was I who had told my counsel of it. At the beginning of each of the two trial sessions following his insinuations to this effect, he asked me if my lawyers had yet told me who had informed them of Cham- bers's trip. In his summation the prosecutor said:

And how about the tipster, the mysterious guy who told Mr. Rosenwald [counsel who had received the report] about "Why not look in the Passport Section for the Breen passport?" How about that guy? Do you think he really existed? . . .

Later he returned again to his unfounded charge of fabrication by the defense:

. . . If Mr. Hiss didn't know, way back in 1935, that Mr. Chambers had applied for and obtained a passport in the name of David Breen when he was going to Europe on another Communist mission, how did they know to go to the Passport Division and ask for passports? They could have written to a thousand places. But why pick out the State Department for passports? . . .

Mr. Davis, their Washington representative, was there last summer. They knew it was there because they were friends together. He confided in him, he told him. . . .

On the subject of the rug that Chambers had given me as partial payment of rent, the prosecutor asserted evidence where none existed. After I had told the Committee of Chambers's giving the rug to me, Chambers had asserted that he had given me the rug on behalf of the Russians. At the trial he attached no date to his story, except to say that it was prior to the alleged January 1937 meeting with Bykov. Cleide Catlett had confirmed my wife's and my testimony that we had received the rug while we were still at P Street (from which we moved in June 1936). The secretary of one of my lawyers had brought Cleide to see the rug in order to identify it as the one she had seen at P Street. She was not even cross-examined by Murphy, an indication of the force and clarity of her testimony.

At the trial the prosecution showed through Edward H. Touloukian, a rug dealer, that on December 29, 1936, months after Chambers had given the rug to me, four other rugs had been delivered in New York to a friend of Chambers's. In no way (except for Chambers's assertion) was any of these shown to have any connection with me or with the rug I had received. But in summation Murphy said:

. . . But just consider the rug by itself. . . . Mr. Hiss says, "He gave me a rug; I have it; I have the damn thing. Clidi [*sic*] Catlett saw it. I have it in my home."

Now, what would you do assuming you were unjustly accused, and the man said, "Why, you got a rug from us," and you had a rug but you did not get it from us? What do you do with the rug? You bring it in and say to Mr. Toulokian [*sic*], "Is this the damn rug?" No. Whom did they show it to? Clidi Catlett. Clidi Catlett said she saw the rug up here in the Village. The thing to do when you are unjustly accused is to come in and prove that that is not the rug. The Government can't go out and subpoena rugs belonging to the defendant. . . . Bring it in here. Let us look at it. Let the expert look at it. "That is one of the four rugs I sold." Bang. Guilty.

No, don't do it that way. . . . He could not bring the rug in because that proves Count II.

There was no slightest hint in Mr. Touloukian's testimony that my rug was one of the later four. Yet Murphy's summation put such words in his mouth. And it is not correct that the prosecutor could not have subpœnaed the rug if he had thought the dealer would give any such testimony. My counsel had announced that I would take the stand, as I had in the first trial. I had thus waived any privilege I might have had to object to a subpœna. More than that, whenever the prosecutor asked for anything in my possession I produced it voluntarily—Murphy must have known that he could have had the rug for the asking.

The prosecutor continuously played upon the prejudices of the times against use of the Fifth Amendment and to this added the imputation of "guilt by association." He read into the record Chambers's charges before the Committee that Nathan Witt, John Abt, and Lee Pressman were members with me of a Communist "underground organization." (The others named in Chambers's story of a group, including my brother and a man I had never known, had not received the same prominence in the press as Witt, Abt, and Pressman, on whom Murphy chose to concentrate.) The three men selected by Murphy for his insinuations had been colleagues of mine in the Agricultural Adjustment Administration; Pressman I had known from the time when we were classmates at the Harvard Law School.

All three men had claimed the privilege of the Fifth Amendment before the Committee. Over and over again throughout the trial the prosecutor brought in their names. Chambers had played the same theme. When being cross-examined about his interview with Martha Pope, he had said:

Q: And she told you in no uncertain terms that she did not recognize you? A: She told me in a quiet pleasant way that she did not recognize me.

Q: Well, there wasn't any qualification in her answer, was there? A: I can tell you exactly what she said.

Q: Tell us. A: She said that she could not remember my coming to the Hisses' house but she remembered Mr. Lee Pressman and Mr. Nathan Witt as being there very often.

Murphy went over this with Martha when she testified, and found that she did not recall seeing these men when she worked for us in New York or at the 28th Street apartment or anywhere except at P Street, where she worked for about half a year of the five years she was with us. And she told him that she had recalled them, when she had been asked about them, because she had read about them in the papers. In answer to Mr. Cross's questions, she also testified, referring to her interview with Chambers and the FBI:

I didn't see them come very often. I said they came there.

· · · ·

Yes, Mr. Jerome Frank [who was Pressman's, Witt's, and my superior at the Agricultural Adjustment Administration] came to the house but they didn't ask me that down there.

Q: They didn't ask you that? A: No.

Q: And that was at the time when Mr. —when did Mr. Pressman and Mr. Nathan Witt come, when Mr. Frank used to come? A: Yes.

On three separate occasions during my cross-examination Murphy returned to the subject of my having known these men. He also brought their names into his questioning of my wife when she testified. He had Mr. Dulles testify as to my having told him that I knew Pressman.

These men were not witnesses at the trial. There was absolutely no evidence except Chambers's assertions that they had had any Communistic relations with me. But in his summation Murphy employed innuendo and an appeal to prevailing prejudices in place of evidence:

. . . I think Mr. Hiss is a prototype. He is the example of what a lot of people here named, we named in the trial, resemble. I think he is the prototype of Pressman and Witt and Abt. . . .

For emphasis he repeated the offense and added to it. Their names, as Martha Pope had noted, had been prominently displayed in the press. The prosecutor knew, of course, that they had claimed the Fifth Amendment and that this meant I could not call them as witnesses to refute those parts of Chambers's statements about them that included me. Yet he told the jury at still another part of his closing argument:

How about Pressman and Witt and Abt, . . . all of these people who were friends? Why weren't they here? You don't suppose it is because perhaps I had a file on some, do you? You don't suppose that they were afraid to sit there (indicating witness chair)? And these were his friends, the maids told us, at the house discussing office affairs on Sunday. They couldn't see enough of each other during the daytime, the week time, but had to come on Sundays to discuss office matters.

The special injury and unfairness of these tactics were made quite evident more than half a year after the trial when Pressman, following the outbreak of war in Korea, withdrew his claim of privilege and on August 28, 1950, stated to the Committee (which, despite my pending appeal, continued to regard Chambers's stories as its own particular preserve) that for about a year he had in fact belonged to a Communist group, which he left when he left the government in the latter part of 1935. He said flatly, in direct contradiction of the whole basis of Chambers's story:

. . . I do know, I can state as a matter of knowledge, that
for the period of my participation in that group, which is the only
basis on which I can say I have knowledge, Alger Hiss was not a
member of the group.

He said that his group consisted of four men (Chambers had said eight) and that "what we did was receive literature of a Communist nature, daily newspaper, monthly magazines, books, and things of that nature, Communist literature;
we would read the literature and discuss problems covered by
the literature." Harold Ware, he said, had brought them the
literature before he was killed in an accident, and Pressman
had "a hazy recollection" that on one occasion Peters may
have brought the literature. He also said that he had "absolutely no recollection" of having met Chambers in Washington
in connection with his membership in the group. After having
left the government, he had once met Chambers (under another name) in New York.

Defense witnesses were subjected to innuendo of the
same nature. Philip C. Jessup, then an important official of
the government, was asked if he had ever met a "Jacob Ara-
noff" and said he had no recollection of the name. He had
already, at the time of the first trial, given the same answer.
The repetition was not, therefore, a genuine search for information for possible use in impeaching Mr. Jessup's credibility. The dragging in of a Russian name could only have been
intended unwarrantably to arouse suspicions in the minds of
the jurors. Mr. Jessup was also questioned about his connection
with the Institute of Pacific Relations, the American-Russian
Institute for Cultural Relations with the Soviet Union, Inc.,
and the China Aid Council—a further attempt to smear
him by association with agencies that had been targets of
widespread attacks as "front" organizations in that period of
ever enlarging charges of that kind.

Mr. Sayre was asked if I hadn't had something to do
with his being appointed to the position he then held as the
United States Representative to the Trusteeship Council of

the United Nations, and the prosecutor pressed him with questions implying that I had been "working behind the scenes" to get him that post.

Clark M. Eichelberger, director of the American Association for the United Nations, was asked about his associations with the American Youth Congress (which he denied) and a Spanish Refugee Relief Committee, in an obvious effort to suggest to the jury some Communist tinge. Mr. Eichelberger had testified to my association with him, both before and after the Hitler-Stalin Pact of August 1939, in his efforts to obtain revision of the Neutrality Act, which stood in the way of aid to the Allies by the United States. He also testified that he had been the National Director of the William Allen White Committee to Defend America by Aiding the Allies, which had been active during the period when the Soviet Union and Communists were advocating strict neutrality toward the Allies. Murphy, trying to convey to the jury that the White Committee's efforts of ten years before had been just the opposite of aiding the Allies, called it "the Committee to defend America by keeping it out of the war" and, again, "that committee to keep us out of war."

Throughout the trial the prosecutor had used the appearance of each defense witness who testified to my good character as an opportunity to argue my guilt. Argument on the evidence should be reserved for the opening and closing remarks of counsel. But character witnesses were asked, in Committee fashion, as if the fact were established when it actually was the sole issue in the long trials:

. . . Did you know prior to 1948 that Mr. Hiss took State Department documents and gave them to someone who was unauthorized to receive them?

When Mr. Cross objected that "this assumes something that the jury is asked to pass upon, and the question is improper," it brought only the mild and equivocal comment from the Judge:

I think you could reframe your question, Mr. Murphy.

The reframing was merely to repeat the offensive statement as if it were fact. Murphy simply asked if the witness had *heard* "prior to 1948 that Mr. Hiss took State Department documents and gave them to people or persons unauthorized to receive them." Mr. Cross's objection that he thought this was "the same question" was overruled by the Judge. With this permission from the Judge, Murphy thereafter sometimes used one form and sometimes the other for his insidious assertion of guilt. One being as bad as the other, further objection could only have intensified the injury by attracting still more attention to the prosecutor's reiterated statement of his basic contention.

Murphy's summation was delivered the day the case went to the jury. Mr. Cross's summary had been completed the day before and thus could not have the continuing vividness in the jurors' minds of the prosecutor's inflammatory and biased argument, to which, under the established rules, we could make no reply. Having used the appearance of the witnesses to my good reputation for improper reiteration of his main contention, Murphy attempted to make the reputation itself suspect and even appealed to prejudices against education and against the position in life my character witnesses had achieved:

> I ask you ladies and gentlemen what kind of a reputation does a good spy have? Of course it must be good. The fox barks not when he goes to steal the lamb. It has to be good. But we are here on a search for truth. We are not concerned with reputations. Poppycock. . . .
>
> Ladies and gentlemen, character witnesses belong to another era. This is the age of reason. This is the age of common people. And what we want are facts. We are here, you are here, Judge Goddard is here to ascertain the facts. We don't want gossip.

He had brought out, as if it were something to be sneered at, that various defense witnesses had been to Harvard. In his very first reference to the evidence in his concluding remarks, he remarked that I "went to Harvard" whereas Chambers went to Columbia. My wife's having been to Bryn Mawr was also brought out. He denounced "the intelligentsia" as detractors of the FBI.

At the same time that he breathed insinuations of Communism into my professional and occupational contacts, Murphy inconsistently treated as camouflage not only my relations with the character witnesses but my positions on issues of policy. My official actions in furtherance of American interests, regardless of contrary Soviet policies, Murphy attempted to pervert into support for his thesis. I had not only assisted Mr. Eichelberger's efforts to obtain revision of the Neutrality Act. On September 26, 1939, during the period of the Hitler-Stalin Pact, I proposed, in a memorandum that went to Secretary of State Hull, a policy of aid to the Allies. Murphy made of my position on this pivotal issue:

. . . When in Rome, do what the Romans do. When you are a spy you do what the spies do. You would be an awful spy if you went around with a sign on you. God! This man was good. That is why he was there. That is why he was so good. He pretended to be an American.

To add to the prejudice, he made again the Committee's unfounded assertion that Chambers's possession of the type-written papers (whose contents Murphy not surprisingly failed to stress) meant that with "a translation of the code . . . the codes were broken."

In dealing with the psychiatric testimony, Murphy once again suggested that he had evidence where there was none in the record. In his closing argument he told the jury that "the Government could afford competent psychiatrists." He said he didn't call any psychiatrists because "There was no suspicion of anything wrong with Mr. Chambers' mind at all." [5] The implication was that the prosecutor had psychiatrists who vouched for Chambers's mental health but that Murphy didn't call them because he didn't "think the question attained that

[5] This in the face of Assistant Attorney General Campbell's admission that Chambers was unstable and abnormal (see pp. 191–2).

dignity." And he emphasized to the jury that Dr. Binger had said in an address that "there was a neurosis going over the minds of the American people called 'the bugaboo of Communism.'" This, out of all the psychiatric testimony, the prosecutor said was "one thing I thought was significant." The jury was meant to conclude that Dr. Binger was tolerant of, if not sympathetic to, Communism.

Murphy's most unjustified and damaging assumption of the role of witness has been described earlier: [6] Toward the end of his final plea to the jury he invited them to take the typed documents with them and to "look for similarity of mistakes," calling expressly to their attention three combinations of letters. Even Mrs. Murray's unfair surprise appearance gave my counsel at least the opportunity for unprepared cross-examination and the chance to point out in final argument that her testimony was manifestly imaginary. But here, in the closing minutes, the prosecutor on a crucial issue suddenly became a "witness" not subject to any cross-examination or subsequent comment by defense counsel:

. . . In going over the documents I notice some common typing errors. . . .

If there had been the slightest evidence linking the typing to my wife, Murphy would have had an expert point it out and give an opinion as to the identity of the typist. Instead, Murphy himself became a "witness" whom my counsel could not cross-examine. And his further direct invitation to the jury to make the same comparison that the first jury had improperly made without his invitation could not be objected to, except by the Judge, without compounding the damage. Counter argument was no longer available. There was, therefore, no opportunity to point out that this comparison meant nothing and was gravely misleading, or to point out that other documents in the case which had not been typed by my wife had typing errors in common with the typed documents that Chambers had produced. The Judge not only remained silent at the time but in his

[6] See pp. 320-1.

charge, which followed Murphy's summation, by ambiguous reference to the prosecution expert's testimony may have misled the jury into thinking that this expert must have done more than merely assert that the same typewriter had been used for both sets of papers.

Judge Goddard in this passage of his charge reviewed the expert's testimony in which he had given his reasons for his opinion that the Chambers papers and personal letters of my wife's had been typed on the same machine. These reasons had been that the same broken characters and other defects appeared in Chambers's papers and in the personal letters that my wife had typed. In restating this testimony, Judge Goddard referred to the expert witness as a "typewriting expert," without explaining that the expert's opinion had been simply that the same typewriter had been used and had contained nothing about who had done the typing. The Judge continued by saying that this expert had testified "that, in his opinion, there were various defects in the type appearing in the letters allegedly written by Mrs. Hiss which were identical with defects in the type appearing" in the Chambers papers. The *defects* in *type* the expert had pointed to were, of course, totally different from the *errors* in *typing* that Murphy had just referred to. But the Judge's silence on this latter point may have led his listeners to think he was referring to the same topic. As we had not disputed the expert's testimony, there was no occasion for the Judge to summarize it. The expert's *conclusion* was quite enough. The ambiguity was thus unnecessary as well as confusing. The Judge had done nothing to criticize and correct Murphy on this vital matter. Thus when the members of the jury retired soon afterward, our supporters among them were left not only without aid on a crucial issue, but with Murphy's crude misinformation uncorrected.

During the trial Judge Goddard was lenient with the prosecution witnesses and brusque with defense witnesses. And though he found no occasion to restrain Murphy's attitude toward defense witnesses, Chambers received his protection when Mr. Cross was questioning him. For example, when Chambers was being asked where he had told of using forged birth certificates, he had replied provocatively that Nixon would be a better judge. When asked again, he began: "I had many talks——" The question was repeated once more and Chambers said:

Well, I could tell you where it would have to be, in the old House office building——

Mr. Cross observed that if Chambers couldn't remember he would pass on. At this point the Judge interrupted.

THE COURT: I think you should give him a reasonable opportunity to answer.
MR. CROSS: If this is responsive.
THE COURT: I think it is and he is trying to tell you it is one of several places.
THE WITNESS: That is right.

When Mr. Cross asked Chambers about details of one of his newly volunteered stories of trips, the Judge implied that he couldn't be expected to remember details after many years:

THE COURT: This is 1935?
THE WITNESS: I believe it is, your Honor.
THE COURT: 14 years ago?
THE WITNESS: That is right.

Interruption of cross-examination breaks the continuity of counsel's efforts and, of course, tends to disparage it with the jury. Great latitude is normally allowed, especially to defense counsel, in the topics and scope of cross-examination. Opposing counsel may be eager to interrupt, but the judge usually prevents this tactic. Yet, when Murphy interjected that Mr. Cross had already covered the subject of how many times Chambers had seen Cleide Catlett (in view of his claim to have come to my house about 4:30 in the afternoon every week or ten days), the Judge observed:

You have been over this, it seems to me, in great detail. It seems to me to be repetition.

Mr. Cross pointed out that he had previously inquired only about Chambers's story of also coming to my house at midnight or later each day that he said he had been there in the afternoon. But the Judge, without warrant, continued his disparagement:

THE COURT: We have had all this about the doorbell ringing and the key and all that.

When he summarized to the jury the inconsistencies in various statements by Chambers to the FBI and other officials, contained in reports which we had compelled the prosecution to produce, the Judge did what Murphy did with my character witnesses. He assumed the very facts at issue when he said that, according to the FBI reports, Chambers did not "make any reference *to the fact* that the defendant Hiss had given any papers to him." [7] Similarly, he said that in the several statements there was no "*mention* by Mr. Chambers *of the introduction* of Alger Hiss to Bykov—that is, *Colonel* Bykov." [7]

On cross-examination Chambers had bizarrely embellished his story of a supposed last visit in December 1938 with his fearing an ambush, then staying to dinner and finally being given a "little child's wooden rolling pin" as a Christmas present for his daughter. He said he didn't tell his wife until much later about the rolling pin and, after keeping it for a while, threw it away. He didn't remember where he had kept it. Mr. Cross asked scornfully if he didn't put it in a pumpkin. At this point the Judge intervened:

Is that a serious question?

As Mr. Cross began to reply by referring to other testimony about hiding things (Mrs. Chambers had said she had hidden the Breen passport in a chicken house) the Judge cut him off:

That does not mean that a lawyer should ask a foolish question at this time because he thinks——

[7] Italics added.

Here Mr. Cross, accepting the admonition, asked if Chambers knew where he had hidden it. The Judge intervened sharply:

THE COURT: Now, wait a minute.
MR. CROSS: Excuse me.
THE COURT: It does not mean that a lawyer may ask a foolish or silly question because he thinks the witness has not given him the proper answer.

In the course of Mr. Sayre's testimony Murphy had objected to a question by Mr. Cross about Secretary Hull's not applying the Neutrality Act in March 1938, a topic directly relevant to two of the handwritten memos. The Judge said that it was not apparent what relevancy the question had. Mr. Cross offered to state the relevancy and was told to do so. Before he had completed two sentences he was again interrupted by Murphy, and he remonstrated:

Will you please let me finish. His Honor said I might state it.

The Judge promptly interjected:

I thought you would give a short answer.

A less stable lawyer than Mr. Cross would have been badly confused by the treatment he received. As it was, the presentation of our case was impaired. Mr. Cross was constantly aware that the discrimination in attitude was marked. He believed that it was due to the Judge's desire to avoid any possible basis for criticism of the kind Judge Kaufman had received for his conduct of the first trial. Mr. Cross hoped and believed that the balance would be redressed in the final charge to the jury. Instead the scales were then tipped still further.

The Judge never rebuked Murphy, despite the latter's frequent lapses, and of his own accord did not restrain or interrupt him. While showing special consideration for Chambers, Mrs. Chambers, Mrs. Massing, and other prosecution witnesses, the Judge told Malcolm Cowley and Dr. Binger that they were not "advocate[s]," conveying to the jury the idea that their testimony was not objective. When Geoffrey May asked if he might complete a sentence which Murphy had interrupted, the Judge said sharply:

Just answer that question.

Despite Chambers's and Mrs. Chambers's unhindered irrelevancies, Judge Goddard supported Murphy's interruption of Mr. Sayre when the latter had said of me: "I found him, sir, an outstanding man——" In so doing, the Judge went beyond a mere ruling on the immediate point, commenting generally:

Yes. Mr. Sayre, if you could give direct answers it would be more helpful.

Not content even with this, when Mr. Sayre was then asked simply if I had performed the duties laid out for me and had replied with the one word "Yes," the Judge remarked pointedly:

That is a good answer.

Additional instances of partiality on the Judge's part are to be found throughout the lengthy record, too many to be recapitulated here. Much of the partiality lay in tone of voice and demeanor, which cannot be disclosed by the record, but which carried great weight with the jury and which were noted not only by my counsel but by others who attended the trial.

Judge Goddard actively assisted the prosecutor in presenting his case. For example, when Murphy was presenting the documents early in the case the Judge volunteered as to the typed papers:

Mr. Murphy, are you sure the jury understands what these papers are or what the Government contends they are?

Another instance of argumentative aid in stating the prosecution's case and belittling defense evidence, an action especially weighty with a jury when coming from the supposedly impartial judge, came late in the trial. When Murphy objected to evidence of public policies I had consistently supported, Judge Goddard said:

I suppose Mr. Murphy's position is that even though he was active in these other committees, that does not exclude his activity in the Communist Party, but we are nearing the end of the case and while this does seem to me remote, I think we had better go ahead.

Largely because our brief on appeal, despite the length and complexity of the evidence, had to be limited to 125 pages, we did not assign as error Judge Goddard's partiality throughout the trial. The subject has been treated here because it was an important, though little-noticed,[8] element in the experiences I am here recording. On appeal, in addition to challenging the Judge's rulings I have discussed earlier in this chapter, we assigned as error his one-sided charge to the jury and his later prejudicial selectivity in rereading portions of it at their request.

Mr. Benjamin's brief stated simply our objection to the charge as "weighted in favor of the Government and against appellant." For example, Murphy's attempt to turn my good reputation against me must have seemed to the jury to have received Judge Goddard's endorsement when he said:

. . . It may be that those with whom he had come in contact previously have been misled and that he did not reveal to them his real character or acts.

Despite Chambers's inconsistent stories and his demonstrated unreliability, Judge Goddard refused to give our requested cautionary instructions to the jury and said only that both Chambers and I, and our wives, were interested in the result, that Chambers and I would both wish to have our statements sustained, and that the result might affect the libel suit. He said that the psychiatric testimony was "purely ad-

---

[8] See, however, Richard B. Morris: *Fair Trial* (Knopf, 1952), p. 476.

visory" and that, even though the jury might accept this testimony as to Chambers's mental condition, "you may still find that Mr. Chambers was telling the truth" (when he said he had seen me after January 1, 1937, and had received the documents). He found no occasion to say that I might be telling the truth.

In contrast, Judge Kaufman had told the first jury:

. . . The Government, in its endeavor to establish the allegations of the indictment, has called as its principal witness Mr. Whittaker Chambers. He is the only person who testified that the defendant furnished, delivered and transmitted to him secret documents belonging to the State Department.

You must, therefore, carefully weigh the testimony given by Mr. Chambers. The testimony of Mr. Chambers is not to be taken like that of a disinterested witness. It was the defendant's denial of an assertion made by Mr. Chambers which brought about the defendant's indictment for perjury, and it would only be natural for Mr. Chambers, in the circumstances, to endeavor to sustain his original assertion. In addition, there is still pending in Baltimore the action commenced by the defendant here against Mr. Chambers for libel. I charge you, therefore, that Mr. Chambers is an interested witness because the result of this prosecution may affect the outcome of the Baltimore suit.[9]

Moreover, in considering the weight and the effect to be given to the testimony of Mr. Chambers as to the delivery of the documents by the defendant to Mr. Chambers, you will bear in mind that he has admitted here that on several occasions between 1939 and 1948, sometimes under oath and other times not, he made statements inconsistent with and contrary to his testimony here, and he tells you that his testimony here is true and that on all those other occasions on which he swore to the contrary he committed perjury, and that when he made previous statements to the contrary not under oath, those statements were false.

In this connection, you will also have in mind the fact that he did not make disclosure of having received documents from this defendant during the years he claims to have had possession of them, although he was under a duty to do so, particularly when

[9] It of course did. After my conviction and sentence it was not practicable to continue the libel suit, which was therefore dimissed.

interrogated in reference to them; that by his own testimony he
failed to disclose them until after he had been examined on two
separate occasions in the libel suit commenced against him by
this defendant in Baltimore. . . .

Judge Kaufman had also told the first jury to take into
account Chambers's previous statements that he had left the
Communist Party in 1937, and said that:

. . . The time of his leaving the Party is an important factor
in connection with the validity of the testimony that he has given
here.

The first jury had been further told by Judge Kaufman to
take into account Chambers's "life, his Communist activities,
his code of ethics, his demeanor on the witness stand, his
apparent success when he joined Time magazine in early 1940,
the plausibility, the logic, and the effect of all his testimony"
plus any other factors that in their opinion bore upon his
credibility.

The issue of corroboration was an especially important
one. The word was constantly misused by Murphy, an instance having been given earlier in this chapter.[1] In his summation Murphy had said that "every one of the facts have
been corroborated" in Chambers's first testimony to the Committee alleging a close association with me. That Chambers
had bought a farm in Maryland in which I had been interested in 1935 he called "another bit of corroboration,"
though he didn't say of what. A photograph of Harry Dexter
White's summer place at Peterboro he called "corroboration"
of Chambers's tale of a long trip to Peterboro. Mrs. Massing,
he said, had been "called to corroborate the association."

In his charge Judge Goddard said that, if convinced beyond a reasonable doubt by Chambers's testimony and by
"corroborative evidence," the jury could return a verdict of
guilty. There was no *definition* of what constituted corroboration—namely, proof of the same point *independent* of the
testimony. On the contrary, the jury was, in effect, told that

[1] See pp. 327–8; see also pp. 306–7.

it could regard as corroborative any evidence it found was corroborative. Then, in the paragraph that followed the brief discussion of the need for corroboration, there was an emphatic statement by Judge Goddard of the prosecution's case and a seeming endorsement of all of Murphy's loose claims of corroboration to the "nth degree":

> Now, the Government says that the affair was carried on with great secrecy so as to escape possible detection, and that no one else was present when the alleged acts took place. The Government, however, urges that facts and circumstances have been proved which, it says, fully substantiate the testimony of Mr. Chambers. This is an issue to be determined by you.

The bias of the charge was markedly added to the next day when the jury asked for further instructions. After deliberating all Friday afternoon and that night, the jury on Saturday morning showed its confusion on the subject of corroboration by asking the Judge, "without reading the entire charge," to define the following: "reasonable doubt; circumstantial evidence, acceptable corroborative evidence and their relation to each other." Judge Goddard still gave no definition of corroborative evidence, but merely reread portions of his charge. The discussion in the charge of circumstantial evidence, unlike that of corroboration, was full, detailed, and explicit. Its main conclusions were that such evidence consists of "circumstances from which you are able to draw reasonable conclusions and deductions." "Circumstantial evidence is entitled to as much consideration as you find it deserves. . . . The law makes no distinction between direct evidence of a fact and evidence of circumstances from which the existence of the fact may be reasonably deduced. . . ." Again, as the day before, there was no statement that for corroboration the facts thus established must *independently* of Chambers's testimony, and as a matter of logical *necessity*, substantiate his testimony. To the jurors it must have seemed that any circumstantial evidence could, if they chose, be used by them as corroboration.

The bias of the last paragraph reread by Judge Goddard
was increased in the rereading. He omitted the final sentence:
"This is an issue to be determined by you." The last words,
therefore, that the jury heard before reaching its verdict four
hours later were these:

> . . . The Government, however, urges that facts and
> circumstances have been proved which, it says, fully sub-
> stantiate the testimony of Mr. Chambers.

THE COURT: Does that answer your question?
THE FORELADY: Yes, your Honor, thank you.

Mr. Cross had not then received his copy of the charge.
As soon as he did so and discovered this omitted sentence
(which he did within half an hour) he urged the Judge to
recall the jurors and to read it to them. He contended also
that the Judge should have reread the next paragraph in the
original charge, which had ended the section on corroboration:

> If, as to either count, you do not believe Mr. Chambers or if
> you do believe Mr. Chambers but do not find such corroborating
> evidence, you must return a verdict of not guilty on that count.

He also objected to the fact that in rereading from his charge
passages on the subject of reasonable doubt the Judge had
left that topic incomplete, too. He had stopped just before
the paragraph on character witnesses that contained the sentence: "Evidence of good character may, in itself, create a
reasonable doubt where, without such evidence, no reasonable
doubt would exist."

The requests were denied by Judge Goddard. The jury did
not even know they had been made. In our brief on appeal
we pointed out that the initial charge, too, had ended with a
heavy weighting of its effect against me. Judge Goddard urged
the jury "to mete out justice," a phrase that carries quite a
different implication from "doing justice." He continued:

> Now, ladies and gentlemen, if you find that the evidence
> respecting the defendant is as consistent with innocence as with
> guilt, the defendant should be acquitted. If you find that the law
> has not been violated you should not hesitate for any reason to

render a verdict of acquittal. But, on the other hand, if you find
that the law has been violated as charged, you should not hesitate
because of sympathy or for any other reason to render a verdict of
guilt, as a clear warning to all that a crime such as charged here
may not be committed with impunity. The American public is entitled to be sure of this.

Here, at the culmination, there was no reference to reasonable doubt, to the burden of proof, to the need for any
corroboration at all. It was at best difficult for these jurors to
be objective. Surely an impartial judge should have told them
that the American public was at least equally entitled to be
assured that a defendant must be acquitted if not proved
guilty.

Judge Kaufman's appeal to the jurors' duty had been quite
different. In his charge in the first trial he had said:

. . . If . . . you ladies and gentlemen of the jury make any
mistakes in your conclusions, there will be nothing to show how
you arrived at them, and there may be no way of correcting them.
It is for that reason that I again impress upon you that it is your
duty to determine the case only on the evidence as adduced in
this courtroom, the inferences properly deductible therefrom, and
the instructions that I am giving you.

And he had concluded his charge with these words:

Finally, you are about to exercise one of the highest functions
that can fall to the lot of any man, the function of participating
in the administration of justice. This high privilege carries with it
the equally solemn obligation to decide the issues solely upon the
evidence and to the best of your ability and understanding, free
from all bias, prejudice or partiality. I am confident that each of
you will exert every effort to come to a just conclusion.

Even in the disposition of the appeal the pervasive influence of the Committee played a major and unjustified role.

Judge Harrie B. Chase, who wrote the opinion for the
court, had also written the decision in a case against Rosen,
holding that Rosen was entitled to claim the privilege of the
Fifth Amendment before the grand jury, for which he had

been charged with contempt.[2] Rosen's defense was that he might be charged with participating in a conspiracy with Chambers and so any testimony of his might tend to incriminate him. On this issue Chambers's testimony and mine before the Committee was relevant, and Judge Chase therefore became familiar at that time with that testimony, though not, of course, with my later evidence of Chambers's many inconsistencies and falsehoods.

The Committee testimony had played no great role in the actual evidence in my trial, however much its wide dissemination in the press and by television and radio may have conditioned the jurors and others. We did not even cover in our brief on appeal the passages that had been read into the record of the trial. The rest of the Committee hearings, held without cross-examination or normal judicial safeguards, had dropped out of the case. Yet one third of Judge Chase's opinion dealt with the August 1948 Committee testimony. Judge Chase, after extended quotation from the August 17 hearing at the Commodore, indicated how much the Committee's bias had influenced him:

. . . The jury might well have believed that the appellant had been less than frank in his belated recognition of Mr. Chambers as a man he had known as Crosley and had admittedly known well enough to provide for him a partly furnished apartment at cost with all utilities free to say nothing of an automobile, old certainly, but still useful. . . .

The extent to which Judge Chase had accepted, as had many others, the Committee's assertions is further indicated by his reference to a period of "about ten years between the time the appellant admitted having last seen and known him as Crosley and the time in 1948 when he denied that he could recognize Mr. Chambers." This assumes that I had said that I had known Crosley in 1938, whereas I had actually last seen him before the middle of 1936. A basic issue was thus, ap-

[2] Judge Chase's opinion in the Rosen case is reported at p. 187 of volume 174 of the Federal Reporter, second series, and his opinion on the appeal in my case at p. 822 of volume 185 of the same reports.

parently unconsciously, resolved against me as if it were undisputed. And Judge Chase's characterizing—as "less than
frank" and as "belated"—my refusing to admit or deny ever
knowing Chambers on the basis of mere photographs and my
identification of him as Crosley when I actually saw him also
shows the influence of the Committee's tireless publicity.

At another place in his opinion Judge Chase described
Chambers's August 7 testimony thus:

> Mr. Chambers was then recalled, thoroughly examined re-
> garding his acquaintance with the appellant, and gave to the Com-
> mittee information in considerable detail concerning appellant's
> places of residence and their arrangement and furnishings, as well
> as about his habits and family. . . .

This can only mean that the Judge had accepted the Committee's assertions that Chambers's recital on August 7 had
been accurate, when in fact his glaring inaccuracies demonstrated his penchant for fabrication and his lack of any intimate knowledge of my personal life (the few facts he included
being, as I have shown in Chapter III, no more than would
have been available to him from the acquaintanceship I had
actually had with him or from standard reference works).

At another place Judge Chase wrote:

> Before the time when the appellant identified Mr. Chambers
> as his former acquaintance Crosley, the Committee had before it
> evidence, much of it testimony of Mr. Chambers, to the effect that
> the appellant was a member of the Communist Party and active
> in its behalf when he was employed in the State Department. . . .

Here he was carried beyond even the Committee's biased assertions, unless he was relying on Mundt's wholly unsupported
statement when Chambers first appeared that "there is reason
to believe that [Hiss] organized within that Department one
of the Communist cells which endeavored to influence our
Chinese policy and bring about the condemnation of Chiang
Kai-shek, which put Marzani in an important position there.
. . ." No witness before the Committee had in any way sup-

ported Chambers's charges of Communism prior to the August 17 confrontation. No witness did so later, with the exception of Louis Budenz, who gave the vaguest kind of hearsay that he had "heard [my] name mentioned as a Communist" and said that he "regarded [me] always" as a Communist. Budenz was not called by the prosecution—strong indication that the prosecutor did not believe that Budenz would aid his case.

Budenz's statements certainly do not belong in any category that an appellate judge would be expected to refer to as "evidence." Judge Chase may have assumed that such charges by a Congressional body would have to be based on some further evidence than Chambers's stories.

In the Rosen case Judge Chase had been justified in taking uncritically the Committee's characterization of the testimony in its hearings, for this represented the maximum possible threat from which Rosen sought to protect himself. But the following quotations from his opinion in that case disclose that such an acceptance of the Committee's point of view may have left him with a residual impression of the hearings quite at variance with their actual contents and with the facts later developed at my trials:

Hiss . . . testified positively . . . that he was unable to recognize a picture of Chambers which was shown to him as that of anyone he knew under any other name [This, of course, is most inaccurate. See Chapter I and pages 133–8.]. . . . Hiss subsequently appeared several times before the committee and its sub-committee and for a time was unable to suggest anyone he might have known who could have been Chambers under some other name [I told all I knew of Crosley on my second appearance. See Chapter II.]. . . . After hearings had been held on several days [again the same inaccuracy],[3] Hiss stated that it had but recently occurred to him that Chambers might be a freelance writer, known to him as Crosley. . . . At a subsequent meeting of a sub-committee in New York Chambers and Hiss were both present. At first Hiss could not recognize Chambers as Crosley but after he had looked at his teeth and had heard him answer some questions, Hiss did iden-

---

[3] The official report here contains a period by typographical error.

tify Chambers positively as the man he had known as Crosley.
. . . [Compare pages 84–91.]

At this point in his opinion in the Rosen case Judge
Chase quite unaccountably said, referring to the August 1948
Committee hearings, that Chambers had testified at length in
regard to espionage, a charge that was in fact not made until
three months later. He continued:

. . . His [Chambers's] credibility as well as that of Hiss was
a material matter for the Committee to pass upon in making its
finding of facts relating to the investigation it was conducting.
[There is here no recognition of the Committee's assumption of
the role of prosecutor rather than objective finder of facts.] And
so the truth as to what Hiss had done with the car he said he had
turned over to Chambers, whom he said he had known as Crosley,
was investigated.

It turned out that the title to this particular roadster, as shown
by the public records of the District of Columbia, had been transferred by Hiss on July 23, 1936, which was a year or more after
the time when Hiss had testified that he had turned over the car
to Chambers in connection with the sub-letting of the apartment.
[Compare pages 30–2, 72–7, 105–7, 115–28.]

In his opinion on my appeal Judge Chase was also inaccurate in important respects in his references to the record
in the case. He said that the documents produced by Chambers on November 17, 1948, were "the fruit of his last such
pick-up before, having lost sympathy with it, he renounced
Communism in 1938. . . ." But Chambers had testified that
he picked up these documents in a series of visits occurring
every week or ten days.[4]

[4] His reference to a "last such pick-up" seems to be another instance in
which Judge Chase, no doubt without being aware of it, adopted a Committee
assertion that had no basis in the record of the trials. The Committee's report
of December 31, 1948, entitled "Soviet Espionage Within the United States
Government," refers to the documents as "only 1 week's fraction of the total
volume which Chambers had obtained. . . ." Perhaps this was based on
Chambers's still unpublished testimony of December 1948, given before he had
fully worked out his story. In any event, it adds to the demonstration of Judge
Chase's misunderstanding of essential elements of Chambers's testimony on
which the trials were based.

Again, his opinion said of the typed papers:

> . . . The jury had ample evidence other than the testimony of Mr. Chambers on which to find . . . that the documents of which Mr. Chambers produced copies were all available to Mr. Hiss at the State Department. . . .

If this means that they were "available" to me simply because they were physically in the building where I worked, it obviously has no bearing on the case the prosecution attempted to prove—namely, that I had normal and regular official access to all the documents copied in the typed papers. It seems more likely that the Judge had failed to examine the lengthy record (ten large printed volumes) closely enough to grasp the demonstration that some of the documents copied or summarized in the typed pages had not in fact come to my office.

Judge Chase referred to both of his misstatements of the evidence as "known circumstances" tending "to fill out a normal pattern of probability. . . ."

Most important of all, he completely misconceived the defense's position with respect to the typewriter. Our position had been made clear: Chambers, by means we did not (and still do not) know precisely,[5] had forged the typed papers (or had had them forged) for the purpose of incriminating me. Judge Chase somehow concluded that we rested the defense on the theory that "one or more" of Chambers's sources, having taken documents from the Department of State, copied them or had them copied on our typewriter without our knowledge before giving them to Chambers. We had never remotely considered or suggested anything of the kind. Having set up this straw man defense, Judge Chase disposed of it shortly as suggesting a not very practical "means of copying" for Cham-

---

[5] My counsel and I had suggested possible methods open to Chambers for carrying out his plan; these have been mentioned earlier. We had emphasized as a likely method his having made the copies from microfilms at some time after my wife and I had given the machine to the Catletts. Evidence discovered after the trials made it evident that methods were available to him in addition to those we had suggested on the basis of the facts known to us at the trials (see the next chapter).

bers's sources to have used in supplying him with material. He made no reference to the inherent weaknesses in Chambers's attempt to account for the typed pages, to the evidence of those pages themselves that they were not typed for espionage purposes, or to the evidence that I had not had access to some of the material copied in them.

It is not surprising that Judge Chase, having arrived at such views on the merits, passed over the conduct of the prosecutor and the errors of Judge Goddard. The complex and elaborate documentary evidence (the logical value of which, as corroboration of Chambers, so "deeply troubled" Judge Kaufman that he thought it left "a very substantial question of law that will continue in this case for all time") was held to be adequate for the jury to pass upon as it saw fit. After all, there had been two long and sensational trials. If a reviewing judge is convinced of guilt, he is not likely to be eager to order a third controversial trial.

The appeal was denied in December 1950. Though rehearings are practically never granted, we felt that Judge Chase's misconceptions about the case were so grave that we should seek a rehearing at which these misunderstandings could be corrected. The request was denied early in January 1951.

The Supreme Court does not attempt to review most cases. It has set sharp limits on the cases it will hear, so that only questions of general applicability come before it. Unless an important Constitutional question or the construction of a Congressional statute is involved, or unless two of the appeals courts in different parts of the country are in disagreement, or the case raises some other legal issue likely to affect numerous other cases or individuals, the Supreme Court will not pass on a case at all. By far the great majority of the decisions of the Courts of Appeals are thus final. In refusing to hear cases that it is asked to consider, the Supreme Court thus does not pass on the merits; individual hardship, an erroneous decision, a miscarriage of justice are not in themselves grounds for review by the Supreme Court.

Despite the Supreme Court's strict limitation of its jurisdiction, my counsel and I believed that the case presented issues that warranted its review. We believed that Judge Chase and his two colleagues had misapplied applicable decisions of the Supreme Court in refusing to hold that no case had been presented by the prosecution which even warranted submission to the jury. We also believed that Judge Goddard's permitting Rosen to take the stand and his truncated rereading of parts of the charge, as well as Murphy's conduct, all involved general issues likely to arise in other cases. However, the Supreme Court was unwilling to review the case.

On March 22, 1951, I went to prison.

CHAPTER ELEVEN

——

THE NEW EVIDENCE
OF FRAUD AND FORGERY

WHILE the appeal was being readied I had intensified the search for new evidence. My lawyers had not had time during the trials to follow up every lead. With time for more investigation, they began to collect new evidence for the new trial that might result from the appeal or for use in a subsequent motion for a new trial. Under the Federal Rules of Criminal Procedure a motion for a new trial on the ground of newly discovered evidence may be made within two years after final judgment. We had, therefore, until January 25, 1952 (two years after the sentencing by Judge Goddard). After March 22, 1951, when I went to prison following the denial of the appeal, I could no longer take an active part in this work. I was not on hand to follow the daily results of investigation. Experts in typewriters, in document analysis, in the chemistry of paper, and in metallurgy made exhaustive tests. Investigators followed up leads in New York and other cities, including London. I heard of their findings only at a distance and from time to time when my lawyers were able to visit me or to write to me at the Federal penitentiary at Lewisburg, Pennsylvania, nearly two hundred miles from New York City.

Consequently, I cannot tell of the course of the investigation and of its results from the point of view of having been in daily touch with this work as it went on. The man in charge of that investigation was Chester T. Lane, a New York lawyer, whom I had known at the Harvard Law School and during my years of government service. In February 1950, I had asked him to be my attorney of record in the appeal (to work with Mr. Benjamin) and to carry out the simultaneous investigation that formed the basis for my motion for a new trial. He was put in complete control of the investigation. My account of his brilliant investigative work in the face of great obstacles, and of the vitally important evidence he obtained, will be taken from the court records of the presentation he made as part of my motion for a new trial.

Mr. Lane made three separate and successive written reports to the court. The first results of his investigation were filed with my motion for a new trial on January 24, 1952— just the day before the expiration of the time limit. At that time his investigation was far from complete. The prosecution, which opposed the motion, at first attempted to have it rejected as filed too late. Failing in this, the prosecution obtained repeated adjournments of the argument on the motion. Mr. Lane used the extra time to continue the investigation. After seven more weeks he was blocked by the prosecution's refusal to let his experts examine the typewritten papers that Chambers had produced and that the prosecution had kept in its possession. On March 12, therefore, Mr. Lane made a further written report of his investigation up to that time and announced that he would ask in open court for permission to examine the Chambers papers. As a result, a conference was held with Judge Goddard at which permission was granted. Following expert examination of the papers, Mr. Lane on April 21 filed his third report.

I shall set out the history of Mr. Lane's investigation,

and give its results, in these same three successive stages. This was the way the investigation proceeded; this was the way it was presented to the court; and this is the way it appears in the court records.

By law, my motion for a new trial had to come before the judge who had presided over the trial I sought to have set aside. The motion was therefore presented to Judge Goddard. In spite of the effect of the new evidence which, my counsel and I were convinced, completed the demolishment of Chambers's charges, Judge Goddard denied the motion. He refused even Mr. Lane's request for the summoning of witnesses for a hearing in open court as a basis for passing upon the motion. In a court hearing, Mr. Lane, by subpœnaing unwilling witnesses, could have brought out still more fully the evidence that he had submitted to the court in affidavits and exhibits. Because there was no hearing in open court, no witnesses appeared and there was no opportunity for the full development of the testimony of any witnesses, ours or the prosecution's, by cross-examination. Of necessity their testimony was submitted in affidavits. Consequently, the important new facts discovered in Mr. Lane's investigation have been largely unknown except to the few people who took the time to read through the affidavits.

In his first written application to Judge Goddard on January 24, 1952, when the motion for a new trial was filed, Mr. Lane set forth a brief summary of the striking new evidence he had already found:

SUMMARY OF GROUNDS OF THIS MOTION [1]

1. Apart from the testimony of Chambers and his wife, the Government's case rested in principal part on the Baltimore Docu-

---

[1] Excerpt from affidavit of Chester T. Lane dated January 24, 1952, and filed in court that day. (To distinguish between Mr. Lane's own footnotes, appended to his original affidavits filed in court, and the footnotes such as this one which I have subsequently added, I have identified the latter with my initials. [A. H.])

ments,[2] which a Government expert testified had been typed on a Woodstock typewriter owned by the Hisses. Newly discovered evidence shows, and we offer to demonstrate on this motion, that a technique of forgery by typewriter exists which was not known about at the time of the trial, and which if it could have been demonstrated at the trial would have fatally undermined the essential identifying testimony of the Government's expert.

2. The typewriter supposed to have typed the Baltimore Documents was put in evidence at the trial as a physical exhibit, and was used by the Government before the jury as a dramatic visual illustration of Hiss's guilt. Newly discovered evidence points strongly to the conclusion that the typewriter found and produced by the defense in the belief that it was the original Hiss machine was in fact a carefully constructed substitute, which could only have been fabricated for the deliberate purpose of falsely incriminating Alger Hiss.

3. Though the Chamberses testified to long and close social relations with the Hisses, in public as well as in private, Edith Murray, a supposed former maid of the Chamberses, was the only person ever produced by the Government to testify to any such relations. She was first produced on the last day of the second trial, thus enhancing her dramatic effect on the jury and depriving the defense of any opportunity to prepare for cross-examination or to test her credibility. Newly discovered evidence demonstrates that her identification of the Hisses as visitors at the Chamberses' home cannot have any foundation in fact.

4. The core of the Government's case lay in the Baltimore Documents and in Chambers's story that they were documents supplied to him by Hiss for espionage purposes. To support Chambers's story it is essential that his alleged conspiracy with Hiss should have continued until a few days after April 1, 1938, the date of the last of the Baltimore Documents. Newly discovered evidence establishes that Chambers quit his Communist Party activities at the latest several weeks before April 1, 1938, and thus establishes that Chambers's entire testimony regarding the Baltimore Documents is a fabrication.

[2] Because the 65 typewritten pages had been produced by Chambers in the course of his testimony in the Baltimore libel suit, they were referred to throughout the trials as the Baltimore Documents. (A. H.)

5. Chambers's story depended upon implicating Hiss in a Communist Party group or cell containing several other designated members. Up to the end of the second trial no other alleged member of the group had been willing to testify publicly as to whether the group had in fact ever existed and, if so, what its membership was. Newly discovered evidence, from one prominent alleged member of the group, in the form of sworn testimony before a Congressional Committee, establishes that while such a group did exist, Alger Hiss was not a member of it.

The typewritten pages that Chambers had produced, it will be recalled, had played a part in the case *only* because the prosecution's expert, Ramos C. Feehan, had testified that they had been typed on the same machine that had been used by my wife in typing various personal letters of hers that were also in evidence at the trials. Feehan's opinion had been based on the assumption that each typewriter has peculiarities or defects in some of its letters that enable the typewriter to be identified from samples of typing done on it. Feehan had told the jury, with the use of photographic enlargements, that both the Baltimore Documents and my wife's personal letters contained some ten letters of the alphabet that showed the same peculiarities or defects. My counsel at the trials had also assumed that Feehan's method of identification of a typewriter was scientifically sound and that the similar typeface defects he had pointed to established that the same machine had been used to type the two separate sets of material that had been put in evidence. Except on the basis of this assumption, made by the prosecution and the defense alike, the typed pages Chambers produced would not have given even seeming support to his charges against me.

The typewriter that the defense had found in Lockey's house was put in evidence by my counsel in the belief that it was the machine my wife had once owned. In the examination my counsel gave this machine it appeared to have some of the same typeface peculiarities as those observable in the Baltimore Documents and in my wife's personal letters. This typewriter had engraved on it the serial number 230,099 and was marked as defendant's exhibit "UUU."

Mr. Lane's initial written statement [3] to the court of the new evidence he had found demonstrated that the basic assumption on which the Chambers typed papers had been accepted as evidence was erroneous:

I

The Typewriter

Following the conviction of Alger Hiss by the jury on January 21, 1950, on what his counsel were satisfied was in essential part perjured and fabricated evidence, the whole case was reexamined with a view to trying to find out how Chambers had been able to produce documents typed, or appearing to be typed, on a typewriter owned by Alger Hiss and his wife. One possibility was that Chambers had simply borrowed the typewriter, either when it was in the possession of the Hisses or after it had been given to the sons of their colored maid. This possibility had been fully explored at the trial—without apparently convincing the jury; and it seemed unlikely that any new evidence could be found to prove that Chambers had conducted what was in all probability a clandestine operation known only to himself.

The alternative possibility was that instead of using the Hiss typewriter, Chambers had in some way forged the Baltimore Documents so as to make them appear to have been written on the Hiss typewriter. This possibility had not theretofore been explored because of a general belief that experts in the examination of questioned typewritten documents were able to detect to a scientific certainty whether two given documents, or sets of documents, were typed on the same or on different machines. The scientific method by which this is customarily done had been demonstrated by the Government's witness Feehan in his testimony in this case, and advice from experts employed by the defense had furnished no reason to question the soundness of Feehan's method or the correctness of his results.

[3] In quoting from Mr. Lane's affidavits I shall omit his citations of exhibit numbers of supporting affidavits and page references to the trial record or to hearings.

But after extended reflection it occurred to me that the method employed by Feehan and other experts rested on an assumption that if two typed documents contained a certain number of *similar* deviations from the norm—a repetition of similar peculiarities in a certain number of the typed characters employed in the two documents—the laws of chance would preclude the possibility that two different machines had been used. This assumption, while doubtless sound enough in the ordinary type of case, appeared to neglect altogether the possibility—if it was one—that a typewriter might be deliberately created, or adapted, so as to duplicate some, if not all, of the peculiar characteristics of another. I decided to explore this possibility—to see whether a typewriter could be created which would duplicate a sufficient number of the peculiar characteristics of another to meet the tests which as applied by Mr. Feehan had satisfied him that the same machine had been used in this case for the two sets of documents. If this—which so far as I know had never before been generally supposed possible—*could* be done, the demonstration of it would, it seemed to me, neutralize the "scientific" evidence which had been necessary to corroborate Chambers's testimony and which hence had been vital to the Government's case.

Accordingly, I consulted one Martin K. Tytell, a noted typewriter engineer in New York City, and explained my problem to him. I asked whether, without ever seeing the typewriter in evidence in the Hiss case—Woodstock #230,099—but working simply from sample documents typed on that machine, he could make another typewriter which would produce typed documents so similar in peculiar typing characteristics to the samples as to meet the tests of identity applied by Mr. Feehan. He said that not only could he do that, but he believed that he could make a machine the product of which would be so exactly similar in *all* respects—not merely in the ten or so characters analyzed by Mr. Feehan—that no expert could distinguish documents typed on the two machines, even if put on his guard by warning in advance that a deliberate effort had been made to construct a duplicate machine. Of course, he said, an expert not so forewarned (as Mr. Feehan was presumably not forewarned) would be even more likely to be mistaken in his attempted identification.

At my request Mr. Tytell undertook to try to create such a machine. The machine he built is now in my possession and, as his affidavit shows, it was constructed solely from samples of typing on the alleged Hiss machine. Neither he nor anyone working with him has been allowed at any time to inspect the machine which he was attempting to duplicate, or to take impressions of the original type on it.

It became apparent early in the experiment that it would be necessary to secure the assistance of an expert document examiner, not participating in the manufacture of the machine, who would inspect the results as the experiment progressed and give suggestions as to where improvement was needed. Finding such an expert proved an extremely time-consuming task. Expert after expert declined to take any part in the experiment, some of them basing their refusal on firm disbelief in the possibility of the experiment's success, and others more or less frankly intimating that they did not wish to contribute to the success of any experiment which they feared would have adverse effects on the profession of document examination. One well known expert placed his refusal on the ground that in order to demonstrate the success of the experiment he would have to try to deceive a brother expert, which he would consider an unethical course of action.

After many months an associate suggested to me that I consult Miss Elizabeth McCarthy, whom he described as the leading document expert in New England. I did so, and found her willing and able to help. Her work during the course of the experiment has been confined to examining and comparing samples from the two machines,[4] advising as to progress, and making suggestions as to improvement. At the conclusion of the experiment I asked her to embody her conclusions as to its success in an affidavit.[5] As it shows, she concludes that the duplication has progressed to such a degree that an expert in the field, however highly qualified, would find it difficult if not impossible to distinguish between samples from the two machines. Her affidavit annexes samples from the

[4] That is to say, machine #230,099 produced by my counsel at the trials and the machine Mr. Tytell had constructed for Mr. Lane. (A. H.)

[5] Miss McCarthy's affidavit and other supporting papers filed by Mr. Lane have not been reproduced here. (A. H.)

two machines, which she believes will demonstrate the soundness of her conclusion.[6]

Of course, any expert now examining these samples in the knowledge that two machines have been used will be forewarned to use much more rigid standards of examination and comparison than would heretofore have been the case. It is Miss McCarthy's opinion that even though an expert so forewarned might on that account be successful in differentiating the products of the two machines, an expert not so forewarned would conclude that all the samples were made on a single machine. Moreover, she expresses the opinion that the relative, even if not complete, success of the experiment demonstrates that the testimony of the Government's expert, Mr. Feehan, at the second trial, basing his conclusion of identity of machines on the identity of only ten characters in the two sets of documents, is absolutely worthless.

As the experiment was reaching its conclusion I also enlisted the aid of Mrs. Evelyn S. Ehrlich, of Boston, Massachusetts, who was for many years associated with the Fogg Art Museum at Harvard University as an expert in the detection of typographic and other forgeries. I submitted to her samples from the two machines, taken in December, 1951, and early January, 1952. Without any key from me she successfully differentiated the machines, but told me that she considered the duplication to be far more precise than she had imagined possible, and that in her opinion only a very small number of minor discrepancies remained on the basis of which an expert could possibly differentiate the machines. I then asked her to read Mr. Feehan's testimony at the second trial and, having done so, to give me her opinion as to whether the products of my two machines would show as many identical peculiarities as Mr. Feehan had relied on in his testimony as sufficient to prove that the Baltimore Documents and the Hiss standards [7] had been

[6] Whatever the Government may have done about Miss McCarthy's samples in the laboratory, it did nothing whatsoever about them in court. The United States Attorney in his affidavits, brief, and oral argument totally ignored the fact that the defense had invited the Government to tell them apart if it could. Judge Goddard, denying the motion, likewise ignored this fact. Some of Miss McCarthy's samples are reproduced following p. 374. (A. H.)

[7] In the trials the personal letters typed by my wife, used by Feehan for comparison of observable typeface defects, were called the Hiss standards. (A. H.)

typed on a single machine. She advised me that that was her opinion and, further, that in her opinion the duplication had proceeded to a point where any document expert who, acting with
reasonable care, applied the Feehan criteria to specimens from the
two machines in the condition which they were in at the time
the samples she had seen were made would reach the conclusion
that a single machine had been used to type the two sets of samples.

At my request Mrs. Ehrlich has embodied her opinion in an
affidavit and has accompanied her opinion with extensive photographic material demonstrating the basis for her opinion. As she
points out in her affidavit, the examples she selects are illustrative
only, as she finds in the two sets of documents [8] far more identical
deviations than the ten on which Mr. Feehan relied in his testimony.

In addition, I asked Mrs. Ehrlich whether, from comparison
of available specimens of the Hiss standards with current samples
from Woodstock #230,099 she could form any conclusion as to
whether Woodstock #230,099 was in fact the machine used to type
the Hiss standards. Her opinion, expressed in her affidavit, again
with illustrative photographic material, raises serious question as to
whether it was, although in the absence of original documents [9] in
better condition she finds it impossible to form a definite opinion.

The significance of the evidence offered on this point is that
it demonstrates a technique of forgery which experts have heretofore not considered practicable, and which Mr. Feehan cannot be
supposed to have taken into account. That technique depends, of
course, upon the availability of specimens from the typewriter to be
duplicated; but there is no question that such specimens would
have been available [1] in this case. The new evidence therefore

[8] That is, in the respective samples Mr. Lane had had typed for this
purpose on machine #230,099 and on the machine constructed by Mr. Tytell.
(A. H.)

[9] At this point Mrs. Ehrlich had only photostatic copies of such typewritten exhibits as had been introduced at the trials by the prosecution. The
original exhibits had been retained in the possession of the prosecution and
were not available to us or to Mrs. Ehrlich at that time. (A. H.)

[1] Mr. Lane is here referring to the fact that when Chambers was my
subtenant for ten weeks at the 28th Street apartment, which we left partly furnished, and when he spent two nights at my P Street house, he had opportunity to obtain samples of typing from our machine either by use of the typewriter itself or by picking up personal papers my wife had typed. (A. H.)

renders valueless the testimony relied upon by the Government to ascribe the typing of the Baltimore Documents to the Hiss machine.

II
Indications of Forgery in This Case

As it became more evident in the course of the experiment described in Point I above that Chambers *could* have created a machine so similar in its product to that owned by the Hisses in the early 1930's as to "stump the experts," counsel for Alger Hiss began to turn their attention to the problem of why Chambers should have done so, and, if he had, what had become of it. As to *why* he should have done so, it could have been because he could not find the original Fansler [2]-Hiss machine when he needed it, or, if he knew where it was, could not or did not dare steal it. The risks of discovery involved in even a discreet hunt for the old machine might have seemed considerable, and would be avoided by using a duplicate machine if the forgery could be made convincing enough.

On the other hand, it could have been that Chambers got hold of the original Fansler-Hiss machine and found it unworkable. This could have been so whether the forgery occurred in 1938 (the approximate date of the State Department documents) or in 1948, when he needed to fabricate some evidence to protect himself in the libel suit; for there was evidence at the trial, *not* emanating from Chambers, that the Fansler-Hiss machine was unworkable in 1938 and also in 1945, when Lockey found it in the rain. In this case, it would have been necessary to fabricate a duplicate, and it would have been most natural, when the work of duplication and forgery was completed, to return the duplicate in place of the original as a means of increasing the deception.

The more this theory was considered, the more tenable it appeared, especially if the forgery and substitution occurred in 1948. When Chambers appeared before the House Committee on Un-American Activities in August, 1948, he gave no hint, any more than he had done in his meetings with Berle (1939) and

[2] My wife's father, the original owner of the machine. (A. H.)

Raymond Murphy (1945-6), that there were any such things as
the Baltimore Documents in existence. Not until the pre-trial deposition hearings in the libel suit in Baltimore in November, 1948,
did he suddenly change his story, assert that Alger Hiss had been
engaged in an actual espionage operation, and produce the Baltimore Documents with the charge that they had been typed by
Priscilla Hiss and given to him by Alger. On the face of it this
switch suggested that the documents had been recently typed; and
the documents themselves showed that they had been typed on a
machine in adequate working condition. Moreover, the machine
recovered by the defense from Lockey and placed in evidence
(Woodstock #230,099; Defendant's Exhibit UUU) was clearly in
adequate working condition; Government witness McCool demonstrated its fitness in court at the trial, and I can state from my
own observation that it is still a relatively efficient machine.

Against this background another peculiarity began to assume
importance. It had been established at the trial that the Hisses
had disposed of their typewriter by giving it to the two sons of
their colored maid, "Mike" and "Pat" Catlett, possibly as early
as December, 1937, and certainly no later than April, 1938. Before
the trials both the Government and the defense had made earnest
efforts to trace the machine. Finally, the defense had been successful in locating a typewriter which, allowing for lapses in
memory over the years, answered the description of the Hiss machine, and which appeared to be traceable through several hands
back to the Catletts. An expert retained by the defense had examined the machine and typing from it, and expressed the opinion
that it was the same machine as had been used for the admitted
Hiss specimens. The defense had accordingly introduced it at the
trials on the theory that it was the Hiss machine, and the Government appeared to take the same view; in fact the prosecutor, in
summation to the jury at the second trial, pointed to the machine, and said dramatically: "They [the Baltimore Documents]
were typed on that machine (indicating). Our man said it was".
And the jury was even instructed by the trial judge that the identification of the typewriter was part of the Government's case.

Yet in fact no Government man had said anything of the
kind. No witness for either side had testified that Defendant's

Subject: ENCLOSING A REPORT ON THE
NEW ECONOMIC ORGANIZATION
IN "MANCHUKUO"

The Honorable
     The Secretary of State
               Washington
Sir:
     I have the honor to enclose herewith a report datedJanuary 6,
1938, entitled New Economic Organization in "Manchukuo". This report
describes the change in the directing force of the economic development of "Manchukuo" from the South Manchuria Railway to a new
company, the Manchukuo Heavy Industry Development Company, which will
be a holding company jointly owned by the "Manchukuo" Government and
the Japan Industries Company (Nihon Sangyo Kabushiki Kaisha).
     Mr. Yoskisuke Aikawa, the promoter of the venture described in
the report, is expected to leave Japan for the United States in a
few days. He will no doubt present his plan for investment with
American capital in "Manchukuo" to possible American investors as
soon as he can arrange to meet them.

                              Respectully yours,
                                   Richard F. Boyce,
                                   American Consul

(Germany)

          March 26. Ravndal, U. S. consul at Buenos Aires cabled:
               "According to best possible source, Germany is
          secretly purchasing large stocks of cereals and linseed in
          Argentina, presumably for excessive fees. Shipments
          since January 15, 1938, have been of unusual volume and
          local shippers are strictly prohibited from divulging
          any information regarding them."

SAMPLES OF TYPING (above, and two following pages) done on the Tytell experi-
mental machine constructed for Mr. Lane and on the Woodstock machine that
was found and introduced in evidence at the trials by the defense in the belief
that it was the typewriter that had been given to Priscilla Hiss by her father in the
early 1930's. These samples were among those offered in evidence on the motion
for a new trial to demonstrate the feasibility of forgery by typewriter. Some of the
sample paragraphs here reproduced were typed on one machine, some on the other,
and some partly on one and partly on the other. The prosecution was challenged to
detect which of the samples offered in evidence had been typed on which machine
(see p. 404). The challenge was never accepted (see pp. 370–1).

Far East

Feb. 11. Lockhart, U.S. counselor of Embassy at Peiping, cabled that
reports indicate that the Japanese are continuing preparations for
advances southward along the Peiping-Hankow Railway, and in Shansi.
The number of Japanese troops going south on that railway has
increased; the number of Japanese forces on the Taiyuan plain
has been increasing; railway materials have been sent south,
presumably for repair of the line destroyed sotuh of Changteh;
Japanese espeditions to cause the retirement of irregular forces
west of the Peiping-Hankow Railway and north and south of the
Shikiachuang-Taiyuan Railway have reportedly increased for the
purpose of rendering flank attack against the Japanese more difficult.
Rumors of a western movement of Japanese in Suiyan can not be
confirmed in Peiping.
Feb. 11. Gauss, U.S. consul general in Shanghai, cabled that the
University of Shanghai in the Yangtzepoo District which was
occupied by Japanese military and naval units was adjacent to
a golf course which was being used as an airfield.

                                        February 15, 1938
                                            4 p.m.

Telegram sent

AMLEGATION
    VIENNA

6.
Your No. 18, February 14, 9 p.m.

The Department has found your recent telegraphic reports, and in
particular your telegram under reference, most enlightening and
extremely helpful.
    I am somewhat concerned, however, by the statements which you
say you made to Schmidt, as reported by you in the sixth paragraph
of your telegram. You should very carefully avoid, in the future,
making any statements which can possibly be construed as implying
that your Government is involving itself, in any sense, in
European questions of a purely political character or is taking
any part, even indirectly, in the determination of such questions.

                                        HULL

London, No. 257, March 28, 8 p.m.

"My 241, March 23, 7 p.m.

    "I have just finished an hour's talk with Grandi who recently returned from Italy.
    "First, he is vitally concerned regarding America's opinion of Italy. Second, he informed me that the agreement with England will positively go through within the next few weeks; the Spanish situation will not stop the agreement, settlement of that problem being taken care of. Third, he impressed me with the fact that the Italians will heave a sigh of relief on making this deal with England which will relieve them of being so closely identified with Germany. In answer to Moffat's letter to me of March 14, I would say that in my opinion the successful conclusion of this agreement would definitely seaken Italy's connection with Germany.
    "Grandi was not particularly flattering in his opinion of Goering. Hitler we did not discuss. He is very impressed with Chamberlain and says that he has enjoyed the last month in England more than the previous five and a half years because of the Prime Minister's attitude."

                            KENNEDY

March 29.
Carr, U.S. Minister at Prague, cabled a summary of the Prime Minister's speech of the 28th. After noting the reference in the speech to future minority measures, Carr said "no mention made of new measures though they are probable since in addition to Chamberlain's suggestion we know that British and German ministers think further measures and improved administration essential."

March 29.
Carr, U.S. Minister at Prague, cabled a summary of the Prime Minister's speech of the 28th. After noting the reference in the speech to future minority measures, Carr said "no mention made of new measures though they are probable since in addition to Chamberlain's suggestion we know that British and German ministers think further measures and improved administration essential."

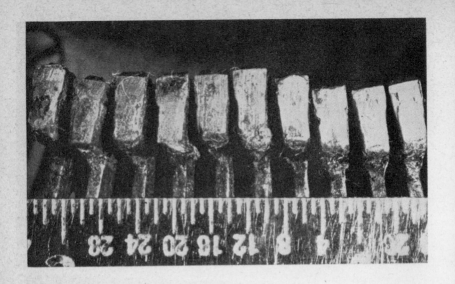

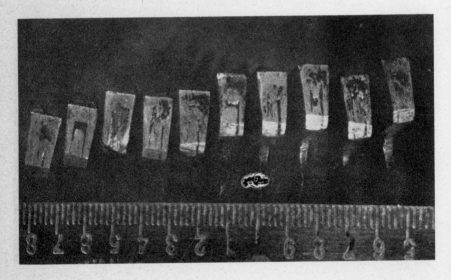

SOME OF THE PHOTOGRAPHS offered in evidence on the motion for a new trial to illustrate the bases for Dr. Norman's conclusion that the Woodstock typewriter which played so prominent a part in the case is an altered machine (see pp. 403–4). This is the typewriter that was found and introduced in evidence at the trials by the defense in the belief that it was the machine that had been given to Priscilla Hiss by her father in the early 1930's. The typebars appearing in the two photo-

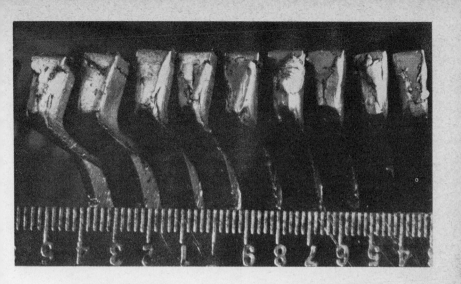

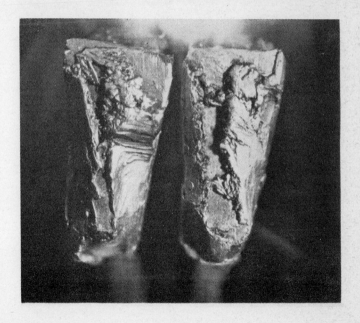

graphs opposite are from ordinary Woodstock machines comparable in age to the machine that was an exhibit at the trials and show normal factory soldering. The photographs above illustrate the unusual soldering of type on to the typebars of the machine that was in evidence at the trials.

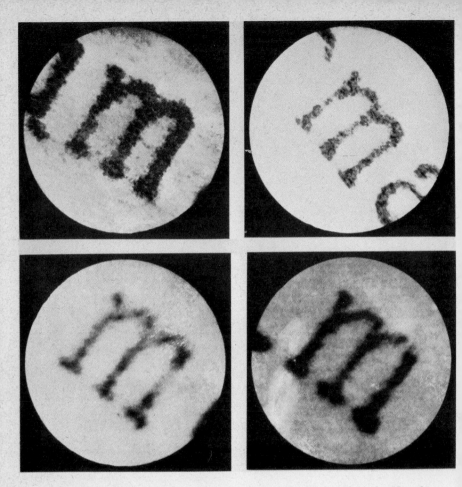

"In almost all of the imprints of the letter m in the photocopy of the Hiss document the highest part of the loops appears to be farther to the right and slightly different in shape than the more rounded loops of the small letter m in the samples typed by the so-called Hiss machine." (Affidavit of Evelyn S. Ehrlich dated January 24, 1952)

SOME OF THE PHOTOGRAPHS offered in evidence on the motion for a new trial to illustrate the bases for Mrs. Ehrlich's conclusion that the so-called "Hiss Machine" (N230,099), an exhibit at the trials, was not—as assumed at the trials—the machine that had been given to Priscilla Hiss by her father early in the 1930's (see pp. 372, 412–3). The two upper photographs on this and the facing page are of typing done on the so-called "Hiss Machine" (N230,099); the two lower photographs on both pages are of genuine typing done on the machine that was in fact owned by the Hisses in the 1930's. Examples of the genuine typing were known at the trials as "Hiss Standards," a term used by Mrs. Ehrlich; Mrs. Ehrlich is also referring to one of these genuine examples when she uses the term "Hiss document."

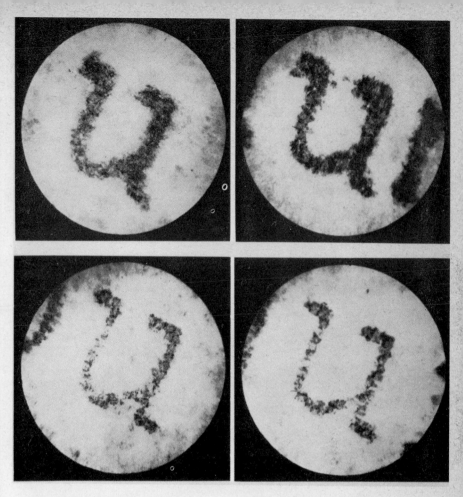

"*The angles where the lower seriph and the loop, respectively, meet the right leg are different in the imprints of #N230099 from those in the Hiss Standards 46-B, 37 and TT.*" (Affidavit of Evelyn S. Ehrlich dated April 19, 1952)

Following page: SOME OF THE PHOTOGRAPHS offered in evidence on the motion for a new trial to illustrate the bases for Dr. Norman's rejection of the authenticity of the "Baltimore Documents" (the typed papers produced by Whittaker Chambers). (See pp. 409–10, paragraphs 4–8.) These photographs show stains appearing on the envelope stored over the dumbwaiter (but not appearing on the "Baltimore Documents" supposed to have been kept therein), and show also the peculiar state of the gummed label.

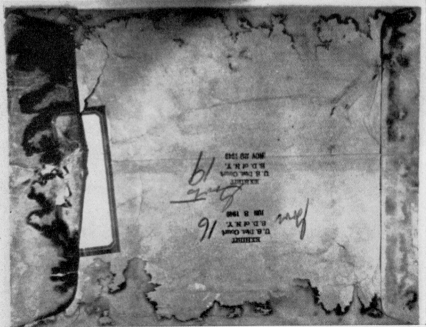

For description see bottom of preceding page

Exhibit UUU was the machine used for the Baltimore Documents, or for the Hiss standards typed in the early thirties. The defense would have had no occasion to make such an identification, but it seemed peculiar that the Government's case had been silent on the matter. The typewriter had been impounded with the clerk by court order at the conclusion of the first trial. I am informed (although I have not been able to verify the fact) that at some time between the two trials the machine was temporarily released to the Government (presumably by authority of the Court) so that for all I know it may have been submitted to expert examination by the Government at that time. Whether it was or not is immaterial; in either event the Government made no effort at the second trial to identify it by *testimony* as the Fansler-Hiss machine. The Government's expert Feehan confined his testimony to comparison of the Baltimore Documents and the admitted Hiss specimens. Could it be that the Government also was suspicious of the machine's authenticity?

In the light of all these considerations, and bearing in mind that the expert who before the trials had identified the machine for the defense had rested his opinion on identical peculiarities in only three characters, apparently without consideration of the possibility of a deliberately fabricated machine, I determined to make a thorough study of the authenticity of Woodstock #230,099. That study has produced results which are startling, as far as they go. Admittedly, for reasons described below, they do not go far enough to demonstrate with any certainty that #230,099 is a fabrication; but I believe that they go far enough to cast serious doubt on its authenticity, and to justify calling upon the Court for its aid in supplying the missing links in the chain of evidence.

The general conclusions from my investigation are as follows:

1. According to the best information I have been able to uncover, a Woodstock typewriter bearing the serial number 230,099 would have been manufactured in or around August, 1929, and certainly no earlier than the first week of July 1929. At the same time the best available information indicates that the typeface style on our machine (#230,099) was a style used by the Woodstock Company only in typewriters manufactured in 1926, 1927 and 1928, and possibly the early part of 1929. These inconsistencies

point to the conclusion that #230,099 is a fabricated machine.

2. The documents admittedly typed by the Hisses on the machine owned by them in the early 1930's were typed on a machine previously owned by Mr. Thomas Fansler, father of Mrs. Hiss. The available evidence points to the fact that this machine was in use in Mr. Fansler's office at least as early as July 8, 1929, and therefore could not have been the typewriter now in the possession of the defense—#230,099.

3. The Government has interested itself in, and has since before the second trial had information about, another machine, bearing a different serial number. There is some indication that the Government has in fact found the machine for which it was searching. In view of the conclusions in paragraphs 1 and 2 above, it would seem probable that this machine, rather than #230,099, is the original Fansler-Hiss machine. Significantly, my investigation of the authenticity of #230,099 is the only phase of my investigative activity which to my knowledge has invoked Government surveillance.

The data upon which the foregoing conclusions are based can only be understood by a somewhat detailed account of my investigation.

HISTORY OF INVESTIGATION OF THE TYPEWRITER

Early in the course of the experiment described in Point I, I sent a representative to the Woodstock factory at Woodstock, Illinois, to secure type of the same kind as used in #230,099. Upon his return he informed me that Mr. Schmitt, the Factory Manager, had advised him that the kind of type he was looking for could not belong to a machine with the serial number 230,-099, since such a machine would have been manufactured in August or September, 1929, whereas the kind of type requested had been discontinued at the end of 1928. He also told me that Mr. Schmitt had mentioned, without elaboration, that his company "had helped the FBI find the typewriter in the Hiss case."

In an attempt to verify the information given by Mr. Schmitt as to the date of manufacture of #230,099, I had an inquiry made by Mr. Robert C. Goldblatt, a typewriter expert of Chicago, Illinois. This inquiry resulted in an affidavit from J. T.

Carlson, Vice-President in Charge of Manufacturing of R. C. Allen Business Machines, Inc., the company which succeeded to the business of the Woodstock Typewriter Company. Mr. Carlson's affidavit, which I annex, indicated that a machine with a serial number only slightly lower than 230,099 would have been made in April or May, 1929.

In view of this divergence of reports, I arranged to have representatives again visit Woodstock to seek an explanation of the discrepancy. My representatives reported to me that at this meeting Mr. Carlson stated that his affidavit had been prepared for him by a clerk and that he himself was not familiar with the facts. He and Mr. Schmitt then produced for inspection certain production records which showed the number of machines manufactured each month during the year 1929, as well as the serial numbers at the beginning and end of that year. One of my representatives, an attorney, further reported to me that after examining these records and discussing their significance with Messrs. Carlson and Schmitt he prepared a draft of an affidavit for Mr. Schmitt's signature, setting forth as accurately as he could the relevant facts from the records and the inferences which he thought could properly be drawn from them as to the date of manufacture of #230,099. According to this attorney, he returned to Mr. Schmitt's office and gave him the original draft affidavit, and was told by Mr. Schmitt that he would have to consult counsel before signing any affidavit in this matter. I have heard nothing further from Mr. Schmitt or Mr. Carlson with respect to the affidavit.

The attorney who prepared the draft affidavit delivered to me on his return to New York what he described as an original carbon copy of it, and I attach this document. I have requested this attorney to authenticate his draft by an affidavit of the circumstances surrounding its preparation; but he has advised me that although he knows that what he prepared represented at the time his understanding of the records he is unwilling for fear of personal consequences to himself to sign any affidavit connected with the Hiss case.

Having in mind that in any event examination of the records by someone experienced in studying typewriters and their his-

tories might be more productive of accurate results, I later asked
one Donald Doud, a document examiner from Milwaukee, Wisconsin (whom I had retained in connection with another aspect
of the case, described more fully below) to see if he could arrange
for inspection of the records at Woodstock. He reported to me that
his written request for an interview and inspection was denied
by letter dated December 6, 1951, from Mr. Schmitt, and he sent
me Mr. Schmitt's original letter. A photostatic copy of Mr.
Schmitt's letter to Mr. Doud is annexed. Mr. Doud has refused
to authenticate this letter by affidavit for reasons I describe below,
and now has the original in his possession.

It will be seen that both the facts reflected in the affidavit
prepared for Mr. Schmitt's signature and Mr. Schmitt's letter of
December 6, 1951, indicate that the date of manufacture of #230,-
099 was not before July, 1929. I have prepared, and attach, a
memorandum explaining how this conclusion is necessarily de-
rived from the records inspected by my representatives at Woodstock.

Paralleling the inquiry as to the date of manufacture of
#230,099, I initiated an investigation to ascertain the date of
original purchase of the Fansler-Hiss machine. The obvious line
of inquiry lay in Philadelphia, where Mr. Fansler had been at
the time General Agent of the Northwestern Mutual Insurance
Company of Milwaukee, Wisconsin. Our files showed that in
December, 1948, before the typewriter had been found, a defense
investigator had reported an interview with Harry L. Martin,
Mr. Fansler's secretary or office associate at the time, in which
Martin had told him that the Fansler Woodstock had been originally purchased in early 1928. This seemed worth checking on
further and I had a representative attempt to interview Mr. Martin
again. My representative informed me that Mr. Martin had declined
to grant him a personal interview, and had stated that he would
not discuss the matter under any circumstances without the formal
consent of the Agent in charge of the FBI in Philadelphia.

I also requested Kenneth Simon, an attorney then associated
with the Hiss defense, to try to locate the dealer from whom
Fansler had acquired his machine. Mr. Simon's affidavit as to the
results of his inquiry is annexed. As the affidavit shows, Mr. Simon

on several occasions interviewed Mr. O. J. Carow, who had been
Branch Manager of the Woodstock Typewriter Company Sales
Agency in Philadelphia from 1927 until its discontinuance in
1938. From these interviews several significant facts appeared:

(a) Mr. Carow had been interviewed in late 1948 or early
1949 by the FBI, and had been asked in connection with the
Hiss case to locate records of the sale of a machine with a given
serial number. He could not remember the exact serial number,
and had not been able to find any record of the sale of the
particular machine; but he recalled that on the basis of other
records in his possession he had advised the FBI that the machine
they were interested in would have been sold in Philadelphia
in November 1927, with a six months margin of error.

(b) Mr. Carow was unable to give even an approximation
of the date on which #230,099 would have been sold because the
FBI had taken away, and never returned to him, all the material
on which he had based his calculation of the date of sale of the
machine in which they were interested, and after their visit he had
destroyed most of the rest of his records.

(c) Mr. Carow thought, although he was not certain, that
the machine the FBI was interested in had a serial number different from 230,099.

(d) Between Mr. Simon's first and his last visit to Mr. Carow
(i.e., between October 23, 1950, and January 18, 1951) FBI agents,
including a Mr. Kirkland, had been in touch with Mr. Carow
to find out what it was that Mr. Simon was trying to learn, and
what Mr. Carow had told him.

Mr. Simon's inquiry thus helped us very little in our effort
to find out when the Fansler-Hiss machine was originally purchased by Mr. Fansler. It did, however, indicate:

> (1) that the FBI, in its search for the original
> typewriter, had had a serial number to work from, and
> that that number was different from the number on the
> machine which the defense had found before the first
> trial;
> (2) that the machine the FBI was looking for had
> been first sold in late 1927 or early 1928, and so could

certainly not be a machine made in 1929, as a machine numbered 230,099 must have been;

(3) that the records which might make it possible for us to prove our point were unavailable, because either the FBI had them or they had been destroyed, and that as late as the end of 1950—nearly a year after the finish of the second trial—the FBI was still enough interested in the problem of the typewriter to be keeping our investigative efforts under surveillance.

This search in Philadelphia for the original sales record of the Fansler machine was only one of the lines of investigation I followed trying to date Fansler's purchase of the typewriter. As a separate inquiry I decided to try to locate letters typed in Fansler's office in the late twenties with the thought that if I could have such letters compared by an expert with the letters typed by the Hisses in the 1930's, the expert could show just when the typewriter first came into use in the Fansler office.

The most likely place to find such letters was clearly the home office of Fansler's employer, the Northwestern Mutual Life Insurance Company, in Milwaukee, Wisconsin. In early October, 1950, I telephoned Mr. G. M. Swanstrom, the Company's General Counsel, and arranged to have him meet with one of my representatives. My representative reported to me that at the meeting Mr. Swanstrom showed him photostats of letters from the Fansler office written in 1928, 1929, and 1930, but would not allow him to see the originals or to borrow the photostats for examination by an expert. The 1929 letters, according to my representative, were dated January 14, June 29, July 8, and August 21; and the July 8 and August 21 letters appeared to him to be typed on a Woodstock, and on a different machine from that used for the earlier letters.

At my request my representative made a further attempt about a month later to persuade Mr. Swanstrom to let him have an expert examine the Northwestern Mutual letters, and compare them with the Hiss standards. He reported that again Mr. Swanstrom declined, this time saying that prominent policyholders of the Company had indicated disapproval of permitting access to the Company's files without a subpoena. As I had no legal right to a subpoena, I could do nothing.

For a while the matter necessarily rested there, but in September, 1951, a private investigative agency which I had retained to cover certain limited aspects of the inquiry for me reported that Mr. Swanstrom might be willing to release the letters for examination to a Mr. Donald Doud, a document examiner in Milwaukee practicing in association with Mr. John F. Tyrrell, a former employee of Northwestern Mutual who had made himself a considerable reputation in the field of examining questioned documents. I went to Milwaukee, and found Mr. Doud already in possession of the originals or photostats of a substantial number of letters written from the Fansler office to Northwestern, running in date from July 23, 1927, to February 14, 1930—including photostats of the July 8 and August 21 letters which my representative had seen in Mr. Swanstrom's office. We talked over my problem at length, and I explained that since I had reason to believe that #230,099 had not been made before July, 1929, it was important for me to know whether, in the view of an expert, the Fansler letter of July 8, 1929, or any of the earlier letters was written on the same machine as had been used for the Hiss specimens in evidence at the trial; for if so it would follow that the machine we had found—#230,099—could not be the original Fansler-Hiss machine. I gave him for comparison purposes the originals or copies of the Hiss standards, and also photostats of some of the Baltimore Documents. Mr. Doud undertook, for an agreed fee, to make the necessary document examination and to give me his expert opinion as soon as practicable.

Mr. Doud sent me his opinion on November 6, 1951. I annex his letter. As will be seen from a reading of it, he concludes:

(1) that the Northwestern Mutual letters from the July 8th letter on were written on an "apparently quite new" Woodstock machine different from the machine used for the earlier letters.

(2) that the Northwestern Mutual letters dated July

8, 1929, and later "agree in typeface pattern" with the Hiss specimens, as well as with the Baltimore Documents, and show a tendency "toward the development of type-face defects that later became so highly identifying in the 1933 and 1935 specimens and the Baltimore Letters."

(3) that he could "find no evidence to show that these early Northwestern Life specimens from July 8, 1929 to February 14, 1930 *could not* have been written on the same typewriter used for the Baltimore Letters and the Standard Hiss specimens."

(4) that the model typewriter all these letters were written on was of a kind made from 1926 "until some time the latter part of 1928 or early in 1929," and that the letters show "complete agreement in typeface style" with specimens of typewriting from his files dated in 1926, 1927, and 1928.

Although Mr. Doud had been working in large part from photostats which necessarily limited the certainty of his conclusions, it seemed to me that his opinion went far to show that I was on the right track: that the Fansler-Hiss machine could not be the one the defense had found, and that our machine, #230,099, must therefore be a fake, deliberately planted on us by somebody. This would follow not only from his opinion with regard to the July 8th letter, but even more strongly from his opinion that the model typewriter used in the Fansler office from July 8th on, and later by the Hisses, was a model made in 1926, 1927, 1928, or early 1929. Accordingly, I asked Mr. Doud to embody his conclusions in an affidavit, with whatever qualifications he might wish to make arising from the limitations within which he had had to work.

To my surprise Mr. Doud declined to make any such affidavit, or even to authenticate the letter which he had received from Mr. Schmitt at Woodstock in answer to his request to be allowed to look at the production records. I attach Mr. Doud's letter of refusal, dated January 14, 1952. His stated reason is quite clear: he does not believe that it would have been possible for anyone to have faked a typewriter, and therefore he declines to make any affidavit which might be used in connection with an attempt to show that that may well have been done.[3]

Nothing in his letter of refusal retreats from the conclusions stated, in however qualified form, in his earlier opinion letter. I attach the letter of refusal for two purposes: (1) to show why I cannot present the original conclusions in affidavit form; and (2) to show to the Court in the most effective form possible the extraordinary difficulties with which the defense has been confronted in its effort to uncover Chambers's methods of operation. Mr. Doud's reference to "evidence [he has] gathered to date" is misleading; Mr. Doud gathered no evidence, but simply made a comparison of certain letters I furnished him with certain letters Northwestern Mutual furnished him. He has never seen #230,099. He has not been asked to give any opinion as to specimens from it. He has not examined the records as to its date of manufacture. He knows nothing about it. He concludes, from "typeface style and pattern," that the Fansler-Hiss typewriter "must have been manufactured during * * * 1926, 1927, 1928, or possibly early 1929," and that therefore Mr. Schmitt must be wrong in saying that #230,099 was made in July or August 1929.

Why must Mr. Schmitt be wrong? Evidently because, unless he is, the experts could be wrong when they say a machine could not be fabricated. But maybe the experts could be wrong too.

The foregoing is an unfortunately but necessarily elaborate account of the investigation into the authenticity of the typewriter. I do not contend that it has produced usable evidence which would conclusively demonstrate that a fabricated typewriter was used to forge the Baltimore Documents, or that such a typewriter was planted on the defense for deceptive purposes. I do contend, however, that considering the extraordinary handicaps which surround any such investigation on behalf of a private citizen, the matters hereby brought to the Court's attention give

[3] As a second reason for his refusal Mr. Doud states that he had to work in part from "blurred photostats," and that "any judgment based upon such poor reproductions must be a qualified one." It will be noted that Mr. Doud's opinion letter of November 6th made no such complaint; and at my conference with him in September, when we both examined the specimens from which he would be working, he raised no question as to the inadequacy of the photostatic reproductions.

rise to such serious doubts regarding that part of the Government's case which rested on the typewriter that justice cannot be done unless the case is reopened for further proof according to law.

It is the handicaps surrounding the investigation which most require the Court's attention. We search for records—the FBI has them. We ask questions—the FBI will not let people talk to us. We request access to ordinary documents in corporate files—corporate officials fear the wrath of their stockholders. We ask people to certify information in files they have shown us—they must consult counsel, and we hear no more from them. We pay experts to give us opinions—and they decline to back them up in court because they "cannot subscribe" to anything which might support the conclusion we believe the facts point to.

And, even worse, honorable and patriotic citizens who have wanted to help have been deterred by the appearance—whether or not it is reality—of official surveillance and wiretapping, and others who have labored to gather information for us in the interests of justice are afraid to come forward for fear of personal consequences which might result to them from public association with the defense of Alger Hiss.

Anyone alive to today's events knows that as a result of Chambers's stories and the trials based on them the name Alger Hiss has become synonymous with treachery and betrayal in high office. If he was guilty, this is perhaps as it should be. But if he was not, it is tragic that the fear and hysteria of the times should be allowed to impede so gravely the efforts of his defenders to unearth and present the evidence which would clear his name.

If a new trial were granted, the defense could then, through subpoena power, present to the jury in evidentiary form much of the information which has necessarily been reflected in this affidavit as hearsay—however reliable. And I urge that the information presented herein is of such significance that if it had been possible to present it to the jury in the second trial, the jury could not but have been shaken from its faith in the genuineness of the Baltimore Documents, the Government's principal corroboration for Chambers's story. A new trial should therefore be granted, without more. But if the Court is not so convinced, I urge, and even more strongly, that in its consideration of this motion the

Court should in the interests of justice invoke its own inquisitorial power. These questions cannot be set at rest unless the Court will bring before it the witnesses who have refused to make oath for us, require the production of documents which have been closed to us, and call upon the Government to show what it knows about the typewriter. And if, as we have deep reason to believe, the Government knows relevant facts about the typewriter which it has during and since the second trial concealed, that alone should require a new trial.

Mr. Lane's third point in his affidavit of January 24, 1952, dealt with Edith Murray, the surprise witness of the second trial. The substance of her brief direct testimony was that in 1934–5 and 1935–6 she had worked daily as a maid for the Chamberses (under their assumed name of Cantwell) at their homes at 903 St. Paul Street and 1617 Eutaw Place, Baltimore, and that in the course of the latter period she had seen my wife four times and me once on social visits to the Chambers-Cantwells. Wherever and whenever she may have worked for the Chamberses, according to this new evidence she did not work daily for them at either of these two Baltimore addresses.

The St. Paul Street address was the Baltimore headquarters of the Woman's Christian Temperance Union. Its housekeeper in the 1930's, up until 1938, was a Miss Hasson, who died about 1946. Miss Hasson's niece married Mr. William Reed Fowler in August 1934. In an affidavit presented by Mr. Lane, Mr. Fowler stated that he and his wife had dinner three to five times a week at 903 St. Paul Street, with Miss Hasson, from the time of his marriage until Miss Hasson ceased to be the housekeeper there in 1938. He remembered a couple with one child who rented the top floor during the winter of 1934–5. He didn't recall their names as being either Chambers or Cantwell. Though he frequently met the man, and had not only seen pictures of Chambers but in 1951 had seen Chambers himself, Mr. Fowler said that Chambers bore no "resemblance whatsoever to the man who was living on the third floor at 903 St. Paul St. in 1935." [4] Mr. Fowler was certain that this couple had no maid:

I am also absolutely positive that no colored maid, or any maid, for that matter, was employed there during that period by any of the people who were tenants during that time, or by Miss Hasson. Miss Hasson did have a colored man who did odd jobs around the house, as well as at another house which she owned and had rented out, but she didn't have any colored maid. Entirely apart from my own observation I am sure that she would have talked about a maid if there had been one there. As a matter of fact, I remember her mentioning that she had quite a lot of trouble even getting the rent out of the couple with the child.

Mr. Louis J. Leisman, in an affidavit presented by Mr. Lane, said that he lived and worked at 1619 Eutaw Place as custodian and rent collector from September 1935 to December 1936. He remembered that one of the apartments at 1617 Eutaw Place was occupied by someone named Cantwell. He also remembered Chambers as having lived there, but did not know his name. He had often seen Chambers in and around the house and had frequently seen him at a near-by tavern. Mr. Leisman said also:

I know from my own observation that Chambers, or Cantwell, never employed a colored maid. If Chambers, or Cantwell, had employed a white maid, I might possibly have mistaken her for a tenant, but no colored maid could possibly have escaped my observation. In the winter time I was regularly in the basement in the morning and in the evening where I lived, in which there was a basement window that reached a little above the street level from which I could see the steps of 1617 and 1619 Eutaw Place. I stood there each day to watch for tenants in my house in order to catch them to collect rents due or to tell them to get out if they had proved undesirable. In warm weather I would either sit on the front steps outside my house or on a chair set against the railing, not more than three feet from the front steps of 1617.

[4] The testimony of Mr. Fowler is at least another indication of the marked change in Chambers's appearance in the period from 1935 to 1948.

It would have been almost impossible for a colored maid to have used the rear entrance of 1617 because the rear of the basement was taken up by the furnace room and there was no exit from the furnace room to the upper floors of the house except through the front basement apartment which was rented to a white tenant. The janitor of 1617 had to use the front entrance to get into the house proper and a white tenant in Baltimore would never have given a colored maid permission to come through the basement apartment. I can further say that it would be very unlikely that she could have escaped my observation by using the rear because it was necessary for me to take out the ashes and trash at 1619 through the rear exit at various times during the day, and certainly I would have seen a colored maid at least once in the time Edith Murray is supposed to have worked there.

I further say that there is no possibility of my being mistaken in my recollection in this matter, since the buildings in the neighborhood, including 1617 Eutaw Place, were generally occupied by very low type white people, paying rents of not more than $8.00 a week at that time, and keeping the police busy at all times checking up on prostitution, illegal sale of whiskey, and other immoral activities. It would have been so unusual for anyone to have a maid in that house that everybody in the neighborhood would have known about it and spoken about it, and if I had seen a colored girl going in or out of any house in the 1600 block of Eutaw Place it would have been so unusual that I would have investigated and found out for myself what new was going on in the block.

The vast importance of opportunity for investigation was again demonstrated. As Mr. Lane concluded, Edith Murray "did not see [my wife and me], as she said she did, and . . . fairness and justice call for giving the defense an opportunity to establish that fact at a new trial."

In the fourth major point of his affidavit Mr. Lane disclosed important new facts as to when in 1938 Chambers broke with the Communist Party, went into hiding, and left for Florida. Mr. Lane pointed out that from 1939 until late August 1948 Chambers had consistently said that his Communist activity lasted only through 1937. Mr. Lane further stated that it was not until late August 1948 that for the first time Chambers moved the date of his break with Communism to the second or third week of February 1938. Mr. Lane continued:

At the second trial, however, the story is changed. According to the new version, his break with the Party occurred approximately in the middle of April, 1938: "I believe it was April 15." Upon this break he moved his family to a room on Old Court Road, near Baltimore, where he stayed for about a month, until he "had obtained a translation to do" from Paul Willert of the Oxford University Press—a translation of a book entitled "Dunant—The Founder of The Red Cross." As soon as he had the translation and an advance he went to Daytona Beach, Florida, where he "finished the translation, and after a month returned to New York."

Chambers himself was aware of—or could not escape from—the inconsistency. On cross-examination he was asked: "Now, did you on a number of occasions say that you broke with the Party in 1937?", and he replied: "Yes, I did." He was further asked: "Is that date correct?" and replied: "It is not."

It is obvious why Chambers had to change his story. He had first produced the Baltimore Documents at a pretrial deposition hearing in the Baltimore libel action on November 17, 1948—when he needed some kind of evidence to protect himself against liability for his charges of Hiss's Communist affiliations. The documents he produced covered dates running from January 5 to April 1, 1938.[5] Once he had produced them, his old story of having left the Party in 1937, or no later than the middle of February, 1938, would no longer do. He had to provide a new date for his break; otherwise he could not sustain his new tale that he had been collecting State Department information from Alger Hiss for Communist espionage purposes through January, February, and March, 1938. So for the end of his Party activity he came up with April 15, 1938—a convenient date which would

---

[5] That is, the State Department documents copied or paraphrased in the Baltimore Documents were shown to have been received in the State Department between those dates, inclusively.

allow for the mechanics of abstracting and copying documents received in the Department as late as 7:45 on the evening of April first.

The suspicious characteristics of Chambers's changed story were evident on the trial record, and are reiterated here only because the defense has now come into possession of evidence showing that the second story, not the first, was the false one. This new evidence establishes that Chambers had left the Party and secured his translation from the Oxford University Press at least by early March, 1938. Therefore his whole story of Hiss as the source of State Department documents running into April is shown up as a fabrication.

First, I attach an affidavit of Dr. Martin Gumpert, of 315 East 68th Street, New York, N.Y., the author of the book which Chambers translated. This affidavit recites in general the history of the translation. It shows that the book was first assigned for translation to Mrs. Rita Reil, at some time before the end of December, 1937. Before very long a new translator, Chambers, was substituted. As soon as he was engaged Dr. Gumpert asked to meet him, but was told by the publisher that he could not do so because "he was in hiding from the Russian secret service, known as the G.P.U. and that because he was in hiding he constantly changed his address, and, also, that because he changed his address constantly the Oxford University Press was unable to contact Mr. Chambers, but had to wait for him to contact the Oxford University Press."

Both by Chambers's own testimony and by Dr. Gumpert's affidavit, the date when Chambers got his translation clearly marks the outside limit of Chambers's Party activity. I have made contact with Mrs. Rita Reil, the first translator, and with Paul Willert, then Vice-President of the Oxford University Press in New York and the editor in charge of publication of Chambers's translation. Together, they confirm the basic facts reflected by Dr. Gumpert's affidavit, and upon a new trial, if one is granted, I intend to call each as a witness; but neither can be any more precise as to the relevant dates than Dr. Gumpert.

However, other records which have now become available to the defense are more precise. I have personally examined the files of the Oxford University Press, 114 Fifth Avenue, New York, relating to Chambers's translation of Dr. Gumpert's book, and I have caused an examination to be made of the files of Dr. Gumpert's London agent, Pearn, Pollinger & Higham, Ltd., 39–40 Bedford Street, Strand, London, W.C. 2, regarding the same subject matter. I attach copies of the relevant documents in those files. Though these documents still do not fix the exact date when Chambers got his translation, they prove beyond question that the date was not only well before the middle of May—Chambers's date in his second trial testimony—but well before April first, the date of the last State Department document covered by the Baltimore Documents. Chambers had made his arrangements, got the bulk of his translation, and an advance of $100, early in March at the latest.

1. Chambers had obviously gotten his translation some time before April 12, 1938, since Willert's letter of that date to him, which the Post Office was unable to deliver, asks how he is getting on with it, and implies that some results are already due. This is confirmed by the fact that a portion of the manuscript had been mailed to him at his Mt. Royal Terrace address in Baltimore on March 18, 1938. The delivery instructions were "RUSH—MUST REACH BALTIMORE SATURDAY EXPRESS"; i.e., the next day, since March 18, 1938, was a Friday. Taken alone, this could mean merely urgency on the part of the publisher, or it could more probably mean that Chambers had advised that after March 19th he would no longer be available to pick up the package. That Chambers went into hiding at or about that time is clear from his handwritten letter dated May 3rd to Willert, in which he says: "I have not been at Mt. Royal Terrace for more than a month." In any event, Chambers had clearly become a translator by March 18th, and therefore by his own account must have been out of the Party by that date.

2. The same proof may be tied in more specifically to the Baltimore Documents Chambers claimed to have gotten from Hiss. The last of the State Department messages covered by the Baltimore Documents was an incoming cable dated April 1, 1938. This message shows on its face that it was received in the Department at 7:45 p.m. on that day, and therefore it could

not have been distributed to the Departmental offices until April 2nd—a Saturday. If Chambers had visited Hiss for a pick-up on April 2nd he would—according to the system he described at the trial—have taken not a typed copy, but the original for photographing that night or over the weekend. There would have been no occasion to paraphrase and type the message if Chambers had visited on April 2nd or 3rd. To have picked up a typed copy he would therefore have had to visit on Monday, April 4th, or some later day. But by April 4th, he was already in hiding, for in the letter of May 3rd to Willert he said that he had not been at Mt. Royal Terrace "for more than a month." [6] Baltimore Document 46 cannot therefore have been received by Chambers in the manner he asserted at the trial—a further proof out of his own mouth that his story of the transmission of documents to him by Hiss is false.

3. Since a portion of the manuscript was sent to Chambers on March 18th, he must certainly have been out of the Party by that time. But the actual date was even earlier, for further correlation of the information in the Oxford University Press and the Pearn, Pollinger & Higham files shows that the March 18th shipment was the *last*, not the first, batch of manuscript. Chambers's telegram of May 22nd refers to the "complete translation including extra chapters you sent"; and as the shipping ticket of March 18th is the only shipping ticket in the file, it must have covered the "extra chapters," and the bulk of the manuscript must have been delivered by hand at some earlier date. That there was such a hand delivery is a natural inference from Chambers's own testimony that he got his translation and an advance [7] on a personal

---

[6] Although Chambers's handwritten letter bears the date "May 3, 1938," it seems probable that it was actually written on May 4th. From the subject matter, both it and the typed letter dated May 4th were obviously in answer to Willert's letter dated May 4th. In view of Willert's urgency and irritation he would undoubtedly have written Chambers air mail, and his letter might well have reached General Delivery in St. Augustine on the same day. The fact that stamped notations show that neither of Chambers's answering letters was received by Willert until May 9th is consistent with the facts that Chambers, needing money, would not have used air mail, and that a weekend intervened, May 9, 1938, being a Monday.

[7] The advance would appear to have been $100, for (a) London was to pay one-half the translation fee; (b) London's half was to amount to $350;

visit to Willert in New York—a visit which now is shown to have been at *some* time before March 18th.

4. Just how much before March 18th Chambers quit his espionage activities is still not certain from the records. However, the records do show that the London office of the Oxford University Press learned as early as March 3rd that a new translation was being made and on March 4th instigated inquiries as to its progress. While this may not establish that Chambers had actually been retained by that time, it should be recalled that at the second trial one of the Government's own witnesses, Henry Julian Wadleigh, who was a self-confessed source of many of Chambers's documents, placed the date by strong inference at some time before March 11th, the date on which he left for Turkey. When "the time came near" for him to go to Turkey, he tried to notify Chambers that he was going, but could not because before that time he had been instructed "not to deliver any document for the time being" and had no means of getting in touch with Chambers.

The conclusion to be drawn from these papers is necessarily that Chambers's break with the Party, and his cessation of espionage activity, occurred at least no later than the forepart of March. The new evidence, while generally supporting Chambers's story of his leaving the Party and getting a translation, definitely contradicts it in the vital features which would implicate Hiss. Even if everything that Chambers at the second trial said had happened in this respect did in fact happen, it did not happen *when* he said it did. It happened earlier—enough earlier to contradict and vitiate his testimony as to the source of the Baltimore Documents. And if Chambers was wrong as to the source of the Baltimore Documents, the Government had no case, and the jury could not fail to acquit.

The final item of new evidence presented to Judge Goddard on January 24, 1952, was the testimony given by Lee Pressman after the trials:

---

and (c) Willert completed the first half of his payment to Chambers with a check for $250.

V

Lee Pressman

One of the major difficulties facing the defense throughout the trial was Chambers's tendency to bring in—as people involved with him in his Communist conspiracy which he claimed also involved Alger Hiss—people who were either dead or unavailable to deny his story. Thus, Chambers and Hiss were supposed to have met originally at a meeting engineered by two Communist Party officials, Harold Ware and J. Peters. At the time of trial Ware was dead, and Peters had flown from the United States. The alleged trip to Peterboro, New Hampshire, was mentioned only after the death of Harry Dexter White, the person whom Chambers claimed to have made the trip to visit. Instances could be multiplied.

In one centrally important phase of his tale, Chambers did use the names of persons who were alive and at least physically available. That was his story of the Communist group to which Hiss allegedly belonged. In the varying versions of this story Chambers nevertheless maintained consistency in his assertion that other members of the group included Nathan Witt, Charles Kramer, John Abt and Lee Pressman. It might reasonably have been supposed that one or more of these persons might have been able to deny Chambers's story, at least so far as Alger Hiss was concerned; but each of them rendered himself as a practical matter unavailable by declining to testify in response to Chambers's charges on the ground of self-incrimination.

Since the conclusion of the trial, however, one of these men, Lee Pressman, has withdrawn his claim of privilege, and has testified before the House Committee on Un-American Activities regarding the Communist group described by Chambers. He has stated publicly and under oath that such a group did exist, that he was a member of it, that it also included Abt, Kramer and Witt, and that Alger Hiss was not a member of it during the period of his own participation, namely, about a year, from 1934 to the latter part of 1935. This period was vital to Chambers's story, for it embraced the period of Hiss's service with the Senate

Committee Investigating the Munitions Industry (the so-called
Nye Committee), during which Chambers claimed that Hiss first
began to turn over to him confidential State Department documents which he had obtained in his official capacity, and it also
embraced the period of Chambers's stay at the 28th Street apartment. I quote relevant portions of Mr. Pressman's testimony before the House Committee on August 28, 1950 (Hearings Regarding Communism in the United States Government—Part 2, Committee on Un-American Activities, House of Representatives,
Eighty-first Congress, Second Session):

> In my desire to see the destruction of Hitlerism and
> an improvement in economic conditions here at home,
> I joined a Communist group in Washington, D.C.,
> about 1934. My participation in such group extended for
> about a year, to the best of my recollection. I recall that
> about the latter part of 1935—the precise date I cannot
> recall, but it is a matter of public record—I left the Gov-
> ernment service and left Washington to reenter the private
> practice of law in New York City. And at that time I dis-
> continued any further participation in the group from that
> date until the present.
>
> * * * * * *
>
> Now, I believe it of interest to comment that I have
> no knowledge regarding the political beliefs or affiliations
> of Alger Hiss. And when I say I have no knowledge,
> I am not endeavoring to quibble with this committee. I
> appear here, as I necessarily must, as a lawyer. I am a
> lawyer. When one asks me for knowledge, knowledge
> to my mind is based on fact, and I have no facts. And
> bear in mind, sir, that as an attorney, to be asked to com-
> ment on a case now pending in court is a very unusual
> experience for an attorney, because anything I say un-
> doubtedly may have an impact one way or another on
> that case, and for that reason I am trying to be very, very
> precise. I do know, and I can state as a matter of knowl-
> edge, that for the period of my participation in that group,

which is the only basis on which I can say I have knowledge, Alger Hiss was not a member of the group.

Now, those two statements of mine are based on
knowledge, which embraces facts within my possession.
I do not believe that this committee would want me to
hazard conjectural surmise. That is not my function. You
want from me, I assume, facts and nothing but facts.

* * * * * *

Mr. Tavenner. What were the circumstances under
which you united with the Communist Party? That is, who
recruited you into the party and all other circumstances
connected with it?

Mr. Pressman. The circumstances are very simple. I
was asked to join by a man named Harold Ware. For
the reasons which I have already indicated, I assented,
and I joined with the group which had, in addition to
myself, three other persons, all of whom at that time were
in the Department of Agriculture.

* * * * * *

Mr. Case. Were there other Government employees
who were members of your group?

Mr. Pressman. No, sir. I have stated there were only
four.

Mr. Case. You have made a distinction between those
who were employees of the Department of Agriculture
and other Government employees.

Mr. Pressman. No. I have said there were four, only
four, no more, no less.

This Communist group was the core of Chambers's admitted
conspiracy to infiltrate the Government in the interests of the
Soviets. Evidence from a self-confessed member of the group that
Alger Hiss, the defendant here, was not a member of it would
have been deeply damaging to the Government's case; and now
that that evidence has become available a new trial should be
had at which Mr. Pressman can be subpoenaed and given an
opportunity to reiterate his testimony before a jury.

CONCLUSION

This motion is made with full appreciation of the fact that new trials are not lightly granted, and that a showing must be made that upon a new trial the newly discovered evidence, if placed before the jury together with the old, would more than probably produce an acquittal.

I believe that such a showing will be made on this motion. I believe that the new evidence now offered hits so deeply at the vital aspects of the Government's case as it was presented to the jury that if it can be presented at a new trial it cannot fail to produce a different verdict.

All the evidence hereby presented is newly discovered since the second trial, and I assure the Court that it has been gathered and presented with the greatest diligence of which I and my associates have been capable. I have referred at length under Point II to the disheartening difficulties with which we have been faced in our search for the history of the typewriter. Furthermore, for approximately the whole of the first year of the two year period since the judgment and sentence the energies of counsel, including myself, were unavoidably in large part devoted to the preparation of the record and briefs on appeal and in certiorari proceedings in the Supreme Court. The investigation has had to be pursued in many parts of the United States and in foreign countries, and many lines of inquiry which looked and still look promising have had to be deferred temporarily, or even abandoned, because of lack of funds and personnel. While it is true that certain portions of the new evidence—such as the evidence under Point III, relating to Edith Murray—could have been presented earlier, I concluded that it would be an imposition on the Court to make successive motions on different points, and that the only proper course would be to defer making any motion until we were in a position to present to the Court the best possible comprehensive showing of the falsity of Chambers's story and the inadequacy of his alleged corroboration to substantiate his story under the rule of the *Weiler* case.[8]

[8] Mr. Lane's reference was to the leading Supreme Court decision of Weiler versus United States, which is printed in volume 323 of the reports of

I believe that such a showing is made. Any fair reading of the record shows beyond question that Chambers's testimony was riddled with inconsistencies and improbabilities, and it is inconceivable that the jury would have believed it, or convicted on either count, if it had not been for the apparent corroboration furnished by the Baltimore Documents, and by the testimony of Edith Murray supporting the Chamberses' story of social relations between the two families. These spurious corroborations we are now for the first time in a position to challenge successfully; and when we can also show by documentary evidence that the event which Chambers himself said marked the end of his Party activity and his alleged conspiracy with Hiss had occurred at least weeks before the date of many of the Baltimore Documents he claimed to have received from Hiss, I believe that no jury could possibly feel sufficient confidence in the Government's case to vote for conviction.

Following Mr. Lane's filing of the motion for a new trial and his affidavits in support of the motion came the series of postponements of the argument obtained by the prosecution. Meanwhile, the investigation continued.

By March 12, 1952, Mr. Lane had discovered still more evidence that Chambers had ended his Communist activities much earlier than he had said in his testimony at the trials. By that time there had also been obtained important new evidence demonstrating that the typewriter produced at the trials (#230,099) was a fake. But to continue with the proof of forgery Mr. Lane's experts needed to examine the typed papers which had been retained in the possession of the prosecution. Permission for this examination had been refused. Consequently, on March 12, Mr. Lane filed with Judge Goddard his second report. This described the evidence he had dis-

the Supreme Court. That case established the rule, which my counsel believed had not been applied by the appellate court in its disposition of my appeal, that in perjury cases the testimony of a single witness is insufficient unless it is corroborated by circumstantial evidence that substantiates the witness's testimony. (A. H.)

covered since January 24 and gave notice that he would ask for a court order allowing him to examine the Chambers typewritten papers:

I

Chambers's Break with the Communist Party [9]

In my original affidavit supporting the motion I outlined briefly the successive versions Chambers gave of his break with the Party,[1] and showed how his original story of breaking in 1937 was necessarily changed to April, 1938, when he had to support his new found tale of having gotten State Department documents from Alger Hiss through April 1st of that year. I referred to those portions of his testimony in which he purported to date his break by reference to his employment by the Oxford University Press as translator of Dr. Martin Gumpert's book, "Dunant—The Founder of the Red Cross"; and I appended to my affidavit copies of correspondence from the files of the Oxford University Press showing conclusively that his employment as translator began well before the middle of March. Further, I attached an affidavit of Dr. Gumpert, the author of the book, to the effect that when Chambers was first engaged as translator Dr. Gumpert asked to meet him but was told by Paul Willert, Vice-President of the Oxford University Press, that he could not, because Chambers "was in hiding from the Russian secret service, known as the G.P.U."

Dr. Gumpert's affidavit was illuminating as far as it went, but it failed to answer the question of just when he tried unsuccessfully to see Chambers. I mentioned in my affidavit that I had been in touch also with Paul Willert, the publisher, and that he too had difficulty in fixing the date precisely.

More recently, Mr. Willert has had an opportunity to review the Oxford University Press records, as well as to reexamine his own records. As a result he has refreshed his recollection and

---

[9] Excerpt from affidavit of Chester T. Lane dated March 12, 1952. (A. H.)

[1] This part of Mr. Lane's first affidavit was summarized on pp. 387–8 to avoid repetition, since the successive variations of Chambers's story about his break with Communism have been covered elsewhere (see the first part of Chapter VIII). (A. H.)

embodied it in an affidavit, which I attach hereto.[2] His affidavit leaves no further doubt that Chambers's story of having stayed in the Party until April 15th, and thereafter secured the translation, is false. He was out of it, and in hiding long before, and could not possibly have been engaged in active espionage operations down at least to April 1st, as he would have to have been if his story is to stick.

Two questions may occur. The first is: Where, if all this is so, did Chambers get the later State Department documents which were copied or paraphrased in the Baltimore Documents? If he was out of the Party, and out of his espionage work, by some time in early March at the latest, how did he come to have access to State Department cables and memoranda dated down to April 1st?

I do not know. Perhaps he "borrowed" them from some one connected with the notorious "Amerasia" incident, which came to light in 1946. If "Amerasia" could so easily stuff its files with hundreds of State Department documents running back over the years, who knows but that there may have been other similar caches of State Department papers which might have been made available to him by some sympathetic acquaintance in 1948. For our purposes, all that matters is that he clearly did not get them when and how he said he did.

The second question may be: Why, if he forged the Baltimore Documents to incriminate Alger Hiss, did he include State Department documents down to April 1st, after he had left the Party?

[2] Mr. Willert's affidavit referred to by Mr. Lane stated, on the basis of Mr. Willert's review of the relevant files, that Chambers had been brought to him "at the end of 1937 or at the very beginning of 1938," as a translator for Dr. Gumpert's book. On one of his first visits to discuss the translation or to collect portions of the manuscript, "Chambers expressed violently anti-communist views and explained to me that he was in fear of his life as he was being hunted by the G.P.U. He gave me the impression of being hysterical and suffering from persecution mania." In these conversations, according to Mr. Willert, Chambers "talked about communist leaders in Europe, particularly in Germany, Holland, France and Belgium in a manner which left no doubt in my mind that he was personally acquainted with them and had in fact been in Europe in recent years." Mr. Willert, on the basis of his review of the files of the Oxford University Press, stated that Chambers "must have been given the translation a considerable time before the 18th March 1938," after which date Mr. Willert "was unable to reach Chambers for about six weeks." (A. H.)

Again, I do not know, but I can suggest. Julian Wadleigh was
an admitted confederate, stealing for Chambers documents of just
the same kind as many of those which Chambers says he got
from Hiss. There must always have been a fear in Chambers's mind
that a judge or jury might believe that Wadleigh, not Hiss, was
the source, unless it were shown that at least some of the documents
could not possibly have come from Wadleigh. Wadleigh left
the United States for Turkey on March 11, 1938. What more
natural than to make sure that some of the documents should
be dated after that happened?

But why should Chambers have run the risk of setting the
date of his disappearance by reference to the time he secured a
translation which we now can show he secured much earlier than
he said he did? Maybe his memory just failed him: he thought
he had not gotten it until April. Certainly, he has emphasized that
he got it on a personal visit to New York, and he may well have
assumed that there would be no record of the exact date of a
personal meeting—forgetting that a last portion of the manuscript
was shipped to him by mail on March 18th, and that the record
of its shipment might be still preserved in the files.[3]

These are speculative answers, and they may be wrong. The
important point, however, is that the evidence which raises the
questions is new, and that it so directly challenges Chambers's
veracity on a matter essential to the Government's case that it
could not fail to raise a reasonable doubt in a jury's mind.

II

Proof of Forgery in This Case

At the opening of Point II of my original affidavit I described
some of the reasons why, on reviewing the record for purposes of

---

[3] Chambers's consciousness of the weakness of his story at the trials is
interestingly betrayed by the emendations he is supplying in his articles being
currently published in the Saturday Evening Post. In the issue of March 1,
1952, at p. 97, he says: "Our life in hiding on the Old Court Road was an
anxious and troubled time. One of my first problems was to find work. By
prior arrangement with a publishing house I got some foreign books to trans-
late." The reference to "prior arrangement with a publishing house" has no
support in his trial testimony; it appears to be a belated effort to explain
meetings with Paul Willert earlier than April 15th. It still does not explain
shipment of manuscript by Willert to him in March.

the appeal, I began to be suspicious of the authenticity of the typewriter—Woodstock N230099—which, though found and put in evidence by the defense, was adopted and used by the Government as one of its principal, though mute, witnesses at the trials. I concluded my introduction to Point II as follows:

> In the light of all these considerations, and bearing in mind that the expert who before the trials had identified the machine for the defense had rested his opinion on identical peculiarities in only three characters, apparently without consideration of the possibility of a deliberately fabricated machine, I determined to make a thorough study of the authenticity of Woodstock #230,099. That study has produced results which are startling, so far as they go. Admittedly, for reasons described below, they do not go far enough to demonstrate with any certainty that #230,-099 is a fabrication; but I believe that they go far enough to cast serious doubt on its authenticity, and to justify calling upon the Court for its aid in supplying the missing links in the chain of evidence.

I still need the Court's aid, particularly in calling upon the Government to show what it knows about the typewriter.

But I no longer just *question* the authenticity of Woodstock N230099. I now say to the Court that Woodstock N230099—the typewriter in evidence at the trials—is a fake machine. I present in affidavit form, and will be able to produce at the hearing, expert testimony that this machine is a deliberately fabricated job, a new type face on an old body. This being so, it can only have been planted on the defense by or on behalf of Whittaker Chambers as part of his plot for the false incrimination of Alger Hiss.

My original affidavit outlines the growth of my serious suspicions. At first, even in a case full of fantastic improbabilities, it seemed futile to question the judgment of experts, our own as well as the Government's, that forgery could not be committed by typewriter; but my experiment in producing a duplicate typewriter began to show that it could be done. Then it began to appear that there was something definitely wrong with N230099:

its serial number did not agree with its type; its date (from its serial number) did not seem to agree with the time when Fansler must have bought it; and the Government seemed to have become interested in another machine. Always I looked towards having a real examination made of Woodstock N230099 to see whether from internal evidence it could be shown to be a fake; but I did not know how to go about it, and in any event I felt that first I ought to be surer from the other leads I was following that I was on the right track. Development of those leads, as I showed in my first affidavit, was discouragingly slow: witnesses were reluctant, records were missing, and experts, to say the least, were coy.

My first real encouragement towards having the typewriter analyzed came only in January of this year. I had, as outlined in my first affidavit, enlisted the aid of Mrs. Evelyn S. Ehrlich, of Boston, Massachusetts, as an expert in the use of photo-micrography for the detection of documentary forgeries. Mrs. Ehrlich's function, as I first consulted her, was to give me an informed judgment on the success of my experiment in duplicating the typing product of Woodstock N230099. I gave her samples of typing from the two machines, and she successfully distinguished them, though only on the basis of a few minor remaining discrepancies. I was not surprised that she could tell them apart; what startled me, in the discussion in which she reported her results, was that she had concluded that the samples I had made on N230099 were the ones on Tytell's fabricated machine. When I corrected her, she assured me that the only possible explanation was that N230099, as well as the machine Tytell had made for me, must be a forgery—and not as carefully constructed a forgery as Tytell's. She said there was no other way of accounting for certain peculiarities of the typing from N230099 which she could observe by photomicrography.

I asked her whether she could confirm this by an actual examination of the typewriter itself, rather than merely specimens of its typing. She said that any comprehensive examination should be made by a metallurgical expert, which she did not consider herself, but that she would be willing to look at it herself under a microscope just to see whether there was enough obvious evidence of fabrication on the types themselves to justify my having a comprehensive examination made. When she had done so she assured me that an expert examination was fully warranted.

I was most anxious to arrange for such an examination in time to incorporate its results in my original papers supporting my motion for a new trial. But again I met the familiar difficulties: those I could find who seemed competent to do the job were concerned at possible adverse consequences to themselves from public association with the defense of Alger Hiss, or were precluded from participation by the "policy" of the institutions with which they were associated.

I finally consulted Dr. Daniel Norman, Director of Chemical Research of the New England Spectrochemical Laboratories, of Ipswich, Massachusetts, and President of its subsidiary, Skinner & Sherman, of Boston, Massachusetts. Dr. Norman's organization was recommended to me as "the best in the business", with long and distinguished experience in the field of metallurgical analysis. Dr. Norman agreed to examine Woodstock N230099 for me. He has done so, and his conclusions are embodied in his affidavit.

What were suspicions before are now translated into certainties. Dr. Norman and his organization have established that the machine the defense found and the Government used as evidence at the trials is a fake. In the language of Dr. Norman's affidavit, this machine

> * * * is not a machine which has worn normally since leaving the factory, but shows positive signs of having been deliberately altered, in that many of its types are replacements of the originals and have been deliberately shaped.

Dr. Norman does not merely state a conclusion. His affidavit outlines in detail scientific proof, annexing photographs to illustrate such of his data as are capable of visual demonstration. From it we learn:

1. That Woodstock type consists of a small detachable piece of metal which fits over the end of the typebar and is soldered into place.

2. That a majority of the types on Woodstock N230099 have been soldered onto the typebars in a careless fashion, quite unlike

the kind of soldering job done at the Woodstock factory or in a regular repair operation.

3. That the solder used for the replacement types has a different metallic content from that used on the types which apparently have not been altered, and from that used on other contemporary machines.

4. That the type face metal in almost half the types contains metallic elements not present in Woodstock type metal until the date of machines of substantially later serial numbers than N230099.

5. That the altered types show tool marks which indicate deliberate alteration of the striking faces of the letters, as well as peculiar finish or polish quite unlike that on types which have worn or aged normally.[4]

In my original motion papers I presented evidence to show that it was *possible* to construct or alter a machine so as to make its typing resemble that of another machine so closely that an expert would be unable to tell the difference, especially if he applied the criteria used by the Government's expert at the trials. I attached specimens of typing from two different machines and invited the Government to have its experts tell them apart if they could. I do not know whether the Government's experts can tell them apart, or even whether the Government will dare accept the invitation to try. However that may be, my proffered proof is now no longer pointed to showing how someone *could* have faked a machine which would fool the experts; it shows rather that someone *did* fake such a machine. Clearer evidence of the plot to incriminate Alger Hiss falsely could scarcely be desired.

At this stage of the case the Court, or the Government, may ask whether I can prove *when* N230099 was fabricated. I cannot. But I can say this: From April 16, 1949, when it turned up in Lockey's house, till the day it was put in evidence at the first trial, it was in the possession of defense counsel. Between the trials it was ordered impounded in the Clerk's office. It was returned to the possession of defense counsel at the end of the second trial, and was turned over to me on or about February 17,

---

[4] See photographs, following p. 374, illustrating some of Dr. Norman's conclusions. (A. H.)

1950, the day I was retained as counsel. From that time until February 10, 1952, when I had it delivered to Dr. Norman in Ipswich, it has been under my personal control,[5] and no one has been allowed access to it except my immediate associates.

Accordingly, the alteration or fabrication occurred before the machine was found by the defense. As to when it was done, there are of course various possibilities. One possibility with considerable logic to support it is that the initial alteration was made between the time Chambers first testified before the House Committee in August, 1948, and November 17, 1948, the day he reversed his story and produced the Baltimore Documents as a defense to the libel suit—enough alteration in the types to produce the deceptive typing embodied in the Baltimore Documents themselves. The fact that between November and April neither the defense nor thirty-five agents of the FBI could find the machine suggests that it was during this period that further work was being done on the types, in an effort to remove at least the more obvious tool marks which would betray the deception.[6] Dr. Norman's affidavit leaves no doubt that such an effort was made, and that though the result could not pass his critical examination it would have been—and in fact for nearly three years was—sufficient to deceive non-mechanical lawyers and even questioned document examiners.[7]

In the last analysis all the proof I am here offering looks to a final showing that the Baltimore Documents are forgeries—that they were not typed on the same Woodstock machine as the so-called Hiss Standards. The fact that the machine in evidence at the trials can now be shown up as a palpable fabrication could

[5] This is subject to the exception that for a period of three days early in 1952 it was in the possession of a distinguished scientist who first agreed and then declined to examine it for me and who assured me that he kept it locked in his safe for the three days he had it.

[6] I plan to show at the hearing, by expert testimony, that the fabrication of such a deceptive machine as N230099 could be accomplished in no more than a few days by anyone who had taken the pains to acquire knowledge of the techniques of how to do it.

[7] As well as the Service Manager of the R. C. Allen Business Machines office in New York (successors to the Woodstock Typewriter Company), who at my request and in my presence gave the machine a quick naked-eye inspection early in 1950.

hardly fail to raise a reasonable doubt in any jury's mind as to the truth of Chambers's story of how and when the documents were typed; and I am confident that careful expert examination of the Baltimore Documents conducted in the light of our proof of the possibility of forgery by typewriter, would show conclusively that they are forgeries.

Unfortunately, I am not in a position to present any proof to the Court on the matter at the moment. Having just this problem in mind, on February 11, 1952, I addressed a letter to the United States Attorney requesting, among other things, that he make the original documents available to me for photographing. As a result of my letter Special Agent Spencer of the FBI visited me at my office on February 13th and asked me to explain in greater detail what I wanted—in view of the fact, as he said, that the defense had already photographed the documents three times. I told him that, whatever photographing might have been done in the past, I was now interested in a photomicrographic examination of the kind made by Mrs. Ehrlich in connection with her examination of specimens from N230099 and from Tytell's machine; that my experts advised me that such an examination could only be satisfactorily done from the originals themselves; and that they assured me that the photographing could be done wherever the documents might be without danger to the documents or expense to the Government.

The United States Attorney refused to comply with my request. I attach a copy of his letter of February 14th.

I have regarded it as my duty, as attorney for Alger Hiss and as an officer of this Court, to bring out the true facts of this case, as far as diligent research can uncover them. The Government, it has seemed to me throughout my investigation, is reluctant to allow me the materials necessary to this result. Whatever may have been the justification in other phases of the case, I can see none in the matter of allowing me access to the original Baltimore Documents for photographic purposes.[8]

---

[8] Nor can I see justification for the refusal, in the same letter, to furnish me with blank parts (of which there are a great many) of a few of the pages of the Baltimore Documents for paper analysis. The three inch square which was furnished by court order—over Government protest—during the second trial, was long ago consumed inconclusively.

Accordingly, I hereby give notice that on the argument of the motion for a new trial I shall further move in open court for an order allowing me to have photographs made of the Baltimore Documents, as well as the Hiss Standards, so that, in the light of the new understanding which my experiments have developed as to how forgery by typewriter may be—and in this case was—accomplished, it may be possible at last to prove that the Baltimore Documents are forgeries, and that Alger Hiss is innocent of the crime charged to him.

Following Mr. Lane's statement that he would ask in open court for permission to have new photographs made of the typewritten exhibits, the prosecution finally agreed—at a conference held in Judge Goddard's chambers—to let Mr. Lane's experts have access to these exhibits for that purpose and to take samples of the paper for analysis.

The results of the examination by the experts were presented to Judge Goddard in Mr. Lane's third and final report of his investigations. This third report was filed on April 21, 1952. Mr. Lane stated in it:

. . . The examination has been most fruitful. I believe that it leaves no vestige of doubt but that Chambers's whole story is false, and that his fraudulent plot now stands exposed.

He went on to summarize Chambers's story that my wife had typed the documents and that every ten days or so Chambers would collect the typed material and original documents. Chambers had said that he had preserved the papers he produced on November 17, 1948, having stored them in an envelope given to his wife's nephew, Nathan Levine, for safekeeping. According to Chambers he had put into the envelope, in addition to the sixty-five typed pages, my four handwritten notes, some yellow sheets supposedly in Harry Dexter White's handwriting, the two strips of developed microfilm that were exhibits at the trials, and three metal cylinders or cans containing undeveloped microfilm. (Mr. Lane noted that in Chambers's articles in the *Saturday Evening Post*, which were then appearing, Chambers, in the issue of April 5, 1952, had said there were also "one or two smaller items of no particular importance.") Levine did not know what was in the envelope and never saw what came out of it. After describing these background facts, Mr. Lane told the court of the results obtained from the new examination of the typewritten papers:

FOREGROUND:
WHAT THE DOCUMENTS THEMSELVES SHOW [9]

If Chambers is telling the truth, the typed Baltimore Documents must have been typed by one person (Priscilla Hiss), on one typewriter (the Hiss family Woodstock),[1] currently over the three months' period represented by the dates of the underlying State Department documents (January 5 to April 1, 1938). They must have been kept together in one envelope, a specific envelope, for ten years, over a disused dumbwaiter in Brooklyn. They must have rested there, in that envelope, with three cylinders of undeveloped microfilm and a "little spool of developed film (actually two strips)",[2] as well as with the "long memo on yellow foolscap in the handwriting of Harry Dexter White [and] one or two smaller items of no particular importance." [3]

I attach affidavits of experts who have at last had an opportunity to examine and analyze the originals of the Baltimore Docu-

---

[9] Excerpt from affidavit of Chester T. Lane dated April 21, 1952. (A. H.)

[1] Baltimore 10, a precis of a long War Department MID report routed to Mr. Hamilton, of the Far Eastern Division of the State Department, was obviously not written on the same typewriter as the others, and the Government made no contention that it was; but Chambers still pressed his recollection: "I believe Alger Hiss gave me that paper."

[2] This particular description comes from page 736 of an advance copy of Chambers's *apologia*, "Witness", shortly to be published. His April 5, 1952, article in the Saturday Evening Post speaks of "two strips of developed microfilm". His second trial testimony emphasizes that while the undeveloped film was in cylinders, the developed film was not. When Agent Appell of the FBI [*sic*—Appell was an employee of the Committee (A. H.)] reached in and found it in the green pumpkin on December 2, 1948 (or when Chambers "took out the documents and handed them over"—whichever may be the fact), they were still not in cylinders; according to Agent Appell, they were "wrapped one in another, wrapped in wax paper".

[3] This description is from his April 5, 1952, Saturday Evening Post article. The text of the "memo on yellow foolscap" ascribed to Harry Dexter White was read into the Congressional Record for January 30, 1950, by Representative Nixon, and the memorandum was there described as consisting of eight pages.

ments and the Hiss standards. Their qualifications have been set out before, in my earlier affidavits and in their affidavits which I annexed to mine. Mrs. Evelyn S. Ehrlich is an expert in the use of photomicrography to detect printing forgeries. Miss Elizabeth McCarthy is an expert in the examination of questioned documents, handwritten and typewritten. Dr. Daniel P. Norman is an expert in physical and chemical analysis of paper, metals and other materials. They have examined the Baltimore Documents, separately, according to their several expertnesses. They have recorded their findings in their affidavits.

They find, and will testify at a new trial:

1. That the Baltimore Documents were not typed by one person, but by two, and probably more, and that therefore Priscilla Hiss cannot have typed all of them, as Chambers said she did.

2. That Priscilla Hiss did not type any of the Baltimore Documents.

3. That neither Priscilla nor Alger Hiss made the pencil corrections on the Baltimore Documents.

4. That the Baltimore Documents, physically observed, fall into two categories of size, one of which is made up of sheets apparently cut down to a particular size (approximately 8" x 10½") after the typing had been done, but before the penciled corrections were made.[4]

5. That the same two categories show such different characteristics of aging and discoloration that they cannot have been stored together for ten years in a single envelope, and therefore cannot all have been kept in the envelope which Chambers recovered from the dumbwaiter.

6. That the envelope in which Chambers said the documents had been kept is most peculiar in itself; its observable stains, both outside and in, and the condition of its flap, and of the two parts of the label which presumably once sealed it, pose questions which defy logical explanation.[5]

[4] Spectrographic analysis of the typewriter ink at the edges of the pages which were cut off in the middle of line-end letters might have enabled us to prove more effectively that the cutting was done after the typing. The Government would not let us make the excisions necessary for this analysis.

[5] For example, Dr. Norman pointed out in his affidavit that the two halves of the label which had sealed the envelope show entirely different degrees of discoloration and staining. (A. H.)

7. That none of the Baltimore Documents can have been kept in that envelope; they are devoid of the stains and pressure marks which they would have had to show if they had been in the envelope.

8. That the absence of stains and pressure marks on the Baltimore Documents cannot be explained by the presence of other protective material, since the envelope could not have held all these and the microfilms too.[6]

9. That the Baltimore Documents are a tricky set of papers, typed on a machine, or machines, closely resembling the original Hiss machine, but with miscellaneously different typewriter ribbons and faked typographical errors, plainly designed to confuse.

10. That the typewriter in evidence (Woodstock #N230099) was certainly not the original Hiss machine, although it probably was the machine made to forge the Baltimore Documents.

In short, the typed Baltimore Documents were not typed by Priscilla Hiss, or by any one person. They were not given to Chambers by Alger Hiss. They were not put in the envelope and kept in the dumbwaiter for ten long years.[7] They are an ingenious set of forgeries.

The affidavit by Miss McCarthy, presented by Mr. Lane to Judge Goddard as part of the final statement of his investigations, contained the following testimony:

[6] I have myself examined the envelope, and seen in it markings which might well have been made by the cylinders of undeveloped microfilm. There is another marking, made apparently by the presence of a squarish box or carton, approximately 3″ x 3″. This mark, from its shape and size, cannot be the mark of Chambers's "little spool of developed film"; and therefore even the "Pumpkin Papers" microfilm may well not have been in the envelope. Unfortunately, the United States Attorney would not permit us to split the envelope so that we could demonstrate photographically the interior markings and stains. The United States Attorney would not, either, let us see the 8 pages of "foolscap" on the ground that it had not been formally admitted as an exhibit at the trial— even though it had been produced in court, and its text has since been made public by Representative Nixon in the Congressional Record. Whether or not the foolscap shows stains or pressure marks, it could not have adequately protected the Baltimore Documents.

[7] See photographs, following p. 374, illustrating some of Dr. Norman's grounds (summarized in numbered paragraphs 4 to 8 in Mr. Lane's affidavit) for his rejection of the authenticity of the Baltimore Documents. (A. H.)

1. No one person typed the Baltimore Documents. There were certainly two typists, whose work varied sharply in evenness of pressure, typing skill, mechanical understanding and control of the machine, style habits, and other similar respects. No one person's work could exhibit such differences. It is quite possible that more than two typists were involved.

2. Since certainly more than one person typed the Baltimore Documents, Priscilla Hiss cannot have typed them all. Furthermore, the characteristics of her typing make it perfectly clear that she was not either of the two principal typists involved. I base this conclusion to a considerable extent upon such factors, not clearly observable except from the original documents, as typing rhythm, pressure habits and variations, quality of touch, pace of typing, relative competence of the two hands, and the like. My conclusion from these factors is borne out by many other differentiating characteristics in such matters as style, mechanical skill, and habits of mind. Priscilla Hiss did not in my opinion type any of the Baltimore Documents.

Miss McCarthy characterized as "grossly misleading" Murphy's invitation to the jury to draw conclusions as to the identity of the typist from "common typing errors" in the so-called Hiss Standards and the Baltimore Documents. One of his three examples she found was not an error common to the two sets of papers at all. As to his other two she stated:

The "combinations" "f" for "g" and "f" for "d" are the commonest kind of typing errors, committed by every typist because of the proximity of the letters on the keyboard. Even if Mr. Murphy's selection of what he calls "common typing errors" were correct—which they are not—or were unusual—which they are not—they are totally insignificant against the fact that the Baltimore Documents contain at least fifty typing errors of a kind which do bear on the personality of the typist and which do not appear anywhere in the standards, while on the other hand nine errors of that nature appearing in the standards never occur in the Baltimore Documents. Only four errors of this kind are common to the two sets of documents.

The typed pages Chambers produced contain a number of handwritten corrections and proof-reading marks in pencil.

Miss McCarthy noted that although Chambers's story was that they had been typed "from day to day over a period of about three months," these corrections "give the appearance of having been made in one continuous operation rather than at the separate times when the separate pages should have been typed," were his story true. "The corrections and proof-reading marks," she said, "were made with a soft, grayish-black pencil, in approximately the same condition of wornness and bluntness throughout, and are quite inconsistent with the idea that the same or different pencils were used at a number of different times over a three months period."

Miss McCarthy's study showed still more:

As to the handwriting and the correctional or proof-reading habits, they show that the pencil notations were carefully done, at one time, by one person, quite probably with stenographic training. I have studied numerous samples of the handwriting of Alger and Priscilla Hiss, as well as samples of documents furnished to me as taken from Alger Hiss's files in the 1930's and showing his correctional and proof-reading habits. In my opinion neither Alger nor Priscilla Hiss could have done the pencil marking on the documents.

Dr. Norman stated in his affidavit filed on April 21 that he had established from ribbon thread counts that "at least four ribbons were used in the typing of these documents. Alternation in the use of the various ribbons bears no discernible relationship to any possible grouping of the documents by their dates; in fact, in a number of instances two documents dated some time apart are typed with a ribbon of a given thread count while other documents with dates in between are typed with a ribbon of a different count." Miss McCarthy also found that "At least four, and probably more, ribbons were used. . . ." The best ribbon, she found, was used only once. Documents of the same date show ink of different shades. This alternation of ribbons, she said, "appears entirely inconsistent with the normal use of a typewriter."

Mrs. Ehrlich's final affidavit stated that she had found that in the Baltimore Documents, due to poor quality of paper and moist ribbons, the characteristics of the type that might have been observable on microscopic examinations were obscured.[8] She also considered inadequate for comparison purposes two samples of my wife's typing that Feehan had used for comparison. However, she found other samples from our machine among the prosecution's exhibits and the defense's exhibits which permitted "reliable comparison." And she had adequate recent specimens from #230,099. With these she was "prepared to confirm the tentative judgment" she had formed earlier on the basis of photocopies of one of the prosecution's usable exhibits:

In my opinion, #N230099 cannot be the same machine that typed Government Exhibits 37 and 46-B and Defendant's Exhibit TT.[9] I base this opinion upon certain differences in type impressions between many of the letters in the two sets of documents [i.e., between letters in the three exhibits on the one hand and letters in the recent specimens from #230,099 on the other], these differences appearing with such a high degree of regularity as to preclude the possibility of their being due to variations of ribbon, typing pressure, or other peculiarities of operation, and being of such a nature that differences in imprint cannot be due to age or wear on the machine.[1]

Mr. Lane concluded his final report to Judge Goddard on the results of his investigation in these words:

After all my investigation, I still do not know exactly what Chambers did, or how he did it, or exactly what motivated him to frame Alger Hiss. Some signs point to the conclusion that, though his personal interest may have been largely to protect him-

[8] The condition of the Baltimore Documents precluded Mrs. Ehrlich from giving a definite opinion that they had been typed on #230,099. On this point she states in her affidavit that "I can only say that the observable peculiarities in the type of the Baltimore Documents in my opinion more nearly resemble the peculiarities in the typing from #N230099 than they do the peculiarities in the Hiss Standards which I used for comparison."

[9] These three exhibits were personal papers that had been typed on the machine my wife's father had given to her.

[1] Mrs. Ehrlich supported by various photographs her opinion that #230,-099 was not the machine that had been given to my wife by her father, Mr. Fansler. Some of these photographs are reproduced following p. 374.

self in the libel suit, the availability to him of the means for such self-protection may have been part of a much larger scheme, involving other people, and far larger objectives than the mere framing of Alger Hiss. This, however, is speculation. For purposes of this motion it should be enough that I present proof that every important point of the Government's case at the trials is vulnerable. Chambers was the Government's witness, its only real witness; and everything that he said, or did, or said he did, is tainted with fraud and forgery. The Government may present evidence to countervail some of my proffered proofs; if so, that will create issues. Those issues should be considered anew, by a jury. Wherever the truth may ultimately be found, in all its details, we have surely borne the burden of showing that on the proofs that went before the last jury a grave miscarriage of justice has occurred. We should be given a chance to rectify this at a new trial.

On May 19, 1952, the prosecution filed numerous affidavits in reply to the affidavits of the defense. In part the answering affidavits challenged conclusions of our experts or facts asserted by Mr. Lane and by our witnesses, frequently on minor or non-essential points.

One group of the answering affidavits attempted to support Chambers's story that he had broken with Communism on April 15, 1938, and had gone into hiding for a month before leaving for Florida: A real-estate broker said that on March 14, 1938, Mrs. Chambers had paid rent on the Mount Royal Terrace premises to cover the period until April 30. Another affidavit stated that gas and electric service was furnished to the Mount Royal Terrace apartment until about April 9 and that someone calling herself Mrs. Chambers had by telephone on April 12 ordered electric service for premises in Randallstown, Maryland (where Chambers had said he was in hiding on the Old Court Road for a month before he went to Florida). An automobile-repair company at Randallstown certified that its records show that on April 1, 1938, repairs were made for a Mrs. Esther Chambers on a 1937 Ford. A letter from both the Chamberses dated April 2 was printed as an exhibit. It had the heading "Mt. Royal Terrace," was addressed to their daughter's school, and expressed regret "at having to cut short her attendance this year. . . ." This letter was enclosed in another letter to the school from *Mrs.* Chambers only, dated April 9, *with a Long Island heading,* which asked for an appointment for her "on Monday" to talk over plans for the next year and stated "we have had to leave Baltimore temporarily but expect to return in the Fall."

Another affidavit stated in effect that it was not feasible to identify the typist (a sharp commentary on the good faith of Murphy's invitation to the inexpert jury to do so) or to pass on the authorship of the penciled corrections or on the number of ribbons used in typing the Baltimore Documents. Other affidavits controverted aspects of Mr. Lane's information about the Woodstock Company's practices and the opinions of the experts. One FBI agent stated, irrelevantly, that paint spots on the envelope Chambers had left with Nathan Levine were of the same color and composition as paint from the Levine dumbwaiter shaft. (My counsel and I had never claimed that *the envelope* had not been stored in a dumbwaiter shaft. Mr. Lane's new evidence showed that none of the Baltimore Documents could have been stored in the envelope as Chambers had claimed.) Another agent denied that the FBI had information about the existence "of any other Hiss Woodstock machine other than the trial Exhibit UUU" and said the FBI had not sought a Woodstock by any other number "than serial number 5N230099" after May 14, 1949, a month after the defense had found the machine of that number in Lockey's house. Mr. Lane's point was that *in the preceding six months* the FBI had searched for a machine with an *earlier* serial number, an indication that the machine we found was not the original Fansler machine and that this was known to the FBI. Feehan restated his trial testimony with some slight expansion and disagreed with a point of Miss McCarthy's about corrections made by striking a second letter over an incorrect one. Mr. Fowler's wife said that after her marriage on August 18, 1934, "until approximately eight months later" she and her husband did not visit her aunt at 903 St. Paul Street more than once every three weeks. She remembered that at some time after her marriage her aunt had said a family named Cantwell lived there.

In the main, however, the prosecution attempted to belittle the significance of our evidence and to obscure the issues. The United States Attorney called the motion for a new trial "frivolous" and contended that all of the new evidence was available to the defense in time for the trials if we had used "due diligence." With no basis at all for his statement, he said that, assuming the soundness of the new "theories" as to the typewriter, there were "other corroborating proofs which are independently sufficient." Most astonishingly, he asserted that the prosecution's case "in no way and to no degree hinges upon who the typist was," because Chambers had said he had no recollection of seeing anyone type the papers. Incorrectly, he said that Chambers had not mentioned Pressman's name at the second trial and that Pressman's testimony did not conflict with that of Chambers. He conceded that Chambers had "erred by a few weeks in fixing the time of his obtaining the translation," but argued that this would not warrant a new trial as it was only of "an impeaching nature." Without producing supporting affidavits, he said that Mr. Leisman had a bad record and was an excessive drinker, that other people said there were colored maids in the neighborhood where the Chamberses had lived in 1935–6, that there was a "readily available rear entrance" to the building where they had lived, and that Leisman had worked where he said he did only for a short period in early 1935.

In a memorandum dated May 26, Mr. Lane replied in detail to the objections made by the prosecution to the principal new facts he had discovered. Where there was an actual conflict of evidence on matters of substance, he pointed out that the conflict could be resolved only by the hearing he asked for. He said also:

The blunderbuss approach of the Government's answering affidavits makes it impracticable to answer them point by point. To attempt to do so would be to bog the argument of our motion so deeply down into controversies on minor irrelevancies, confusions, and inaccuracies that neither side nor the Court would any longer be able to tell just what the issues on the motion were, and the motion might well lose simply because we had failed to make clear its import and its merits.

The motion was finally argued on June 4, 1952. Like so many other events in the case, even the disposition of this motion had a political setting. The case had begun four years earlier in the midst of a Presidential election campaign. Judge Goddard denied the motion for a new trial on July 22, during the sessions of the Democratic Convention that was to nominate Adlai E. Stevenson, who had been one of my character witnesses. Judge Goddard's decision reached the press before it reached my counsel, and when Mr. Lane applied at the courthouse for the opinion, he found that all copies had been distributed already. It was many hours before he could learn authoritatively just how the motion had been disposed of.

Judge Goddard's opinion [2] said that my counsel had "submitted no proof, which would support a finding by a jury that the typewriter received in evidence at the trial was constructed by or for Chambers or that the typewriter was not the original Hiss machine." Yet he had refused to order a hearing to which we could have summoned by subpœna those witnesses whose testimony we could not otherwise obtain. More generally, he found no newly discovered evidence which "would probably result in a verdict of acquittal."

In his brief on appeal from this decision, Mr. Lane said of Judge Goddard's opinion:

However decorously we may phrase our criticisms of the trial court's action, they will inevitably be recognized as amounting to

[2] It is printed in volume 107 of the Federal Supplement Reports at page 128.

a charge of predetermination of the motion, without hearing of the witnesses and without that just and fair consideration which even once-convicted defendants are entitled to receive at the hands of our courts when evidence of a miscarriage of justice is offered. We cannot make any lesser charge. We believe that the trial court's handling of the motion displayed such predetermination, without fair hearing, as to amount to an abuse of its discretion, and thus to constitute error requiring reversal by this Court.

He pointed out that the Judge had misstated or misunderstood much of our evidence, and had resolved disputed issues of fact in favor of the prosecution without even hearing the witnesses. He called attention to:

. . . such features as the language which the court chose to select from the supporting affidavits for quotation, as contrasted with the language it chose to omit, the characterizing phrases which the court chose to use in introducing quotations or in discussing evidence, and the court's uncritical acceptance of unsupported, irrelevant, or patently fallacious assertions made in the Government's answering affidavits.

And he drew the conclusion:

The opinion, we respectfully submit, bears all the earmarks of a document gotten together to justify a fixed determination—i.e., that in no circumstances must Alger Hiss be allowed a new trial—rather than a reasoned statement of the considerations leading to an exercise of true judicial discretion based on the evidence presented.

At the special request of the prosecution, my appeal from Judge Goddard's decision was heard by the same three judges who had heard the original appeal. It was denied on January 30, 1953—a result hardly unexpected, since by long precedent decisions on motions for new trial are largely non-reviewable, being left to the discretion of the trial judge. We felt that every possible effort should be made to show that the failure even to grant a hearing constituted a grave abuse of discretion;

we therefore asked the Supreme Court to review the case. On April 27, 1953, it declined to do so.

_____

In what I have written about my case I have tried to let the record speak. But now that the book is completed I want to add this personal comment:

My mind has been occupied with this book for much longer than the year or so its writing took. I wanted to start it when I first went to prison, but arrangements to have the necessary source material sent to me were forbidden by the authorities. Then after I returned home and had begun work on the book I was interrupted by illness and a stay in the hospital. However, during the times when writing had to be postponed I gave much thought to what I wanted to say in the book and I gained an increased sense of perspective.

The ordeal of fighting false charges has disrupted my life and has brought pain to me and to my family. But nothing can take away the satisfaction of having had a part in government programs in which I strongly believed. I feel deep satisfaction that I took part in the creative efforts of the New Deal and in the formation of the United Nations.

The democratic ideals which motivated me in government service continue to shape my outlook on life.

APPENDIX A

22 East 8th Street
New York 3, New York
August 18, 1948

J. PARNELL THOMAS, ESQ.
Chairman, House Committee on Un-American Activities
Washington, D.C.

DEAR MR. THOMAS:

In the course of my testimony in executive session day before yesterday before the Subcommittee at which you presided I was asked to reply to the Committee by today whether I would be willing to submit to a "lie detector" test to be administered by a Dr. Leonardo Keeler of Chicago. I was informed that Dr. Keeler has what is known as a polygraph machine and that in the Committee's opinion he is the only individual interested in "lie detector" machines whose methods have had "broad acceptance." Mr. Nixon said he had made a study of the general subject in the past two months [1] and has confidence in Dr. Keeler's machine as a device which he thought might be helpful in the circumstances. I was also informed that Mr. Chambers is willing to submit to Dr. Keeler's methods of procedure.

As I told the Subcommittee Monday when this question was raised with me, two newspaper men in the course of last week had informed me that the Committee was giving consideration to making such a suggestion to me. As a result of these conversations I had made some cursory and informal inquiries into the subject. You will recall that I told the Subcommittee Monday that my inquiries had not been re-assuring.

Both the scientific and legal experts whom I have consulted confirmed the impression which I, as a practicing lawyer, had obtained some years ago that the scientific validity of mechanical tests for veracity have most definitely not been established by Dr. Keeler or anyone else.

Yesterday and today I have initiated further inquiries and again the result to date has been uniformly negative. My information is that no Federal Court in the United States relies upon any "lie detector"

---

[1] Mr. Nixon had said two "weeks." The word "months" is a stenographic error not noticed at the time the letter was sent.

machine and that scientists who are most familiar with psychiatric and emotional questions repose no confidence in any mechanical device thus far developed.

Dr. Keeler's machine, I understand, does record changes in certain physical indices of emotion, such as fluctuation in rates of perspiration, in rapidity of heartbeat, in blood pressure, etc. It is *not*, however, a "lie detector." The information I have received thus far is further to the effect that the reading of the record of any such machine, including Dr. Keeler's, is necessarily a matter entirely within the subjective discretion of the operator of the machine and is not capable of objective scientific check by impartial observers. In other words, only the deviser of the tests utilized in the operation of the machine is able to interpret the results. I am in addition informed that no Federal agency, including the Federal Bureau of Investigation, accepts the scientific validity of any "lie detector" machine.

I am much impressed by the Committee's statement to me on Monday that it, on the basis of its investigations, has confidence in Dr. Keeler's machine. However, I believe that the Committee's suggestion is unprecedented in Congressional procedure. The matter is therefore one of some general importance as well as of significance to me as an individual. Before reaching a definite conclusion I think the importance of the decision warrants my obtaining more searching and definitive information and opinion from legal and scientific experts. It has not been possible for me to obtain the results of the inquiries I have initiated by today, the date on which the Committee asked for a reply from me. Under the circumstances I can only say that I do not at present feel in position to make a final decision with respect to the Committee's suggestion. I shall do my best to expedite the inquiries I have under way. In this connection I might mention that the middle of the summer when many people are on vacation is not the most favorable time in which to pursue such inquiries with despatch. I shall communicate further with you as soon as I am in position to speak with more certainty on this subject.

Very truly yours,

ALGER HISS

APPENDIX B

Some of the State Department documents included in State 5–47 are neither incoming nor outgoing cables. Except for State 10 (the typed excerpt from which [Balt. 10] was not typed on the Woodstock typewriter . . .), they are either despatches received by diplomatic pouch or memoranda prepared and circulated within the Department. No information copies of such documents were prepared by DCR [Division of Communications and Records], and the distribution of such documents within the Department is evidenced not by distribution copies but by receiving stamps or other notations on the face of the documents (see, e. g., R. 765, 795–7, 800, 802). The practice was for every office to which such a document was circulated to stamp the document, or some other document part of a single circulating file, to evidence receipt. Mr. Sayre's secretary, Miss Lincoln, testified that this was always done with respect to documents routed to his office (R. 928–9).

The evidence is conclusive that one of these documents, State 13 (copied in full in Baltimore 13), was never in Sayre's office. There is therefore no basis for inferring that State 13 could have been copied by appellant or his wife on their typewriter and the copy given by appellant to Chambers. The only reasonable conclusion is that State 13 was given to Chambers by someone else, presumably someone in FE, the Division of Far Eastern Affairs of the State Department, and copied (with the other typewritten Baltimore Exhibits) as we shall hereafter suggest.

State 13 is a brief memorandum, referred to in the State Department as a "chit" (R. 797), dated February 9, 1938, by J. M. Jones of FE. It is a practically verbatim summary of the essential content of a short despatch from Richard F. Boyce, Consul at Yokohama, dated January 18, 1938 (part of Def. Ex. VV),* which, as appears from stamps on its face, was received in the Department on February 7, 1938, and in FE on February 9. The content of State 13 shows that it was intended to, and did, circulate with the Boyce despatch of January 18 as a quick summary introduction. The Government does not dispute this (as will appear from the later discussion of State 13-A).

State 13 bears no receiving stamps. The routing of the Boyce despatch of January 18, which circulated with State 13, is shown by pencil notation in the upper right-hand corner; that routing was to FE, A-M/C (Commercial Office of Assistant Secretary Messersmith) and EA (Office of the Adviser on International Economic Affairs). Receiving stamps on the face of the despatch show receipt by FE on

---

* Copies of State 13 and the Boyce despatch of January 18, 1938, stapled together, were marked Defendant's Exhibit VV.

February 9, receipt by A-M/C on February 12, receipt by EA on March 16, and filing in DCR on March 21. No stamp of Sayre's office appears on the despatch, and it is thus demonstrated that the despatch, and State 13 which circulated with it, were never in Sayre's office unless they can be shown to have accompanied some other paper which does bear his receiving stamp. There is no credible evidence that the Boyce despatch of January 18 and State 13 were circulated with any other document in the State Department. The conclusion is that neither the Boyce despatch of January 18 nor State 13 was ever in Sayre's office.

The Government sought to remedy this state of the record by advancing the hypothesis (disproved as we shall show) that State 13 and the Boyce despatch of January 18 circulated in the Department with State 15, a memorandum ("chit" or "tag") of Stanley K. Hornbeck (then Adviser on Political Relations), dated February 11, 1938, addressed to Sayre among others. It attempted to support this hypothesis by introducing State 13-A, made up of State 15, State 13 and the Boyce despatch of January 18, stapled together in that order. It elicited testimony from Walter H. Anderson, an employee of the Department, who produced the original State Department documents at the trial, that he had produced State 13-A from the State Department file, so stapled together (R. 915). On cross-examination, Anderson admitted that he had no real knowledge what papers were circulated together (*e.g.*, R. 852, 919), that the stapling together of papers in the files did not necessarily mean that the stapled papers had actually circulated together in the Department (R. 844), and in effect that he did not even know whether the papers presently stapled together as State 13-A had been so stapled together when the documents in this case were delivered by the State Department to the FBI on April 7, 1949 * (R. 919–20; see

The Government's hypothesis just discussed is refuted by the internal evidence of the documents. State 15, Hornbeck's memorandum of February 11, addressed to the Secretary of State, the Under Secretary, Mr. Sayre, Mr. Feis of EA, and Mr. Murphy of A-M/C, reads:

> "I feel that you will wish to have knowledge of the facts and appraisals given in Mr. Jones' very informative memorandum hereunder (based on Consul Boyce's report)."

It is obvious on the face of State 15, that it cannot refer to the Jones chit of February 9, State 13, since that is neither a "very informative memorandum," nor is it based on a "report" of Consul Boyce (but only on the brief Boyce despatch of January 18). Clearly it refers to what was in fact a very informative memorandum by the same Jones, an

---

* The documents were returned by the FBI on May 10, 1949 (R. 885). also R. 853–4, 885).

eight-page memorandum dated February 7, 1938, State 12, which is in
turn explicitly based on a long report of Consul Boyce, State 6–8,*
enclosed with a despatch from Consul Boyce dated January 6, 1938,
State 5. Hornbeck himself so testified, and testified that it was these
documents, and not State 13, that circulated with his memorandum,
State 15 (R. 1354–5).**

What is clear on the face of the documents and on Hornbeck's
testimony is finally confirmed by other intrinsic evidence in the documents. The receiving stamps on State 12 and State 5 (enclosing
State 6–8) show that these documents reached Hornbeck's office on
February 9, and had thus been available to him for several days before
he wrote his memorandum of February 11 (St. 15). The receiving
stamps on the Boyce despatch of January 18 (part of Def. Ex. VV)
show that it and State 13, which concededly circulated with it, never
went to Hornbeck's office.

The only hypothesis by which the Government sought to show
that State 13 was in Sayre's office comes to nothing. The evidence is
conclusive that it was never there.

*   *   *

Because of the restrictions on the length of the brief, the text of
State Exhibit No. 13 could not be included. The text of the exhibit
reveals that it was not a "very informative memorandum" and that
its unimportant contents, based on newspaper items, would not
have made it an item of any interest for espionage purposes. State
Exhibit No. 13, the text of which was copied verbatim on one of the
typed pages produced by Chambers, reads as follows:

DEPARTMENT OF STATE
_____

DIVISION OF FAR EASTERN AFFAIRS

February 9, 1938.

Yokohoma reports that Mr. Aikawa is scheduled to sail from Japan
on the M.S. *Chichibu Maru* February 24 for the United States. According to a newspaper item in the *Japan Advertiser* Mr. Aikawa hopes to
raise $300,000,000 in the United States. Another Japanese newspaper
item states that the success of Mr. Aikawa's efforts in the United States
depends upon Mr. Aikawa's ability and upon *the attitude of the American government toward his venture.*

FE:Jones:NN

* State 6 is the title page of the report, State 7 the table of contents,
and State 8 the 22-page body of the report.
** In reading this testimony, it is necessary to know that copies of State
15 and State 12, stapled together, were marked Defendant's Exhibit WW.

INDEX

A NOTE ON THE AUTHOR

ALGER HISS was born in Baltimore, Maryland, in 1904. He received his A.B. from Johns Hopkins University in 1926, and his LL.B. from Harvard Law School in 1929. He served as secretary to Supreme Court Justice Oliver Wendell Holmes (1929–30), and then practiced law in Boston and New York City (1930–3). From 1933 to 1947, Mr. Hiss held various United States government positions in Washington; from 1936 to 1947 he was with the Department of State, where his last position was as director of the office in charge of U.N. affairs. He attended the Yalta Conference, and served as Secretary-General of the San Francisco Conference, at which the Charter of the United Nations was drafted. He was President of the Carnegie Endowment for International Peace from 1947 to 1949. Mr. Hiss is married and has two children, and now lives in New York City.